HUNGERING FOR AMERICA

HUNGERING FOR AMERICA

ITALIAN, IRISH, AND JEWISH
FOODWAYS IN THE AGE OF MIGRATION

Hasia R. Diner

HARVARD UNIVERSITY PRESS
Cambridge, Massachusetts, & London, England

First Harvard University paperback edition, 2003

Library of Congress Cataloging-in-Publication Data
Diner, Hasia R.
Hungering for America : Italian, Irish, and Jewish foodways in the age of migration /
Hasia R. Diner.
p. cm.
Includes bibliographical references and index.
ISBN-13: 978-0–674–00605–8 (cloth)
ISBN-10: 0–674–00605–4 (cloth)
ISBN-13: 978-0–674–01111–3 (pbk.)
ISBN-10: 0–674–01111–2 (pbk.)
1. Italians—Food—United States.   2. Irish—Food—United States.   3. Jews—Food—
United States.   4. Immigrants—Food—United States.   5. Food habits—United States.
6. Food habits—Europe.   7. Famines—Europe.   I. Title.
GT2853.U5 D54 2001
394.1′ 2′ 08691—dc21

TO MARTY AND NANCY DINER,
AT WHOSE HOME ONE NEVER HUNGERS

ACKNOWLEDGMENTS

This book has been a long time in the making. It brought together the several fields I work in—American Jewish history, the history of the Irish in America, and immigration history more generally—and reflects the insights I have derived from other projects. Its structure reveals my belief that immigration historians need to study the experiences of more than one, more even than two immigrant groups in order to understand the balance between the particular and the general. My years of teaching and writing about women's history convinced me that the private side of women's lives was not so private after all, and that in the homey details of domestic life we can see the workings of the public arena. Recent developments in gender history also pointed me to the realm of food. Men and women have both have had a share in the answer to the question "what's for dinner." Their shares were, however, often, indeed usually, separate and unequal.

In the largest sense, my thanks go to all the colleagues, students, and teachers who over the years shaped me as a historian, helped me develop in new directions, and exposed me to new ideas. I note in the Preface that over the course of my ten years with this material, nearly everyone to whom I revealed the fact that I was writing a book about food, immigration, and ethnic identity offered me stories about their own food memories. Hopefully those hundreds of people will remember that they helped make this book possible. Their smiles, anecdotes, and even recipes are here, even if not referred to specifically. The skeptics helped me as well, forcing me to prove the historical gravitas of food in the context of immigration.

But I did rely very strongly on the advice and careful reading of a number of colleagues and owe them a special thanks. David Riemers, Thomas Dublin, and Elizabeth Pleck read the entire manuscript. They marked it up and made it better, bringing their expertise in immigration history, social history, and women's history to bear upon it. My dear friend Robert Scally, as well as Marion Casey and Thomas Archdeacon, read the chapters on the Irish. Gary Mormino did more than read the Italian chapters. He provided crucial primary materials which helped frame the interpretation. Steven Zipperstein and Ruth Abusch-Magder, herself an emerging specialist in Jewish food culture, read the two chapters on east European Jewish food on two continents.

Other scholars provided me with crucial information. Lawrence Schiffman, Jeffrey Rubenstein, and Judith Hauptman led me into some Judaic sources which I knew but could not quite locate. Barbara Kirschenblatt-Gimblett, Jeffrey Shandler, Cormac O'Grada, Stephen Whitfield, Alan Kraut, Deborah Dash Moore, Riv Ellen-Prell, Joyce Antler, and Linda Raphael offered various data and asked difficult questions. Some special assistance came from Linda Alameida, Marion Jacobson, Sara Pesce, Emmalina DeFeo, Barbara Natanson, Laura Jockusch, Nancy Carnevale, Jerri Sherman, and Shelby Shapiro. Michael Birch of Shrewsbury, Massachusetts, shared with me his grandfather's letter collection, and I thank him. Laura Beveridge helped me tap the rich collection in the Rochester Jewish Community Oral History Project housed in the Rare Book Collection of Rush Rhees Library at the University of Rochester.

Joyce Seltzer of Harvard University Press played a pivotal role in the evolution of this book. She gave me insight and advice starting from the first and offered me formative guidance for structuring the manuscript. Through years of writing, thinking, editing, and revising she was there, firm, clear, and determined. I am honored that she wanted to work with me.

Ten years is a long and costly amount of time to spend on a scholarly book. The cost was eased by a National Endowment for the Humanities Summer Fellowship, a Distinguished Faculty Research Fellowship at the University of Maryland at College Park, and a sabbatical at my present institution, New York University. I received invaluable assistance from both the University of Maryland and New York University in the form of student research assistants and owe a debt to Psyche Williams, David Weinstein, Hartley Lachter, Alex Molot, Lauren Shedletsky, and Jane Rothstein.

In the decade that this book was growing, I gave numerous papers on parts of it as scholarly presentations. While I cannot here thank all of the many panelists, chairs, and commentators of the various sessions at which I did my "food" talk, many offered helpful remarks. They include Gail Twersky Reimer, Jenna Weissman Joselit, Marilyn Halter, Amy Bentley, Yong Chen, Warren Belasco, Jack Wertheimer, Donna Gabaccia, Barbara Haber, and Ewa Morawska, and many others. Likewise, presentations at the University of Wisconsin (courtesy of the Stanley and Sandra Kutler Lectureship), the University of Louisville, the Center for Judaic Studies at the University of Pennsylvania, Stern College, Dickinson College, Georgetown University, the College of Charleston, the University of Hartford, the University of North London, and the University of Haifa brought me in touch with other scholars who challenged and endorsed my efforts. Audiences that attended my lectures at museums, libraries, synagogues, and other community settings allowed me to try out some of the ideas that are developed here.

Work at New York University and particularly the Skirball Department of Hebrew and Judaic Studies, under the inspired chairmanship of Robert Chazan when I first joined it, has been exhilarating. New York University also houses one of the country's richest centers for the study of food and culture. Marion Nestle and Amy Bentley, along with the other participants in the "Feast and Famine" group, cheered me on. My colleagues in the Meyerhoff Center for Jewish Studies at the University of Maryland also gave me support and space to pursue this subject and present some thoughts on it.

Librarians and archivists at the Library of Congress, McKeldin Library at the University of Maryland at College Park, the New York Public Library, and Bobst Library at New York University have been most helpful. At Bobst the staff of the Robert Wagner Labor Archives and Tamiment Library, particularly Andrew Lee, extended valuable aid. The Historical Society of Wisconsin, YIVO, the Archives Center at the Smithsonian Institution's National Museum of American History, the

American Jewish Historical Society, Trinity College in Dublin, Regenstein Library at the University of Chicago, the Center for Migration Studies located on Staten Island, and the Schlesinger Library at Radcliffe were all invaluable to me, and their staff members extremely helpful. Marion Smith, the archivist for the Immigration and Naturalization Service, and Mary Ann Bamberger at the Jane Addams Memorial Collection at the University Library of the University of Illinois at Chicago directed me to crucial material.

There is an important, much-cited food book, *Much Depends Upon Dinner*, by Margaret Visser. I take the liberty to paraphrase her title by saying, much depends upon family. And what a family I have. Steve: you know what you mean to me and how little I could accomplish without you. My wonderful children, Shira, Eli, and Matan—a living embodiment of his name—clipped articles for me, directed me to books about food, told me food stories they heard in random places, and sometimes even mocked the idea of my "cookbook." But always they made me feel that my work mattered to them. They made it all worthwhile.

New York City
May 2001

CONTENTS

ILLUSTRATIONS

PREFACE

At meetings and dinner parties, in libraries and at conferences, old friends, relatives, professional colleagues, and new acquaintances ask me: what are you working on? I hesitate momentarily, knowing full well what will follow. But I tell them anyhow: I am writing a book on immigrant foodways and ethnic cultures in America. I then brace for the predictable response.

First, they smile, perhaps even laugh. Some just think it a strange subject for an historian. Treaties and wars, strikes and elections, rallies for equal rights, protests against discrimination and exploitation, these are the stuff of history. Food seems ephemeral, the subject for cookbooks. But the smile also reflects a love of food. Food is fun and gives pleasure. Since it is linked psychologically to sex, people may feel slightly excited or embarrassed. Mentioning it elicits a twinkling of the eye, a broad grin, a ribald chuckle.

But after this response, conversations quickly shift to memory, going from smiles of surprise to rhapsodies of remembering. Talking about food is a way of talking about family, childhood, community. Remembered foods open the floodgates of the past, as friends and acquaintances describe who they are, where they came from, and the textures and tastes of the time gone by.

In exquisite detail they describe a mother's lasagna, a beloved grandmother's kugel, the curries, chiles rellenos, lutefisks, goulashes, moussakas, pierogis, and other hearty and sensuous reminders of childhood, all seemingly brought intact to America and now the salient part of their ethnic repertoires. They recreate for me the kitchen smells and tastes of their pasts. They recall iconic meals, certain that these cherished foods were the treasured recipes of someplace called "back home," wherever their families originally hailed from. Remembered food connects them to those places. It, more than language, clothing, home furnishings, even religious rituals, launches their journeys back in time and across borders to long-finished family meals. Through the talk of authentic ethnic foods they make their claim to being insiders of communities they may no longer live in. It would never occur to them to ponder the authenticity of these dishes or to think that such foods have histories. The food which came out of ancestral ovens represents to them powerful legacies of continuity, linking them to faraway places, most of which they have never visited.

Like all memories, these tales of immigrant foodways reflect more about the rememberer than about the actualities of history. The dishes described require elaborate preparation and call upon high levels of skill. Those who cooked them—mothers and grandmothers—owned and used bowls and pans, spatulas and turning forks, measuring cups, rolling pins, and ladles. These succulent foods came out of ovens of gas or electric which gave off a uniform and predictable heat. These dishes, chock-full of expensive ingredients—meat, cheese, oils and other fats, eggs, fresh vegetables, noodles, rice, sugar, salt—represented the investment of much money and time.

Most of the millions of women and men who chose to immigrate to America in the century of European migration, the hundred years stretching from the 1820s through the 1920s, came from precisely that class which could never afford to eat such fine foods. Had they eaten so well regularly in the "old country," they might not have needed to come to America. While religious persecution and political turmoil also pushed people out of their homes, by and large the ranks of the immigrants were drawn from among people who did not eat such wonderful dishes. They may have tasted them at feast days a few times a year, or taken some from an employer's pantry. Meat in particular lay beyond their reach. Nor did they have the time, the tools, or the space to regularly produce such wonders of culinary delight. Just the basic chores, like finding fuel for cooking and heating and drawing water, amounted to an unending burden.

The women and men who came to America came hungry and in part because of hunger. America had achieved a deserved global reputation as a place where food could be had for relatively little money. Immigrants never believed that the streets of America were paved with gold. Instead, they expected that its tables were covered with food. Newcomers knew that they would have to work hard, but that was nothing new. The difference was that arduous labor before migration had gotten them little food, while in the United States equally hard work in factories, mines, mills, railroads, and farms would be rewarded with tables sagging with food unimaginable to them back home. Only in the imagination of later generations did the people who came to America eat such a varied diet and consume regularly dishes laden with meat and oil, sugar and eggs, fresh fruits and vegetables, hearty soups and stews, crusty breads and soft rolls.

To all the people who over the last decade shared with me their wonderful stories about foods eaten, then lost, but now remembered, I offer this book. Without minimizing the images of their parents and grandparents as the custodians of tradition, or dispelling the warm glow of the mnemonics of childhood meals, I explore how those grandmothers and grandfathers negotiated between what they had eaten and, equally important, not eaten before migration, and what they found in America. How did they experience the search for bread (and meat, sugar, cheese, oil), and how did finding it transform them into new people, Americans from particular places? Their memories of hunger remained, playing a considerable role in the communities they created. Their memories originated in the mingling of recollections of being hungry in one place and finding once unattainable food in another place. This book explores how the memories of hunger and the realities of American plenty fused together to shape the ethnic identities of millions of women and men from Italy, Ireland, and Jewish eastern Europe.

HUNGERING FOR AMERICA

WAYS OF EATING,
WAYS OF STARVING

"People," novelist Isaac Bashevis Singer wrote, "do not love alike." "Neither do they starve alike," he observed in his commentary on *Hunger*, the grim novel first published in 1892 by another Nobel Laureate, the Norwegian Knut Hamsun. Although Hamsun, according to the Yiddish author, explored hunger as a "highly individualistic sensation," the comment suggests a relationship between food, scarcity, and the social history of immigration.[1] How people experienced hunger in one place and then recalled its pangs in another had everything to do with who they were, where they came from, and where they went.

In the hundred years following the 1820s, a massive transfer of population sent about 30 million Europeans to the United States. They came from the Continent's tens of thousands of villages, towns, and cities; from hundreds of regions and dozens of countries. A mass migration, it was yet the sum of decisions made by individuals coping with the specific difficulties of specific places. All of the individual and collective movements were, however, shaped by the powerful draw of America, a place where newly arrived immigrants could find work. To work as a laborer in a mill or as a hired hand on a farm, as a miner digging for coal or as a stevedore unloading cargo on some waterfront, as a peddler in the hinterlands or as a grocer in a small neighborhood shop, meant being able to feed oneself and one's family. There are millions of stories about how this happened and what it meant. None exemplifies the whole. Even on the level of the immigrant group, no single experience represents the totality of the many, in terms of when migrations took place, who migrated, how, and why.

The bulk of the Italian migration occurred in the last two decades of the nineteenth century and the first two of the twentieth. In those years 4 million individuals left the Italian peninsula, initially young men from villages in the regions south of Rome. About half of the men who came to America ultimately returned to their home communities, although an untold number re-emigrated. The emigration from Ireland began earlier, with the 1840s, the decade of the Famine, a crucial moment in the creation of a visible Irish presence in the United States. But the flight from "the Great Hunger" did not account for the largest number of Irish immigrants, nor did they cease to arrive after 1880. In the forty years from 1880 to 1920 over a million Irish people made their way to America. Theirs was a heavily female migration, with young women bound for domestic service constituting the majority. Irish immigrants evinced little interest in returning home, other than perhaps to visit parents. East European Jews began their immigration to the United States in the 1870s. In 1880 only one-sixth of America's Jews hailed from the regions east of the Elbe, but after that the relentless exodus from regions then ruled by Russia and Austria-Hungary—Russia itself, Poland, Rumania, and Galicia—transformed American Jewry into an east European outpost. The two-and-a-half million Jewish women and men migrated in equal numbers, and they came to America with no intention of returning. The immigrants, who counted many older people and children among them, arrived with a keen sense of themselves as Jews, bound to each other regardless of place of origin.

Despite the differences between these three groups, they shared many aspects of a pre-migration reality. Those who emigrated had little prospect of sustaining themselves and their families if they stayed put. Economic changes were shaking up their home communities, and the potential migrants saw and felt that conditions were worsening. The best off in their communities—the well-fed—had little motive to leave. The worst off also did not join the flow, as the truly destitute and starving did not have the means to do so. Those who emigrated knew hunger and envisioned America as a place where they could alleviate its pangs.

For all of human history people have contended with the stark reality that they must eat to live. Fulfilling this most fundamental need never was easy. For most people at most times, food choices depended upon what was available locally. Food shaped basic forms of social organization, and human societies were structured according to how they hunted, gathered, farmed, or fished. Human beings created and invoked deities, constructed religious systems, and coined money to trade beyond their limited resources. They killed each other over food, and left their homes and journeyed far when the food they expected ran out.

Even in ordinary times, daily chores of gathering food and fuel, transforming raw ingredients into something edible, distributing finished products within a community, and storing foodstuffs for future use took up most human energy. Natural disasters, floods, earthquakes, droughts, and infestations diminished already precarious supplies. Wars impeded the process of getting, preparing, and consuming food. Human destruction of rivers, forests, fields, and herds also jeopardized food supplies. Conquests by outside invaders changed food systems, putting barriers between the occupied people and food. Class and gender distinctions within any community also decreed who ate what, where, when, and how.[2]

But amidst all these universals, consumption of food has always been culturally constructed. What was tasty to one group invoked disgust and loathing in another. Different communities variably defined some items as edible and others as utterly inedible.[3] Many cultures built rigid systems of dietary taboos, carving up the world of food into the permitted and the forbidden. A people might decide to move on to a new home because of a lack of food, although their region teemed with plants and animals which they technically could eat. How people respond to scarcity and hunger and what food means to them offers both a window into and mirror of their culture.

The history of food and its cultural underpinnings involves more than just the sad story of famines and flights from hunger, or restrictions and rules. Food has provided people with great pleasure. We enjoy food, its tastes, its smells, and the sense of satisfaction of consumption. We yearn to eat what we regard as good, and eating well represents the good life.

In this, food very much resembles the other zone of sensuality to which it is usually compared: sex. In most societies the ways people think about food and sex are linked. Both make people feel good. Both are defined as either acceptable or taboo. Both involve practices which sometimes are sanctioned and sometimes are not. Varying by culture, some foods and some sexual practices are never allowed. Others are sanctified and enshrined in official practice and ritual. Societies often link periods of sexual abstinence with fasting, while the pleasures of the table and the pleasures of the marital bed offer regulated times for indulgence. Many cultures deprecate wanton overindulgence of both zones of sensuality, condemning gluttony and promiscuity. Likewise, both systems of food and sexuality strengthen bonds between group members and create barriers to interactions with outsiders. Put bluntly, the person with whom one cannot eat (and whose food cannot be consumed) is often the same person with whom sexual relations must be avoided.[4]

Food, like sex, intensifies group identity. The overly quoted statement of Jean Anthelme Brillat-Savarin, "tell me what you eat, and I shall tell you what you are,"[5] rephrased in common American parlance as "you are what you eat," works. Sex is not the only kind of human interaction connected to and refracted in the world of food. In its literal definition, a "companion" means one with whom bread is shared. Preparing and consuming food together solidifies social bonds within families, between households, and among individuals who consider themselves friends. The notion of the common table connecting people exists in many cultures as an embodiment of communal trust. We might define a community as a group of people who eat with each other.

While we can talk in general about the history of food habits in particular places, food differences existed within each individual society. People in most communities did not all eat the same foods in the same ways. The distribution and consumption of food has been historically determined by age, gender, and class, and its unequal allocations highlight internal group differences.

Food differences reflected the complexities of parent-child relations and the meaning of growing up. Certain foods have been considered appropriate for children, others for adults. The transition to adulthood involved the right to partake of certain foods and to give up others. At ritual moments adults relived childhood by eating its foods. Children usually had a different role in the acquisition and preparation of food than parents and other adults. They may have helped in the process as they learned, but fathers and mothers hunted, farmed, fished, made fires, and cooked. Adults distributed food. Children received their age-appropriate share.[6]

Food is also modified by gender. Given the close connection between food and sex, it would seem obvious that gender, understood as any culture's knowledge of, and beliefs about, sexual difference, would come into play around food.[7] Women and men usually had different roles to perform when it came to getting and making food. In some societies women did the most difficult, backbreaking labor to bring up a crop from the soil. In other places they worked in fields only in moments of crisis, ordinarily doing only farm work defined as ancillary to the family's main enterprise. Men might grow wheat, and women might cultivate kitchen gardens, collect eggs and make butter, can fruit and prepare preserves. In some cultures men never cooked, while elsewhere they prepared certain items at certain times. Societies with religiously prescribed dietary laws invested in men the authority to regulate and guard the gates of the food system. Where religion and food have been more loosely connected, women had a freer hand in food preparation, and men less interest in the workings of the kitchen.[8]

Food in most places has been squarely associated with sociability, and within families it provided a common expression of love and affection. Family celebrations and community feasts marked sacred time. Weddings, birthdays, coming-of-age ceremonies, good harvests, military victories, small personal triumphs, historic re-enactments, religious ceremonies, even funerals and rites of mourning had their iconic foods served in ritualistic ways. These moments expressed community and family cohesion. Women did most of the cooking and serving of the foods which made such moments possible. As such women and the foods they prepared articulated a society's deepest-held values.

Changes in the food supply and in the tasks involved in food preparation affected women more heavily than men because of their primacy in matters involving cooking. When scarcity set in, they had to figure out how to feed the family. The crisis of the empty larder fell upon their shoulders first. When novelties showed up in the marketplaces, they decided what would, and would not fit into the family's food culture. These changes could enhance women's power or reduce it, depending on the context.

Men and women often do not eat the same foods in the same amounts. In many places women serve men the food which they have cooked, but they eat only after the men have finished.[9] Or women prepare an array of foods, but some items, usually meat, are denied to them. Some cultures impose food taboos upon women, which are defined as necessary and natural to menstruation, pregnancy, and lactation. Other food practices, which divide the table, metaphorically, into a female and male sphere, persist throughout a lifetime.[10] So it is important to keep gender in mind when describing "Japanese food," "French food," "Chinese food," "Mexican food," or the food of any other system.

The same applies to class. Class is the mechanism by which an elite allocates resources within a community, and food *is* a society's most precious good.[11] Once in place, class structures exist to replicate themselves. Those who have the most and the best expect such bounty to continue. Those who have less are expected to accept the inevitability and naturalness of inequities. Class differences profoundly divide any society's foodways. These differences play themselves out in various ways: ingredients, modes of preparation, the very acts of consumption, and basic ideas about food. Distinctions in diet between rich, poor, and the various gradations in between have been observed in most places at most times. The better-off eat more varied food, of higher quality, more often, than do the members of the poorer classes, who eat less and have few choices.

Historically, those who ate at the lower end may have learned about better food, its possibilities and its complexities, through encounters with the elite. Poor women worked as servants in the homes of the wealthy and saw, smelled, and even tasted the richer food of the richer people. The elite at particular moments shared food from the top down, giving the usually hungry people a sense of what it meant to eat well. Those experiences of eating across class lines had important implications for people who suffered deprivation but knew what it was to eat better and desired it for themselves.

In the modern era, class-based differences in food manifested themselves in part through the emergence of national cuisines. In Europe, the development of distinctive foodways linked to the nation accompanied the rise of nation-states and the flowering of ideologies of nationalism. As France, Italy, Germany, England, Russia marked themselves off as distinct from each other and as greater than the regions within their newly drawn borders, their national cuisines took shape. National cuisines came to represent the nations themselves and were created and consumed by elites.[12]

The poorer people of the nation, particularly in rural areas, continued to eat in familiar ways, untouched by the emergence of national cuisines. Bouts of scarcity, disruptions of their food system caused by wars, and the daily struggle to put bread on their tables, rather than aristocratically inspired dishes concocted at courts and castles, shaped their food world. They adhered to local food practices, undisturbed by the talk of cuisine in capital cities where the privileged few experimented with elaborate blends and mixtures of the foods indigenous to certain regions, but with new ingredients and styles imported from abroad.

But as masters and landlords—those who owned the lands which rural workers farmed and upon whom they depended for a livelihood—came to develop the national food culture, the poorer classes increasingly learned about new tastes, foods, and ideals of eating. They may have experienced moments during the year—holidays, religious festivals, events of national celebration—when they saw, or even better, tasted morsels of the foods of the well-off, given to them as gifts. Through these occasional tastings they encountered the idea of their own national food. With the growth of the nation-state, some members of the lower classes were allowed, or compelled, to participate in national institutions—notably the military—which fed them and exposed them to a national standard. National educational systems also provided ways to learn about cuisine.

In addition, the rural poor, in search for work, came to the capitals and large regional urban centers. Here, they broadened their knowledge of and exposure to the idea of the nation and its foods. In the cities, the world of food expanded for rural newcomers turned urban dwellers. They came to link certain foods with national identity and came to prefer city food to the simple, rougher fare they were used to.

The relationship between food, class, and identity was connected to specific historical developments that attended European expansion across the globe, and the great changes in food brought by exploration and colonization.[13] The European conquest of the Americas revolutionized eating for all of Europe's people. The introduction, most importantly, of corn and potatoes transformed Europe, and those two New

World foods played a key role in Europe's demographic leap forward at the beginning of the eighteenth century. The exponential growth in Europe's population did nothing less than make possible the industrial revolution and European dominance of much of the world. Indeed, the emigration to America would not have taken place without the socio-economic revolution unleashed by potatoes and corn. Less powerful in shaping population, sugar, coffee, tea, and chocolate also altered what the rich, the poor, and the emerging middle classes ate, how they ate, and what food meant to them.[14] The industrialization of food production and technological changes upset the previously simple paradigm that most people ate what they found nearby.

In that transformation of historic food systems, new foods, new ways of eating, and new ideas about food entered peoples' homes, no matter how poor. The introduction of food novelties and changes in local foodways challenged traditional patterns.[15] The dialectic between tradition and novelty informs the history of food.

Human beings are brought up into particular worlds of taste. At very young ages they learn that certain tastes and forms of food are acceptable, ordinary, normal, and natural. Other tastes they learn to dislike, considering them abnormal and deviant. According to social theorist Pierre Bourdieu, "It is probably in tastes in *food* [emphasis in the original] that one would find the strongest and most indelible mark of infant learning, the lessons which longest withstand the distancing or collapse of the native world and most durably maintain nostalgia for it."[16]

Childhood tastes are strongly internalized. Over the course of a lifetime, individuals learn to eat new things and even like them. But the likings formed earliest endure longest. Because food is so tightly woven around childhood, family, and sensuality, it serves as a mnemonic, an agent of memory. The often cited literary example by novelist Marcel Proust in the opening section of the first volume of *Remembrance of Things Past* offers a handy case in point.

> Many years had elapsed during which nothing of Combray . . . had any existence for me, when one day in winter, as I came home, my mother . . . offered me some tea . . . She sent out for one of those short, plump little cakes called "petites madeleines" . . . and soon I raised to my lips a spoonful of tea in which I had soaked a morsel of

the cake. No sooner had the warm liquid and the crumbs within touched my palate than a shudder ran through my whole body . . . an exquisite pleasure had invaded my senses.

With the taste of the madeleine, "memory returns," and the narrator's past rushed back to him.[17]

Food conservatism grows out of the sensory link between food and memory. The "wrong" tastes or "inappropriate" formats jar with long ingrained ideas about food. Conservatism informs food habits. What one group eats and enjoys—dog, snake, insects—causes utter revulsion in others. Some tastes—spicy, bland, salty, pulverized, lumpy—seem just right to some and abominable to others. So too combinations and standards of what goes with what, as well as modes of preparation and consumption, differ from place to place and are deeply felt in the everyday, year-in and year-out foodways of the people who prefer them.

That people like what they remember from childhood fits an almost universally observed phenomenon. Migrants, when they settle down in new places, regardless of how long they plan to stay in their new homes, attempt to recreate familiar foods. They find ways to prepare them, cooperating with each other to make them available on a community basis. Their stores, bakeries, boarding houses, cafes, and restaurants all bear witness to the desire of the newcomers to relive the foodways of places left behind.[18]

Yet, as a counterweight, human beings are not only biologically omnivorous, but they can be easily tempted by foods once unknown or disdained. They experience new smells, see new dishes, watch others eat and derive pleasure from their food, and want to try it too. Much of the history of the contacts between different peoples tells of mutual fascination with new foods. In heterogeneous societies, it is possible to look into someone else's pot, sample from—and ultimately crave—new spices, meats, grains, fruits and vegetables.

To study any society is perforce to look at what the women and men in it have eaten, how they got it, with whom they ate it, who prepared it, and what it meant to them. What happened when they could not get their staples, the core of their diet? How did they engage with new tastes, new formats, new ideas about food? Foodways include food as material items and symbols of identity, and the history of a group's ways with food goes far beyond an exploration of cooking and consumption. It amounts to a journey to the heart of its collective world.

Journeys, in the form of migrations, have facilitated contact with new foods and made it possible for people to construct new identities. Much of human migration, extending back to prehistoric times, has been a physical response to the diminishing of resources in one place and the knowledge that elsewhere food could be found. The Latin aphorism, *ubi est pane, ibi est patria* (where there is bread, there is my country), echoes in the historic experiences and canonical texts of people everywhere.

The linkage between food and migration remains valid at the end of the twentieth century, in terms not so different from those recorded for eras long past. An immigrant from Nigeria living in Houston, Texas, explained to a writer for the *New York Times Magazine* why he made the move. "Here," explained Murphy Popoola in 1999, "you work, you have money, you eat."[19] Like him, immigrants were historically women and men who experienced want of work, want of money, and hence want of food. Their hunger propelled them outward. When they settled in new places they recreated elements of familiar foodways, at the same time that they embraced novelty and enjoyed greater abundance. The history of each immigrant group entails a particular negotiation between the memories of past hunger and the realities of new foods available in greater quantities than previously encountered.

True for all destinations of immigration, this reality in particular shaped the lure of America, the place of choice for so many immigrants from around the circle of the globe. From early on in its history, food was available in America in great abundance, at low cost. Soon after the European discovery of the "new world," the land became associated with the idea of plenty.[20] In a 1605 comedy, *Eastward Ho*, by George Chapman and John Marston, a fellow fresh from Virginia answered the question, "is it a pleasant country withal?" by declaiming, "As ever the sun shined on: temperate and full of all sorts of excellent viands: wild boar there is as common as our tamest bacon is here, and venison as mutton."[21] Hector St. John de Crevecoeur wrote his *Letters from an American Farmer* as a tribute to his new country, contrasting it with Europe's limitations.

> We have no princes, for whom we toil, starve, and bleed . . . Can a wretch who wanders about, who works and starves . . . call England

or any other kingdom his country? A country that had no bread for him, whose fields procured for him no harvest . . . ? No! Europe and America here stood as polar opposites. Wives and children, who before in vain demanded from him a morsel of bread, now, fat and frolicsome, gladly help their fathers to clear those fields whose exuberant crops are to arise to feed . . . them.

In the name of America, Crevecoeur proclaimed to the "foreigner from any part of Europe, 'Welcome to my shores, distressed Europeans; bless the hour in which thou didst see my verdant fields. . . . If thou wilt work, I have bread for thee; I will give thee fields to feed and cloath thee.'"[22]

Commentators in the eighteenth century described Pennsylvania— but it could have been New York or Maryland, Rhode Island, or just about anywhere in America—as the "best poor man's country in the world," where "wheatbread is eaten in almost all places." Europeans who settled in early America noted that "scarce a house but has an apple, peach, and cherry orchard"; "we who are Country people used always to think of it a great matter that the gentlemen in Scotland had orchards."[23]

This theme carried through into the twentieth century. In 1906 the German sociologist Werner Sombart speculated on the political implications of plenty for the working class. American workers, in contrast to those in his native land, were "well fed and . . . not acquainted with the discomforts that must necessarily result in the long run from the mixing of potatoes and alcohol." He observed that American laborers consumed meat daily, while those in Germany filled up on potatoes, washed down and calorically augmented by brewed or distilled beverages. The outlook of the American working class, composed largely of European immigrants, millions of whom hailed from Germany, needed, Sombart wrote, to be understood in light of the "extraordinary" differences between the American worker and "his continental-European counterpart." The title of Sombart's essay, *Why There Is No Socialism in the United States*, indicated his larger interest, and he concluded that "all socialist utopias come to nothing on roast beef and apple pie."[24]

Sombart correctly saw in America a less vigorous and powerful socialist presence than in his native Germany. But his words ought not to be taken as the sum total of the history of radicalism in the American working class. Some of them, native-born Americans and immigrants and their children, did join protest movements, condemning the cruelties of capitalism and the hollowness of America's rhetoric of offering a good life to all who worked hard. They had ample evidence of millions who labored and received little in compensation.

The deprivation experienced by so many immigrants in America was, however, mild compared to what they had known back home. Even critics of the excesses of American capitalism saw that when immigrants measured their material lot—particularly their food consumption—against old world realities, they saw that they could earn more money more regularly and purchase more food for themselves and their families.

Two years before Sombart's book, Peter Roberts studied the residents of Pennsylvania's anthracite coal towns. Inhabited principally by immigrants from Wales and from the Slavic lands of central and east Europe, coal towns symbolized America's deepest economic exploitation. No apologist for the coal companies, Roberts documented life in these wretched towns. He charted the low wages, "at $1.50 or $2.00 a day," for nine hours of difficult, often deadly, labor. But he recognized that the terms of oppression were relative.

> The Sclav standard of living in the coal fields is low, but if compared to that in vogue in his home, it is rich and varied. Bread made with the best wheat flour the market affords, meat of some kind every day unless religious considerations forbid it; on fast days eggs, sardines and cheese take the place of meat; a plentiful supply of cabbage, potatoes, pickles, apples and coffee—these give the Sclav a sumptuous living, while they drink beer more freely than they did water in the hills of their ancestral home. It is not astonishing that many of these people regard this land as a "goodly country" where they have realized more of the good things of life than was ever dreamt of in the fatherland.[25]

The American workers Sombart saw, and the transplanted Europeans Roberts studied, ate precisely those items which in Europe were defined as luxuries, foods reserved for the upper classes, with meat and white-flour bread high on the list.

From the period of the early republic onward, both foreign visitors and guidebooks written for prospective immigrants repeatedly stressed with wonder the vast amount of food, meat in particular, available on the tables of the boarding houses where workingmen lived.[26] They marveled at the amounts of meat that Americans of all classes bought and ate.[27] By the middle of the nineteenth century the American population, including its working class, experienced relatively little hunger, and of the foods it ate, meat ranked high on the list. An 1864 visitor from England, coming during the Civil War, a period which should have produced civilian food shortages, found the opposite:

> As a flesh-consuming people, the Americans have no equal in the world. They usually have meat three times a day, and not a small quantity at each meal either. I have seen gentlemen choose as many as seven or eight different kinds of animal food from the bill of fare, and after having all arranged before him in a row, in the national little white dishes, commence at one end and eat his way through in half a dozen minutes.[28]

Such commentaries might be dismissed as hyperbole, overstatements written for one political purpose or another. Other kinds of data, however, are more difficult to attribute to ideology. For one, political economists and statisticians computed and contrasted food prices in America and parts of Europe. From the end of the eighteenth century onward, American food prices dipped below those in Europe.[29] They edged downward immediately after the American Revolution, and with the opening up of the trans-Appalachian West, and then the completion of the Erie Canal, the vast lands of the Midwest produced even more massive amounts of food to be piled on city dwellers' tables. The first incursions of the railroads into what had once been remote and undeveloped sections depressed food prices even more and increased variety.

Food prices tumbled downward even further in the postbellum period. By the 1880s, the decade in which the tidal wave of east and south European immigration flooded the United States, the cost of flour, rice, tea, coffee, sugar, mutton, pork, beef, butter, lard, and milk dropped again.[30] The decline meant that European immigrants who had eaten meat a few times a year, considered coffee a luxury beyond their means, and wheat bread the privilege of their social betters could in America have these foods regularly. It also led to the late nineteenth-century crisis of American agriculture, which drove millions of modest farmers off the land and paved the way for the triumph of American capitalist agribusiness. This transformation brought the cost of food prices down even further, putting more food within the grasp of the urban working class.[31]

The bounty of the American diet manifested itself physically in American bodies. From the eighteenth century onward, while the country was still a British colonial outpost on the Atlantic, Americans grew taller than their kin who had stayed put in England or elsewhere on the Continent. They ate more and better and that gave them greater stature. Even American slaves exceeded the height of the Europeans who had remained at home.[32] Average European stature did not approach that of Americans until the middle of the twentieth century.[33] As evidence of the beneficence of American opportunity (and to demonstrate the power of environment over heredity), anthropologist Franz Boas measured immigrants and their children in the early twentieth century and found that the American-fed children of Europe's poor were taller and stronger than their European-fed parents.[34]

In the late nineteenth century, working in the emerging field of nutrition, scientists began to measure, calculate, and compare the American diet and that of other peoples. W. O. Atwater, one of the pioneers of the field, wrote for the United States Department of Agriculture in 1894 that "the most remarkable thing about our food consumption is the quantity; for comparable occupations the Americans ate more than the Europeans." The comparisons testify to the distance European immigrants traveled when it came to matters of food in America. They had come to America from places where everyone, including those who were fairly well-off, ate less than ordinary Americans. Atwater commented that "living in the midst of abundance, our diet has not been regulated by the restraints which obtain with the great majority of the people of the Old World where food is dear and incomes are small."[35]

This history of food abundance corresponded to an analogous abundance of just about every other gift of nature: land, coal, oil, wood, water, minerals, the basic resources needed to stoke massive economic development and to put a virtual cornucopia of food on the tables of ordinary people. America experienced constant expansions of agricultural frontiers, producing bumper crops of whatever people at home and abroad cared to consume. Those who lived in the path of the juggernaut of geographic and economic expansion—particularly America's native peoples—paid a steep price. They were removed for the development of abundant and cheap resources.

Broad expanses of cheap land put nature's bounty of grain, vegetables, and fruit within the reach of most Americans. Farmers cultivated holdings far larger than those which characterized "old world" farming. They gave over much of their land to raising and grazing vast animal herds, pigs and cows in particular. The bounty of the land was consumed in large part by the animals, who then showed up on American tables as pork and beef.[36]

Fuel was also easy to come by. Americans did not have to devote hours each day scouring the land for kindling sticks or lumps of coal, something which consumed the strength of much of the world's population. Neither did they have to rely upon techniques of food preparation which economized on these precious bits of fuel. They had enough of it, easily within their reach to fry and bake and roast and simmer, stew and boil whatever they wanted.

Not only did Americans have access to vast amounts of fertile land which produced the food they ate and the fuel which made the cooking easier, but those realities also made possible the accumulation of wealth that in turn allowed for technological changes. Changes in shipping, slaughtering, freezing, and packaging expanded the amount and the variety of foods that could be consumed as costs dropped.

In the long sweep of American economic history, the one element that until well into the twentieth century was in short supply was human labor. Unlike Europe, which endured overpopulation, America suffered from chronic labor shortages. The European, Asian, and Central American migrations to the United States were set in motion by the worldwide knowledge that here work could be found and food could be obtained. America's greatest and most enduring tragedy, the forced enslavement of African people, also grew out of a shortage of hands to exploit the vast, seemingly endless lands that in turn produced the food, fuel, and other "natural" resources of the American soil.

This need for workers helped bring down the price of food. American workers commanded higher wages than their counterparts elsewhere, a fact not lost upon the millions of people who migrated to America for the work which they could not find at home. Americans could produce more food with less energy than any other people in the world. The transportation revolution of the mid-nineteenth century produced roads, waterways, and railroads, all of which linked Americans more closely to each other.[37] This meant that Americans rarely endured localized famines. From the end of the eighteenth century onward, food went from one frontier to another, from the hinterlands to the cities, and in finished form, from the cities back to the hinterlands, through a well-articulated transportation network.[38]

That food existed in abundance had profound cultural implications for the development of American history and identity. Americans came to believe in their right to an acceptable standard of living wherein hunger played no role.[39] They believed that as Americans they *all* deserved to live life free from want. A conservative politician at the end of the nineteenth century looking to be elected president, William McKinley, promised America's workers that voting for him would get them a "full dinner pail." In 1928 working families considered themselves entitled to the twin icons of modern America, "a car in every garage and chicken in every pot." Members of groups excluded from the national bounty demanded their right to "a piece of the pie." That an idea was as "American as apple pie" embodied a deep truth about the United States. Americans expected to live well, and living well meant never being hungry.[40]

This theme played itself out in immigrants' lives. They learned—by way of guidebooks, recruiters, returnees, and most importantly the "America letters," which went back across the ocean—that in America they could expect to eat well and relegate old hungers to memory. Here they could find work and with their wages they could afford food in plenty and even foods previously deemed luxurious. That encounter with food structured their continuing encounter with America.

As it happened, America actually welcomed the immigrants with good food. Emblazoned on a panel at the museum which now stands on the former receiving station at Ellis Island is a quote from a Swedish woman describing her first encounter with America. "When I arrived at Ellis Island," she recalled, "they served us coffee and donuts. This was the first time that I saw or ate a donut and I thought it was great! It tasted so good. Of course at home we didn't have anything like that." America to her was associated with that sweet and filling taste.

The chance to have a full belly could not be resisted. Margaret

1. European immigrants poured into America in unprecedented numbers in the late nineteenth and early twentieth centuries. For these hungry women and men who made the journey, this meal at Ellis Island revealed much about what America meant to them.

Byington, surveying the grim realities of life in Homestead, Pennsylvania, in 1910, compared the reactions of native-born Americans with those of immigrant Slavic families, two groups that made up the mill town people. The long-time Americans, rural Pennsylvania poor who had abandoned failing farms to work in the mills, responded to hard times by eating a bit less, putting their resources into housing. Conversely, "the Slavs . . . put up with poor housing, [but] will not skimp to a great extent on food." How could they, when America's "more varied and palatable food" had impelled their migrations, much more than the quest for better housing?[41]

Obviously, even in America not all people ate well nor did they eat the same. The poor ate less well than the rich. Rich folk employed servants to cook their multicourse meals, served in elegance on expensive dishes.

2. The sign above the heads of a group of immigrants detained at Ellis Island reads, "No charge for meals here."

They read magazines and cookbooks which included recipes using new, elaborate, and costly ingredients. They had no need to improvise and plan to ensure a full table.

Immigrant women and the others who swelled the ranks of America's poor economized and stretched their limited budgets to make food for their family meals. They found ways to turn scraps of land into kitchen gardens so that they could grow produce. They shopped every day for food, relying on neighborhood merchants from their ethnic communities to extend credit, and they prepared meals from lesser cuts of meat and overly ripe vegetables.[42] Sympathetic Americans saw their hunger. Carl Sandburg, for example, exposed the cruelty of "Chicago" in poetry and wrote: "On the faces of women and children, I have seen the marks of wanton hunger."[43]

But hunger, like food, is relative. Immigrants did not eat as well as middle class, native-born white Americans. They spent more of their family incomes on food, and fretted and worked out strategies to produce meals. But they ate better than they had back home, and better than they would have had they not made the move to America.[44] To them the point of reference was not what America's rich ate. Rather, they constantly measured their American tables against the ones that they had known back home.[45] For most, America was a place of increased nutrition, stocked pantries, and groaning tables.

Sophonisba Breckenridge in 1921 described "Mrs. P. from Posen," and how she perceived the change immigration had brought in her standard of living. "The meal" that Mrs. P. remembered as typical back home "was one dish, from which the entire family ate; here there is variety of food and each person has his own plate and eating utensils."[46]

To "Mrs. P from Posen" hunger remained a potent memory. She carried it with her to America, and it colored the way in which she experienced her new life. In America she, like millions of other immigrants, found that hunger came less often, that choices about what to eat and how to eat well were theirs quite frequently, and that everyday life took its shape more as a result of new tastes and possibilities than from the omnipresent fear of empty bowls.

No single story encapsulates the linkages between immigrants' past hungers with America's relative plenty. Rather, the ability of particular immigrants to seize the pleasures of American food depended upon how they had experienced deprivation, and what was the nature of their relationships to their new American homes. What they had endured "back home" influenced how they used American plenty. They employed food in particular ways in order to shape ethnic communities and identities.

For some immigrants, such as Italians, the migration to America represented the revenge of the poor against the inequities of a hated class system. The once hungry could now feast upon the good things that had been the preserve of the rich. For east European Jewish immigrants, America was a land not just of "milk and honey" but of meat and cake and ice cream—indeed, of seemingly limitless food possibilities. But for the Irish, who had just endured Europe's worst (and last) famine in modern times, and who had been dispossessed by the British from their land, it was different: powerful memories of hunger prevented them from using American food as a source of Irish identity.

The histories of these immigrant groups as they fashioned ethnic identities around food stand on their own. They serve as exemplars of the multiple ways in which people do not, in Singer's words, "starve alike."

BLACK BREAD, HARD BREAD:
FOOD, CLASS, AND HUNGER IN ITALY

As Nanni, on his death bed, closed his eyes for the last time, his children, now bereft of father and breadwinner, imagined the hunger awaiting them. Would they "have bread to eat"? Young Santo deferred marriage, knowing that "bread is scarce, and children come quick." Another son married a well-off widow, "out of love for daily bread." Lucia, the daughter, went into service in Don Venerando's home. Despite the dishonor such work brought, there she would have "as much bread and soup as she wanted, a glass of wine every day, and a plate of her own with meat on Sundays and festivals."[1]

Set in the Sicilian countryside near Mineo, Giovanni Verga's 1880 tale, "Pane Nero" (Black Bread), wove together the many strands of food—its reality and ideology in late nineteenth-century Italy. Like much of his literary output, Verga's "Pane Nero" detailed how the poor scrambled for food, knowing full well that much existed close at hand. Not just a literary image, this reality pervaded the lives of the Italian poor. The tasty information about what they did not eat mattered as much as the mundane details of what they did. While poor people were limited to a meager and precarious diet, they could see that a few in their midst ate better. Measured amounts of better food consumed at sacred times heightened the contrast between the ordinary and the good. This too whetted their appetites.

New political realities, ushered in with the unification of Italy in 1860, played a considerable role in shaping the food culture. A project of modernization, the *risorgimento* set out to destroy feudalism and transform Italy into an independent, unified European nation on par with its powerful industrialized neighbors to the north.[2] But rather than liberate the poor from economic exploitation, the creation of a modernizing Italy complicated their relationship to the land and its products and compromised their ability to feed themselves.[3]

The history of food in modern Italy, especially the ever present prospect of hunger for the poorer classes, reflected both the Italian class structure born of modernity and the politics of united Italy, which then persisted until the end of the World War II. From Rome, the central government introduced new taxes to finance the building of a modern country, a burden much resented in formerly more isolated regions. These levies made it even more difficult for the poor to feed themselves. The *fuocatico* taxed each and every hearth. The *macinato* (grist tax) placed a levy on every bag of grain brought to the mill. This tax in particular raised the ire of marginal growers, and in Sicily and Naples peasants rose up dozens of times against this threat to their subsistence.[4] Taxes were also imposed upon draft animals, like mules whose labor made low-level agriculture possible.[5]

The rich easily evaded taxes on fireplaces, food, or animals. Armed with franchises and able to trade upon political connections, they had friends in high places. Even when authorities successfully enforced assessments, those with means felt little pinch to their comfortable standards of living. For the poor, in contrast, the smallest tax chipped away at already thin margins of survival.[6]

Given the tax evasions of the rich, authorities turned upon the poor for revenues to finance industrial development and military ventures. The poor in turn devised elaborate strategies to circumvent taxes. Francis Clark, an observer sympathetic to the plight of the Italian poor, described to American readers in 1919 the social drama surrounding food taxes: "As one enters an Italian town . . . he is sure to see a little customs house. . . . The official comes out, peers . . . to see if perchance a bag of flour, or a bottle of wine, or a dozen oranges are concealed . . . every load of provisions . . . must pay the *octroi* duties, or the local tax."[7] A traveler in 1915 described "an old woman fined fifty francs for having in her possession a pound of sea-salt . . . no wonder the women of the country-side, rather than waste three precious hours in arguments about a few cheeses, will smuggle them past the authorities under the device of being *enceintes* [pregnant]."[8]

Poverty had long been a fact of Italian life, but it worsened under the pressures of modernization and overpopulation. In the late nineteenth century the emergence of the unified nation coincided with a vast increase in population.[9] For the country as a whole, numbers climbed from 26.8 million in 1871 to 28.46 million ten years later. By the dawn of the new century, 32.4 million people lived in Italy.[10] In the two decades before Italian statehood, Sicily's population had grown by 19 percent, but in the next 40 years it doubled.[11] Between 1861 and 1901 the population of the Italian south as a whole doubled as well, and this despite constant emigration.[12]

Italy's new poverty lacked the cushions associated with feudal inequities. In their long history before unification, the peninsula's poor people had by tradition enjoyed wide access to common and noble lands for hunting, fishing, and foraging. They had once benefited from common rights to collect wood for fuel and heating, and could comb baronial estates for wild fruits, mushrooms, acorns, grasses, and herbs to supplement their diet. With the end of feudalism such privileges disappeared, and their fare declined.[13]

Instead of the past's simple feudal relationships, a new social order emerged, based on an intricate system of clients and patrons.[14] Patrons, for a price, brokered on behalf of clients in need of resources, favors, and privileges. The former occupied a higher class position, the latter a subordinate one. A good relationship with a patron spelled the difference between a stable or an unstable contract for a sharecropper, a modicum of protection against an overly zealous tax collector for a peasant proprietor, some privileges of gleaning fields or gathering wild food for a tenant farmer's family, or a lease on better plots not located miles away from home. The more clients a patron amassed, the greater his wealth, influence, and status in the local community.[15] Salvatore Salomone-Marino best described Sicily's system of classes, patrons, and clients in 1897. Agricultural life, he noted, functioned by means of "multiple intermediaries between land and labor."[16]

Complications of class, relations between patrons and clients, and the gap between the small number who ate well and the majority who did not, expressed themselves in ways specific to the multiplicity of towns and regions. Despite unification into a political entity called "Italy," geographic variability created a patchwork of agricultural, social, political, and economic patterns.[17] Italy contained radically distinctive agricultural zones, soils, climates, degrees of forestation, and sources of water, which in turn produced different crops, regional staples, and landholding and labor arrangements.[18]

The conventional bifurcation of Italy into north and south distorts the variegated realities of class, geography, and food.[19] Some very poor people lived in the supposedly affluent north. They eked out their lives as sharecroppers, subsisting on rice or corn, rarely enhanced by protein. At the same time, some better-off peasants in the impoverished south acquired economic stability, and with bits of extra land planted gardens that broadened their bread-based diet.

Geographic diversity ruled. In the Apennines alone, "every village had its own peculiar characteristics," making it impossible to generalize about all Montefegatesi, let alone all northerners or all southerners.[20] Sicily did not have a singular economic system or agriculture either. The island consisted of several ecological zones, roughly running along east-west, coastal-interior lines. Each area supported particular crops, grown under idiosyncratic land and class systems.[21]

Crops differed by region.[22] In some parts of Italy rice predominated, in others maize (corn), and yet others grew wheat. In the north, assumed conventionally to have been less ravaged by poverty and hunger, the poor since the sixteenth century existed on a diet of corn. As a result, the northern Italian poor suffered repeatedly from the scourge of pellagra, a disease which made no inroads in the *mezzogiorno*, the south, where wheat, as bread for the poor or macaroni for the better off, was the staple of daily eating.[23]

Some areas, mainly although not exclusively north of Rome, supported small-scale peasant landownership, while south of Rome and in Sicily large landowners, through their intermediaries, the *gabellotti*, entered into sharecropping arrangements with peasants. In some places in the north there were extensive *mezzadria* (estates). Here tenants gave half their crop to the landlords, keeping half for themselves. Some villages in the south included peasant owners, however impoverished, functioning somewhat independently.[24] Even within regions a kaleidoscope of landholding systems distinguished town from town. Based on tradition, topography, and climate, distinct local practices persisted through World War I.[25] In some places, local variation survived into the Fascist era. Localism, *campanilismo*, predominated. Calabria contained a great "internal diversity," rather than a unified regional culture.[26] In the Alto Molise region of the south Italian Appenines, vast "community differences" separated neighboring villages and produced distinctive "dialects and dietary peculiarities."[27] Antonio Gramsci, writing about the south, a region usually constructed as singularly poor and barren, saw instead "a great social disaggregation" and little uniformity in social practice.[28] Luigi Villari, in 1902, likewise attributed Italy's lack of development to his perception that "in no country in Europe are local differences so marked as in Italy."[29]

Class divisions trumped all others. In the decades following national unification through the end of the 1920s, class positions remained relatively fixed and were crucial. The Italian rural class structure consisted of four broad groupings, unequal in size and influence.[30] A small elite, usually known as the *galantuomini*, topped the hierarchy and owned most of the land.[31] In the south and in Sicily members of this class often did not live on the lands they owned, but made their homes in Palermo, Naples, or some other city with greater amenities. They appointed underlings, *gabellotti* (sometimes called *fattori*), to supervise their estates, the *latifondia*.[32] This intermediary class made sure that crops got cultivated and brought to market, and that taxes got paid, all at the bidding of the *galantuomini* on the backs of the poor.[33]

The *gabellotti* bridged the chasm between the landowners and those below them, the vast bulk of the Italian population in every region. Some of these peasants, the *burgisi*, owned small plots of land, although at moments in their lives and at critical times of the year they also farmed a landowner's estate as tenants or hired themselves out as *bracciante*, day laborers. Peasant owners of small strips of noncontiguous land (the more substantial strips were called *massari*) maintained at best a tenuous hold on their land, rarely deriving great material benefit from its produce.

The single largest group of land tillers, the *contadini*, owned no land and scrambled to enter into tenancies.[34] Families differed from each other in terms of the quality, number, size and locations of their holdings, as well as the quality of their relationships to the middlemen, who had the power to dispense favors. Some *contadini* got good deals from landowners for nice-sized holdings relatively close to each other and to their village. Others got bad deals and ended up with *fazzoletti,* or handkerchief-sized plots separated by long distances, far from home. Some worked out multiyear contracts. Others renegotiated annually.

But the *contadini* did not constitute the bottom of the pyramid. Below them could be found *giornaleri* (day laborers), who gathered every morning in the village piazza to sell their services. They hired themselves out to *contadini,* to *gabellotti,* or directly to landowners depending on season and place, and truly lived a miserable and precarious existence.[35] A study of the causes of the food riots in Palermo in 1893 and 1894 asserted that the unrest had been spearheaded by one distinct group at the bottom of the local class mosaic, those "who watched over flocks and herds . . . [and] do not know pasta, while very often they eat greens cooked without condiment of oil."[36]

The *contadini* saw the misery of those below them. They actually knew that life at first hand. When crops failed or when some other exigency disrupted the status quo, they too hired themselves out as day laborers.[37] Movement between various strata of poverty, and the bewildering internal splintering within the ranks of the poor, offered the *contadini* "a field of knowledge which gave the humble experts, even when they were illiterates, an envied authority" on the implications of class status.[38]

Individuals negotiated separately with landowners, usually through agents, for work or land, and as such did not constitute a class when their numbers were added up. They did not all enjoy, or endure, the same status or share the same stake in the preservation or disruption of the economic system, nor did they stand in a similar relationship to their social and economic betters or inferiors. "In Italy employer-labour relations," one economist wrote, "are so many and varied that contracts assume a pattern which in certain regions is as intricate and overlaid as that of land ownership."[39]

The *contadini* were ever mindful of the implications of contracts and of their relationships to those with power over them.[40] Social bonds in Italy encompassed the complicated "relationships between various categories of peasants." The minute differences between one rank and another corresponded to crucial differences in standard of living and consciousness.[41] In this class system food emerged as a powerful symbol and tangible reality of the differences between being on the top or on the bottom, or at a particular place in between. Scant food and dependence went together. The poor ate a poor diet, and what they ate, they did not determine themselves.

A Calabrian *contadino* testifying to a parliamentary inquest headed by Francesco Nitti articulated this dependence. "How can we survive?" he asked. "The better soils are far away. I am old and it takes me four hours to get to a piece of land I work on . . . It is the bitter mountains here . . . We are dying of hunger here."[42] Lucio Barbarossa, a day laborer in Apulia, told a government commission about the hard work and the meager resources which people like himself drew upon: "When you get home you eat an anchovy. We bought those and put them on our bread. Then we sat by the door and ate, and that was what we had. What did we know of soup in those days? We didn't know about anything. Four, five children, the mother and the father all ate from the same plate."[43] "*Una vita di misera,*" a life of misery, was what Maria Torno endured in her Lombardian childhood. "We ate *pan gialo* [corn bread], *minestra* [vegetable soup], pasta, *polenta* and meat maybe twice a year."[44]

Various intermediaries stood between the workers and food. Much of what the *contadini* family ate came to it in the form of payment in kind. Landowners, through the *gabellotti*, dispensed rice, corn, flour, oil, and a few times a year, meat. The amount and type of food included in the peasants' remuneration package was up for negotiation. Landowners could decide to put more, or less, food on the tables of the poor. In one southern Italian town the largest landowner in the early 1890s decided to increase his wealth by shifting from growing grain, corn, and pulses to cultivating sugar beets and opening a sugar refinery. Fine for him. But it meant that the *contadini*, who depended on growing staples and receiving a share for their own consumption, now had even less food to eat. One observer from Tuscany, on traveling through Abruzzo, commented in the 1870s that "the peasant, in order to eat, depends from one year to the next on the proprietor."[45]

Well-off Italians, however, lived comfortably in their homes, be they absentee landowners in urban villas or occupants of estates in the countryside. They enjoyed an elaborate diet. They employed servants and cooks and had access to the bounty of Italian agriculture, wine, olive oil, cheeses, pastas, meats, rice, vegetables, and fruits, as well as imports from abroad. They ate a range of complicated dishes that achieved world renown and self-consciously wrote down what they ate, boasting of its complexity and richness.[46]

The foodways of the well-off were linked in their own minds and in the consciousness of foreigners with the new Italian nation. Pellegrino Artusi's cookbook, *La Scienza in Cucina e l'Arte di Mangiar Bene*, published in 1891, deemphasized regional styles and elevated the cuisine of the middle classes as the embodiment of Italian food.[47] These pastas, meats, cheeses, oils, wines, alone and in combination with vegetables and fruits, made the idea of Italian cooking synonymous with high-class taste throughout Europe and the United States.[48]

In the public spaces and their homes the rich ate well. A 1902 description of a typical lunch of the upper and middle class depicted a leisurely two-hour meal consisting of

> a dish of eggs, or else macaroni or some other variety of *paste asciutte* (of the macaroni family) [dried pasta]. Then follows meat— stewed, roast, or boiled. The latter, called *lesso*, is a specialty of Italian cookery, and when properly done, is very appetizing. Often there is a *fritto misto* as well—a mixture of fried vegetables, bits of chicken, sweetbread, etc. Then comes a dish of vegetables, in which department Italian cooks are masters. Cheese and fruit end the repast.[49]

Even modestly well-off Italians enjoyed good food and wrote about their tastes and smells. Constantine Panunzio grew up in an economically well-placed, although not dazzlingly rich, family in Apulia. His parents entertained often, and lavished upon their guests "almonds, walnuts, raisins and stuffed dates or figs, with home-made cakes and candy. They served the best of the year's wine and 'rosolio'—a delicate liqueur." Evenings found the family strolling to the town's piazza, and "we would sit in groups around the marble-topped tables of the cafes to eat a 'gelato' or sip a delicious 'orzata'—an almond drink."[50] A woman who spent her youth in Lombardy celebrated the "rich cabbage soup" of her childhood and the thick slices of bread whose taste she remembered seventy years later.[51] Clementina Tedesco from the Veneto region came from a economically secure landowning family. She recalled a childhood fragrant with pork and veal sausages. "Oh boy," she remembered, "when you fried a little of that sausage, the smell was sent all over the town." In her childhood, coffee, risotto, fried salami and eggs, salty vegetable soups, fresh fruits, artichokes, tomatoes, lentils, ice cream, pastries, and polenta showed up regularly on the family table. Her father hunted the lands he owned for grouse, partridge, and pheasant, and she gathered wild mushrooms, asparagus, and berries from their land.[52] Guido Orlando came from a "sturdy gray stone house" in Barisciano, Aquila, in eastern Italy. In their garden his family raised cabbage, tomatoes, zucchini, eggplant, and artichokes. While he claimed that they were actually "very poor people—as was almost everyone in our town," the garden and the "number of painfully purchased patches of ground . . . out of town" allowed his modestly well-off family to buy pepper, sugar, and salt, something most *contadini* could not afford.[53]

In 1935 Fascist authorities banished Carlo Levi to a remote village, Lucania, for his opposition to the invasion of Ethiopia. As he described his isolation and boredom and the lives of the town's women and men, he also delineated the town's two food cultures. In Don Luigi's home Levi ate "excellent jams, preserves, cakes, baked olives, dried figs stuffed with almonds, and sausages with Spanish peppers." But, "as for the poor," he wrote, "they ate plain bread the whole year around, spiced occasionally with a carefully crushed raw tomato, or a little garlic and oil, or a Spanish pepper with such a devilish bite to it that it is known as a *diavolesco*." Despite a government ban on fishing in the local rivers, some of the poor defied the law out of hunger, because "the poor people . . . had so little to eat all the year around that a plate of fish was a gift from the gods."[54]

The lives of *contadini*, day laborers, small-farmowner peasants, low-grade artisans, and struggling townspeople pivoted around the search for food. Their narratives resonated with the details of hunger, scarcity, privation, and a desire for the good foods eaten by others.[55] In the first decade of the twentieth century, Calabrian *contadini* ate "green soups . . . made of cabbage and beans, scarcely dressed with lard or oil."[56] An exhaustive survey of Italian life in the 1920s emphasized scarcity. "Dry bread," wrote Robert Foerster, a Princeton economist, "soaked in oil and salt, is the staple diet of many a laborer."[57]

Personal narratives echoed these observations. Leonard Covello, born in the town of Avigliano described how his family, occupying a notch above most *contadini*, still struggled for food: "To make ends meet, my mother rented a little cubby hole on the *piazza*, where she sold small quantities of olive oil and bread and other staples. Sometimes she would make enough money for our food, but more often we ate *acqua sale*, which was nothing more than hard bread soaked in boiling water with a little olive oil and salt added for flavor."[58] Rocco Boffilo remembered his native Calabria as a place where "Many *contadini* . . . do not eat bread. They live on potatoes and beans."[59]

The great majority spent most of their income on food. In 1890 Maria Pasolini computed that in Ravenna, for example, a family consisting of husband, wife, a son, and two daughters earned 587 lira a year, 73 percent of which went for food.[60] A series of government surveys beginning in the 1870s and extending through World War I estimated that the average poor family used up 75 to 85 percent of its income to feed itself.[61] An 1885 inquest estimated that better-off peasants "feed on vegetable soup and pasta, bread and a little wine. Only rarely does the menu include meat."[62] An American investigator estimated that an "average" family living south of Rome consumed 21 pounds of wheat flour weekly, 17 pounds of corn, or "Indian meal," 19 cents worth of oil and condiment, 4 cents of meat and bacon, four eggs, and a half pound of salt.[63] Nearly every first-person account of Italian life, from the end of the nineteenth century through 1945, brings up the subject of food and scarcity. Government reports, travelers' accounts, and imaginative literature provided snapshots from all regions, and concurred that hunger pervaded the lives of the poor, who worried that conditions would worsen.[64]

The constant fight for food informed almost all the writing of Giovanni Verga.[65] The fictional characters he created, the women and men of the peasantry, expressed Verga's understanding of the intricacies of the class system as the poor fretted over every meal and morsel. In such stories as "Pane Nero," "I Galantuomini," "Cavalleria Rusticana," "L'Osteria dei Buoni Amici," and his masterpiece novel of peasant life, *I Malavoglia*, published in 1881 (in English, *The House by the Medlar Tree*),[66] Verga wove together his perceptions of the hunger of the poor with their knowledge of the food of the elite, and he defined as his task recording the voices of those who only ate "black bread."[67] In an 1878 letter to a friend, he expressed his hope of capturing in literature "modern Italy, from the lower classes where the struggle is limited to the conquest of one's daily bread," to the elite who dominated political life.[68]

He did just that in *I Malavoglia*, a novel as focused on food, hunger, and class difference as on fate, family, and village life. The novel's protagonist, 'Ntoni, aspired to a better lot, and his aspirations took the shape of dreams of food. One of 'Ntoni's kin, skeptical of his ambitions, interrogated him, asking what more money would bring. "What shall we do when we are rich?" For an answer, the young peasant repeated the question, and "scratched his head . . . We shan't do anything at all! . . . We shall go and live in town and do nothing, and eat macaroni and meat every day." 'Ntoni had once actually been to Naples and wrote his family fantastic letters about the city's wonders, a place where "that *pizze*, the kind that gentlefolk ate, were on sale for two centesimi each."[69]

The novel's poor all thought about food. One particularly perceptive character, Piedipapera, "sniffed in the direction of the priest's house and said to his poor friends, 'Don Giammaria is having fried vermicelli for dinner to-night!'" At just that moment the well-fed priest walked by, greeting those who were about to eat a much more Spartan fare. Piedipapera, "who still had the appetizing smell of fried vermicelli in his nostrils, called out: 'Eh! Don Giammaria! Fried vermicelli this evening!'"[70] Macaroni, the priest's food, fried in oil, smelled good, and for the poor of this fictional Sicilian village it was a luxury. They ate pasta only when friends brought platters of it to each other when someone had died, as a meal of consolation. "All her friends," Verga wrote of a newly widowed villager, "brought something, as is the custom—macaroni, grapes, wine, and all God's good gifts."

Verga's scenarios of eating, talking of food, and comparing who ate what, when, and where reflected the reality of food consciousness of the Italian poor. People knew the extent of their neighbors' hunger and compared their own to that of others. Stories circulated in towns about the lengths to which people went to find food, and oral accounts of poverty and hunger haunted the villages. A commentator on the conditions of life for the lower class in Apulia in the Tavoliere region opined that "a man who ate every day was reckoned to be wealthy, and his sons were 'catches' in the local marriage market."[71] In Montegegatesi in north central Italy, villagers talked about a poor family which came "up with an imaginative and inexpensive way of adding a bit of flavor to their monotonous diet." They hung a smoked herring above the dinner table and rubbed slices of thick porridge, the daily *polenta*, on it.[72]

The poor generally fed upon regionally determined staples—rice, corn, or wheat—with little to supplement their single foodstuff, other than the vegetables which they might grow if they had a garden.[73] Sometimes they negotiated the right to forage, or they took a chance and gathered greens, mushrooms, nuts, and herbs without permission.[74] Few had gardens, however, and breaking the law risked punishment.

However skimpy their usual diet, even that could diminish. In most regions winter represented a low in the dietary calendar. Families knew days when they had nothing. The mercurial fluctuations in the price of bread sent the urban poor into a terror of starvation, and that in turn sent them out into the streets, begging or demanding food.[75] A 1909 study, based heavily on Italian government reports, noted that "cases of death from starvation are very rare, but there is a terrible permanent lack of food."[76]

Natural disasters—crop failures, droughts, storms—further jeopardized the food supply. Each region and village had its own history of crises, and in each case, the staple's disappearance brought the poor into direct confrontation with starvation. In Sicily's Nissoria region peasants subsisted on fava beans. They experienced three fava bean crop failures in the 1880s. Bad roads made it impossible to bring in food relief, leaving the poor with few resources to alleviate their desperation.[77]

No matter how little the poor had to eat, they always had to pay landowners first.[78] When food supplies dwindled, they turned to family members for help, foraged illegally, or stole. But if they did not pay the landowner, they had no place to live. If they had no place to live, then true starvation followed. Food, even if negligible, became a luxury.[79]

Meat they almost never ate, although if they happened upon the carcass of a dead animal, they were usually allowed to scavenge it.[80] In Apulia, landowners on the great estates maintained an explicit policy of granting *bracciante* a share of the flesh of dead beasts of burden. Such beneficence was useful to landowners. They got a slightly better-fed work force at no cost, and dead animals were disposed of.[81]

Two or three times a year, on Christmas, Easter, and the local saint's day, the landowner, directly or through *gabellotti*, distributed meat.[82] A child of poverty in Santa Teresa di Riva in Sicily experienced great excitement at eating a piece of meat fat at Christmas. "Over there," he remembered, "if you had a piece of fat you was lucky, and boy, it tasted good."[83] Government reports confirmed the meatless diet of the *contadini.* "Agriculturists," noted the 1909 inquest on Calabrian conditions, "see meat when they are about to die and cannot eat it anymore."[84]

Visitors noted the paucity of food available to the poor. Alexandre Dumas commented in 1862 that in Naples, "while a *signore* feeds his dogs on white bread, the people live on roots and grass, eked out with an insufficient quantity of coarse bread."[85] A writer who traveled in Sicily several times at the end of the nineteenth century remarked that to the poor, death was not to be feared, as "life [is] a place where there is not always enough to eat."[86]

Food for Italy's poor fit directly in the patron-client nexus. Most *contadini* and casual laborers received part of their payment in kind. Sharecroppers earned almost no cash, taking their compensation in food and seed. Up until the 1880s southern *latifondia* owners typically shipped 75 percent of the olive oil to Naples for export, keeping the other quarter of the yield for themselves to feast upon, and a minute amount they dribbled out as *minatici,* monthly allotments to underlings.[87] Miners took part of their compensation in food as well.[88] Thus food, rather than the money to purchase it, was the currency in the class-based world of employers and employees. Day laborers in Caccamo near Termini, for example, relied upon their employers to supplement their bread with other food, usually cheese, olives, and "bad wine."[89]

In Sicily, during the crucial times of the year when laborers, mostly men, worked in gangs among olive trees, grape arbors, and wheat fields, it was gang bosses (*corporali*), who fed workers. Sometimes whole families, men, women, and children picked, harvested, and threshed together.[90] According to Salvatore Salomone-Marino, Sicilian *contadini* ate during harvest time a mess of vegetables, *minestra,* as well as "salted sardines and onions or a bit of cheese," with some wine to supplement the bread they had brought from home. What the boss provided they called *companatico,* that which accompanied the bread baked by wives and mothers. During harvest time laborers ate up to "seven moderate repasts a day," which were "likely to be wholesome."

This distribution of food was no act of kindness. The owners of the fields, vineyards, and orchards needed well-fed workers.[91] Lombardian rice-picking crews working the *risaie,* rice plantations, received remuneration as well as their sustenance on the job in rice. Mostly women and children, these seasonal rice pickers remembered that "for food we got a big bowl of rice three times a day."[92]

Importantly, not everyone on work crews ate alike. Workers negotiated on their own, and not as a class, for what they were fed. The fastest and ablest pickers demanded "a taste of gravy" to enrich the common fare. Higher paid workers ate best, and the others saw what better meant. Employers worked with hired hands at these peak moments, and "the greatest complaints," Salomone-Marino observed, "are because of what is given as *companatico* and almost always when seeing (oh, how different and how tempting!) what is taken from the employer's sack, and seeing what he and the stewards eat." This chant of the grape gatherers puts it bluntly:

> And now that I have eaten and drunk,
> I praise my boss who has given it to me!
> He eats steak, he has drunk wine,
> I filled up on sardines and water;
> He gulped dainty tidbits
> I've made do with the smell!
> And always every moment,
> The grapes to the vats.[93]

Food was limited, getting it difficult, but knowledge about it was widespread, and its meaning powerful. Peasants and laborers processed raw crops into food, but tasted it rarely, and never on their own terms. They prepared olive oil and wine for the *galantuomini* and the *gabellotti*, receiving only tantalizing drops. In Sicily, the *gabellotti* took for themselves all the milk and the *ricotta* cheese which peasants made. All over the Italian peninsula, the poor made the food, saw it, knew how to assess its quality, but could only eat what those with power allotted.

That so much of the foodstuffs the poor produced were out of their reach contributed to a widespread reverence for food. Individuals perceived it as a precious commodity, the possession of which meant the difference between life and death, comfort and distress. They carefully constructed a highly regulated system to share food amongst themselves. While they maintained active village social lives, they rarely invited one another for meals. They functioned within a culture of hospitality wherein hosts felt obligated to feed guests.[94] Because of that, little visiting in private homes ever took place among the poor. They lived in small cramped units, making indoor socializing nearly impossible. Individuals extended food hospitality only to their social betters, because they knew those visitors could reciprocate. To invite one's social and economic peers or inferiors into one's home and feed them, obligated the guest to do so as well, placing upon them an onerous burden.[95]

The only exception to this took place at one key moment in everybody's life, the hour of death and bereavement. Neighbors commonly brought cooked and uncooked food to houses of mourning.[96] Residents of Palermo called it *conolu*, while in the Sicilian town of Montedoro it was a *conzu*. Whatever the name, the practice confirmed communal responsibilities among the poor and limited food sharing to the heightened spirituality of ritual time.[97]

Food, its preparation and consumption, otherwise took place within the home, confirming assumptions about the primacy of the family. The matrix of food-family-sanctity served as an Italian peasant ideal, in part because it so often lay beyond the grasp of the poor. Families had little control over what they ate. Young women left home for lengthy periods of time to work in silk mills and textile factories, or to labor as domestic servants for local elites. Men, the *contadini* in particular, left home and walked many miles from holding to holding, unable to return home for the midday meal. At various seasons they were absent for extended periods of time, eating, with other men, what employers gave them, and what they cooked themselves.

"Family" as the unit of everyday life could not be separated from food. An ethnographer who lived in a Sicilian village in the 1920s with a poor family declared that "the real symbol of the household unity is the common table."[98] While in reality men ate daytime meals away from home, and women and children took theirs out of doors in the courtyard with peers, the notion of the family consuming a meal together dominated popular ideas about how human beings should live. Central to that common table and to the reality of food as fundamental to family life were women. They, within their sphere of influence, shaped family consumption patterns.[99] Salvatore Salomone-Marino asserted in 1897 that "the housewife, too, has her portion of absolute domain," the home where food was cooked and consumed.[100]

Women determined, within the limited range of choices dictated by class, what the family ate. Their culinary skills spelled the difference between good and bad food. If bread, or polenta, or rice represented the boundary between life and death, between hunger's pangs and a meal's satisfaction, then women as the bakers of bread and preparers of polenta were hardly ancillary to Italian social life. As custodians of the family's money and guardians of its larder, women made sure they had a bit extra at hand so that holy days might be marked by better meals. They made sure that daughters learned to cook, since without adequate food skills girls made poor candidates for marriage. Women made sure that husbands and sons consumed enough so that they could work and everyone could eat again.

Italian peasant women did not use that power to enhance their own personal consumption. They operated within a system of gender deference based on male superiority. The *contadina* "keeps the least possible for herself and the children; she always keeps the best for" her husband.[101] Men generally ate first and women later.[102] A "well-to-do Italian peasant near Alba in Piedmont" detailed his daily life in a 1909 interview. "The men sit in the kitchen round the table, the women serve and eat, the boys squat by the chimney or on the doorstep, eating greedily porringer [*polenta*] on knee."[103] Carlo Levi observed gendered eating at the upper end of the class spectrum in Lucania. He sat down to eat with a local aristocrat, a Signor Orlando, and "in his house the old Lucanian customs were observed: his wife did not come to the table with us."[104]

Despite separate seating, men recognized the importance of women in the universe of food. They complimented wives and mothers on their cooking. In recalling their childhoods, they lovingly recalled mothers as good cooks, able to transform meager raw products into tasty dishes. A consumer of polenta praised the women in his family for enhancing its inherently bland taste. "If polenta is the dish, the women prepare a sauce, and what sauce it is!"[105] Women's food worlds blended public and private. Although families ate their evening meal at home around family tables, town life, the basic residential pattern of Italy, fostered the spread of food knowledge. Even small villages had a communal oven. In larger towns several were scattered among the *robba*, the clusters of houses which constituted neighborhoods.[106] While the very wealthiest residents did not bake in these ovens, most everyone else did. At the community ovens women learned about skills, class difference, and food. Women bringing their bread to the ovens saw other women's bread, and could measure their own loaves accordingly.[107]

In Sicilian towns women brought their cooking and sewing to the courtyards, the *cortilli*. Some owned little portable stoves and daily carried them out of doors. The women sat and cooked and talked and assessed what was simmering in everyone else's pots.[108] In the 1890s Salomone-Marino recorded that women fed their children out of doors, "as well as herself; and all this not silently, but chatting and joking loudly with her neighbors."[109] The impact of such close contiguity meant that women constantly compared their food and status with that of others. [110]

Women's culinary skills reflected on the family. The bread they baked their husbands took to work, and its quality symbolized the family's position. When necessary, wives carried meals to their men in the fields, and how good it looked, smelled, and tasted represented the family among the community of laborers. Women transported food knowledge from the homes in which they had cooked as servants to the homes they set up as wives. When foraging was possible, women and children hunted down mushrooms, nuts, berries, and greens.[111] Women brought whatever dishes and pots they could afford to their new homes upon marriage, and if foodstuffs were to be bought, women did the purchasing. Women with some cash dealt with storekeepers. Those without money bartered with peddlers or merchants. In the one act of food gifts among the poor, the meals of consolation, women brought the food.

While women ruled the world of food, men played a supporting part. Landowners negotiated with men. Part of that negotiation involved the amounts and types of in-kind food remuneration. To see men cooking was not unusual. Particularly during harvest time, when they lived in groups away from home, they cooked for themselves. Men bought the rare piece of meat and knew what ingredients went into what dishes.

But women played the biggest and most constant role. Only they consistently traded upon their relationship to food and culinary abilities. Men were judged by their ability to provide for a family, but women stood at the center of the food cycle and their work linked the family's fate to the rituals and skills of the kitchen. Husbands earned the flour or oil, but wives stood on the front line, changing raw products into the edible, something which satisfied the body's need for calories and produced the pleasures of taste. A man who lived in Sicily until 1920 in a very poor family remembered how, "To feed the family in winter, my father would buy a hundred kilograms of dried beans. My mother would soak them the night before and the following day get some macaroni and that's how we fill the family. And naturally, she baked her own bread."[112] He got. She transformed. His abilities were prosaic: lugging a heavy sack. Hers were almost magical.

Women also served as agents of food culture through their work as domestic servants in the homes of their towns' elites. The poor by necessity sent daughters off to work for better-off families. They not only contributed to the family, but they stood to better their prospects when it came to marriage. A daughter who could cook meant a great deal to a family living at the margins of subsistence. Domestic service confirmed for women the need to teach their daughters kitchen skills.[113]

These young girls learned to cook the richer and more varied foods that money could buy.[114] They cooked, and the well-off ate. Charlotte Chapman noted in her 1928 research in Sicily that in the homes of the very wealthy, servant women shopped for food. Girls from poor families in the service of wealthy employers got extensive first-hand information about what food there was, how it should be prepared, and how it tasted.[115]

Domestic work also exposed young women to the humiliations of the class system. A woman who had been a domestic servant in Italy, laboring in a home in Ponte di Serra, recalled that "the lady" of the house "counted the potatoes she gave me at supper. Can you imagine! A young girl like I was, full of life and get-up-and-go, leaving the mountains for the city. I had such an appetite I could have eaten rocks."[116]

Women's role as intermediaries between the reality of the food of the poor and the tastes of abundance grew out of Italy's long history as a tourist magnet. For centuries foreigners journeyed to Italy to look at the glorious ruins of the ancient world. Pilgrims came to venerate the shrines of early Christianity, and students of art contemplated the treasures of the Renaissance. Italy's magnificent palaces, paintings, statuary, and churches drew artists, writers, and lovers of beauty to the cities and countryside. Italy's urban dwellers vacationed away from the big cities, experiencing briefly the pleasures of simple country life.[117]

Visitors needed to be fed and lodged. Women in modest families augmented their family income by doing precisely that for tourists, and in doing so learned what "rich" city people expected to eat.[118] Angelo Pellegrini grew up in a moderately poor home in Tuscany in the early twentieth century. His mother supported the family by cooking for tourists. "I was frequently puzzled," he wrote in an appropriately named memoir, *The Unprejudiced Palate*, "as a child by the . . . dinners Mother prepared for wealthy Italians who came to our country home from the city." The visitors ate "fine broth," with escarole, boiled beef, turnip greens and dandelion salad, wine, cheese, and "an immense amount of homemade bread."[119] The Pellegrini family never ate so well.

Through the Heel of Italy, the travel journal of Katharine Hooker, an American tourist in the 1920s, confirmed Pellegrini's childhood recollection of tourists being fed in private homes. She reported extensively on the meals villagers served her in their homes, contrasting that fare with what she ate at cafes, inns, and restaurants. After visiting one town in Potenza, she noted that in cafes throughout the peninsula proprietors will not serve "native Italian dishes," because they assume that travelers prefer "something they consider cosmopolitan." But in private homes, the women conformed to "local and traditional forms of cooking." Her travel narrative made the point that Italians, women in particular, recognized the linkages between food and class and knew that travelers and foreigners demanded "higher" standards. Hooker and other tourists chronicled such knowledge and behavior in Trani, Gravina, Potenza, Bari, Barletta, and dozens of other places along the peninsula, in the heel and up the boot.[120]

Basic residential patterns also fostered food knowledge. While most Italians were tied to agriculture, few lived in isolated rural areas. They lived in villages at some distance from the fields to which laborers went out each day.[121] Even small villages manifested urban characteristics. People lived close to each other, with little physical segregation between the homes of the poor majority and the elite minority. "Not far from the villa" where Constantine Panunzio grew up in comfort and plenty, "and in bold contrast to it, stood the crude huts of the 'contadini.'"[122] In one Sicilian village the houses not only abutted upon each other, but "there is no pronounced pattern of settlement . . . following class lines. Mansions are dispersed rather than clustered."[123]

Visitors to Italy repeatedly commented on the urbanism of agricultural villages. Writing about Calabria in 1915, Norman Douglas remarked that "even a small Italian town would be incomplete without its piazza where streets converge and commercial pulses beat their liveliest measure."[124] An "elegant high street lined with the palaces of the local *signori*" ran through most Apulian villages.[125] These towns maintained a common public space, usually around a piazza, with a church, a cafe where men spent time away from the family, and in some places a store or two where those with some money could buy sugar, salt, tobacco, or foodstuffs.[126] Comfortable families took evening strolls to the town center for light refreshments, and were observed by those unable to buy *gelato*, cakes, and liqueurs. The poor saw what comestibles appeared on the store's shelves. Town life taught them that those foods existed far beyond their means, yet very close by.

In a different way from the close relations in villages and market towns, Italy's great cities—Naples, Palermo, Turin, Milan, Genoa, and Rome—also gave the poor the chance to see, smell, and sometimes taste the foods of their social betters. Home to both the very rich and the very poor, the cities played a key role in the diffusion of food knowledge from the rich to the poor.[127] A constant flow of people from the countryside to the cities contributed in part to the growth of Italy's urban population by the middle of the nineteenth century. Those searching for work went in and out of cities, and, while there, assimilated new knowledge about food and standards for consumption.[128] For many, a brief sojourn in Naples or Genoa constituted a first exposure to a big city. Guido Orlando, whose village family occupied a notch above most, remembered his amazement during a week in Naples. "I never had such food before—food I hadn't had to work for, and as much as I wanted to eat. It was, almost literally, like manna from heaven. My only trouble was learning to use a fork."[129]

City stores advertised their wares by festooning exteriors with "great rings of bread," "long loaves tied to a pole," "bladders of lard and curious looking piles of cheese," all designed to attract consumers.[130] The cities' fish markets, fruit stands, vegetable stalls, butcher shops, and bakeries demonstrated that food could be had if one but possessed money. Hucksters roamed the streets selling food. In Naples, the *maccaronaro*, the vendor of macaroni, set up shop outside, with "two tall stoves on which stand two ample pots forming the front of the booth. . . . He wears an apron and holds a long-handled ladle. On his right is a bench with a platter of

3. Italian cities, unlike towns in the countryside, supported restaurants, bakeries, and stores selling cheese, macaroni, sausage, fish, and other foodstuffs. In this 1903 stereograph, a group of people eat in front of a Naples macaroni restaurant.

grated cheese, a large pan of tomato sauce, a pile of bowls . . . His customers eat on the spot, the richest take cheese and sauce, others only cheese, while the poor content themselves with a little water from the pot."[131]

In cities rich people and travelers from abroad ate in restaurants, public places designed to show people eating where others would see them.[132] Poor people walked past these palaces of consumption and witnessed the drama. George Gissing sat in a restaurant in Reggio and noted with disgust that during his meal "I saw children's faces pressed against

4. Vendors, like this one selling bread, roamed the streets of Naples and other Italian cities. Rural visitors marveled at the amount of food available there.

the glass, peering little faces." Every time the door opened, he heard those children begging for *un pezzo di pane*, a slice of bread. The waiters dutifully pushed the hungry children away from the restaurant, helping patrons eat in peace.[133] In Naples beggars stood outside the *maccaronare*, the public macaroni stands, and hoped to "collect alms in the coin of macaroni."[134]

Food knowledge traveled from the top down along the sacred rhythm of the Christian calendar as well. The poor who lived on polenta or bits of bread experienced moments of relief at holy days. Sundays for better-off *contadini* and artisans brought a slight improvement. Rosa Cassettari's family, a middling-poor one in Cuggiono, Lombardy, operated an *osteria*, an inn. Every day they ate polenta with "sour wine." Sundays and holidays meant extra business, which translated into a little extra cash in the family's coffers. So on the Lord's day, after church, they ate *minestra*, a vegetable soup, and "Oh, we were happy! We only got that good rice soup on Sundays and holidays. We examined our own and each other's and ate very slow to make it last." Rosa was puzzled by the behavior of her wealthier neighbors, the people who owned the house she lived in. They ate *minestra* every day, and Rosa wondered, "How will they know it's a feast day?"[135]

At moments of communal celebration, with the arrival of holidays, the *gabellotti* or the *galantuomini* demonstrated their largesse by passing out food and wine to the poor.[136] At Christmas,[137] Easter, and carnival, the onset of Lent, and local saints' days, food passed from the wealthy to the usually hungry, and "the peasant expects and claims from his *padrone*" on Christmas special pastries, either *cuccidata*, *nucatuli*, or *mustazzoli*.[138] Towns and regions varied as to what patrons gave—chicken, goose, oil, eggs, capon, pasta—and for which holiday, but whatever the local tradition, food flowed from the powerful to the dependent.[139]

Throughout the south and Sicily, holiday time meant a chance to eat macaroni and a bit of meat, foods eaten regularly by the elite.[140] Life histories resounded with stories of holidays being days of eating better. A man recalled how the town's grandest landowner gave meat to those who worked his land three times a year, Christmas, Easter, and the festival of the Madonna of Mount Carmel.[141] Another, from a town east of Naples, reported that the rich gave the poor sweets, not "regular food," on Christmas.[142] In Sicily, local elites used March 19, the festival of Saint Joseph, to demonstrate their commitment to the poor and their obligation to feed them. They held banquets and invited the poor, with orphans a particular object of concern, into their homes for a meal. Intended to re-enact the poverty of Mary, Joseph, and Jesus, this festival, like other annual food distributions at sacred times, fixed class relations through food. The gifts relieved hunger, making sacred time truly special. The gift-giving confirmed the obligation of those with little power to those with more. As long as *contadini*, tenants, and *giornaleri* fulfilled their obligations, they could expect holiday food. Any disruptions of the chain of command disrupted this sacred food chain.[143]

Holy time food performances demanded highly public venues.[144] On Sicilian holy days, bread, olives, almond candies shaped like olives, cheeses, were paraded through the streets and then marched into the church to honor St. Agatha the patron of Catania, St. Biagio of Salemi, St. Cono of Naso, and other saints who protected other towns. To honor Saint Calogero, dear to the women and men of Agrigento, loaves of bread in the shape of human feet, legs, arms, and heads wended their way through the town and to the church.[145]

In one central Italian village, an elaborate carnival ceremony marked the beginning of Lent. The men who participated in the public festivities assembled at the bakery and were served spaghetti in tuna sauce, all expenses covered by the wife of the town's wealthiest merchant, the "community's patroness."[146] In Bari, during the Festa di Maria Santissima degli Angeli di Quasoni, all who volunteered to bake festival bread were rewarded with wheat, which they carried through the town to their homes.[147] The theatricality of these food festivals was planned so the poor saw the patrons' largesse.[148]

Food itself was holy and venerated. In Taranta Peligna in Abruzzi, on the Feast of San Biagio, the town crier traversed the streets, calling out the names of the people who had made bread for the public celebration. In Marta, on the Feast of the Madonna del Monte, townspeople encircled the picture of the Madonna with loaves of bread, framed by artichoke, cherries, lemons, apples, and oranges, while local fishermen filed into church, making offerings of live squid and eel.[149] *Feste* confirmed the sanctity of food. Food could hardly be mundane and prosaic if women and men carried it to the Madonna in acts of devotion. Far more than supplying the body with energy, the consumption of food through public religious ritual on sacred days of the Christian calendar emphasized its sanctity.[150]

During *feste*, the local clergy and the upper classes arranged for lavish public displays of food. They gave handouts of food directly to the poor in the form of oil, wine, cheese, and macaroni. Beginning in the seventeenth century, the gentry and priests in the towns of the Emiliana-Romagna region passed out *polenta*, their staple, to the poor to celebrate the maize harvest. Visitors to the festival described how "people used to open their doors and offer wine to friends and foreigners."[151] Being impoverished meant knowing viscerally the difference between sacred and ordinary through the sense of taste and the periodic satisfactions of a fuller belly. The poor experienced these temporary, seasonal increases in calories and pleasures of the palate through the beneficence of patrons. Food thus gained a place in the hierarchical class structure, and ritual gifts of food confirmed the rightness of the every day reality that the poor did not control their own consumption. What they ate came from the top down. The *feste* in Italy wove food into the skein of class relationships held together by patrons' power and clients' deference. That the rich staged these festivals, centered around food and performed in public, showed the poor in one more way exactly what poverty meant.

The Italian poor had one more source of information about food. The worldwide migration of the Italian people shaped the understanding of those who remained in Italy with regard to taste, wealth, and consumption. Italian life of the late nineteenth and early twentieth century took part of its shape from the constant back-and-forth movement between home villages and sojourns in the wider world, and America in particular.

Italian men by and large defined their initial migrations as temporary, brief periods of "exile" in which they went abroad, earned money, saved as much as they could, underconsumed, and then came back home. Italians far outnumbered any other group in the statistics of return migration to place of origin.[152] The ubiquitous presence in Italian towns, villages, and cities of men who had once lived in America transformed past practice and shook up popular consciousness about food.[153]

These men came back different than they had left.[154] Their clothes bespoke American success, measured by village standards. Their encounters with American food also demonstrated the impact of America and the creation of American tastes. Angelo Pellegrini recalled his village in Tuscany "before the ravages of Fascism and war," and depicted the "gay event" surrounding the "return of an emigrant. "All the townsfolk," Pellegrini remembered, were impressed by his "fine woolen garments, amazingly handsome shoes of real leather, his bleached complexion and smooth hands." They soaked up his tales of America, "of wheat fields so vast that no fast train could traverse them in a single day; of meats and sweets and fine clothes so universally enjoyed that it was impossible to distinguish the rich from the poor. And of incredible waste! No American, he would assure his fellow peasants, "ever eats an entire sandwich; he always throws away the fringe of crust."

Returnees did not just talk about American foodways. Their trunks, of "immediate interest to the villagers," were "crammed full of sweets. The most prized were the chocolate bars."[155] Giuseppina Spoto reluctantly returned to Sicily with her husband in 1902. He wanted to go back. She did not. Upon her forced return, she regaled her neighbors with stories about America, particularly Florida's Ybor City, where "they make coffee in a big pot." Coffee, for Italy's poor was an extravagant luxury. But now one of their own described how she drank it regularly in America.[156]

Ironically, even when the *americani* complained about conditions abroad, they heightened popular consciousness about the bounty of America compared to Italy's meagerness. A man who returned to his village in Abruzzo in 1908, moaned that in Canada "we ate together and lived in one small bedroom. . . . Once or twice a week we ate meat." This level of meat consumption was meager by Canadian standards, but in Vasto in the first decade of the twentieth century, meat weekly constituted a bounty unheard of except among the rich.[157]

Returnees had money to spend, unlike most natives, and wanted to replicate tastes developed in America. They bought food and other goods that their peers could not afford and that they themselves had not eaten before their sojourn abroad. In rural villages in the Apennines, the *americani* were criticized for preferring "meat and fancy dishes" to the familiar "wholesome chestnut concoctions."[158] In one southern town, the men who spent a few years in America stood out, according to local wags, for their love of beer and "steak," neither of which they could get. As a result they developed a "nostalgia for foggy Pennsylvania or Canada."[159]

Americani in hometowns opened food establishments, coffee shops in particular, with the money squirreled away during their sojourns abroad. In a few towns, returned Americans invested in food-processing plants, particularly macaroni factories. They then exported pasta to Italians in America. This export of macaroni, as well as cheese and olive oil, forged a transoceanic Italian-American food chain.[160]

That the returnees had developed these tastes but could not fulfill them back home may have pushed some to go back to America yet again, a common phenomenon among these "birds of passage." The heightened experience of the *americani* had a direct impact upon the continuing migration. Later Italian emigrants, those who left after some had come back, went out into the world with greater expectations about what awaited them in America. The poor knew that food was scarce, precious, and sacred. They knew that it could be taken away from them. They also recognized that just beyond their doors lay a world of good food, tasty items, and rich dishes eaten by their social and economic superiors. They had learned about the abundant fare eaten by those from their town who had emigrated to places of plenty.

Food, its scarcity in Italy and knowledge of its availability in America, underlay the emigration. Poor Italians believed that America offered good prospects for good food. Francesco Ventresca wrote in his immigrant autobiography that he had heard that in America workers always got three meals a day, something unimaginable at home.[161] Pietro Militello's parents left him in Italy and went to North Philadelphia, "to find a job, a house and plenty of pasta and vino."[162] Millions like them did likewise.

"THE BREAD IS SOFT": ITALIAN FOODWAYS, AMERICAN ABUNDANCE

Sometime toward the end of the first decade of the twentieth century, Giuseppe Mormino, a resident of Alia, a town in Sicily's Palermo province, received a letter from his brother Rosolino. Rosolino composed his letter on the other side of the Atlantic in Napoleonville, Louisiana, where the young man labored on a sugar cane plantation. "In America," wrote Rosolino, "il pane e'molle, ma la vita e' dura" (bread is soft, but life is hard). Rather than read the letter as just an indictment of America's harsh working conditions, Giuseppe focused on the tale of food. After all, he had never eaten any bread other than the *contadini*'s familiar hard, dark loaves, and Rosolino tasted soft bread only in America.[1]

Rosolino's letter was not the hyperbole of an immigrant trying to impress stay-at-home kin. His words exemplified the experience of four million other Italians who came to America between the end of the nineteenth century and the 1920s. A quarter of a century after this letter went from Louisiana to Sicily, Italian immigrants living in San Francisco told anthropologist Paul Radin similar stories of American hardships cushioned by plentiful food.

They measured their American lives against remembered Italian scarcity. A laborer who came to the United States from near Milan, said that back home his family had been "forced to raise their own vegetables and could afford very little meat . . . were too poor to buy wine." In San Francisco, on a slim salary earned in a tile factory, he bought imported rice, "antipasto, wine," and meat, which he ate in his "roomy, comfortable kitchen." A "miner from Girgenti," now a California packing house worker, brushed off the question of Italy versus America. "Forget it," he told Radin, "there is no comparison." There he had been fed "the regulation rations of the poor Italians." In America, he "has all he wants to eat . . . America is a great country and no matter how bad things go, is still a great country."[2] The packing-house worker, once a miner, recounted what he had eaten in Italy in a passive voice. His fare had been rationed to him, grudgingly meted out to fit his class position. But he extolled his American present with active verbs emphasizing personal choice and individual tastes.

In this grammatical turn, as in Rosolino Mormino's understanding of the benefits of migration through soft bread, Italians in America erased the class barriers of the world they left, at least in terms of food. Their subversion of old-world hierarchies shaped their attitudes towards America, Italy, and themselves.

Italians' behavior in America, their taking advantage of abundance, seemed to mimic that of the rich of their hometowns who had so thoroughly dominated their everyday lives. Their American rhetoric resonated with the cadences of American choice and plenty. An immigrant to Oneonta, New York, from San Donato in Cosenza in 1886, interpreted the meaning of the migration in a 1931 speech, "Americans and Americanism." "To all of us" Italian immigrants, he explained, "the privilege to work at whatever job we prefer, eat and drink whatever we like, and say whatever we please" encapsulated America.[3]

The immigrants spoke of food, abundance, and choice; they did not dwell on past hunger, scarcity, or limitation. They called their American food "Italian," and spent their precious small earnings on "Italian" olive oil and "Italian" cheese, on meat and macaroni, foodstuffs that had once been doled out to them in minute quantities by haughty *galantuomini* through their intermediaries, the *gabellotti*. In America they bought what they wanted and decided on their own whether to buy domestic products or imports, and if imported, whether from Italy or the Italian diaspora in Argentina. Nowhere in descriptions of *contadini* life had they eaten these foods in this way. After migration, these foods became the everyday.

The act of taking possession of rich food associated with the well-off and the cities played a role in making immigrants from the scattered towns and villages of the Italian peninsula into Italians. It contributed mightily to the emergence of their new identity. By grafting onto their everyday life the foods of the holidays and holy time, these immigrants derived not only an ethnic identity but a sense of well-being. And as sacred food was turned into everyday food, it became more sacred. Connected as it was to the essence of being Italian, this food culture emerged as a pillar of identity and, as such, worth whatever it cost.

The encounter of Italian immigrants with food in America took place against a backdrop of real poverty. They had come to America poor and continued to suffer hardship.[4] They lived in cramped quarters. Children went to work young. With their mothers, they fabricated artificial flowers, sewed, stitched, and hemmed garments around kitchen tables. Children suffered from rickets, a disorder associated with a lack of milk, a partner of poverty.[5] Fathers faced constant bouts of unemployment, and when they worked, earned low salaries. They experienced only slow, painstaking economic mobility. Poverty in these initial years never lay far away and was often brought on by accidents, illnesses, and the vagaries of the American economy.[6]

Yet the poverty of the vast majority of the immigrants was not a permanent condition. Immigrants experienced modest mobility from within the ranks of the working class, moving from unskilled to somewhat more skilled positions, and from one working class neighborhood to slightly better ones. Some of them became self-employed as they tried their hand at small-scale enterprises, with food businesses a particularly popular choice. Until about 1900, many immigrants from Italy worked for and through a labor boss, a *padrone*. These *padroni* themselves had come up from the masses of the poor, but by helping to recruit and organize new immigrants for the labor force, they moved into the strata of the communal elite. So did immigrant bankers, who operated in most "little Italies"; they too occupied a higher rank than most. Their banks often doubled as grocery stores, financed by the capital they amassed in America. By and large, until the early twentieth century, Italian enclaves in America supported a small elite which knew at first hand the vulnerability of life in the laboring class. The migration out of Italy had been a relatively single-class phenomenon, and most of the individuals who rose above the masses did so as a result of taking advantage of various American opportunities.

Despite the ubiquity of poverty, few narratives of Italian immigrant life depicted the painful hunger as told by those who stayed in Italy.[7] Joseph Lazzaro from Agrigento came to America in 1920 and settled in Bridgeport, Connecticut. An unskilled worker, he remembered two decades later that despite his family's deep poverty, they ate "Italian style . . . macaroni five-six times a week, sometimes on Sunday we had a chicken and for some other time we had beans with greens, broccoli, asparagus, *ceci* [fava beans], 'minestre,' lentil soup, pork, gelati [ice-cream], spinach, and all kinds of green things."[8] Philip Bonacorsi came to Lawrence, Massachusetts, in 1904 as a child. In his chronicles of his family's poverty, he admitted that "we were lucky we never went hungry."[9] Antonio Mangano surveyed the lives of his *paesani* in New York in 1903 and declared that the typical Italian "has a greater variety of food and more of it" than back home.[10] A woman who grew up at the turn of the century in an immigrant home in New York's Italian enclave of Greenwich Village confirmed this. "We had enough to eat."[11]

American observers agreed. Italian immigrants placed a high premium upon eating certain foods and eating them well. A writer in the 1890s described the Italian poor in Chicago, "the lower class of Italians, born and bred," and marveled how, despite widespread poverty, "every person, of whatever sex or age seems to be provided with all food necessary to sustain life though perhaps not to the rudest health."[12] In 1897 Carroll D. Wright studied these same people and found the same commitment to eating well. Despite low-paying, unskilled jobs, they ate, for "Breakfast and lunch; One pound round steak (beef), three times per week; one-half for breakfast and one-half for lunch; red peppers instead of round steak three times per week; every morning 5 cents' worth of beer; bread with all three meals. Supper; Macaroni and beans, or round steak fried with potatoes; always bread and 5 cents' worth of beer."[13]

Throughout the migration era, Italians in America gave high priority to enriching their daily fare.[14] Robert Woods, a social worker associated with Boston's West End House at the beginning of the twentieth century, praised America and the Italian immigrant, who "eats much more meat than he did in Italy."[15] Frank Sheridan conducted a survey in 1908 for U.S. Department of Labor. The unskilled Italian workers he studied purchased imported pasta and cheeses and built their daily lives on meat, sardines, tomatoes, potatoes, oil, beer, and wine. "The Italians," he concluded, "consume a better quantity and variety of food than in Italy."[16]

5. Italian American memoirs, community histories, and fiction all emphasize the family meal as a common social experience. Here is a New York family at table in 1915.

Louise Odenkrantz concurred, in her 1919 observations of poor Italian women and their families in New York. After computing what they spent on food, rent, and clothing, she summarized that "they are more generous in providing food for themselves than for any other need of life. Bread and milk are bought and consumed in large quantities. The typically Italian spaghetti and *pasta* are popular, but meat and fish also form an important and regular part of their diet."[17]

The consumption of those foods helped to define the migration and the immigrants' new lives. Looking back upon his migration, one immigrant in upstate New York remembered that he had intended "to make a fortune and return to settle in the old country." He changed his mind. "I saw that the great thing about this country is that it is good for the working man. Italy is good if you can work for yourself, otherwise no. . . . *Here I can go out to eat in a restaurant and sit next to anyone I want*" [emphasis added].[18] With a similar sense that eating well justified the migration, a Philadelphian commented that when in the late 1920s he finally bought a house of his own, one which needed vast repairs, "the first thing I built," he boasted, was "the kitchen . . . modern kitchen."[19]

Migrating to America, a place of abundant food at low prices, empowered the newcomers not only to raise standards of consumption, but to do so as Italians. By engaging with American food realities, immigrants created an Italian American cultural system heavily centered on food. The women and men who had lived in Lucanian, Foggian, Cuggionese, Catanian, and Sicilian villages inhabited mixed neighborhoods in America, interacting with each other and with people from hundreds of other Italian places.

Some American communities fostered greater retention of home traditions than others. Isolated towns like Roseto and Carneta, Pennsylvania, exemplified the extreme of continuity. Immigrants and their children living in these two mining towns, the former founded exclusively by people from Roseto Valforte, the latter by Foggians from Carneta, ate pretty much as they had at home. Dishes continued to bear Italian names, *minestra* (vegetable soup), *ciambotta* (mixed vegetables), *scarola* (escarole), *cocozza* (squash), and the like. Residents of these communities interacted with few Americans or Italians from other towns and regions, so the process of fusion and invention took place at a slower pace.

Yet even here, dishes got richer and more complicated. Pizza in Roseto Valforte was a flat, thin disc of bread with salt and oil. In Roseto, Pennsylvania, tomatoes, onions, and anchovies gradually covered the dough.[20] In Carneta, Pennsylvania, the addition of meat transformed the fare of Foggia's poverty to that of Italian American abundance.[21]

Most Italians settled in America's larger cities. Here they lived in proximity to each other and saw, smelled, and over time, tasted each others' local and regional foods. Angelo Pellegrini commented that immigrants came to America "ignorant of cuisines beyond their own regions. In the Little Italy of the American metropolis the Southern Italian ultimately learned about *osso buco* and veal *scaloppini*, and his neighbor . . . from the north met up with pizza and eggplant Parmesan."[22]

Although utterly invented in America, certain dishes, spaghetti and meatballs as a case in point, became fixtures in Italian homes.[23] Moreover, foods blended the names and styles of noncontiguous Italian towns and regions. Niccolà de Quattrociocchi, a native of Palermo, came to America in the 1920s, representing a northern Italian business concern that marketed Sicilian canned tuna and artichokes. Eventually becoming a restaurant owner, he learned early on how far Italian American cuisine had evolved from anything he knew. "One evening," while strolling around New York, "we went to an Italian restaurant where I was introduced to two very fine, traditional American specialties called 'spaghetti with meatballs,' and 'cotoletta parmigiana.'" Since such dishes were usually served in Italian restaurants, he wryly remarked that they must be "just for fun called Italian. As a matter of fact, I found both extremely satisfying and I think someone in Italy should invent them for the Italians over there." He observed the world of Italian American food "in wide-eyed fascination . . . Italian antipasto, minestrone, beefsteak Milanese . . . with broccoli Siciliano."[24]

These foods played a considerable role in the formation of communities and in shaping the identities of those who lived in them. The daughters and sons of dozens of "little Italies" built and supported vast communal infrastructures to sell and buy food labeled Italian. The social events of their neighborhoods, clubs, and churches showcased that food, and those events allowed them to sample the many foods of the Italian places they had never called home. The foods of their American marketplaces and places of meeting—benevolent societies, parishes, street festivals, and family gatherings—had once belonged to the rich people upon whom they had depended for a livelihood. Feasting upon dishes once the sole preserve of their social and economic superiors enabled them to mold an Italian identity in America around food. Plentiful, inexpensive, American foods transformed the former regional *contadini* into Italians and their food into Italian food.

Culinary invention, a fusion of some southern Italian staples with a hodgepodge of foodstuffs and dishes from other regions, mixed with American styles of consumption, particularly the eating of meat, created a cuisine that combined new and old. Much of what these migrants did was to incorporate into their daily diet foods they had known about but had not tasted before; in this way they innovated and preserved tradition at one and the same time. They created new foods and food practices but skillfully draped them with the mantle of tradition. In all the places they settled in America, they built families, communities, and ethnic practices out of a set of iconic foods and dishes.

None mattered as much as macaroni. A food of affluence for southern Italians, it embodied Italian food culture for the masses in America.[25] In Italian American communities, small and big alike, entrepreneurs operated macaroni factories.[26] In the early years of the migration, macaroni was prepared in tenement sweatshops by family labor, and "then sold up and down" the streets of the neighborhoods.[27] Larger macaroni factories "symbolized in brick and stone a recognition that the ethnic colonies had moved from a transitory mentality to a more permanent status." Giuseppe Nicotera's macaroni factory in Utica, New York, opened in 1903 and was the grandest structure on Bleecker Street, the heart of the city's Italian neighborhood. The five-story building housed the plant which produced the precious foodstuff and dominated the streetscape, marking the area as Italian.[28]

Macaroni shops abounded in Italian neighborhoods, and huge strands of it hung from the outside of these shops, waving almost as flags to proclaim the Italian presence in American urban space. Italian parishes, social clubs, and mutual benefit societies staged "spaghetti dinners" as their most common events. The women of the parish who prepared the suppers made all sorts of food, but the presence of pasta gave the event the cachet of Italian authenticity. In 1911 the Italian women of the Ladies' Auxiliary of St. Joachim's Parish in Trenton, New Jersey, held a fundraising "spaghetti dinner" at which they served chicken, roast beef, ham, salads, olives, and fruit. But it *was* a spaghetti dinner. The spaghetti made it Italian.[29] So too when Holy Rosary Parish in Indianapolis found itself in debt, the women mobilized and staged monthly spaghetti dinners to raise the necessary funds to sustain community life. They cooked all sorts of food, but it was the spaghetti which saved the church.[30]

Pasta did more than symbolize Italian culture. Immigrants and their children ate pasta in some form much of the time. All surveys of Italian domestic life and consumption revealed macaroni's daily presence. No matter what else graced the table, meat, fish, vegetables, pasta in some form had to be there. The United States Department of Agriculture in conjunction with Chicago's Hull House studied the dietary practices of Italians in the surrounding neighborhood in the 1890s and reported on "some peculiarities" among Chicago's Italians, the first being that, "The Italian oil, wine, cheese, which even the poorest families use, are all imported, and of course expensive. . . . They consume a great deal of macaroni."[31] The author of a memoir describing life in the 1930s in upstate New York declared that "some form of pasta was served every single night with dinner . . . Each family member would consume two or three dishes of pasta. . . . Four or five pounds of pasta would be cooked in order to satiate the voracious appetites of my hardworking family."[32]

Olive oil also assumed deep meaning to Italian immigrants in America. Its widespread use, despite its relative scarcity in America in the early years of the migration, testified to how much the immigrants desired the foods once reserved for the rich. Even when they had to import it from Italy or Argentina they bought it, defining it as a necessity. The oil seemed to be essential to Italian identity. The novelist John Fante, who declared that he hoped in his fiction "to cover the true Italian-American scene,"[33] described the troubled relationship between Maria and Svevo Bandini in his 1938 novel, *Wait Until Spring Bandini*. "Looking at her," Fante wrote, Svevo "was seeing her through olive oil."[34]

Despite poverty and criticism by Americans for wasting their money on such a luxury,[35] Italians considered olive oil a basic staple.[36] When Saul Alinsky began his career as a community organizer in Chicago he noted that

> during the depression when Welfare workers came down among our Italian people, they would give them a certain amount of money to spend each week and some education on what they called "nutrition" so they could get the most food for their money. These Welfare workers would get upset because our Italian families insisted on buying very good olive oil to cook with . . . Italians have to have olive oil . . . it's something much more important than budgets or stuff like that.[37]

Meat too, one or more times a week, came to be the norm. In Italy few from the lower classes ate it more than three times a year. In America meat appeared regularly on their menus.[38] The steadier their incomes, the more meat they ate. It seemed to be the first item to appear when salaries rose, and thereby it represented the American standard. But even when money was tight, meat graced their tables more regularly than before migration. Whether added to stews, soups, or combined with tomato sauce to accompany spaghetti, or spaghetti and beans, meat became enshrined as a weekly, and as soon as possible, daily, part of the Italian diet in America. "A taste for meat . . . is acquired in this country," observed one nutritionist about America's Italian immigrants in 1922.[39]

All descriptions of the Italian culinary adjustment to America mention the addition of meat. In 1904 Louise Boland More collected dietary information among New York's wage earners. The Italians she studied *all* ate meat. Indeed meat—beef, veal, mutton, ham, pork, bacon, chicken, and fish—constituted the single largest expenditure in their diets. In one of many documented cases, the family of an Italian stone-cutter, often out of work, spent $9.00 a month on rent, $5.36 on beef, veal, and mutton, $2.45 on chicken, and $2.07 on macaroni.[40] In a 1911 government-sponsored report, researchers documented the experience of another possibly "typical" Italian family, "Family No. 4." After describing the family's migration history, work patterns, and household composition, it noted that "The diet of the family was principally macaroni and bread. When all were at work they had better food. . . . The woman stated that when they were all at work and had money they could eat meat and have beer with dinner."[41]

In family and community events meat, an American accoutrement, fused with ingredients deemed to be Italian. In the 1920s, for example, immigrant families in Madison, Wisconsin, feasted at summertime picnics on "steaks rubbed with olive oil and garlic," and some families built their big Sunday dinners around "meatloaf with Italian herbs."[42] Italian immigrants themselves reveled in the reality of eating meat. In a letter from St. Louis to Cuggiono in 1900, Antonio Ranciglio boasted to family and friends. "Here I eat meat three times a day, not three times a year." He advised those back home who could to do the same: *fare fortuna, trovare l'America*—to make a fortune, find America.[43]

Pasta and olive oil, along with meat and cheese, defined a good life, a life of choice. Italians had come to America in part to eat more and better. They "had often known the meaning of hunger and would not knowingly repeat the experience."[44] Once in America, Italians built their lives and diets around the consumption of foods that were familiar but had been inaccessible, since they had been the preserve of the elite back home.[45] Immigrants did this by acquiring an American standard of eating, articulated in an Italian upper-class style.[46]

Italian American memoirs and other communal sources abounded in talk of pasta and oil, meat and cheese. That talk was couched in comparative terms, measuring America against their Italian home towns. Immigrants and their children recounted years of poverty and poor housing, frugality and improvisation. But interspersed among these words were lavish descriptions of abundant good food. Even so grim a text as Pietro di Donato's 1937 novel, *Christ in Concrete*, included amidst hardship and brutality the pleasures of plenty of good food and sensuous tastes:

> And men's tinged faces of spilled lust and breaths of undigested meat, spaghetti, wine, garlic, and sour tobacco . . .

> They are tired but happy that today is Good Friday and we quit at three o'clock. . . . he swelled in ecstasy at the anticipation of food and drink.

> Annunziata and Cola passed the platters of antipasto as the paesanos found their seats. Bitter green Sicilian olives and sweet Spanish olives, whitings and squid pickled in saffron, Genoese salami and mortadella, pickled eggplants, long pointed peppers and cherry peppers . . . The chicken soup was rich with eggs, fennel, artichoke roots, grated parmesan and noodles that melted on the lips.[47]

A Sicilian woman in New York asked Leonard Covello to listen to her food memories: "Who could afford to eat spaghetti more than once a week [in Italy]? In America no one starved, though a family earned no more than five or six dollars a week . . . Don't you remember how our *paesani* here in America ate to their heart's delight till they were belching like pigs and how they dumped mountains of uneaten food out the window?"[48]

Angelo Pellegrini juxtaposed memories of the meager fare of his Tuscan boyhood, daily *polenta* and little else, with what he found in his new land: "Fed on this meager and monotonous fare, hungry for white bread, coffee, and sugar, flesh and fowl, I came to America. Against the background of . . . *polenta* what I found here, in this land of refugees from hunger and oppression, remains for me a dramatic and very fascinating story. . . . Thus food, bread and meat in sinful proportions, was my first discovery."[49]

Pellegrini's words complemented those of Rosa Cavalleri, who remembered that "in Italy the people were feeding their pigs better than their children."[50] She came to America, unhappily, to join her husband, a laborer in a Missouri iron mine. Her attitude towards him and the migration was bitter, but her negativism—at least towards America—evaporated when she ate her first American meal. "Bread! White bread! Enough for a whole village! And butter to go on it! I ate until I no longer had any pains in my stomach." She reacted just as passionately to her first American breakfast, rhapsodizing about "white bread again and butter and coffee with cream and sugar and sausages and eggs besides! Mamma mia! Did all the poor people in America eat like kings?"[51]

Rosa knew that she had developed an American palate and an American standard of eating when she returned home to get her little boy, whom she had left behind. Her family and friends in Cuggiono gathered together upon her arrival. They wanted to "hear her story of life in America. *Mamma Mia*, but that was hard [for them] to believe—poor people in America eating meat every day!" In their incredulity at what had become standard for her, she and they witnessed the meaning of America. She commented: "After all that good food I had in America, I was no longer content with the sour-tasting black bread, or the thin onion-and-water soup, or a little polenta. I wanted to make thick soup with rice in it every day or cook the rice the way I had learned to cook it in America."[52]

In 1918, researchers helping University of Chicago professor Sophonisba Breckenridge compile her book, *New Homes for Old*, interviewed Italian immigrant women.[53] Each woman indicated that her foodways had changed, for some more than others, but most consumed meat and rich foods at a level unknown back home. "Sadie Campisi," born in Palermo, mother of 5 daughters, herself the daughter of "farm laborers," now ate meat 3 or 4 times a week. Other days she and her family alternated meat with spaghetti. Campisi aspired to an even more American diet. She had no interest in sweets, yet "would like pie, but it is too expensive." She drank coffee every morning and told the investigator that she had learned about American dishes at a local settlement house.

Her daughters had picked up ideas about food in school and brought those ideas home. Another woman, the keeper of a bar in her family's saloon, the daughter of a linen factory operative in Italy whom she described as "poor," purchased barrels of olive oil imported from Argentina. A third family wanted to eat more meat, but as yet could not afford it, but they spent money on Italian cheese imported also from Italians in South America.[54]

Jerre Mangione's classic, *Mount Allegro*, described the author's growing up in the Italian, primarily Sicilian, community of Rochester, New York, in the years before the 1930s.[55] In Rochester these relatively poor Sicilians who had once been *contadini* ate as *Italians* of the upper classes, precisely because they were now in America. Sunday afternoons his immigrant parents and their extended family got together for the men's game of *briscola*, for music, and for the women's talk. By evening, "when the wives got hungry," one of the men went out to the "saloon for a bucket of beer" and "the women would spread out a tablecloth over the table and pile it high with fried Italian sausages, *pizza* made with cheese and tomatoes, and fried artichokes if they were in season."[56] The Sunday meal was "a Lucullan banquet consisting of at least three meat courses."[57]

So much of what these individuals described represented effortless blendings of new and old, fusions of innovation and tradition. Yet they innovated within boundaries. An informal consensus developed as to which foods could be added to their repertoire without violating "Italian" standards. They went only so far in testing the boundaries of imagined Italian authenticity.

New elements crept into their foodways. They drank beer as an accompaniment with their food.[58] As early as 1897, Frederick Bushee wrote that among Boston's Italians, "beer has now become their most common beverage."[59] Italian fondness for beer developed all over America, confirming stories told by returned emigrants who described it to the folks back home as one of the tastes which made America a place of good food.[60] The feasters at Mangione's typical Sunday dinner drank beer as they enacted their family ritual.

They also ate "Italian sausage." The notion that sausages could be "Italian" belied the vast regional diversities where even so common a staple as bread varied from town to town, region to region, as to ingredients, methods of preparation, and shape. Sausage back home was not only a rare dish, usually reserved for some religious *feste*, but it was specific to particular towns, primarily in the north. Mangione's Sicilian family had most likely *never* eaten sausage, let alone called it "Italian sausage." Yet it became a mainstay of their diet. Finally, they ate pizza. Verga's fictional peasant 'Ntoni had found pizza something amazing when he journeyed to Naples. However, to slather cheese and tomato sauce on it, and to eat it at a table rather than on the street, took it far beyond Neapolitan practice and made it standard Italian American fare.

Innovation involved more than what got consumed. In Italy *contadini* did not use food for socializing. That was something the rich did. Only at special ritual moments, particularly when consoling the bereaved, did food go from one poor household to another. But in America the poor took up the practice of hospitality with food, behaving like the elites of their former towns. Perhaps because migration had truncated families, friends and neighbors came to be included increasingly in the circles of sociability, and food came out onto the table to mark companionship. Antonio Mangano observed in 1903 that the friendly former *contadino* now in America manifested great "hospitality . . . by inviting people to share what he may have in the way of food." He is, Mangano asserted, always ready, "to share a meal. . . . The coffee pot is constantly on hand." If the host had no coffee, then "beer is sent for."[61] For Italians, inviting visitors into their homes for food came to be a hallmark of their behavior in America.[62]

Urban foraging also represented new and old behaviors. In feudal times, the Italian poor roamed the countryside, finding wild food to supplement their diets. The abolition of feudalism in the nineteenth century brought that to a close, at least legally. Yet commentators on American cities in the immigrant era described Italians, particularly women, as adept foragers. Together with their children, and sometimes with men, they canvassed city parks, vacant lots, or empty fields on the outskirts of the cities looking for dandelions, other greens, mushrooms, and berries, plants that most Americans disdained as not being food. In Chicago "old Italian women . . . [spend] all day long in the dumping grounds of the city prying out for articles they could use," including celery, carrots, cauliflowers, and the like.[63] In Boston in 1903 Italian children went through the "discarded vegetables" from the markets.[64] Italian immigrant men in Greenwich Village spent their time off work traveling to rural areas of Staten Island and New Jersey to find wild-growing edibles, which the women then "prepared in the traditional manner."[65] In Italy they or their parents may have never foraged, but in America they could revive a traditional Italian strategy to deal with poverty and add food to their tables.[66]

Likewise, the ubiquitous Italian American practice of urban gardening and raising small animals for domestic consumption demonstrated the upward movement of foodways and the fusion of Italian styles with American economic realities.[67] Italians, starting with the earliest years of settlement in America, found scraps of urban land, patches of city soil to grow tomatoes, corn, parsley, onions, various greens, zucchini, artichokes. They creatively engineered small spaces to raise goats and chickens. In Tampa's Ybor City the "Italian neighborhoods developed into urban farm spaces, replete with garden plots and small livestock."[68] In New York's dense Little Italy people openly raised rabbits, chickens and birds for family consumption.[69] Miners in Oklahoma from the Piedmont region cultivated tiny patch gardens in their time off work.[70] Such a bit of yard plays a role in Mari Tomasi's Italian American novel, *Like Lesser Gods*, which takes place in Vermont, among immigrants from Turin who worked as granite carvers in the 1910s. Maria, the heroine of the novel, kept a vegetable patch with chicory for salad and onions, to go into the "soups, meats, and salads which invariably constituted the summer evening meals," while the other immigrant hero cuts dandelions to augment his fare.[71] Robert Woods and Albert Kennedy studied the Italian neighborhood in Boston's Dorchester section from 1907 to 1914 and marveled at how "each house has a vegetable garden in front or side yard."[72] Settlement workers at Boston's North Bennet Street Industrial School had no trouble organizing Italian children and their parents during World War I to cultivate gardens. The "little gardeners" in the neighborhood grew bumper crops of lettuce, radish, beans, turnips, potatoes, and "basilico . . . the herb which is a great favorite among the Italians."[73]

The desire to cultivate a plot of land, no matter how small, and eat from its produce shaped Italian behavior in America and reflected the changes they experienced *vis-à-vis* food and class. In Italy they worked a piece of land for family consumption if a patron had given them the right to do so. If they had won that right, they had to pay a tax on the produce they grew. In America they seized the opportunity to use a few yards of land to grow what they liked and to do so with no outside interference.

So too Italian American agriculture, gardening on a large scale, represented the fusion of old and new. Throughout Italy, agriculture functioned as a way of solidifying class differences and retaining class privilege for those with means. The land, owned by the few, worked by the hands of the many, produced foodstuffs mostly for export. It also produced the foods which graced the tables of the elite. What shreds were left ended up in the mouths of the poor. The best and the most of the wine, olive oil, flour, fruits, and vegetables went to the landowners, precisely the people who did not come to America.

In America, a nation-wide Italian agricultural system developed, bringing foods grown by former *contadini* in New Jersey, Missouri, Florida, Connecticut, New York State, Arkansas, Pennsylvania, Nebraska, California—and many other places—onto the plates of others, like themselves, living in big cities.[74] Italian Americans' intensive farming practices allowed them to sell at low cost, from pushcarts, stands, outdoor urban fruit and vegetable markets, and stores of every size. Much of that produce went to other Americans. This truck farming and the larger-scale agricultural enterprises ringing the large Italian enclaves of New York, Boston, Providence, Newark, St. Louis, Tampa, New Haven, New York, Rochester, Philadelphia, Pittsburgh, Omaha, and San Francisco made it possible for the formerly hungry to now eat a broad range of fruits and vegetables every day. Broccoli, a vegetable Italian Americans claim they brought to America, zucchini, tomatoes, mushrooms, and a variety of salad greens showed up in the markets and on Italian American tables in profusion.[75] Konrad Bercovici took readers on a ramble, *Around the World in New York*, in his 1924 book, and advised: "Turn around and go into Mulberry Street, where both sides are lined with fruit-stand push-carts. What strikes one first is the beauty and the variety of the vegetables and fruits sold there in what is supposed to be one of the poorest quarters."[76]

For many Italian immigrants, selling fruit and vegetables was their entree to the American economy. Many got their start selling to Italian customers. Later, the ones who stayed in the business branched out to the larger, more lucrative general market with its mixed clientele. Some, particularly in California with its abundant possibilities, transformed their modern business into giant corporations. Del Monte and Italian Swiss Colony began as small immigrant ventures.

Successful and visible Italian fruit and vegetable handlers served as role models for the more modest peddlers and owners of marginal stands. In Indianapolis, the first Sicilian to show up in the *City Directory* was Frank Mascari, who opened a fruit stand in 1888. His shop grew as he started to supply fruit to new Sicilian immigrants who peddled the merchandise on the city streets. They in turn opened their small stores once they had amassed enough capital. In 1906 the mayor appointed Joseph Foppiano, one of the Sicilian immigrants who began as a peddler outfitted by Frank Mascari, to be the Master of the City Market.[77] Mascari, Foppiano, and many other Sicilians of Indianapolis used food as a step up out of poverty. Food no longer functioned as their badge of class subjugation.

The vast panoply of Italian stores selling Italian foodstuffs to economically marginal customers demonstrated how changes brought about by American abundance enabled immigrants to capitalize on the idea of tradition. The agro-towns of Italy supported few stores. Some had none, most had one. Out of what people received and gleaned they not only made most everything they ate, but they ate so very little that towns had no need for an elaborate commercial infrastructure. What food stores existed catered to the comfortable classes.

Not so in America. Wherever Italians settled, some went in to business to provision others. Utica, New York, for example, by the first decade of the twentieth century supported enough Italian bakeries to churn out "thousands of loaves" of Italian bread daily.[78] The big cities, New York, Philadelphia, Chicago, Boston, and San Francisco served as the main centers of Italian food buying and selling.[79]

These food shops, larger and smaller ones, wound the fabric of the community around food. Merchants made it possible for the economically marginal immigrants to eat, even well. They did so by extending credit, particularly in hard times. Italian immigrants and their children typically shopped only at neighborhood stores, owned by other Italians with whom they had face-to-face relationships, and for whom credit was a communal obligation.[80] In New Jersey, Italian neighborhood merchants "extended credit . . . and enabled workers to strike beyond the limits imposed by their pocketbooks."[81]

Selling food represented a chance to go into business for oneself and capitalize upon community taste.[82] The existence of a vast infrastructure of Italian stores providing Italian foods to Italian customers is symbolic evidence for the migration's unspoken mission: to enable former *contadini* to have what had been denied them or meted out to them stingily in their homeland. For the growers and the food-business merchants, the food itself provided an avenue to increased economic comfort.

Many Italian immigrants constructed stable family economies by feeding other Italians. Angelo Merlino showed up in Seattle in the late nineteenth century. He "became so homesick for his native food, that he wrote to relatives in Italy, asking for cheese, pasta, and olive oil. Later, while still a miner, young Merlino began to import cheese and oil in bulk." Soon he was bringing in shiploads of it, and he opened a store in 1900.[83] Guido Orlando came to America in 1917 to join up with his brother in Cleveland. They first marketed olive oil and cheese in the Italian neighborhoods. Later on they branched out, selling malted hops with the onset of Prohibition.[84] Bernard Mistretta, like hundreds of other young men from his region, came some time in the late nineteenth century from Sicily to labor in Louisiana's sugar cane fields. He decided to do a bit better by peddling olive oil and cheese on the side to his plantation co-workers. After securing his employer's permission, he spent his Sundays going around to the plantations taking orders for the imported, and now essential, foods. He struck a deal with the planters. He would also recruit fresh workers from Sicily. He therefore both brought food to the workers, who now wanted to consume olive oil and cheese regularly, and facilitated the migration of other Sicilians.[85]

This food merchandising operated throughout immigrant communities and shaped something distinctively Italian in America. Different groups of Italians cornered particular parts of the food world, but they learned to co-operate with each other. In San Francisco, the Colombo Market was the heart of the Italian community. Initially it was the sole domain of the Genoese, the earliest immigrants. Over time they gave later arrivals access to sell there. They worked out a system, and at "5:00 A.M. . . . the Florentine dialect took over. At that hour Luccans began distributing the produce, and the Genoese went back to their farms." The city's other Italian food hub, the waterfront, had also been a place where Genoese owners of fishing boats and fishmongers predominated. Slowly they began hiring Sicilians to work with and for them. By 1913 "both Genoese and Sicilians were entrenched in the fishing industry."[86]

What happened in San Francisco demonstrated how immigrants from different regions of Italy, speaking different dialects and used to eating different foods, fused into an Italian and Italian American entity. This fusion played itself out in the marketplace, with food at its heart. The entrepreneurs who controlled the provisioning orchestrated the means by which Italians from different regions competed with each other and then worked out a *modus vivendi*.

The community infrastructure of merchandising Italian food made the regional fusion possible. Food merchandising gave Italian neighborhoods their distinctive appearance. In Omaha's Little Italy in the 1930s, "the stores display foods dear to the hearts of the people—salamis, cheeses, olive oil, macaroni, spaghetti, braided lengths of garlic, strings of gleaming red peppers drying in the sun."[87] Merchants advertised goods as genuinely Italian olive oils, authentic Italian breads, sausages, cheeses, and pastas. They did not pitch them to consumers as genuinely Sicilian or Calabrian.

Certainly regional loyalties informed the food culture, and merchants used the imagery of specific Italian places to demonstrate the authenticity of their goods. Frank Palescandolo's parents bought a small restaurant in Brooklyn's Coney Island in the 1910s. Like many of the "two-bit eateries" opened by Neapolitans in the beach area, they catered to all Italians, not just Neapolitans, from New York City who came to spend a day in the sun. To advertise the restaurant, they printed up postcards which depicted Mt. Vesuvius, with the caption "A Little Bit of Naples in Coney Island." The menu cover initially depicted Brooklyn's prevalent willow trees. The Palescandolos subsequently capitalized on nostalgia for back home. They replaced the pictures of American trees with the Neapolitan volcano and drawings of the "emerald shores of Amalfi."[88]

Italian food establishments continued to play on regional and local sentiments. Mulberry Street, like many other Italian American thoroughfares had a "Ristorante del Bella Napoli,"[89] while loyal Sicilians in Greenwich Village opened an eatery named Rocco's. By this, they paid homage to a hometown patron saint.[90] But a more powerful countertradition made food merchants the bearers of a unified Italian commu-

6. Italian streets in American cities abounded with food. The Mandaro dairy store on New York's Bleecker Street, in 1937, prominently displayed rounds of Bel Paese cheese, literally, the bounty of the "beautiful land," Italy.

nity in America. They enveloped food in the themes of pan-Italian identity, submerging local loyalties. A restaurant on Mulberry Street was named Villa Vittorio Emmanuele III, honoring the king.[91] An early State Street spaghetti house in Chicago, the Roma, promised diners that its fare tasted "such as one gets in Italy."[92] Newark's Italian community in the First Ward, made up of the sons and daughters of Campania's Avellino province, mixed with Calabrians, Apulians, and Sicilians patronized a Cafe Roma in 1906, and a Tripoli Pasticceria to celebrate Italy's imperialist venture.[93]

Merchants linked the food they sold to the idea of a nation, embellishing the word "Italian" with such adjectives as "fine," "fresh," "genuine," "imported," "real," and "tasty." They did so at a period when residential patterns in America changed. Within a generation or less, local and regional clusterings in American cities were replaced by mixed Italian neighborhoods.[94] In enclaves which housed the former residents of dozens of towns and regions, it made good business sense to highlight the idea of Italian as opposed to Calabrian or Apulian.

Little conflict emerged in these mixed communities over food. Parents and children, husbands and wives, neighbors, boarders, and customers achieved a communal consensus on what should be eaten and how. Housewives in Italian neighborhoods rarely confronted their co-ethnic merchants over exorbitant food prices. Few Italian American workers in the community's food industries organized themselves against employers.

Certainly some exceptions existed. In May 1910, the Italian Butchers' Union of Bronx and Harlem and the equivalent body representing Brooklyn and lower Manhattan held a meeting. They vowed to close down the butcher shops if the price of meat did not go down and marched on City Hall. According to *Corriere della Sera*, it seemed more like a parade with music than an angry demonstration of enraged workers, supported by enraged customers. The butchers wanted Mayor William Gaynor to "say a good word for them in public," so that they should not be blamed for increases in the cost of meat. They launched a two-day strike, hailed as it began as a "beautiful and noble success." Two days later the Brooklyn branch withdrew, and the strike ended.[95] In Providence in 1914, Italian men in the Federal Hill neighborhood launched a campaign against a neighborhood pasta merchant, Frank Ventrone. Accusing Ventrone of charging too high a price for this essential food, they marched through the neighborhood, broke some windows of buildings Ventrone owned, and heaved piles of pasta on to the streets.[96]

In general, however, Italian immigrants supported the merchants who sold them food, extended them credit in bad times, and empowered them

7. Italian American food companies emphasized the connection between the products they sold and the idea of Italy. This label depicts Mount Vesuvius in its majesty and marks the product as authentically Italian.

to eat Italian food as Americans. So too with regard to labor organizing, the communal food industry inspired little worker-employer conflict. Italian communities from the end of the nineteenth century supported factories that produced Italian food. Most were macaroni factories, owned and operated by local entrepreneurs. By the 1920s, some larger national firms such as La Rosa, Ronzoni, La Perla, and Caruso employed thousands of Italian American workers, producing pastas in various sizes, shapes, qualities, and prices.[97] Other Italian American industrialists had, by the 1910s, opened plants for large-scale production and marketing of olive oil, Italian cheeses, and tomato sauces. These too relied on Italian workers.

Workers in these plants rarely organized into trade unions. Some Italian locals of the Bakers, Confectionery, and Tobacco Workers' Union were formed in New York, Brooklyn, Newark, and Philadelphia.[98] A Società di Mestiere Bakers' Union had its headquarters at 127 Delancey Street in 1910, and in Wilmington, Delaware, the bakers were the first group of organized workers in the Italian community.[99] But Italian food workers did not threaten the supply of food to their own communities. In the massive strikes which agitated New York bakery workers in 1910, only "a few . . . Italian" laborers joined in.[100]

This reluctance to unionize Italian food businesses defied ordinary behavior among Italian workers in America. Although labor organizers met some resistance among Italian immigrants in the early years of the migration,[101] that reluctance evaporated. Italian garment workers, as well as laborers, construction workers, shoemakers, textile operatives, stoneworkers, even barbers and piano makers banded together for better wages and conditions.[102] Italian laborers organized against Italian employers and targeted the *padrone*, their co-national labor agents, as the objects of protest.[103] But they did not strike, and rarely organized, when it came to making pasta, processing tomatoes, or manufacturing the foods so deeply enshrined in their cultural landscape. Food had become sacred to them, and Italian foods in particular symbolized their communities' lifeblood. Making food existed therefore outside the boundaries of normal economic activity. To deny those foods to others, their brethren, would have violated an unstated communal norm.

The reality that Italian life in America pivoted around food played itself out in the newly created voluntary associations. Like all immigrants, Italians formed mutual aid and benevolent societies, combining assistance with sociability. Some societies reflected places of origin in Italy and sustained localism. Most, however, reached out to potential members across geographic lines. Clubs served as conduits for sending money back home, for instilling pride in Italy, and supporting local Italian charitable endeavors in Philadelphia, New Haven, Baltimore, San Francisco, and elsewhere.

Food played a key role in these clubs, as members consciously or unconsciously strove to create a unified Italian identity. Part of this involved serving a singular Italian cuisine. Among Cleveland's Italians, "these associations were . . . pizza and sausage clubs."[104] Thus pizza and sausage drew together Italian men regardless of their place of origin and their lack of exposure to these foods before coming to America. A speaker at the initial meeting of the Circolo Italo-Americano di Boston in 1898 sounded the note of Italian unity through food: the club should "have more of those informal talks when some Southern member wanders in fields of memory and calls to his Northern brother. We like our informal music, our singing together, our occasional little plays, our chatting while having a sociable bit of refreshment."[105] The Collandia Club of Chicago, founded in 1933 by immigrants from Lucca, hosted "monthly birthday *cenettas* [small dinners], a Presidential Banquet, dinners for all the American holidays as well as other occasional festivities."[106] In some social clubs, men staged food events for themselves, cooking up their own banquets and bridging the geographic divides of Italy. The Italian Men's Club at Hull House, for example, was founded in 1914. It sought to create a unified Italian presence in the neighborhood. The men held a lavish formal dinner every year, which they cooked together for themselves, and forged social bonds through the common communal table.[107]

Italian charitable societies also played a part in the emergence of a singular Italian American food culture. Organizations such as the Italian Welfare League in New York distributed food to newly arrived immigrants in need, to stowaways detained at Ellis Island, to people being sent back to Italy after failing to pass inspection, and to the distressed in the community. Relying upon local food merchants for donations, volunteers for the charity distributed spaghetti, canned minestrone soup, tomato paste, fresh fruit, cheese, beans, rice, chicken, veal, sausage, "food that Italians like."[108] They defined as such the idea of *an* Italian food culture, no longer splintered along town and regional lines.

Street festivals, *feste*, usually associated with devotions to local saints, also played a pivotal role in the shaping of Italian American communities, linking food with a broad expression of Italian identity.[109] Food merchants and restauranteurs set up booths out-of-doors.[110] Food could be purchased from these booths, and Italians from different neighborhoods and different places in Italy converged to share "traditional" foods on American streets.[111]

A dazzling array of food was available at, for example, the East Harlem *festa* for the Madonna of Mt. Carmel: "From the street vendors, located around Jefferson Park, the devout could buy beans boiled in oil and red pepper, sausage, pies filled with tomato, red pepper and garlic, bowls of pasta, hot waffles, fried and sugared dough, boiled corn, ice cream, watermelon, dried nuts, nougat candy, raisins, pink and blue tinted cakes and pastry rings."[112] *Feste* like this one played a considerable role in fostering a general Italian culture, while the foods served demonstrated that the once poor could now feed themselves.[113]

In Omaha, in 1924, Sicilians recreated for the first time the *festa* of Santa Lucia. They draped the streets of their neighborhood with Italian and American flags. They carried the "richly dressed image of Santa Lucia" through the streets, followed by a parade of children in "Italian costume," and the women standing in their doorways cried out their thanks and supplications to the saint. With "the celebration . . . at its height," the food festival commenced. In Sicily, the *feste* provided the *galantuomini* with an opportunity to distribute food to their dependent inferiors. In Omaha, a working-class egalitarianism prevailed. "Everyone keeps open house and serves Italian wine, *spumoni* and *gelati*" to their neighbors. In the 1920s, as Sicilians paraded their adoration of their patron saint on the streets of the Nebraska city, they also carried the Italian flag. They dressed their children in invented "Italian" costumes and consumed wine bearing the name of the nation. The presence of the American flags indicated the simultaneous acquisition of an American identity. And they fed each other, rather than being fed from the top down.[114]

Class renegotiations took place in conjunction with these *feste*, and without fail, visitors saw the linkages between food, sanctity, class, and identity.[115] In 1940 a folklorist visited a Sicilian community in Southern California staging a St. Joseph's day *festa*. Families throughout the enclave sat down to "cooked vegetables, fish dishes decorated in various ways, rice, many kinds of cookies, cakes (some made or stuffed with figs), numberless loaves of bread of different shapes, wines, and the very characteristic roasted chickpeas, almonds, and horse-beans . . . In addition, each table must always have a large square cake with 'Saint Joseph' written on it." (Meat was absent that year because St. Joseph's day fell during Lent.)

All families served this meal at the beginning of the *festa*. Later, after the street activities had ended, families settled down for another equally elaborate and lengthy repast, said to have taken three hours. One woman confided that on that day she served in her home "no less than ninety pounds of spaghetti." In Sicily such "festivities are held mainly to help the poorest people of the community." But "in California, and probably in all parts of the United States where Sicilians honor Saint Joseph, the altars are prepared in fulfillment of a promise made to the saint in a moment of need." The sumptuous feasts in California appeared on tables in "humble dwellings," prepared by working-class women who prided themselves on being able to cook so well for their families and neighbors. The visitor asked "several women whether in Sicily they prepared such elaborate and costly tables." They resoundingly answered him in the negative. "They invariably told me that because of the much lower standard of living, what they or their parents used to do there hardly compares with what they can afford to do here."[116]

Merchants provided Italian food to Italian neighborhoods. Societies served as venues for eating food that became authentic by tacit agreement. The *feste* showcased the emergence of an Italian consciousness in America through food. But the most formative setting for the preparation, consumption, and sacralization of food took place in the millions of individual immigrant homes.

In their homes, women and men transformed food into the essence of identity and as the focal point of loyalty. Women as cooks and men as arbiters of taste drove the process by which the *contadini* in America became Italians who ate like the rich folks back home. Before migration the preparation of food had been very much the province of women. Women cooked the food, contending with scarcity's crises. They measured their worth in terms of how well they fed their families. Men prepared food in some situations, but food and its preparation were intimately linked to women's performance of role and responsibility. This division of labor did not come to an end in America, but circumstances made it necessary for men to become more actively involved in the process. By investing food preparation and the quality of the food they ate with great weight, men heightened women's understanding of themselves and their role in family foodways.

The very nature of the waves of Italian migration shaped this shift. Men, generally, migrated first. They lived in America for some length of time, in cities, mining camps, railroad crews, and other kind of collective labor gangs, in all-male groups. Many went back to Italy for good. Others went back but returned to America, likely accompanied by a wife and children. Some married men who journeyed to America alone eventually sent for wives and children once they had saved enough money to support a family. This meant that Italian enclaves in America existed with pronounced imbalances between men and women. Antonio Stella scanned the U.S. Census data and commented with regret that more than any other immigrants, the Italian men have "their own womankind . . . left behind." Italian men, unlike others, "were deprived of the regulating home influences."[117] In 1910 in Greenwich Village, 129 Italian men could be found for every 100 women; in 1920, the figure was 119 men per 100 women.[118]

Since men outnumbered women, they had to find ways to feed themselves.[119] In some cases they did their own cooking, something they might have done in Italy, where in the course of seasonal work they prepared their own meals, either singly or cooperatively. In America men cooked and baked on their own to save money. Many claimed that they disliked American food. For men intent on earning, saving, and going back, or sending for wives and children, this frugality made sense. It also brought men into the food process and kept them there.

Wherever Italian immigrant men lived in groups without women they found ways to cook.[120] A plantation owner in Louisiana commented on the Sicilian laborers who worked his sugar cane fields: "They were good gardeners, raised goats, made and baked their own bread, made and formed their spaghetti, made their clothes."[121] In "bachelor societies" one of the men often stayed back in a house or apartment and cooked for the others. Other times they rotated cooking chores.[122] Among Gimaldesi railroad workers, the men formed pairs, and the twosomes alternated cooking and shopping.[123] In her massive study of Chicago tenement houses, Edith Abbott considered this idiosyncratically Italian. The men, she noted, had formed "cooperative clubs" whereby they banded together for living, shopping, and cooking.[124] The circumstances of migration fostered conditions by which "Italian men have a lively interest in food, many of them know a good deal about it, are good cooks and better critics."[125]

In some settings the gang boss, the *padrone*, provided food for his men. Some complained about the spoiled, low-quality stuff he distributed as part of their wages. In other cases the *padrone* let the men fend for themselves and cook their own meals. But they were obliged, at least initially, to shop at the commissary he owned. The *padrone* made a handsome profit on selling food to the men.[126] Constantine Panunzio met up with a *padrone* in Boston when he first arrived from Apulia. The contractor fixed him up with a job in a Maine logging camp. "We smelled food," Panunzio remembered, "and then and there I had my first taste of pork and beans, molasses cookies and coffee and cream." What he thought about this food he did not share in his autobiography, but he did condemn the *padrone* for making the workers shop at his "storro."[127]

The *padrone* derived power and wealth from the commissary system. But the system worked because Italian immigrant men knew what they wanted to eat and would go to great lengths to avoid foods they did not like. The spaghetti, cheeses, oils, and tomato products which they opted for were the familiar but high-end food back home, and that was what these new Americans preferred.[128]

They demonstrated this same commitment by producing their own food. In the Utah mining frontier Italian men raised animals, grew produce, and what they did not eat themselves they sold to other Italian immigrant men. They did this despite the anger of the mine owners, who maintained stores where they wanted the men to shop.[129] Except when desperate, they refused to share in the fare of their non-Italian co-workers. Italian gold miners on Angel's Creek, California, built their own beehive ovens to bake bread, eschewing the biscuits, cornbread, and sourdough bread consumed by other miners.[130]

Italian men living in or near towns with an Italian enclave had more food choices. Here Italian merchants opened inexpensive restaurants, serving food defined as Italian. The demographics of the migration helped create Italian restaurants in America. The first Italian restaurants in San Francisco, as elsewhere, had been adjuncts to small hotels, basically boarding houses for single Italian men. Over time, as the bachelor community dwindled, restaurants reinvented themselves to stay in business. Both Palumbo and Corona di Ferro, Philadelphia's oldest Italian restaurants (which traced their origins to the 1870s), began as boarding houses for single men. Later on they shifted to catering to Italian families, with occasional non-Italian culinary cosmopolitans gradually venturing in.[131]

Well through the 1920s, the general American public was not the intended customer. At Coney Island's Village Giulia, guests in the 1890s could eat "thinly-sliced imported bologna, made of asses' meat and hog product," "sardellen, a long and narrow fish, salted and skinned," spaghetti with tomato sauce and Romano cheese, veal fried in olive oil with garlic, beef stuffed with ham, with a sauce of oil, tomatoes, and onion.[132] None of this fit American tastes, but these dishes appealed to Italian immigrants.[133]

In other places men entered into various arrangements in order to eat the food they wanted. They boarded with Italian families, usually townspeople from the same village or region. They generally "paid the usual three dollars a month for rent and cooking and washing, and they either paid collectively for the food at the end of the month, counting as their own the food consumed by the woman, or each man bought his own food and brought it to the woman to be cooked."[134] The daughter of one landlady of a Long Island Italian boarding house remembered that "my mother would sometimes cook for our family and they [the boarders] ate with us. Other times my mother would start the gravy [tomato sauce] and when they came home they would finish their own meals, cooking their own macaroni."[135]

The reuniting of families when the women arrived broadened husbands' eating options. Wives liberated men from having to fend for themselves. Women used their cooking skills to enlarge the family economy. The wives of men who had boarded could now take over and cook for a new crop of boarders. In America in every Italian enclave women commodified their cooking and other housekeeping skills, feeding unattached men. What had previously been done by women for their families now translated into a commercial asset, and good cooking meant the difference between having a paying boarder or losing him to another family with better food. The numerically outnumbered Italian women gained a powerful and profitable function.[136]

The Italian woman as the center of the boarding enterprise, with food as its heart, emerged repeatedly in Italian American literature. Zia Nuora, for example, a figure in Garibaldi LaPolla's novel *The Grand Gennaro* (1935), "presided over the table, filling the plates of the hungry boarders." She fed these workers soup, chicken, pasta, and beans, and earned more money than her husband, whose job was "bossing railway gangs." She may have done so well, according to LaPolla, because she fed them so well, never "stinting on the food which she piled up on their dishes. She had worked hard to prepare it and was glad to see it go." She always prepared a special meal when her husband returned from his work on the railroad gang, and her boarders looked forward to the banquet she prepared for him. Upon his arrival they too got "macaroni with the Bolognese sauce that was so different from what they knew, roast chicken, plenty of wine, and the good cheese that Nuora was always at great pains to buy."[137]

Discussions of Italian women as cooks, good ones at that, and as the ones who stood by their food as the symbol of their indispensability, ran through the remembered details of immigrant and first-generation life. Men and women who grew up in immigrant homes praised mothers for putting much tasty food on the table. They described their mothers as the ones who ruled the table. Anthony Gisolfi, whose parents came from Campania, grew up in New York before World War I. His grandmother, he recalled, "presided" over the family's food.[138] In a 1920s study of Chicago's Italians, sociologist Harvey Zorbaugh noted that "within the home . . . the wife directs the household, and it is not unusual for her to take the lead in family affairs, such as the expenditure of money" on food, as well as furnishings and rent.[139] In Italian American novels like those by John Fante, Guido d'Agostino, Pietro di Donato, Garibaldi LaPolla—all men—mothers stood over stoves, mixed and kneaded, stirred and ladled. In *Grand Gennaro* the mother, guardian of the family's food, made sure that if her sons "were to stay out late, she waited for them, and had coffee and food ready."[140]

The migration imposed upon women a higher standard by which their cooking skills would be judged. Men had endured years as bachelors fending for themselves. The arrival of wives must have been a relief, a chance to be fed. But having eaten in restaurants and boarding houses, men now expected much from their wives. Having baked their own bread, simmered their own sauces, and set their own tables, they could be more critical of what was served in their homes. Sitting down to those canonical meals, Italian men articulated an aesthetic appreciation for food. Their own experience gave them ideas about quality, and they judged critically what they ate. This in turn affected women, who had to defend their positions as cooks and as the ultimate arbiters of what went onto their families' tables. They could not assume that their husbands would eat whatever was served without comment.[141]

This challenged Italian women in America. The old standards of subsisting on a few staples no longer sufficed. They had new kitchen appliances to draw upon, new ingredients to incorporate, and loftier ideas of quality to measure up to. They might indeed have been perfect candidates for the many cooking classes offered in American cities, in adult education classes in public schools or in settlement houses.

But most Italian women disdained such classes. In 1917 Antonio Mangano listed the many classes Italians in New York availed themselves of at social settlement houses. Cooking did not appear among them.[142] Since its opening at the end of the nineteenth century, Boston's North Bennett Street settlement house served the local Italian population and offered many cooking classes. The only Italian women who showed up as students were enrolled through an arrangement with the public schools. As for the evening classes, in the academic year 1894–95, 38 women attended dressmaking classes. None, however, showed up for cooking. By 1899–1900, 79 neighborhood women hoped to sharpen their sewing skills, but only 15 signed up for cooking.[143] An Evening Elementary School for Adults opened up in East Harlem in 1920. About half of the adults who took classes came from the surrounding Italian community, and the school offered homemaking courses on food budgets, low-cost meals, and nutrition. Hardly any of the Italians, who avidly attended the other classes, chose these.[144]

This general pattern predominated in most settlement houses and other sites for immigrant adult education. American ameliorative organizations tried hard to appeal to Italian women to modify their cooking habits.[145] But Italian women mostly ignored them.[146] They might have refused such classes because they saw them as intrusions into their personal and family lives. Many had experienced directly, or heard of, "social workers [who] burst into their homes and upset the usual routine of their lives, opening windows, undressing children, giving orders not to eat this and that."[147] Moreover, attending a class on a particular subject amounted to an admission of ignorance, incompetence, a need to improve. Since Italian women in America defined much of their personal worth in terms of cooking, cooking classes were cultural land mines. Much of women's power in their families derived from their ability to put a good meal on the table and reap the praise of husbands, children, boarders, and guests. For a woman to sign up for a class would be tantamount to a public declaration that her family somehow found her cooking skills wanting.

Italian women believed that "proficiency in housework should be the first criterion by which a man picks a wife." Eighty-nine percent of those interviewed in 1934 in East Harlem, affirmed this statement.[148] They understood that their authority began in the kitchen. This shaped their relations with daughters. Mothers considered themselves obligated to teach daughters to cook and pass on the skills they had.[149] Girls at very young ages helped their mothers with all kinds of domestic chores, cleaning, tending to younger siblings, and cooking. A 1924 report of the heavily Italian Reed Street Neighborhood House in Philadelphia criticized the Italian mothers who "believe that their daughters are supposed to do the family wash, scrub, cook, take care of all the children."[150] Genoeffa Nizzardini and Natalie Joffe, writing in the 1940s for the National Research Council, recognized the gendered nature of Italian American childhoods. "Little girls at very early ages learn to assume many of the responsibilities of the household. When quite small they can be trusted to go shopping alone, but boys do not do so, for it is decidedly beneath the dignity of the male to shop for food. Traditionally it is woman's work, and she is a skilled bargainer, one not to be fooled into taking wilted vegetables and stale fruit."[151]

Although much of the discussion about Italian families and food centered on mothers as cooks and daughters as apprentices, men and women together engaged in the home production of food. Italian men often worked outdoors and endured constant seasonal slack periods. When not employed, men "dried fish and salami in their cellars"[152] along with their wives, or conserved tomatoes for sauce, made wine, pasta, and other foods that lent themselves to home production. Men prepared food on a regular basis.

Men in Italian families ate at home. Although they may have eaten at restaurants when they lived as bachelors, upon marriage the family meal became *the* norm. Beginning in adolescence, men spent much, and indeed most of their non-work time away from home in all-male places of recreation and sociability, the cafe, club, saloon, and street corner. Eating and sleeping brought them home.

The common meal emerged as an inviolable part of Italian culture.[153] In the 1930s, 96 percent of all East Harlem Italian families ate their meals together, perhaps owing to the number of unemployed workers in each family and to the practice of working close to home.[154] An Italian

American man who grew up in New York's Greenwich Village recalled that "whoever was not present when Papa sat down for dinner did not eat, since the door . . . was summarily locked."[155]

Women showed their cooking skills in public as well, heightening the competition and strengthening communal bonds. Much of Italian public life functioned around food. Weddings, baptisms, funerals, holidays displayed the products of women's kitchens. Women cooked together for parish events, spaghetti dinners, picnics, banquets, and measured their sauces, breads, cakes, and other dishes.[156] In Madison, the women of St. Joseph's Church got together every August to make tomato paste together.[157] In many Italian American communities women exchanged pizzas with each other at Easter. "The pizza exchange, a tradition which extended back to the first decade of the twentieth century between families . . . had . . . symbolic significance. Each family's pizza contained a variation of the customary ingredients and had a unique shape, often having the family's name baked into the crust or spelled out with strips of dough." Neighbors sampled each others' goods and women's reputations rose or fell with those tastings. Collective cooking and cross-household tasting led to the articulation of community standards of excellence to which individual women had to conform.[158]

The public selling of food at the *feste* created a commercial marker of quality. Although families did not eat in restaurants, during the festivities neighborhood families often brought their own plates to the vendors (usually restaurant owners) to be filled, and ate the food outside or carried it up to their apartments. Husbands and sons could then compare and contrast their usual nightly pasta with the restaurant food. Women and their cooking were revered, but reverence had to be earned. That Italian communities provided ample opportunity for women to be judged as cooks heightened the importance of food and women's role in the process.

Italian American children expressed little interest in transcending the food boundaries of their families and communities. Memoirs and other texts written by immigrants and their children never mention the temptation of eating out in restaurants serving other than Italian foods. Few described the pleasure of visiting with friends and co-workers from other ethnic groups and sharing their foods. They pushed the limits of their foodways but only within a constructed definition of "Italianness." In the evolution of an Italian American food culture based on a fusion of certain iconic Italian foods, pasta and sauce, olive oil and distinctive cheeses, with American foods, particularly meat, Italian Americans created a distinctive way of life in America. While they no longer ate as they had back home, neither did they eat like all other Americans. Yet they evinced little personal anguish or familial discord over the distance between standard American fare and their own.

Memoirs by Italian Americans, the immigrants' children, rhapsodized about food as a densely positive experience, often the most meaningful part of their recollections. One memoirist stated frankly, "my recollections of years of dinners as a child are very pleasurable. I do not recall any constraint. . . . The dinner hour was essentially for the enjoyment of the dinner." After rattling off two pages of remembered foods, Anthony Gisolfi apologized for his long exegesis on food. "I have been at some pains to describe the culinary world of my early years—before the nineteen twenties—because enjoyment of meals in the company of adults is an important part of a child's life."[159]

Few of the memoirists indicated any culinary restlessness or desire for greater personal freedom in what and where they ate. Nor did they, as young people, express boredom with a relatively fixed repertoire. If they felt discomfort it was in situations where they had to consume as Italians in public places. Jerre Mangione experienced embarrassment at the food habits of his Sicilian family only when they ate their meals in public. He dreaded the warm weather, when Sunday feasts took place in the park. "As long as the celebrations were held indoors away from public scrutiny I could enjoy them . . . But in the summer months . . . when they invaded the public parks . . . I would be tormented with the worry that they were making a bad impression on the Americans around us."[160] An East Harlemite similarly confessed that "We seldom took our home prepared lunch to school, although we much preferred Italian bread and Italian food."[161] They ate different food than the others and felt discomfort at what Americans must think of them and their food.

Such revelations of shame at eating Italian food were rare and limited to the public sphere. Children ate, with appreciation, the foods in their homes.[162] Italians prided themselves on "knowing" food and judging its quality better than other Americans. They cited, even at the beginning of the twentieth century, their particular contribution to America through food. Physician Rocco Brindisi of Boston defended his fellow immigrants and their diet in *Charities*. "It is the Italians who have introduced in the American kitchens the dandelions, the celeries, the fennels and many other greens," which should be considered "a real blessing to all."[163]

The harmony in Italian homes in America over food contrasted with a deep generational chasm between immigrant parents and American children over much else in their cultural repertoire. This disjunction provided the basis for the work of Leonard Covello, first as a teacher and principal in East Harlem, and as a scholar analyzing the difficulties endured by Italian children in American schools.[164] He emphasized the cultural dissonance Italian youngsters felt between parents' ideas of obedience and loyalty and American values of freedom and individualism. Covello posited that "an outstanding trait of the Italo-American school child is the feeling of inferiority which he experiences in his dealings and contacts with the American world."[165] Another researcher articulated it as a "sense of inferiority, [a] rejection of the parental home."[166]

Yet little of that rift divided American-born children from their immigrant parents when it came to food.[167] A study conducted in New Haven by psychologist Ivan Childs demonstrated that even rebellious Italian American young men, the ones most at odds with families and communities, considered Italian food to be the best. Home cooking represented for them the most—and often only—element in the cultural repertoire which kept them "Italian."[168] Childs delineated three archetypal Italian men, an "in-group," which proudly asserted its Italian identity; "rebels" at the other extreme, who resented their misfortune of being Italian; and in the middle, the "apathetic" group who neither celebrated or ran away from ethnicity. The three converged only when it came to food. In discussing marital prospects, most informants indicated that they preferred Italian girls, because, "They know just what we eat, the way of the house, and so on. I'm used to eating Italian food; that's the main reason." Another put it differently, but conveyed the same sentiment, "It's mostly on account of cooking. I've been brought up with Italian food."[169]

The young men whom Childs interviewed were apt informants. They revealed the dense nexus of food and Italian identity in America. In the process of selectively sampling from American culture, they used food as the focus of their ethnicity. Although opting for American furnishings, American popular culture, American clothing, they kept to their own food, invented though it may have been in this country. A Protestant minister serving an Italian church in Hartford, Connecticut, noted that "the younger generation born in Italy" but now in America was "still attached to Italian cooking . . . but wants American things."[170]

Food, and the ever present danger of hunger, drove the exodus of men and women from Italy who wanted to eat better and who resented their dependence upon others to feed them. In America *they* ate what *they* wanted. They took foods once denied to them, and reveled in consumption. They ate better, not just than they had, but than their social superiors had. By feasting every day in America upon Italy's holiday foods they made those foods more than just good. They made them sacred, symbolic of their communities and of American abundance. They measured the changes they had experienced in status and well-being by inventing new foods and calling them Italian. Food embodied where they had come from and what they had achieved.

4

"OUTCAST FROM LIFE'S FEAST":
FOOD AND HUNGER IN IRELAND

Mary Butler contributed to the early twentieth-century crusade to revive Irish culture in the name of Irish political independence. In a pamphlet addressed to the women of Ireland she crafted a list of fifteen ways to foster authentic Irishness in their homes. "Make the home atmosphere Irish," she admonished Ireland's mothers, by making "the social atmosphere Irish." Wives and mothers should insist that children be given Irish names, learn the Irish language in school, listen to Irish music, and enjoy Irish dance. She articulated an overriding principle: "Consistently support everything Irish, and consistently withhold your support from everything un-Irish." In this way she situated the movement for political and cultural autonomy in the home. It too should join the struggle against colonial rule.

Yet not one of her tips to enhance a distinctive Irish domestic culture involved the world of food. She considered no traditional recipes, foodways, food names, or food practices as instruments for building Irish identity. Language, dance, emphatically yes; but no menus to embody the idea of an Irish nation.[1]

Butler's omission of food as a potential vehicle for creating Irish identity was not an oversight. Food lay on the margins of Irish culture as a problem, an absence, a void. The Irish experience with food—recurrent famines and an almost universal reliance on the potato, a food imposed on them—had left too painful a mark on the Irish Catholic majority to be considered a source of communal expression and national joy. In James

Joyce's words, they were "Outcast from Life's Feast."[2] The history of modern Ireland is revealed through its unique engagement with food. That engagement alienated Irish women and men from using it as a way to structure a positive identity.

Located on the far western edge of Europe, Ireland in the nineteenth century differed fundamentally from its regional neighbors. Colonized rather than independent, it existed in a state of subordination to a foreign imperial power well into the twentieth century. The locus of one of Europe's most protracted and contentious battles for national liberation, Ireland also exported a staggering proportion of its young people as permanent exiles. By the middle of the nineteenth century emigration became a fact of life whose demographic implications reverberated through the social and political landscape. At the same time, unlike the rest of Europe, Ireland experienced only partial industrialization and minimal urbanization.

Ireland also failed to develop an elaborate national food culture. Unlike other peoples, Irish writers of memoirs, poems, stories, political tracts, or songs rarely included the details of food in describing daily life. Those who observed the Irish and recorded their voices rarely represented them as wanting to eat better or craving particular items. They hoped to eat more so as to not be hungry, but dwelt little on particular tastes or special dishes. To the contrary, when the Irish remarked upon food, they did so negatively. They spoke of hunger and lamented the absence of food in general.

Alcohol, rather than food, played an integral role in the Irish social system and through it the Irish consumed their collective identity. Alcoholic beverages long provided them with an inexpensive source of calories that never spoiled and that enhanced sociability.[3] Drink had long roots in the Irish economy and culture, and permeated the folk repertoire. The *shebeen*, literally a hidden public house, offered a venue for male bonding. It and its successor, the legal public house, gave men a place to relax in good fellowship enhanced by the physical sensations, however addictive, that accompanied alcohol consumption. They sang and wrote about alcohol, not food. It linked them to being Irish. The Irish were a people "whose social life was hinged to cheap drink."[4]

The history of drinking in Ireland involved the intersection of numerous subhistories, including agricultural competition between the growing of potatoes and grains, Irish defiance of British monopolies and taxation policies, the evolution of village pubs as male alternatives to female-dominated homes, and the search by poor people for economic security.[5] In a colonized society with few options for marginal people to secure an economic safety net, some small farmers distilled grain to make *poitín* (in English, poteen). This drink provided cash, and the money earned from it could purchase food when hunger set in.[6]

The vast majority of Irish also subscribed to a particular religious system, a distinctive form of Catholicism that made little room for religious celebration by feasting. Instead, it emphasized fasting, total as well as periodic abstentions from meat, eggs, and milk products. Before the Famine Irish church fathers propagated strict regulations governing fasting during Lent, Ember Days, the vigils of Christmas, Pentecost, Assumption, and All Saints Day, on the Wednesdays and Fridays of Advent, and weekly on Fridays.[7] After the Famine a devotional revolution swept through Ireland, and the culture of fasting intensified. No religious festivals brought food into the church to complement the joyous world of sacred time.[8] Abstention from food, it seems, heightened Irish spirituality.

Finally, being Irish also meant consuming potatoes. Potatoes, a product of the Americas, traveled to Europe through the great Columbian exchange which also brought corn (maize), chocolate, and sugar to Europeans.[9] The foods of the New World revolutionized the daily fare of the urban working classes and the rural peasants of the Old World. Potatoes in particular shook up the diets of most of Europe's poor, in Scandinavia, eastern Europe, Germany, parts of Italy and France, England,[10] and the rest of the Celtic Fringe, Wales and Scotland. With important regional variations, the potato expanded the diets of the lower classes, offering a low-cost, easily grown, high-calorie source of nutrition.[11]

The Irish reliance on potatoes grew to a monumental degree and was unique. According to Redcliffe Salaman, author of the highly detailed, meticulous *The History and Social Influence of the Potato*, Ireland and its potato-based culture differed from every place else:

> The potato has, in the minds of more than half the world, an inalienable and time-honored association with Ireland, comparable to the age-long dependence of many Asiatic people on rice. Examples of a rather different nature will readily occur to the mind, where

some special food or dish has acquired a regional or national affinity, such as the eating of bouillabaisse in Provence or the importance of macaroni in the dietary of the Italian. The former is a regional custom and has no bearing, important or otherwise, on the economic life of the people; the latter has assumed the status of a national dish in Italy, and its sudden withdrawal would undoubtedly inconvenience and annoy the people but would not necessarily have any serious economic repercussions.

Ireland and the potato were intimately bound together. Its people, up to three quarters of them by the 1840s, had, wrote Salaman, "for some reason chosen to make a specific . . . food . . . its sole or almost sole supply of nourishment . . . the people have but one available lifeline which, if severed, must bring disaster in its train."[12] He estimated that by 1800 the potato dominated the diet of 90 percent of the Irish population.[13] Such a number, even if a bit overstated, pointed to a culture of potato eating, and a world in which potatoes dominated. The German traveler J. G. Kohl also may have overstated the case in his 1844 account of Irish life, generalizing that Irishmen, "on every day," except Christmas, ate "nothing but potatoes."[14] Eating potatoes was part of the Irish way of life.

It was precisely that essential food item which fell victim to disease. Thus it was only in Ireland that the fungus *Phytophthera infestans* (which, like the potato itself, originated in America) threatened not just one crop, but a way of life. The blight devastated potato crops throughout Europe. It denied other poor people their potatoes, and caused them also to look for alternate sources of nourishment. But only in Ireland did it inevitably wreak "disaster in its train."[15]

Whole classes of Irish people disappeared—the very poor, the cottiers (agricultural laborers who rented a cabin and potato patch), and the landless laborers. The Famine, sometimes referred to as the Great Hunger to distinguish it from the other hungers endured by the Irish poor, loomed large in the lives of those who experienced it, in the memories they passed on to their children, and in the political and cultural repertoire of Ireland for decades to come.

The Famine truly devastated Ireland. In the years from 1845 through the next census of 1851, its population dropped from 8,175,000 to 6,552,000. Had a normal rate of increase taken place, the population

8. Potatoes were not only Ireland's staple, but lay at the heart of antagonistic relations between landlords and tenants. When landlords evicted tenants, their hungry neighbors rushed in to seize potatoes left behind.

should have topped 9,000,000 by 1851.[16] About one million Irish people died, the poor, the old, and the young in particular. Despite the broadly circulating narratives of people dying in droves of actual hunger, and as a result of eating grass out of crazed desperation, most succumbed to famine-related illness such as dysentery, typhus, and cholera.

The massive deaths by disease, and the subsequent hemorrhaging of the population through emigration represented only part of the Famine's impact on the Irish and their food culture. Much of the discussion at the time and in later political rhetoric focused on the British response to the crisis. John Mitchel, the nationalist leader, succinctly summarized the popular Irish view on what had happened to Ireland and what that meant to the Irish. "The Almighty sent the potato blight," thundered Mitchel, pointing an accusing finger, "but the English created the Famine," both as owners of Irish lands and as policy makers in London.[17]

Mitchel's attribution of blame rested on the belief that as the potatoes rotted and the Irish starved, the grains and livestock which belonged to the landowners flourished. The Irish economy had since the eighteenth century been based on an inequitable arrangement, imposed by the English, by which Irish Catholic laborers or small tenant farmers worked lands owned by the Anglo-Irish that were dedicated to the tillage of grains and the grazing of cattle. The produce flowed out of Ireland to England to feed its swelling factory population.

This arrangement had prevailed for decades before the 1840s. In exchange for their labors the Irish existed on potatoes, which they either purchased with meager wages or grew on the scraps of land surrounding their cottages. In good times, the system worked, and a kind of reciprocity kept the Irish fed on potatoes, even though the balance of trade tilted decidedly in favor of London.

But in famine times the first part of the social equation, the ability of the Irish to feed themselves fell apart. Because the single-crop diet was so close to the bone, those who endured the Famine and the generations who imagined it magnified the basic truth that Ireland continued to export vast amounts of food as the corpses of the dying lay along the edges of the road. The Irish scholar Peter O'Leary, who lived through the Famine, stated, "There was sent out from Ireland that year [1846] as much—no! twice as much—corn as would have nourished every person living in the country. The harbors of Ireland were full of ships and the ships full of Irish corn; they were leaving the harbors while the people were dying with the hunger through the land."[18] John Mitchel gave the same figure, claiming that Ireland produced and exported enough food during the Famine to feed 18 million people, more than double the Irish population.[19]

In the late 1840s, as in several earlier and later potato crop devastations, the wheat, rye, millet, and other grains continued to grow, immune to the potato disease. The cattle grew fat. The herds increased, and the landowners themselves felt no pinch in their standard of living, although they did suffer the loss of rents. Pictures of wagons laden with food streaming to the ports to be shipped to England, to be eaten there while Ireland starved, emerged as one of the most potent images in Irish political thinking both at the time and in generations to come, and this starvation became a political matter.

This image suffused literature written during the Famine. The poet Denise Florence MacCarthy published in *The Nation* in 1847 one of the most anthologized literary works of the Famine, in which the poet posed "A Mystery."

> They are dying! they are dying! where the golden corn is growing,
> They are dying! they are dying! where the crowded herd are lowing,
> They are gasping for existence where the streams of life are flowing,
> And they perish of the plague where the breeze of health is blowing.

McCarthy, like Mitchel, knew who was responsible. To them, as to many Irish women and men, it was no mystery at all. They located starvation in the context of politics.

> We have ploughed, we have sown,
> But the crop was not our own;
> We have reaped, but harpy hands
> Swept the harvest from our lands;
> We were perishing for food,
> When, lo! in pitying mood,
> Our kindly rulers gave
> The fat fluid of the slave,
> While our corn filled the manger
> Of the war-horse of the stranger![20]

The stranger had stolen the land, and the stranger sold off food, while its rightful owners starved.[21]

Mitchel accused the British of causing the Famine because they had usurped the land and grew crops which its legitimate owners could not eat. Moreover, the British pursued their heartless policies even after the Almighty had sent the blight. Like his fellow Irish, Mitchel believed that the British reacted too slowly and too parsimoniously. The people who remained in Ireland and those who went abroad firmly believed that the

British did nothing and cared little. In the eyes of the Irish masses the English worried more about stemming civil unrest, particularly food rioting and violence against landowners, than about genuinely finding ways to feed the hungry. The English wanted to keep their own tax rates down, and did so on the bodies of the Irish dead.

Actually, the colonial policy was probably more a matter of too little too late. Official Britain did not want to swerve from policies of free trade, not liking the idea of tampering with the marketplace. Parliament hesitated to deviate from its commitment to *laissez-faire* economics and refused to divert the loads of grain from their foreign destinations to feed the hungry. Prime Minister Robert Peel, early in the Famine, proposed lifting the Corn Laws, and within eight months voters, largely representing landowning classes, turned him out of office. Subsequent governments learned a lesson from Peel's fate. British policy favored creating public works projects, so that the Irish poor could earn money to buy food. But starving people can hardly build roads and break rocks.

Eventually, the government realized that it had to feed the starving masses, and under the Destitute Poor (Ireland) Act it put into operation soup kitchens to feed millions. Doubtless more would have starved and succumbed to disease had those soup kitchens not been opened. In July 1847, for example, over 3 million Irish people ate daily at soup kitchens, although the hungry in remote regions had no way to get to towns where kitchens ladled out the soup.

Even when the British provided direct food relief, the Irish were enraged. In some places relief workers humiliated the crowds waiting to eat, pressuring the Catholic poor to convert to Protestantism in exchange for their mean bowl of gruel. The Evangelical Union, a militant Protestant group, passed out religious tracts to those in food lines.[22] Ironically, the stuff that the soup kitchens distributed, including the soup concocted by one of Europe's most famous chefs, Alexis Soyer, fell below the potato's nutritional value. Soyer and the others involved in providing food relief not only wanted to feed the hungry, but used the occasion to condemn the Irish for their potato-eating ways and attempted to change their attitude towards food. He hoped to teach the poor to give up the fickle potato which had done them in, and replace it with corn and fish.[23] He commented that "The country produces plenty of vegetable and animal substances, and the waters washing your magnificent shores teem with life, which the all-wise Providence has given as food to man, and that they only require to be properly employed to supply the wants of every one." Soyer's cookbook offered the Irish 22 recipes, 21 of which ignored the potato as an ingredient.[24]

In famished Ireland the potato had pushed almost everything else off the table and came to be the centerpiece of most people's diet. The better-off augmented their meals with some cabbage and buttermilk. As a rule, though, most lacked these supplements. Only about Ireland could it have been said, "The whole economic structure . . . rested ultimately on the potato."[25] Only in Ireland were potatoes synonymous with food and with the people who ate them.[26] Only the Irish were imagined by others as the degraded eaters of potatoes. Historian E. P. Thompson asserted that the English working classes resisted potatoes in part because they saw this particular food as degrading, potentially reducing their level of civilization to that of "Erin's root-fed hordes." Thompson celebrated the English workers who refused to become "victims of a conspiracy to reduce them to the Irish level."[27]

The Irish did eat a lot of potatoes. In the 1830s a cleric from Kildare estimated to a Parliamentary commission studying the plight of Ireland's poor that "in 24 hours a labouring man will require at least three stones of potatoes, that is 21 pounds." One historian asserted that "day in day out, except when the crop was poor, the adult Irishman ate some ten pounds of potatoes a day."[28]

In Ireland the details of potato culture meshed with the details of human culture. Their homes and communities lacked the physical infrastructure to prepare and cook other kinds of foods. Families owned few implements for cooking. They needed only a pot on the fireplace to boil potatoes but were ill-equipped to prepare anything else. Most larger towns had mills to grind grain, but few existed in the countryside, particularly in the west of Ireland. Consequently, corn (maize) imported to feed the famished masses could not be ground. Most towns had no technology to make hard kernels edible, nor did the people generally possess knowledge of how to transform it into bread.[29]

The power of the potato in the Irish diet persisted even after the economic and social changes brought by the Famine.[30] Well after the 1850s, even as poverty slowly decreased and significant numbers of Irish people bought modest farms, they continued to eat potatoes often.[31] Even though the potato crops failed again, in 1859, 1879, 1890, and beyond, the Irish continued to place potatoes at the center of their food system, depending upon them almost alone for their nutrition.[32]

Personal testimonies from Ireland charted the tuber's longevity. Sara Walsh was born in 1919 in County Kerry, late in the history of the potato. She recalled many years later, "We were very poor; our diet consisted of bread, tea, potatoes, cabbage, once in a while some salt pork from a pig we killed once a year." Walsh's family were not landless laborers. They owned a small farm with "6 or 8 milking cows and sold the milk at the creamery. . . . The only thing that wasn't sold was enough milk for our tea."[33]

The transition from almost total reliance on the potato took place gradually. When potato crops failed in the west of Ireland in 1879, the local population suffered. This helped launch the Land Wars of the 1880s.[34] Crop failures in the 1890s meant that tenants could not pay rents, had nothing to eat, and faced eviction. Annie Greeley, a poor woman from County Galway, wrote to nationalist leader John Dillon in 1896, begging "to your honor for a trifle to enable me to buy a little fuel and potatoes," while another applicant for assistance from County Kerry sadly noted, "The potatoes are out now and times are very hard with us."[35] It took a full thirty years after 1850 for the Irish diet to shift away from the potatoes, evidence of the conservatism "in their domestic habits."[36]

Other foods did gently nudge potatoes out of their previous centrality, but never banished them completely.[37] By the end of the nineteenth century and the beginning of the twentieth, with the lifting of trade restrictions, shops in small Irish towns began to stock their shelves with more varied goods, including imports.[38] But the potato did not disappear even from the tables of those who moved to cities.[39] Rather, the tubers shared space with bacon and other kinds of meat, oatmeal "stirabouts," cabbage, onions, butter and cheese, and eggs. Tea emerged as the hallmark of Irish domestic drinking and the center of sociability within the home.

Memoirs, literature, and other first-hand accounts of post-Famine Ireland demonstrated that potatoes continued to be on the menu, although increasingly not by themselves. In Maurice O'Sullivan's memoir of his childhood, he recounted his move to the Blasket Islands in 1911. On his first night in this fishing community, "When everything was ready we sat in to the table. And a fine, wholesome table it was for good, broken potatoes and two big plates of yellow bream—the custom of the Island at the fall of night."[40] Conrad Arensberg, in *The Irish Countryman* of 1937, the first scholarly ethnographic study of rural Ireland, commented: "They eat very little meat, confining themselves to bacon and occasional poultry. Eggs are a great staple and the potato has only slowly retreated from its place of honour, though the countryman makes sure he shall not allow it to betray him as it did in the time of the Famine."[41] In Patrick Kavanagh's 1948 novel, *Tarry Flynn*, the hero of the same name helps his mother prepare Sunday dinner. No doubt in this middling farm all sorts of foods would have been served, but Kavanagh shared with his readers only the fact that Tarry "washed the potatoes for the dinner in the tub before the door and put on the ten-gallon pot."[42]

The potato's persistence and its widespread consumption had deep implications for Irish social life. Every foodstuff has its own cultural and natural history. Any crop—corn, wheat, potatoes, olives, beans—offers its cultivators and consumers idiosyncratic challenges and opportunities. Nature endowed potatoes with certain characteristics which made them a good choice for poor people with access to little arable land. They grew pretty much anywhere, including boglands and rocky hills, unsuitable for grain cultivation. They grew on small patches of land and produced, in good years, bountiful yields. They had a brief growing season and required little tending, making it possible for those dependent on them to work the fields of the landowners from whom they rented their houses.[43] And they provided reasonable nutrition if supplemented by milk or butter.[44]

The essential nature of potatoes, however, complicated their use. In their beds they were terribly vulnerable to adverse weather conditions, particularly wet, damp air, a common characteristic of Ireland. The high yield of the good years always had to be balanced off against the dangers of bad weather which ominously threatened. Bulky, potatoes did not transport well, particularly in a rural country without many roads. Shortages in one place could not be easily remedied by importation from another. Potatoes also did not store well. Regardless of quality, they deteriorated within a few months of harvesting, and wet conditions during storage hastened sprouting and rotting. The Irish by and large lived in small cottages with little adequate dry storage space. Even the most prudent individuals could not lay away much of a store as a buffer against yearly hard times.

These natural problems inherent in the potato were exacerbated by the political context of their consumption, which hit with full fury in the nineteenth century. Every year the Irish poor, those most vulnerable to famines and most dependent on potatoes, faced a few hungry months sometimes called "meal months," falling between the end of the old batch and the bringing in of the new. Potatoes, particularly the low-grade variety, "lumpers," most common by the 1830s, usually went bad by August. The next crop would not be ready until October. Laborers found themselves hungry as early as June, and in those months of privation they foraged for nettles, seaweed, consumed some fish, and relied on the largesse of friends and family. Most of the Irish population had no cash reserves because of prohibitive rents, so they had few options when potatoes ran out. When potatoes got damaged, the Irish had neither potatoes to eat nor money to buy alternative food.[45]

Reliance on the potato had other consequences. Potatoes needed little, indeed no technology to render them edible. Potato preparation demanded little in the way of cooking equipment, cooking skill, or even cooking and eating utensils. A listing of *all* material possessions in a parish of 4,000 people in Donegal for 1836 included 243 stools, 8 brass candlesticks, but only 10 table forks, and no other utensils dedicated to cooking or eating.[46] Estyn Evan, a geographer and an eminent Irish folklorist wrote as late as the 1940s:

> One very rarely sees a table of any antiquity in an Irish kitchen. . . .
> The table is not a centre of social activities and has nothing like the
> same importance as in an English farmhouse. There *are* [emphasis
> added since he described Irish material culture a century after the
> Famine, when very different economic and political conditions pre-
> vailed] crofters' dwellings in Donegal where no table is used; in-
> stead, at meal times, the shallow potato basket or skeehogue is
> taken on the knees of the members of the family as they sit in front
> of the fire.[47]

Other folklorists noted that the Irish ate their potatoes without utensils, and that typically they grew the nail of the thumb of their right (or left) hand long, to facilitate peeling the skin off the potato.[48]

9. The vast majority of the rural Irish population lived with few material goods. Tables, chairs, dishes, cutlery, pots and pans were rarely seen in the Irish country-side. This 1903 stereograph depicts a woman of Keel, a poor village in the West of Ireland.

The potato diet neither demanded nor produced cooking virtuosity. Potatoes required simple preparation, plain boiling in their skins over an open fire, just to the point when the jackets burst. Whoever tended the potatoes transferred them to a shallow basket, a *sciathoga*, from which the water drained out. Irish women did not need to learn much about cooking and mothers had scant knowledge to pass on to daughters when it came to the rituals of the kitchen. Neither daughters nor sons in memoirs celebrated their mothers as the source of tasty, nurturing food.

Some forms of potato preparation demanded even less effort. Commentators on the Irish and their diet noted that many consumers preferred potatoes half cooked, believing that the softer the potato, the less energy it released. One traveler in the 1820s in County Tyrone, described a cabin scene: "The father was sitting on a stool and the mother on a kreel of turf; one of the children had a straw box, the youngest even sprawling on the floor, and five others were standing around the potato basket. The potatoes were half-boiled. 'We always have our praties [potatoes] hard, they stick to our ribs and we can fast longer that way.'"[49] If hard potatoes represented a preferred culinary standard, then the need for cooking declined even further. The cook in charge of the pot merely needed to make sure that they did not sit in the boiling water too long.

From the pre-Famine days through the early twentieth century, commentators remarked on the lack of popular interest in food. Even when times got better, when the Famine and mass migration had removed the very poorest from the countryside, Irish women and men still said little in memoir and literature about food. Historical studies pointed to a narrow diet and a general disinterest in foodways.[50]

Meals were not a focal point around which people, as individuals and as family members, organized their time. Interested visitors and scholarly observers in the 1930s noted the ubiquity of the pattern whereby men and women ate separately, men first, women picking among the cold leftovers.[51] John Millington Synge, a member of the Anglo-Irish class best known for his controversial play *The Playboy of the Western World*, spent a few weeks yearly on the Aran Islands between 1898 and 1902. An outsider to the community, he rented a cottage and employed a local woman to see after his meals. He found the generally desultory attitudes of the Aran Islanders toward meals a notable characteristic of the community, one that he later used as the setting for his drama. "The general ignorance," he speculated,

> of any precise hours in the day makes it impossible for people to have regular meals. They seem to eat together in the evening, and sometimes in the morning . . . but during the day they simply drink a cup of tea and eat a piece of bread or some potatoes, whenever they are hungry. . . . For men who live in the open air they eat strangely little. Often when Michael has been out weeding potatoes

for eight or nine hours without food, he comes in and eats a few slices of home-made bread, and then he is ready to go out with me and wander for hours around the island. They use no animal food except a little bacon and salt fish. The old woman says she would be very ill if she ate fresh meat. Some years ago, before tea, sugar, and flour had come into general use, salt fish was much more the staple of diet than it is now.[52]

A culture which pushed food to the margins rather than to the center of social life had special implications for women, since usually food preparation fell within their domain. Women in Irish families did not have to spend much time in intricate food preparations, nor did they develop a repertoire of skills or definitions of personal worth through cooking. Potato cooking did not lend itself to communal preparation. Women from different households had no need or opportunity to work on food preparation cooperatively or in each others' presence. They had no repertoire of food lore to share with each other, and they did not compete amongst themselves for praise. Men did not measure women's worth by a culinary yardstick.

Well into the early twentieth century, when potatoes still played an important although no longer central role on the Irish table, Irish elites (no longer British administrators) believed that Irish women made poor cooks and that efforts had to be made to improve their culinary skills. The United Irishwomen, founded in 1908, hoped to upgrade the Irish diet by upgrading women's cooking. Its founders lamented that Irish women and men knew only potatoes, cabbage, and onions,[53] and in one of the organization's earliest pamphlets, *The United Irish Women—Their Place, Work and Ideals* (1911), the authors mourned that "It will help little if we have the methods of the twentieth century in the fields and those of the fifth in the home."[54]

Women seemed to expect little praise for their cooking. Frank O'Connor, born in 1903 in Cork, remembered his mother and her non-aesthetic relationship to the food she cooked for her family: "After a huge meal of stockfish and boiled potatoes she [his mother] would shrug and bless herself and then add her own peculiar grace: 'Well, thanks be to God, we're neither full nor fasting.'" As to his grandmother, who came to live with him and his parents, "when I glanced into the kitchen and saw

Grandmother at one of her modest repasts—a mess of hake and potatoes boiled in a big pot, with the unpeeled potatoes afterwards tossed on the table to be dipped in a mound of salt and eaten out of the fingers, and a jug of porter besides these—I fled for very shame."[55]

Can the Irish reluctance to talk about food, the generalized Irish disconnection between food and national identity, be understood as a long-term reaction to the trauma of the Great Hunger? Had a diet of potatoes left little room for other tastes and pushed food out of the realm of pleasure into that of mere biological necessity? Neither the potato diet itself nor the Famine, however devastating, suffice to explain why the Irish did not celebrate their culture through food and why they pushed food to the margin of their expressive culture. Other societies have relied heavily, at times, on a staple food eaten every day at every meal. Rice, for example, triumphed over a series of other foods to become the staple and symbol of Japanese culture. Once enshrined as the essence of their food, rice represented the notion of a meal and of Japanese national identity.[56] Japanese artists painted rice, poets wrote about it. Ordinary people gave rice as gifts and placed grains of it on sacred spaces at ritual moments.

Ojibway Indians lived on wild rice. They endured yearly shortages, and had to engage in short-term "switching" to something else between one year's crop and the next. But the Ojibway made wild rice the marker of group membership and the icon of their past, placing it "above being a food for consumption or barter" into the "status of sacred food." Indeed, as contact with white people intensified, so too did their veneration of wild rice. They "associate[d] wild rice harvesting with . . . aspects of traditional culture which are disappearing." Wild rice helped them know who they were and gave them a protected zone impervious to outside white influence.[57]

Similarly, since the age of Spanish colonization Mexican identity came to be expressed with *tamales*, a food embodying the resistance of the poor *mestizo* population to interference. They ate *tamales* at every meal. Daily life for women and men functioned around the tempo of *tamale* preparation. They evaluated *tamales* as good or bad, and the women who prepared them did so conscious of standards of quality. When they had to, they defended their corn *tamales* over tortillas made of wheat. They incorporated them into their cultural repertoire. *Tamales* told who they were.[58]

So famine, long-term exposure to hunger, and trauma did not have to push the Irish to separate food from pleasure and collective identity. Africans forcibly removed from their lands, taken into slavery, did what they could to recreate familiar foodways. They brought seedlings of rice to America.[59] In the slave communities on plantations women and men found pockets of time and moments of leisure to feast on the food they grew, and they gave their own foods names of African derivation.[60]

In the post-Emancipation South, the sharing of food within family, church, and town circles, and women's communal cooking events, bound black people together, even as the increasingly hostile white world mocked the idea of their freedom. African-American migrants from the Jim Crow South to the North in the early twentieth century may have been fleeing a place of hostility and physical violence, but they continued to eat and celebrate "back home" foods. One African American street vendor in Chicago of the 1910s plied his wares through the streets of the "Black Belt" with this piercing cry: "Water-mel-lone, jes' like from down home; roasten' ears, tatoes-tatoes-tatoes; nice ripe toma-toes; tommy-tommy-tomatoes; o-o-o-ochree and dry ingyuns." The list of foods may not have been notable, but the linkage of those foods to a place called "down home" was. By 1919 black restauranteurs in Chicago felt, recognized, and capitalized upon the nostalgia for traditional cooking and opened food establishments such as Southern Home Cooking, the Southern Lunch Room, and the Carolina Sea Island Candy Store.[61]

Ralph Ellison may have best expressed the northern urban African American culture of the early part of the twentieth century. In *Invisible Man*, his simple statement about a simple food, the yam, demonstrated that very mundane foods, despite their origins in oppression and poverty, could be mnemonic triggers for deep emotion. Ellison took the yam, a food commonly assumed to have been transplanted from Africa to America, and invested it with sacred memory, regardless of its association with subsistence living. "I took a bite," Ellison wrote, "finding it as sweet and hot as any I've ever had and was overcome by such a surge of homesickness that I turned away to keep my control."[62]

No matter how much fear and loathing the idea of the South played in the construction of their political identity, when it came to food, black migrants to the urban north carried positive memories of smells and tastes linked to that place, albeit a place they had to leave. No matter how much they defined the South as a world that terrorized them, they transformed certain of its "poor" foods into symbols of group life.

The trauma of starvation also did not stop Jewish men, and particularly women, in concentration camps from talking about food all the time. The women of Terezin not only suffered and starved, but they talked in exquisite detail about the foods of normal times. "Food," wrote Ruth Shwertfeger, "memories of it, missing it, craving it, dreaming of it, in short, the obsession with food colours all the Theresienstadt memoirs."[63] When they got together and talked, they systematically swapped recipes for foods that most would never live to eat again. One of the women, Mina Pachter, transcribed by hand the food lore the women talked about behind barbed wire. In a handwritten manuscript that miraculously survived, she wrote the *Kochbuch* of the women of Terezin. The inmates with empty stomachs talked food to each other. They talked of strudel, *knodel* (dumplings), *Kartoffel Herringspeise* (potato herring dish), Linzer torte, and other tasty foods that had once graced their tables.[64]

The Irish attitude toward food seemed to have been very different from that of these other men and women. They did not relish pre-trauma food memories, nor did they take the one powerful food they had and transform it into an icon of group identity. When they struggled for national and cultural renewal, they did not include food as an element of pride in their distinctive communal and folk culture. They did not transform the potato from a food which kept them alive into a symbol of cultural resistance and integrity.

This is particularly notable given the long Irish struggle against things English. Some nationalists tried to revive the Irish language because they understood the intimate connection between speech and identity. They created a vast and powerful literary and dramatic culture that explored the meaning of Irishness. At home and in their places of exile they produced music, dance, and athletic feats to announce to others that they possessed a distinctive culture which they themselves controlled.

Irish novelists and short story writers who emerged with great panache on the English-language literary scene of the last half of the nineteenth century and the early twentieth, dwelt little, or not at all, on food. James Joyce allowed one character in *Ulysses* to enjoy his food. But Leopold Bloom was a Jew, an outsider to parochial Dublin. He "ate with relish the inner organs of beasts and fowls. He liked thick giblet soup, nutty gizzards, a stuffed roast heart, liver slices fried with crustcrumbs, fried hen-cod roe."[65]

Typically, when Irish writers "fed" their characters, they did no more than mention the fact, as did William Carleton in his 1829 short story, "The Death of a Devotee": "I had dined with the priest"; "After dinner, we amused ourselves"; and the like. What did the protagonist of this story and his curate eat? Who prepared it and what tastes lingered in their mouths?

Food often functioned as a symbol of interpersonal hostility and conflict, not pleasure as lived through family or community. In Sean O'Casey's 1924 play *Juno and the Paycock*, bitterness emerged over the sausages Juno Boyle offered to her husband, Captain Jack, for breakfast. She hoped to bring some respectability and order to their tenement home. He reveled in male company, alcoholic drink, and nationalist bravado. Irritated that Jack had not come home from a night of "strutting about town," Juno muttered that if he "doesn't come in soon for his breakfast, he may go without any." The Captain scoffed at her desire for orderliness, symbolized by the proffered breakfast sausages. "I'll have no breakfast of yours—yous can keep your breakfast," he roared at her. "Sassige! Well let her keep her sassige," he told a friend.[66]

Liam O'Flaherty's Old Paddy Moynihan, in "The Pedlar's Revenge," ate voraciously. "The side of a pig, or even a whole sheep, would make no more than a good snack for him." A glutton, he "loved bacon." But Old Paddy Moynihan was also "not quite right in the head. Lord have mercy on him, he's been half-mad these last two years." His gargantuan appetite killed him. The "pedlar" who took revenge on Paddy for insults accumulated over a lifetime, melted down candles and gave them to Paddy with his potatoes, claiming it was bacon grease. "He'd eat anything" was the village consensus, and food killed him.[67] Neither Carleton, O'Casey, O'Flaherty, nor any of the architects of modern Irish literature used food to imagine Ireland.[68]

These writers and other bearers of the Irish cultural revival could have looked to Ireland's history before the potato for inspiration. Folklorists in the early twentieth century uncovered an alternative food tradition, one predating the potato and the British domination of Ireland. They revealed an early food system based on local resources which could have been claimed as authentically Irish. Their forbears had baked a variety of breads of barley, oats, wheat, and rye. Wheat breads generally showed up on feast days and at important social occasions, while breads made of oats and barley served as ordinary fare and dominated the diets of the poor.[69]

Before the potato, the Irish consumed great amounts of dairy products, butter, milk, and distinctive Irish cheeses, including one known as *banbidh*, made of curds.[70] They had meat, which they roasted and stewed, and oats, prepared in various ways, which they ate in quantities unimaginable by the early nineteenth century.[71] In the 1730s the administrators of the Irish Charter Schools, institutions for the "support of the children of the poor natives of Ireland," made a point of not feeding the children in their care beyond the normal dietary standard of the children's class. The schools therefore served them potatoes, about four and a half pounds a day, meat one time a week, except in the summer when it was given twice a week, as well as on Christmas and New Year. School officials doled out to the children small servings of sugar, butter, and barm, a brew made of potatoes.[72] A half century later meat had disappeared from the diet of the Irish poor on any day other than on Christmas, and sugar was an item which grocers in country towns kept on their shelves only for a tiny minority.

Students of Irish folklore revealed a rich world of pre-Famine and pre-potato Irish foodways, which associated food with holy time. September 29, Michaelmas, had been observed by eating goose; the earlier Irish Christmas table called for spiced ox tongue prepared with raisin wine.[73] One work on Irish custom noted that in centuries past—the author pinpointed it no more precisely than "long ago"—"the Lenten fast was kept much more rigorously than now . . . people did not eat eggs. So the custom arose that all the eggs were used up, in pancakes and so on, on Shrove Tuesday, a sort of 'last fling' before Lent."[74] *Barm brack*, a fruit bread, represented the February 1 feast of Saint Brighid and also New Year's eve, while *colcannon*, a dish of kale or cabbage mixed with potatoes, milk, and onions figured in Halloween rituals.[75] *Boxty*, like *colcannon*, was an elaborate dish made with potatoes, often rotting ones, and was connected to special events. One form of it, *stampy*, made with cream, sugar, and caraways seeds, also marked the festivities of Halloween and harvest celebrations.[76] Folktales referred to a "thick black pudding," "a pointer of mixed griddle bread," and roasted goose with potatoes, cabbage, and bacon as elements of the folk repertoire.[77] "'Sowens' or porridge made from soured 'meal seeds' sifted from the oatmeal," recorded folklorist Estyn Evans, "was traditionally eaten at Hallowe'en; and the Irish name for the 1st of November is Samhain, or 'Sowin.'"[78] Oral narratives of these foods persisted, but the foods died out.

The Irish did not turn to pre-potato foodways for culinary inspiration when times got better. Nor did they look to the elite as a model whose practices they wanted to emulate when more and better food became available to the masses. Ireland's better-off class, the Protestant landed gentry, ate well, and their foodways, visible to the Irish poor, could have appealed to them in better times.[79] The shops of market towns and cities catered to a small resident population of consumers of eggs, butter, fresh meat, fruit, meal, white bread, and the like. For instance, in Carrick, County Monaghan, in the 1820s, ten bakers, five butchers, and 11 grocers sold their wares to those who could afford them.[80]

In their homes, the families of the Irish landed class reveled in the elaborateness of their varied diet, and they socialized around full dinner tables.[81] Selina Crampton, for example, kept a journal of the meals that her family of landowners ate. Choosing a day at random from her diary, January 5, 1817, the family sat down to "2 Boiled Fowl," bacon and greens, roast beef, mutton pies, veal patties, baked potatoes, jelly, and custard with an apple tart. The following week the family hosted one of its many dinner parties and host and guests together enjoyed "Round of beef; Roasted turkey, 2 Woodcocks, Plumb [sic] pudding, mince pies, apple pie, custard, parsnip, mashed potatoes."[82] By the 1840s, indeed at the height of the Famine, her daughter Charlotte recorded recipes for "Gusaldo [sic] Espanol," a dish made of "beef or mutton, browned in butter," with broth, pepper, salt and onions, and then cooked with small pieces of cut up potato. She, like her mother, listed dishes eaten: macaroni ragout, cream cakes, curd cheese cakes, Yorkshire pudding, dumplings of various kinds, charlotte of apples, celery soup, rice pudding, croquettes of meat or fowl, and so forth, prepared in profusion and preserved in written form in exquisite detail.[83]

Jane Alcock, of Wilton Castle, County Wexford, also busied herself with the details of domestic food preparation and the staging of dinner parties for friends. She fretted over the aesthetics of what she served. "It is best," she jotted down in her notebook on cooking, that pastry dough be "rolled on marble or a very large slate. In very hot weather the butter should be put into cold water to make it as firm as possible." She used local ingredients, including potatoes for various dishes, and noted for herself, and no doubt for her servants, tips on how best to prepare potato paste. In this rendering of potatoes, a pot of boiling water and a basket for draining hardly sufficed: "Pound boiled potatoes very fine and add, while warm, a sufficiency of butter to make the mash hold together or you may mix with an egg. Then before it gets cold, flour the board pretty well . . . and roll it to the thickness wanted."[84]

Even the small Catholic elite, closer to the masses of the peasants than the Protestant landowners, also had something of a food culture. An account from the 1750s described the cooking of "a sheep boiled on top, half a sheep roasted at bottom, broiled fish on one side, and a great wooden bowl of potatoes on the other." Another narrative from the mid-eighteenth century recounted "black and white pudding" and a post-Mass gathering at which guests ate "brown barley bread, bacon . . . and roast beef, boiled beef, ducks, chickens, pullets, and turkeys."[85]

Hence the Irish had various options for the way they thought about food. They did have an array of folkloric foods which they could have reinvented. They had a tradition of more elaborate foodways which they could have invoked as part of the culture robbed from them by the English and which, like their language, could be reclaimed. Irish women and men with increasing access to money might have adopted those food practices as their own and boasted about the good stuff they ate.

But such borrowing across time or class lines did not take place. The Irish who came to eat better over time did not dip down into older food traditions and revive them. Nor did they, once they began to worry less about day to day subsistence, celebrate food any more than when they had lived on potatoes. If newly middle-class Irish farmers or city dwellers adopted some of the food practices of their previous social betters, they did not revel in them, nor did they link any food practices to being "Irish."

Although neither the potato diet nor the Famine (or continuous famines) alone determined Irish food practices, together they combined powerfully to repress an expressive culture based on food. The potato, after all, proved to be the source of their sorrow. Potatoes fed them, but also starved them and forced them to leave Ireland. The potato was their root of evil, causing them to experience life on a "pervasive note of sadness."[86]

Composers wrote songs which linked potatoes and suffering. In "The Song of the Black Potatoes," "The Blighted Potatoes," "A New Song on the Rotten Potatoes," their lyrics conjoined food with pathos.[87] In tandem with this, they understood that the potato did not come to them as nature's gift but as Britain's importation. The despised colonizers had imposed it upon them. They ate it but did not venerate it. In this they proved to be good historians. They accurately recalled how, as British control over Ireland tightened and as Irish control of the land weakened, they consumed more and more potatoes. Until the mid-seventeenth century, even the Irish poor ate a fairly varied diet, based on milk, cheese, grains, and game, particularly boar. English owners of Irish lands shrank the amount of land usable for the subsistence of the masses. The land instead went to produce crops for export. Thus the subordination of Ireland's economy to English markets went hand-in-hand with the constriction of Irish foodways. This elevated the potato from one food among many to the universal foodstuff of most. Had the Irish celebrated the potato as the symbol of identity, they would in essence have celebrated the English stranglehold on their native lands.

Nor could the good food of the Protestant landowners serve as a model for the Irish to aspire to. Members of this class bought the butter, cheese, meat, fish, and other local produce of the Irish countryside produced by Irish labor on what many considered stolen land. Landowners did not have to poach the salmon from the rivers since the salmon belonged to them, as did the game in the forest. They bought food luxuries in the towns, and their journals and day books proved that they sat down on a regular basis to elaborate meals strikingly different from the foods consumed by the Irish masses. Their eating so well may indeed have been a potent reason why the Irish masses could not later on adopt an elaborate and intimate relationship with food.

Irish social patterns functioned around a rigid divide between the less well-off Catholic majority and the small, privileged Protestant minority.[88] The stratum of modest Irish Catholic "strong" farmers who owned their land made up a small proportion of the population, about 10–15 percent, and only a thin line separated them from those who rented land. They lived relatively poorly, and indeed, "the Irish landed class was, at its own level, scarcely less beggared and debt-encumbered than the cotti-ers."[89] In Ferbane in 1841, for example, 68 percent of those in the town and 75 percent of the rural dwellers lived in the lowest classes of housing, defined by the Census Bureau as 3rd and 4th class structures.[90] That left little in the way of a native Catholic population who could afford the better grades of housing and better food. An even more extreme eco-nomic profile held for the Catholic residents of Ballykilcline. According to the 1841 Irish census, *all* lived in the worst classes of housing, and they included laborers and even small holders.[91] These figures pointed to a pre-Famine reality that a few people at the top enjoyed an extremely comfortable existence, while most Irish people endured poverty with its concomitant crisis of food.

Irish social relations derived their dynamic from the commonality and ubiquity of poverty. The poor perceived themselves as poor and there-fore bound to each other, just as they constructed an identity which sepa-rated them from the small number of outsiders who lived well. They em-phasized the convergence of Catholicism, Irishness, and exploitation and devised intense networks of cooperation and sharing within the world of the poor.[92] They supported each other by direct aid in times of need and through the development of a "moral economy" that generally con-demned private initiative and accumulation as something alien and inim-ical to the community.[93]

Commentators noted the strong bonds of support among the poor and particularly how despite—or perhaps because of—the shared dis-tress, they fed each other.[94] Alexis de Tocqueville visited England and Ireland in the early nineteenth century. When he asked a village priest how the poor kept from starving even during ordinary times, the priest told him that they sustained each other. "A farmer," he informed the French visitor, "who has only thirty acres and who harvests only a hun-dred bushels of potatoes puts aside a fifth of his harvest annually to be distributed among those unfortunates who are most terribly in need."[95] In the 1820s James Ebenezer Bicheno saw the same intra-class bonding through food:

The most compassionate class will always be the poor themselves, not only because they can sympathize . . . with want, but among them the affections of the heart are the chief medium of communication. . . . A beggar goes into their cabins without invitation, is supplied with a few potatoes and a little butter-milk, and then departs; and this is submitted to by the poorest of the farmers as long as they have anything to spare.[96]

Traditional practice such as *cooring*, or co-operation among the poor, flourished in times of food shortages to mitigate suffering, and in the process "aided inadvertently . . . the general hostility and fear of the classes above." [97] Irish social life among the vast majority of the poor involved the nearly universal goal of the "equalization of subsistence opportunities within each community."[98] Within the ranks of the Irish Catholic poor, despite some stratifications between laborers, cottiers, and small farmers, similarities outweighed differences. The absence of significant and visible gradations of class created a situation in Ireland of an "impermeable, vertical wall, which cut the entire people into two unequal groups."[99] In the imagination of the majority only two relevant groupings existed, the hated Protestant English landowners who had stolen the land, and the Irish Catholics who deserved to have it.

However significant the inner divisions within the worlds of the landowners in Ireland and among the poorer Catholics, to the masses all landowners seemed the same. Poverty and sharing within the communities of the poor intensified distance from and hatred of the gentry. While many of these landowners considered themselves Irish and were defined as Irish by the English, the masses of Irish Catholics persisted for generations to exclude them from the category of "Irish." The Irish poor lashed out at the well-off with violence when the right combination of circumstances came together.[100]

The Protestantism of the landowners set them apart. The Anglican Church in Ireland bore the name "Church of Ireland," although it represented a minuscule percentage of the Irish population. In some places it was slightly greater. In Roscommon all who owned land were Protestants, while Catholics who owned none made up 96 percent of the population.[101] In County Clare in the immediate pre-Famine years "the poor, and most of the people were such," dovetailed with the 99 percent of the population adhering to the Roman Catholic faith.[102]

The gap between the well-situated landowners and the majority went far beyond issues of cultural identity. Distinctions loomed too large for the former to serve as positive, upper-class role models, exemplars of taste whose foodways the poor would mimic someday when circumstances changed. Little real contact took place between them. The fact that the poor and the rich functioned within two separate and antagonistic religious institutions meant that churches could not be meeting places where class divisions could fade, even if temporarily, in the powerful merging of common worship. Occupying two different churches also meant that charity did not link the rich with the poor under the sacred canopy of religious obligation.

Physically as well the two nations lived separate from each other. In some rural towns no gentry resided at all.[103] In one rural community in Meath in the 1840s, just before the Famine, "the majority of the large landowners resided outside the parish and apart from leasing the land for various terms few of them had a regular, ongoing involvement in the area."[104] Non-resident gentry had little opportunity to set a standard to which the poor might aspire.

In most places, if landowners were present, they lived in the town centers, whereas the poor occupied the geographic margins. An 1844 visitor to Drogheda portrayed how classes occupied different spaces. "The suburbs," wrote J. G. Kohl, "are genuinely Irish, miserable, filthy, falling cabins."[105] Despite much variety, the town of Bandon in Munster province during the early nineteenth century typified Ireland's social geography:

> The area delimited by the town walls remained the most salubrious part of the settlement. Here were located the most valuable and elaborate houses. Many of these had highly ornamented gardens, several of them possessing individual orchards . . . On the leading approach roads into the town a range of house-types was apparent. By and large, thatched cabins were most frequent. Here labourers and servants resided, nearly all of whom were Roman Catholics . . . The centre of the settlement, however, remained Protestant. Up to eighty per cent of the residents of the town's main streets are returned as such.[106]

Bandon, like other Irish country towns, did not support any common public space, no public courtyard or town green where rich and poor brushed up against each other, had a chance to observe each other, and see perhaps what each consumed. The poor had no reason to visit shops and therefore no opportunity to see what kinds of goods money could buy.[107] The poor lived out their lives with relatively little exposure to the rich and what they ate.

Landowners and comfortable town families employed servants. The wealthier the family, the more likely it availed itself of Protestant servants imported from England or Scotland.[108] Otherwise, the English and Anglo-Irish gentry sought out non-Catholic servants from the handful of poor Protestants in Ireland.[109] Historian David Fitzpatrick observed that "in Ireland the proportion of women employed as servants was rather low by European standards." He cited a figure of 7 percent in 1861, followed by a drop to 5 percent by the end of the century.[110] Since rural communities supported only a small resident gentry, most women who went into domestic service, pre- and post-Famine, worked for farmers just a rung or two above them, and did not receive on the job exposure to richer and different foodways.[111]

Likewise landowners in Ireland did not regularly dispense food to tenants and laborers as wages, as largesse at moments of community celebration or as charity to ease distress. A historical ethnography of Thomastown in County Kilkenney starting in 1836 stated directly that "all wages were paid in cash rather than in provisions or conacre."[112] Drawing upon extant estate books, one study of life among the Irish landowning elite surveyed the practices of 23 owners of country houses. Not a single owner of the big houses provisioned tenants with food, nor did any provide food as charity during the hungry months or as gifts on special occasions.[113] Indeed, it was the rare estate book or memoir of a landowning family that recorded providing food to tenants or laborers.[114]

In nineteenth-century Cork, "when they [the laborers] were dieted by farmers, the most that laborers could expect to receive was four or five pounds of potatoes and one quart of sour milk a day." So when employers did pay in food, they did not do so in the form of prepared food. Rather, they gave out the familiar staple which the laborers then had to prepare for themselves. The food payment did not allow laborers to vary their diets with something better.[115]

The somewhat better-off Irish Catholic farmers behaved like the poor in their dietary practices, rather than like their Protestant peers. Although the Catholic farmers had more "side dishes" to accompany the

10. The repeated potato famines which visited nineteenth-century Ireland and the enormous social and cultural upheavals which followed in the wake of the great Famine of the late 1840s sent a tidal wave of emigrants from Ireland to America.

potatoes, and when the potato crop faltered they had alternative sources of sustenance, by and large they too lived on potatoes as did those economically below them.[116] An 1834 traveler observed that "A little buttermilk added to the potatoes, made the chief difference between the living standard of the small farmers and that of the laboring poor."[117] Modest farmers who had to pay rents, as opposed to the laborers who earned a wage, often "literally starved themselves to pay rents in an intensely competitive land market," further removing distinctions in foodways between the poor at very bottom and their co-religionists slightly above.[118]

Changes in the Irish class structure took place only gradually in the three-quarters of a century after the Famine.[119] In those decades the very poorest layers of Irish society disappeared, either because they had died out in the Famine, left Ireland, or experienced gradual social improvement. These years also witnessed the gradual dethroning of the potato from its pre-Famine dominance. In their cultural repertoire at home, or as the legacy which the emigrants took with them as they left, food played almost no role. It did not matter much as an element in daily life, only inasmuch as it kept them alive. It did not contribute to making sacred days more special than ordinary ones. It did not symbolize the essence of Irish identity, even as that identity stood squarely in the struggle for liberation. The emigrants, those who would construct a new identity, an Irish American one, and who would invent a series of social practices to inform their private and communal lives, brought with them few images of food as pleasure or comfort. They lacked a positive memory of people who ate well whom they wanted to emulate, and whose foods would represent the markers of mobility as they fashioned families and communities. They had no reason to remember Ireland by way of food. Food would continue to be a palpable absence in their articulation of Irishness, an absence they brought with them to America.

5

THE SOUNDS OF SILENCE:
IRISH FOOD IN AMERICA

Elizabeth Gurley Flynn, flamboyant orator on behalf of the Industrial Workers of the World and the Communist Party, was born in America long after the Famine. Yet the "Rebel Girl" carried memories of the Great Hunger through her Irish grandfather's stories. The cataclysm came down to her as the hunger and rage of a colonized people.

Tom Flynn, a sixteen-year-old from County Mayo, a veteran of nationalist skirmishes despite his youth, fled Ireland after committing an act of sabotage. According to the family narrative, "the river was considered the private property of the landowner. Enraged because hungry people could not have the fish for food in a famine year, Tom Flynn threw lime in the water so the fish floated bellies up, dead, to greet the gentry." He told this story to his descendants in America, and they repeated it amongst themselves. Flynn did not choose to steal the fish instead and bring them home to be cooked, eaten, and enjoyed. He made no mention of wondering what the salmon might have tasted like, how it would have been prepared, or who would have done the cooking. The story as told was of destruction unleashed by hunger and anger; of empty bellies and national outrage at the usurpation of Irish land and food.[1]

The great Famine of the 1840s, which sent young Tom Flynn to a logging camp in Maine, launched an exodus from Ireland that continued into the early twentieth century.[2] Between 1851, the first Census after the hunger's end, through 1921, when Ireland liberated itself from England, four and a half million Irish women and men emigrated. Of them, the largest number, 3,794,852 arrived in the United States.³ They and the 800,000 who had settled in America during the Famine years, and the Irish Catholics who arrived prior to the 1840s, transformed themselves into Irish Americans.

They built social institutions and fashioned ethnic practices which met their Irish and American needs, creating a powerful communal network and eloquent expressive culture. Wherever they settled in America, they used music, dance, theater, poetry, politics, athletics, and storytelling to explore and perform identity.⁴ Wherever the Irish found work, they sought each other out and carved out Irish neighborhoods. Within those neighborhoods they extended hospitality to each other and formed Catholic parishes stressing the common Irish origins of both clergy and laity. Parochial schools enculturated generations of youngsters into an American Catholicism that functioned essentially as Irish American Catholicism. They published newspapers and magazines, reams of fiction, poetry, and discursive literature on politics and history. Musicians created a repertoire blending styles reminiscent of home with the American tones of sentimental parlor music, the rhythms of vaudeville, and later the tunes of Tin Pan Alley. Military companies, fire brigades, dance clubs, county societies, athletic leagues, all "wore green." The Irish in America played a considerable role in the politics of Ireland, taking sides on the issues of the day. They funded and agitated for political causes in Ireland for no less than two centuries. Their support stretched from the United Irishman of the 1790s to the Catholics' struggles during the Troubles in Northern Ireland of the 1990s.

In all these manifestations of ethnic cohesion, food was the one element missing. It exercised little power and occupied no special space. The memory of famines, the ubiquity of the potato, and the legacy of the Irish class structure made it impossible for the immigrants and their children to use America's plenty as a way of celebrating being Irish. For sure, they partook of America's plenty and ate better than they had. But that richer and more varied diet played no role in the performance of Irish American identity. They rarely talked about food, neither did they sing about it, nor did it contribute to community institutions and rituals.

For Irish immigrants food in America offered a stark contrast to that at home. Here they found staples at modest prices and in a profusion unimaginable in Ireland. They lauded America's inexpensive food.

Margaret McCarthy wrote home to her parents in 1850 and described New York as a place where "no man or woman ever hungered or ever will."[5] McCarthy did not, however, rhapsodize about the foods she had found nor did she describe their smells and tastes. For her and her peers, food prevented hunger, but they did not look to it as a great pleasure either.[6] Not only did Irish immigrants and children fail to wax eloquent about America's new tastes; they did not even invent newer and richer ways to fix the food they knew best, potatoes, and did not celebrate them as embodying Irish tradition. When they had local parish suppers, communion breakfasts, fund-raising fairs to support charitable endeavors, or communal and organizational banquets, they did not stamp this food with the honor or mark of Irishness.

The absence of food in the construction of Irish American identity grew as much out of the structural realities of the migration and settlement as it bore witness to the persistence of a pre-migration culture that did not focus on food. The character of the migration itself, the gendered nature of Irish family and community formation in America, and the creation of a new kind of class system all conspired to keep food in the background.

Irish immigration to the United States took on its essential characteristics from the fact that throughout the post-Famine era women outnumbered men as immigrants. Over time this became more pronounced.[7] Women came to America in such large proportion because they had no options in Ireland. Economic scarcity provided the centrifugal force which propelled them outward. Economic opportunity in America drew them in. Domestic service provided the most powerful magnet for their migration. The young Irish women who came to America in order to make a life for themselves and to help their families in Ireland, entered America through the back door, arriving through the kitchens of Yankee homes.[8] They, in contrast to the men whom they would marry—if they did—learned about America through its food and cooking, as well as clothing, furnishings, and general housekeeping standards. They observed, literally in their work, what middle-class Americans ate and how they ate it. They understood this food as typically American.

Irish women, veterans of domestic service, functioned as agents of middle-class consumption back in their communities. Settlement workers Robert Woods and Albert Kennedy commented in their 1913 study that across the country young Irish women who had worked in service brought into working-class homes American practices learned on the job. In this way, Irish women brought their families "up."[9] Working in American homes exposed them to middle-class styles of food preparation and eating, decidedly different from what they knew at home. If they copied them later when they married and set up their own homes, they knew that such foodways, however good, belonged to someone else. They did not claim these foods as Irish. They wanted to replicate what they saw in their employers' homes, and presented it as American.

At times this took a remarkable ethnic twist. Emmett Corry's mother, an immigrant from County Galway, went to work in 1927 for a Jewish family in New York City. According to her son, looking back many years later, Bridget Cosgrove "would share her happy memories of her years with this family when she would cook Rosh Hashonah [Jewish New Year] treats for us." Every fall she cooked "gefilte fish made from scratch, fresh beef brisket with gravy, latkes with sour cream, big lemon meringue pies, and her wonderful 4 'Ps' preserve made from peaches, pears, pineapple, and plums."[10] He recalled nothing, however, which she cooked as being Irish.[11]

This enculturation into American domestic life, its food in particular, did not take place without deep conflict between employers and the women who cooked for them. Americans believed that Irish women made horrendous cooks. The women's magazines fixated on the pitfalls of the Irish cook, "whose sole training for domestic service has been in her native cabin."[12] The Irish in general were thought to be inordinately stupid on all matters, but women's ignorance about food received vast commentary.[13] A cartoon of the late nineteenth century, which appeared on the back of a business card for the Atwood & Eldried Merchant's Cafe of 17 Essex Street in Boston, depicted a distinctively Irish woman dressed only in her undergarments holding a plate of food. Titled "How Biddy Served the Tomatoes Undressed," the caption then put into Biddy's mouth the words, "Indade, Ma'am, an I'll not take off another stitch, if I lose me place."[14] The *Women's Journal*, the organ of the women's suffrage movement, included a joke in 1895 that featured an Irish servant negotiating the world of American food purchases. "A Brooklyn woman," the joke ran, "said to her girl, a fresh arrival on the latest boat from Cork: 'Bridget, go on, and see if Mr. Bock, the butcher on the cor-

HOW BIDDY SERVED THE TOMATOES UNDRESSED.
"Indade, Ma'am, an I'll not take off another stitch, if I lose me place."

11. Middle-class Americans depended upon Irish women to cook their meals for them, but simultaneously ridiculed them. This nineteenth-century cartoon joined in the ubiquitous mockery of Irish domestic servants, always called "Biddy," and poked fun at their ignorance of bourgeois food culture.

ner, has pigs' feet.' The dutiful servant went out and returned. 'Well, what did he say?' asked the mistress. 'Sure, he said nothing mum.' 'Has he got pigs' feet?' 'Sayeth, I could not see, mum—he had his boots on.'"[15]

One writer in 1860 sought to rationalize Irish women's failures in the kitchen. "Being the daughters of laborers," wrote Dr. D. W. Cahill, "or needy tradesmen, or persecuted, rack-rented cotters, they are ignorant of the common duties of servants in respectable positions. They can neither wash nor iron clothes. They don't understand the cleaning of glass or silverplate. They cannot make fires expeditiously, or dust carpets, or polish the furniture. Many of them never saw a leg of mutton boiled or roasted. Several of them cannot even prepare their own dinner bacon or pork."[16] However sympathetic Cahill's motivation, he accepted the "truth" that Irish women could not cook, despite the reality that hundreds of thousands were doing just that at any given moment in American kitchens.

Rhetorical associations between Irish servant women and culinary disasters abounded in private writing and journalism. Women's rights leader Elizabeth Cady Stanton confessed in a letter to a friend that she feared her own low frustration level, and that some day she might smash "the pate of some stupid Hibernian for burning my meat or pudding on some company occasion."[17] Harriet Spofford wrote an 1881 book for others of her class vexed by *The Servant Girl Question*, exploring the difficult relationship between the American woman and "Bridget,"—or her diminutive, "Biddy"—the stand-in name for all Irish women in domestic service. Spofford wrote that "viewed aesthetically, and we may say of course, rather superficially, the exile of Erin is something all very fine to have in your house as an object of sympathy and compassion; but when the exile shatters the delicate edges of every piece of your best china . . . burns your dinner to a crisp with neglect," employers had every right to "look at her more critically than casually, and inevitably [you] find yourself wishing she were an exile from America too!"[18] In 1883 *Puck* graced its May 9 cover with a cartoon of a simian-faced Irish servant girl and a sweet but cowed-looking American woman with pleasant facial features. Between them loomed a stove. The cartoon bore the caption, "The Irish Declaration of Independence That We Are All Familiar with." The editorial inside noted, that, "The Irish declaration of independence has been read in our kitchens . . . many times to frighten housewives. The fruits of that declaration are to be seen in . . . ill-cooked meals on ill-served tables."[19]

Employers focused on the misfit between Irish cooking skills and the needs of the American home. They worried about the propensity of Irish servant girls to steal. Employers lamented "Bridget's" tendency, usually considered racial and fixed by nature, to raid the larder. Hundreds of articles and other narratives accused her of stealing food, of dipping into the pantry for extra butter, bread, sweet cakes and tasty meat, or whatever edible treasures employers might have at hand. What infuriated American employers in particular was that the maid pilfered to feed her Irish relatives and friends. *Harper's Monthly* ran a drawing in 1856 featuring a shocked employer who stumbled into her own kitchen and saw a crowd of stereotypically depicted Irish men feasting at her table. The aproned servant girl looked her directly in the eyes. The caption read, "Who is them Fellows, did you say, Mum? Them Gentlemen's my Cousins, Mum, jist dropped in to kape me company, Mum!"[20] James Michael Curley, mayor of Boston, retold his mother's story in his autobiography. A servant in a well-off Back Bay home, she served the family's Thanksgiving turkey, minus one leg. When the irritated mistress of the house asked her as to the whereabouts of the other drumstick, the future Mrs. Curley answered that she had given it to the cop on the beat, who had to work despite the holiday. Incensed, the mistress fired her, calling her, "an Irish pig." "I'm not fired," Curley reported his mother had said, "I quit," and with that she flung the turkey by its one remaining leg at the mistress.[21]

Irish women, according to American concerns, were using American kitchens and food to sustain Irish social networks. Accordingly, the *New York Times* in the 1840s editorialized on the subject through its invented prototypes, Bridget and Patrick. "The behavior of Bridget," wrote the editor, "was certainly very reprehensible . . . The beefsteak that her mistress left her cooking for breakfast . . was burnt to cinders while she was talking to Patrick."[22]

Negative public discussion about Irish women as domestic servants and their defects as the preparers of food seemed almost boundless. An American public health hysteria of the late nineteenth century, for example, began with, and was discussed as, a raging epidemic crisis borne by an Irish cook, one Mary Mallon of County Tyrone, better known in her lifetime and beyond as Typhoid Mary.[23] Such scapegoating reinforced the Irish tendency to view food as a necessity, not as a pleasure, as something of concern to others but not to them.

Having cooked and eaten in American homes as servants did not translate into power and influence for Irish women in the families they created upon marriage. The cooking learned on the job for American families dissolved any links which might have existed between food and Irishness. Irish women neither came to their jobs with a tradition of cooking and women's culinary virtuosity, nor did they derive any pride or acclaim for what they learned in America. The preparation of food was a chore that they had to get through, for employers or their own families. Cooking had little connection to self-esteem or to the esteem given them by husbands and children.

Few of the Irish American memoirs, autobiographies, or other texts that described first-hand accounts of growing up in Irish American families included the details of meals as shaping family life. Nor in those remembered fragments did grown daughters and sons of immigrant Irish parents compliment their mothers on the foods they prepared or the commensality of the family table. American-born women of Irish families rarely recalled being taught to cook by their mothers, nor did they describe groups of women bonding with each other to prepare communal meals. Most Irish American writers of autobiographies, men in particular, wrote about their mothers in deep emotional detail, shunting fathers to the margins of memory, but their veneration of their mothers made scant reference to tasty meals which generally became the stuff of memories.[24]

The failure to mention food in these reminiscences grew out of a particular matrix of class and family relationships. Large numbers of Irish people never married. Unmarried women obviously did not have the opportunity to feed husbands and children who might praise—or criticize—their cooking. The enduring poverty of the Irish and the sluggish rate of their economic mobility no doubt also made food a problem.[25] Even in America, although they ate better than they had at home, the Irish had little disposable income and often ate poorly.[26]

A small cadre of well-to-do merchants and professionals served as the communal elite among the immigrants, but the majority in the working class faced a range of social problems which challenged family life and made leisurely family meals a luxury. Irish women who married—many remained in domestic service and stayed single—ran a high risk of spending years as the heads of households, struggling to sustain a family with many children because of desertion or widowhood. High levels of domestic distress further marginalized food.[27] Had food been important to begin with, poverty and family difficulties would not have stood in the way of enjoying meals. Even a meager repast could have provided an opportunity to transcend the stresses of life. But poor Irish families did not seem to use the shared experience of meals to do more than consume calories.

The Irish elite in America did not urge newcomers to cook better and confer more sanctity upon the family meal. Community leaders, male and female, clergy and laity, did not address food issues in terms of nutrition or aesthetics. Women were not urged to create a domestic culture which celebrated the family table. Better-off Irishwomen and men did provide a whole range of services to lift up the new immigrants. They launched vigorous campaigns to eradicate Irish male drinking. They founded orphanages, hospitals, schools, vocational training classes, and shelters for abandoned wives.[28] Even when they turned their attention specifically on Irish wives and mothers and attempted to upgrade Irish domestic life, they did not set up classes or other kinds of programs to help Irish women improve cooking skills. In 1860 some members of the Sisters of Notre Dame de Namur, "the grey nuns," called together a group of poor Irish women in Boston

> who stood most in need of instruction, direction, and special assistance in the management of their homes . . . teaching the untaught and overworked creatures how to make everything clean, tidy, and bright about them; helping them to have the children regular in their attendance at school, neatly dressed, with their clothes mended and all mark of degrading poverty removed . . . aiding every wife and mother to be herself, a model of sobriety, thrift and gentleness.[29]

The nuns wanted the women to be neat and respectable and to make sure their children went to school appearing respectable. But these advocates of community uplift did not mention "well-fed," nor did they see any reason to enhance family life through the enjoyment of food.

Obviously, Irish women, immigrants and first-generation Americans, fed their families. Mostly they replicated pre-migration foods. They ate potatoes on a regular basis, and where they could, they grew them, along with cabbage.[30] An Irish woman living with her family in Hannibal township, New York, in the 1840s wrote to a former employer in New York City who had lent her some money. "We have got along since last spring," she reported, "and have a fair prospect of making our next payment." All would have been well with Minerva Donovan and her family but "for the failure in the potato crop, which is the only article we raised on our land." She needed another loan to "buy our bread and potatoes."[31] Henry David Thoreau noticed the potato diet of the Irish in Concord.[32] Visitors to Irish Paddy Camps, the villages that sprang up among the Irish canal and railroad workers before and after the Famine migration, commented on their resemblance to peasant communities in Ireland, as "each shanty appeared to have those sterling Irish comforts, a cow, a pig, and a 'praty garden.'"[33]

A handful of Irish American texts drawing upon the details and memories of the early twentieth-century working class also demonstrated the continued reliance on potatoes and cabbage, as well as the low priority of food in family time, rhetoric, and memory.

Jack Walsh sent a steady stream of letters from his home in Worcester, Massachusetts, to his parents "and all" in Limerick from the time he came to America in 1911. The only reference to food in any of his letters were to potatoes and cabbage growing in the "little garden around my house." Worcester's soil and climate were better than those back home, and "when we get our summer heat crops," they grow "twice as fast as they do in Ireland."[34]

Sara Walsh, born in 1919, came to Chicago in the 1930s and lived in a house on the South Side with her father and an array of other relatives. She remembered only casual meals. An uncle did the cooking because his chronic alcoholism kept him from holding down a job. "He really did cook pretty well for a drunk. Irish standards for the table were, in any case, forgiving." He baked soda bread and boiled potatoes. He prepared "tea and soup or potatoes and cabbage." One of the most remarkable points, small in the total sweep of Sara Walsh's memories but revealing for a study of food culture, was her memory that "If he hadn't saved food for her" when she got back from work, "there would have been nothing for her to eat." It shows that this group of Irish kin, living together and pooling resources, did not sit down to a common meal on a regular basis, nor did they consider that one family member had not eaten and something ought to be kept warm for her.[35]

Frank McCourt, who achieved worldwide celebrity in the 1990s with his wildly popular *Angela's Ashes*, described through the eyes of a child the life of his poor parents in Brooklyn in the 1930s. Food vexed the family. His father spent money, when he had it, on alcohol. He left his wife and children with little to eat. Much of the time the children were hungry and their determined mother, Angela, fretted dreadfully about their hunger. When she had some household money, she gave her children potatoes and cabbage, bread and tea, sometimes smeared with jam. At times others fed them. An Irish-born aunt brought them potatoes. In McCourt's memories of childhood, hunger was relieved when their Jewish neighbor, Mrs. Leibowitz, offered them soup, "lovely and hot and tasty," so unlike Angela's foods. Mrs. Leibowitz made him aware of the connection between their hunger, their undernourished bodies, and their Irishness. "So glass milk, piece cake," Mrs. Leibowitz prodded them to eat. "You boys so thin, Irish don't eat."[36]

Sara Walsh, Frank McCourt, and Jack Walsh told their stories of Irish American hunger set late in the migration. The Irish focused on hunger and want rather than on abundance and pleasure. These were the stuff of both experience and lore. Their memories of hunger were indeed what bound them together as a people and thus became a part of their ethnic repertoire. Food could not become a delicious marker of identity.

Even by the third and fourth decade of the twentieth century, Irish people described an Irish American world of poverty where food and meals were precarious. Their words coincided with the findings of reformers and social workers of the same era. Concerned about sluggish rates of Irish economic mobility and the continued presence of large numbers of Irish Americans in the working class, social reformers studied their home conditions, analyzing what was eaten and how much money was spent on food.[37] These reports unanimously concluded that the Irish poor were notably underfed and spent relatively little of their earnings on food. They spent less on food than did other equally poor residents of the same neighborhoods.

Ruth True's 1914 study conducted in the heavily Irish neighborhood of Hell's Kitchen on New York's West Side, asserted that "nourishment is inadequate" and meals decidedly casual. Charting the eating pattern of a "typical" day, True described how for breakfast "everyone takes as they want," while at lunch the children come back from school "to snatch a hasty lunch served in the same impromptu way as breakfast." In the evening the families did have their "one family event . . . eaten in the kitchen." But since families were large and furnishings scanty, "each one takes his turn for a chair." They could not all sit around the table together.[38]

Most of the social reform commentary about the Irish and food emphasized the connection between poverty and poor eating. Irish American fiction dealt with individuals rising out of the laboring class. This body of imaginative literature connected food to getting out of poverty, but not to ethnic identity. Katherine Conway published novels and short stories about the Irish in Boston, and the Boston *Pilot*, the city's premier Irish Catholic newspaper, featured much of her work. She wanted to dispel the notion that the Irish could not form themselves into stable, two-parent households free of family pathologies. Her novel *Lalor's Maples* (1901), for example, provided a counter-narrative to the grim portraits more commonly given. Set in the late 1860s, *Lalor's Maples* featured a family just recently liberated from its poor immigrant origins. At its center stood the family's new home, which, in the style of the gentry, bore the name "Lalor's Maples." Conway presented the Irish family as successful and acquisitive. She filled their newly purchased home with mirrors, pictures, and the mandatory piano in the parlor. She allowed her readers to imagine what a successful Irish family, flush with the pride of home ownership, would eat on their first night in their first house: "Mrs. Lalor served a supper as substantial as well might be on a Lenten evening, when they had 'only a bite' at noon, and dispensed steaming dishes of stewed oysters to her flock with a proud face and a steady hand."[39] While ample, the meal was neither defined as Irish nor as tasty.

James T. Farrell's dark masterpiece, *Studs Lonigan* (1932), showed a family that did very little common eating. When they did eat together, food represented class mobility rather than Irish ethnic identity.[40] "Old man Lonigan," father of the book's anti-hero, remembered the days of his own youth when, as the child of a "pauperized greenhorn . . . often there had not been enough to eat in the house." Now he ate beef. But he did not particularly enjoy the sensuality of the meat's taste. He consumed it to prove that he was no longer poor. Eating meat was, for the father with "his red, well-fed looking face," a biological class act. He sat devouring his "juicy beefsteak," and all the while "his innards made slight noises as they diligently furthered the process of digestion."

Farrell, writing without any of Conway's apologia for the respectability of the middle-class Irish, depicted meals as moments of tension, opportunities for the enactment of family conflict. Returning from Sunday Mass, the family, except for Studs, sat down to the week's only obligatory common meal. "The old man bellowed that dinner," consisting of roast beef and mashed potatoes, "was ready." Studs showed up late, arriving after his father had started carving the meat. He chided Studs for his tardiness. "He said," Farrell wrote in decidedly unsentimental tones, "that he spent good money for food, and that Studs' mother slaved over a hot stove so that they could have a decent meal." They sniped at each other and Frances, Studs' sister, complained that "She was tired of sitting down to a Sunday dinner and being forced to listen to this interminable ragging." Then "Studs got sore . . . so far as he was concerned, he wouldn't eat Sunday dinner if there was going to be the same fighting." Once the fighting subsided, "they awaited their plates, and then they concentrated on eating."[41]

Personal memoir, presented as fiction or autobiography, disconnected food from the celebration of identity. That disconnection obscured the reality of socializing around food that went on in Irish communities. Women in particular consumed food together in friendship. Tea, accompanied by soda bread and cake, dominated women's social life in post-Famine Ireland. It played a key role in women's leisure moments with each other in America too. Irish women in Butte, Montana, in the early years of the twentieth century, got together while their husbands worked the same shift in the Anaconda Copper mines, and they "just visited, talked about the old country, and they always had to have their tea and soda bread."[42] John Francis Maguire visited with Irish immigrants all over America in the 1860s. Looking for all the markers of success and respectability, he overflowed with praise of their homes and their honesty and sobriety. He described one family in Charleston, South Carolina, in which the husband behaved "as simple in manner—as natural and as Irish—as he was the day he saw the last of 'Kildare's holy shrine.'" He observed that "a more pleasant cup of tea I never drank in America than that which I received from the hands of his wife." Maguire linked Irishness with simplicity, and pleasantness with a cup of tea.[43]

The Irish poor in America also fed each other. Newcomers who showed up in Irish enclaves got their first meals at the homes of family and friends or with other Irish folk who had set up communities in

Lowell, Worcester, Troy, or any Irish neighborhood of any American city.[44] During illness, families provided meals to those who could not prepare their own food, and at weddings, christenings, and wakes, the Irish hosted each other with food.

The reality of the Irish involvement with food in America extended beyond the generosity of community culture into the realm of commerce. Since the eighteenth century and through the early twentieth, Americans had been eating Irish food. Irish butter, beef, pork, salmon, cheese, and herring showed up in American shops and graced American tables from the earliest years of English settlement of North America.[45] Irish Americans took pride in the fact that Americans consumed high-quality Irish products. One magazine, *The Gael*, boasted in 1902 that in American stores "the costliest of all smoked meats are the fine hams and bacon that come from Limerick, Ireland."[46] Irish Americans also played an important role in the direct provisioning of food to urban Americans in the nineteenth century.[47] They operated grocery stores, boarding houses, hotels, and restaurants.

As early as the 1810s, Irish entrepreneurs showed up among the ranks of New York and Philadelphia's small-scale grocers and owners of food establishments. By 1850, 200 Irish-owned grocery stores dotted the working class streets of Boston.[48] Until 1855 Irish women and men made up a majority of New York City's peddlers of fruit, vegetables, and other foodstuffs. Irish vendors also predominated among the city's fish and oyster dealers.[49] In Philadelphia in 1857, 22 percent of all grocers had distinctively Irish names.

Irish grocers, at least the more successful among them, rose to positions of stature within their communities, particularly in the decades before the creation of a substantial professional class. James Butler had come to New York from County Kilkenny and by 1909 owned 200 stores, doing over $15 million dollars in business a year. James Reeves, an immigrant from County Clare, got his start in the grocery business in New York by working for Butler, and by 1911 he and his brother operated 35 stores of their own.[50] Irish grocery stores functioned as centers for informal socializing, but the food itself did not serve as a source of emotion and identity.[51]

Irish immigrants and their children also made a living throughout much of the nineteenth century as the owners of boarding houses where lodgers took their meals. Some of the more successful of these evolved into hotels, but most operated at the fringes of the economy. In Butte, Montana, the "most Irish" city in America, half of all the Irish men between 1900 and 1910 "lodged and/or ate in one of the many miners' homes." The copper town had 16 Irish-owned, or Irish-run boarding houses in 1889, most located in the Irish section of town, dubbed Dublin Gulch.[52]

Irish-owned boarding houses sprouted in all American cities. Like those in Butte, they probably catered primarily to Irish boarders, for these establishments tended to be ethnically specific. First-hand accounts of Irish life in America, like Maguire's *The Irish in America* or Jeremiah O'Donovan's narrative published in 1861, detailing his ramble across America in search of "His Countrymen," abounded with references to boarding houses run often by Irish women for Irish guests.[53] O'Donovan told for example of a Mrs. Murphy, "a countrywoman of my own," who kept "excellent accommodations" at 17 Chestnut Street in Philadelphia. He described the fare as sumptuous, although offered little detail on what this "respectable widow lady" served. In New York, at 177 Grand Street, he boarded at an Irish-owned establishment also operated by a widow from Ireland. He indicated that all but one of the boarders, men and women alike, "emigrated from the Emerald Isle." In Paterson, New Jersey, he found "shelter under the friendly roof of a Milesian mansion, where I expected to find shelter, prayer, piety and protection, disunited and disconnected with . . . impurity or irreligion or, mongrelism." He found what he sought at Mr. Lynch's boarding house. The all-Irish group of boarders made him feel at home.[54]

The ubiquity of the Irish boarding house grew out of migration patterns. This was a young people's migration. Parents stayed put in Ireland. This also was a late-marrying population, so women and men experienced years alone before they formed their own families. It was also a poor population, and families strategized to meet expenses. In the mid-1930s romance writer Mary Higgins Clark's mother, an immigrant from County Sligo, found herself newly widowed with three small children. She turned her home in the Bronx into a boarding house. As her daughter recalled, "It was impossible to get a job. So . . . A sign, 'Furnished

Rooms, Kitchen Privileges' was bought and tacked over the doorbell."[55] Many Irish women like her turned their homes into boarding houses when they found themselves bereft of a breadwinner.

The Irish concentration in the grocery and boarding house trade was matched by Irish ownership of urban restaurants. From the middle of the nineteenth century into the early twentieth, Irish men and women operated many city eating establishments. In New York Irish immigrants dominated in the low-end places, oyster houses in particular. Oyster houses clustered along Canal Street in the 1830s and 1840s allowed patrons to eat an unlimited number of bivalves for 6 cents, washed down with beer or other alcoholic beverages.[56] Daniel Sweeney achieved fame in New York as the "father of the cheap eating establishment" at 11 Anna Street, where working people purchased plates of meat for 6 cents or vegetables for 5 cents.[57] Over the course of the nineteenth century Irish and Irish-Americans opened numerous restaurants, such as Gallagher's Steak House on West 52nd Street or Cavanagh's, which opened its doors in 1876 on West 23rd Street.[58]

The Irish grocery stores, boarding houses, and restaurants resembled each other in that, despite dealing with food, they disassociated it from Irish ethnicity. Places which purveyed food did not name themselves after places in Ireland nor did Irish symbols emblazon their exterior or interior walls. Irish travelers like O'Donovan and Maguire provided only fleeting references to the food in the boarding houses. Men and women who grew up in these neighborhoods did not discern linkages between the Irishness of the grocery store owners and the food that crossed their counter.[59] If Irish boarding house owners prepared particular foods enjoyed by Irish guests for their mnemonic power, or if grocery stores stocked special foods to satisfy Irish tastes, those who went to such establishments and left documents about them did not record such matters.

In the commercial and communal realms, as at home, the Irish in America did not use food to celebrate Irishness. Two examples from the 1890s epitomize this. In 1896 Irish New Yorkers banded together as the Irish Palace Building Association. They wanted to construct an Irish building in New York City, a structure to house the county associations, a place where Irish New Yorkers could meet and socialize with each other, and through which they could represent themselves in the city's multiethnic landscape. The plans called for "drill rooms and administration quarters," for organizations, an auditorium, ballrooms, a fully equipped gymnasium, a labor bureau, a library with books from and about Ireland, a training school, and meeting rooms.[60]

In May 1897, the "patriotic daughters of Erin" staged a giant fair to raise funds for the ambitious project. At the fair the 32 county associations set up booths which sold "authentic" crafts and other objects associated with places in Ireland from which the visitors or their parents had come. Music flooded the hall. Dance competitions amiably pitted the counties against each other, vying for first place in keeping alive and excelling at this art form so deeply associated with Irish culture.

According to the *Irish World*, at the heart of the fair,

[in] a long, rectangular space, fenced off within a space that forms a promenade around the four sides, and entered by five columned archways, surmounted by a huge green shamrock, [lay] upon the floor, a topographical map of Ireland, marked off into 32 county spaces, cast in the exact from of the Irish county it represents. These spaces are filled with the veritable Irish soil of the county . . . duly attested as truly genuine.[61]

Some older women, immigrants likely, knelt on the soil of their county, prayed, and made the sign of the cross with deep reverence.

Chicago's Irish also conceived of such a building that same year. To be called Great Emmet Hall, it was to be dedicated to the memory of the Irish national hero, Robert Emmet. It too, its planners hoped, would proclaim the Irish presence in the city. It would offer space for meeting rooms for Irish lodges and societies, multiple venues for athletics and dance, as well as classrooms and an auditorium to seat up to 2,000. Like the New York Irish, the Irish in Chicago organized a fair to raise money for the building. Their event, held in December 1897, also featured 32 booths selling crafts native to the 32 counties. The Chicago event showcased Irish athletes demonstrating their manly prowess. And, at the heart of the fair, just as in New York, visitors could touch down upon a topographically correct giant map of Ireland, made with "Irish earth, each particular county to be formed of earth from that region." Authenticity mattered. They transported to the shores of Lake Michigan "bog oaks from Killarney," and "a piece of the coronation stone from the hills of Tara."[62]

Something was curiously missing from both the plans for the buildings (which were never built) and the fairs. Food did not show up in either. The blueprints for the building showed no banquet halls, no dining rooms, no kitchens. The county booths did not offer the public a chance to recall the "ould sod" through taste. Concerned with the authenticity of the crafts they sold and the maps they constructed, those who planned the fair seemingly ignored the possibility of inventing Irishness through food.

At some Irish communal events food was in fact sold or served. At picnics, fairs, dinners, and communion breakfasts Irish men and women ate together. They often staged meal functions to support an Irish cause or institution. In some cases event planners printed up the list of food items available to those in attendance. In Milwaukee in 1912, for example, the Ancient Order of Hibernians held their Annual Irish Picnic and Games. At the picnic grounds those in attendance could buy "Cold Roast Beef, Cold Tongue, Cold Boiled Ham, Wiener Potato Salad, Sliced Tomatoes, Pickles, Red Beets, Celery, Bread, Hot Coffee, Pie." None of these had any Irish resonance, and the potatoes of back home appeared here in Germanized form, no doubt influenced by Milwaukee's most numerically significant immigrant group.[63] Irish Catholic Ladies' fairs in New York in the nineteenth century offered their patrons oysters, chicken or lobster salad, salmon, sardines, turkey, cold cuts, and various deserts, and to drink there was lager, beer, wine, sherry, claret punch, or ale. Like their Milwaukee counterparts in the early twentieth century, the charitable Irish women of New York felt no reason to connect food and Irish identity.[64]

Certainly the most important and regular Irish communal banquets were those marking St. Patrick's Day. Lavish meals associated with March 17 began to be organized in the second decade of the nineteenth century.[65] Public celebrations of St. Patrick's Day were intended to demonstrate to other Americans the strength and prosperity of the local Irish community. City newspapers covered the banquets, described the scene, recounted the lengthy roster of toasts and who offered them, and often reprinted in full the speeches. Non-Irish dignitaries and city officials sat at the head tables, particularly at the more elite banquets, and they had a bird's-eye view of Irish American culture as the Irish wanted them to see it. It was a show of political power designed to impress and elicit respect from outsiders.[66]

The St. Patrick's Day banquet also met an internal group need. It became a yearly communal ritual which aided the construction of Irish American identity. Its formulaic quality, repeated year after year, gave it sanctity. It allowed Irish community leaders to orate on the meaning of Irishness. They draped elegant ballrooms in green, festooned them with shamrocks, harps, maps of Ireland, portraits of great nationalist leaders. They congratulated themselves on how far they had come as Americans and on how steadfastly they continued to fulfill their obligation to Ireland. In this way they performed their Irishness for themselves.[67] Here, then, should have been a moment when Irish Americans displayed their ethnic identity in tandem with food. After all, at banquets people ate. Someone had to decide what to serve, how to present the food, and how to describe the items on the menu.

At the yearly March banquets of New York's Friendly Sons of St. Patrick, graphics on the elaborate menus linked the banquet with the icons of imagined Irishness.[68] They bore the visible markers of Irish culture recognizable to Americans: harps, shamrocks, Celtic-style lettering, Celtic crosses, all potent reminders of Ireland. In comparison to the pictorial images, the Irishness of the food amounted to little.[69] Indeed, almost all of the dishes bore French names: "Selle de mouton Colbert," "Tomates farcies," "Ris de veau Montebello," "Ailes de poulet à la Finnoise," "Cotelletes de pintades a la Reine" accompanied by "Petits pois français," and the like. Even simple items such as platters of radish and celery became "Radis," and "Celeri." In this reliance on French food words, the Irish American elite bought into an Anglo-American culinary value system. If it was to be high cuisine, it must be French. The successful Irish communal leaders, merchants, professionals, and politicians who organized and attended the dinners used that cultural standard to mark their achievement of prosperity and civility.[70]

Even potatoes lost their Irish particularity. They too became French, as did the lamb, the chicken, the pastries, and the soups. "Pommes de terre persillade" appeared repeatedly, while some years banqueters could dine on "Pommes laurette" or "Bermuda Potatoes Rissolees." Banquet planners neither elevated potatoes to the symbol of Irish identity nor treated them as digestible symbols of Irish persistence despite English occupation. Only "Irish bacon and greens" appeared yearly as food meant to convey the homeland. Bacon may have been the perfect food vehicle to link their Irish and American selves. Americans, on the one hand, had been savoring Irish bacon for a century or more. On the other, Irish farmers who had long produced massive amounts of it, only began to eat it regularly themselves by the end of the nineteenth century. By the time these menus were being printed up, bacon had become a ubiquitous item on the dinner tables of modest Irish farm families. Hence, unlike potatoes, bacon carried no stigma of shame. It rather announced the successful progress of Ireland, from a nation of impoverished tenants eating a Spartan and dangerous diet, to one of small but independent farmers who had some choice in what they ate.

The connection between the political fortunes of Ireland and the menus surfaced most fancifully on the banquet tables of 1919. That year something had changed. The first course, the grapefruit, became "Grapefruit Irlandaise," the soup, whatever its ingredients, appeared as "Potage Londonderry," and along with the annual "Irish Bacon with Greens," guests finished up their celebratory meal with "Frozen Pudding Killarney."[71]

It matters little that Killarney *never* boasted a special pudding, frozen or not, and that Londonderry's kitchens never produced a distinctive soup, much less a *potage*. Cooks in neither Irish place distinguished themselves by their puddings, soups, or any other food for that matter. Rather, this curious menu points to the fusion of food, politics, and identity. The time was right. By the 1920s and 1930s Irish Americans began to experiment a bit with the presentation of identity through food. In the 1920s corned beef and cabbage came to have some association with Irish American cooking. In 1935 Dinty Moore beef stew, based on the character by that name from the cartoon strip "Bringing Up Father," was frequently eaten in working-class homes. It associated a hearty, inexpensive food with an Irish-sounding name.[72]

Changes in the Irish class position also explained the shift, as did distance in time from the Famine. Increasingly, Irish Americans came to occupy a modestly comfortable niche in America as middle-class homeowners, several generations removed from the memory of the Great Hunger. Food no longer carried the same stigma of shame and want. But more importantly, the political moment proved propitious for London-derry soup and Killarney pudding. An armed struggle was raging in Ireland to drive the English out at last and achieve national independence for Ireland. In the aftermath of World War I, and given the victors' lofty global rhetoric about self-determination for colonized nations, the Irish pressed their claim for independence. In 1918, perhaps when the banquet organizers held their first meetings to prepare the 1919 St. Patrick's Day event, Sinn Fein, the political wing of the Irish nationalist movement, captured 73 out of 105 Irish seats for Parliament. The middle-of-the-road home rulers won a scant 6. Sinn Fein refused to go to London to take seats there since it considered Irish representation in Parliament meaningless. Instead, they assembled in Dublin, declared the creation of the Dail Eireann, the Irish Assembly, and elected Eamon de Valera President of the Irish Republic to which they swore allegiance.[73] The Irish in America could think about Ireland as a source of pride and strength rather than as a place of shame and sorrow.

In the 1920s, with the creation of the Irish Free State, Irish American activists for the first time used the marketing of Irish-produced foods to support their "homeland." The Irish Women's Co-operative League of America, headquartered in New York, launched a campaign to get Irish Americans to "buy Irish," in part by not "buying British." They encouraged Irish American consumers to express Irish loyalty by purchasing food from Ireland. Irish food businesses, which had long divorced their goods from the idea of Irish identity, now married them. A Manhattan baker, J. J. Nolan, put a sign in his shop window proclaiming, "Sinn Fein for Your REAL IRISH SODA BREAD AND GENUINE IRISH TEA."[74]

The year 1919, when guests at the Friendly Sons of St. Patrick banquet consumed Irishness through Irish-marked foods, was a momentous year in Ireland's recreation of itself as a nation. It also happened to be the year that the 18th Amendment to the United States Constitution went into effect, prohibiting the manufacture and sale of alcoholic beverages. The consumption of alcohol had long been part of Irish social and cultural practice. Alcohol provided calories, and Irish immigrants brought with them a tradition of using alcohol in part as a food substitute. It also represented Irish identity, embodying a defiance of outside authority and valorizing sociability for those inside the community circle.

Alcohol was business as well. Irish immigrant men and their sons showed up in great numbers as owners of saloons across America. In 1820 in Philadelphia, for example, one-fifth of all liquor licenses went to men with Irish names. By the 1890s the percentage reached one-third.[75] These figures represented just the visible tip. Much Irish alcohol merchandising took place in home *shebeens*, unfettered by license requirements set by municipal authorities.

Owners of saloons played conspicuous roles in Irish communities, wielding influence and enjoying the respect of their Irish neighbors. Saloons and other liquor establishments dotted Irish neighborhoods. In the nineteenth century, both before and after the Famine, most Irish grocery stores also sold liquor, as did boardinghouses, inns, hotels, and oyster shops.[76] In New York City's heavily Irish Sixth ward, half of all stores sold liquor, and almost *all* of the Irish people who owned any land either operated liquor stores or played some other role in the liquor trade.[77] Not uncommonly, liquor-grocery stores occupied the basement or ground level of tenement buildings in the larger cities, while in Worcester, Massachusetts, and Portland, Maine, Irish families ran grog shops in their homes.[78] In the earlier part of the century, before municipal (and later state and federal) authorities regulated the sale of alcoholic beverages, Irish people in places like Lowell, Massachusetts, "obtained their liquor in unlicensed 'common dram shops' which flourished in the front rooms of tenements throughout the Irish neighborhoods."[79]

These drinking establishments functioned as hubs of communal social life, particularly for men. Removed as they were from women's interference, men found them good places for talk, politics, and conviviality. Among the Chicago Irish a local custom flourished whereby men gathered at local saloons, without wives, sisters, and daughters, for all-male wakes.[80]

Although some saloons set aside a separate women's section, these establishments served men primarily. Michael Donohue remembered Irish life in New York at the turn of the twentieth century as a world dominated by the culture of male drinking. He described the bars of Avenue A, around 54th Street, as places governed by

strict rules of order. It was like a church, in a sense, in that they had the women's section, the family section, and the men's section, and people never made the mistake of violating these rules. . . . .I got to go in the bars' when my father sent me for beer . . .

Going for beer was like a ritual. Before your parents sent the growler down—the growler was a big can—they all did the same thing to it; they got their dinner lard out and greased the sides. The grease was meant to take the head off the beer so that you'd get more.[81]

Donohue's memories resonated with the details of life lived around the rituals of a world that had passed with time. By this he sacralized the mundane as remembered and told through alcohol.

The saloons, whether licensed or not, played a crucial role in the social and political life of Irish communities. Here men got together and acted out communal equality by the institutionalized practice of the treat, men taking turns paying for drinks for all. Saloons served as job centers, and contractors with work to give out often hired directly from their smoky interiors. Political life got played out in the saloons, be it the politics of the urban machine or of Irish nationalism.

To mark off the centrality of saloons and their connection to Irish ethnicity, they often bore the names of either Irish heroes or Irish places. They displayed icons of Irish distinctiveness inside and out.[82] A saloon with Daniel O'Connell's picture painted on the signboard and the slogan "Hereditary bondsmen, who would be free, themselves must strike the blow!" sat in the heart of Philadelphia's Irish community in the 1840s. Another saloon in that city boasted an ornate mirror over the bar written over with the words:

> Romantic Ireland never dies,
> She lies beyond all time.
> The bread of angels gives her strength,
> The blood of martyrs is her wine.[83]

Well into the late nineteenth century Irish men in their saloons broke out into sentimental songs about Ireland, belting out "Where the River Shannon Flows," "Wearin' of the Green," and "The Harp That Once through Tara's Halls," songs extolling Ireland and holding up the English as the incarnation of evil.[84]

Irish American writers rhapsodized about alcohol as sensual pleasure that was integral to Irish identity. In 1851 Seamus O'Daoir, owner of a "porter house" on New York's Duane Street, sent a poem in Irish to the *Irish-American*. He had pecuniary reasons for writing this poem, since it extolled his particular establishment. Beyond the self-advertisement, his words fused the celebration of alcohol with the celebration of Irish identity:

> Let every stout, spirited, well-met young fellow
> who wants to spend some time in pleasure
> Come quickly to Duane Street and into the Daisy
> where music is playing like the song of the birds.
> There he'll find moderation and decency without boasting
> Brandy in plenty and wine being poured
> No lack of gin, I believe, and beer for the asking
> from that brave Lion of the noble lineage of the Gaels.
> James is the cheerful, mindful guardian
> of the true blood of the Plain of Banba of great fame.
> O'Dwyer never cowardly at the break of battle in blasting the
>   enemy
> with a high noble deed, defeating them, crushing them, and
>   destroying them.[85]

Alcohol symbolized who they were, and demonstrated Irish cultural distinctiveness. In one of Mr. Dooley's vignettes, his ever-present side-kick Hennessey asked him, "D'ye think ye-ersilf it [alcohol] sustains life?" Mr. Dooley answered affirmatively. "It has sustained mine f'r many years."[86] In another Dooley sketch, the sage of Archey Road speculated in the *Boston Globe* in 1907 on the meaning of alcohol: "Dhrink never made a man betther, but it has made manny a man think he was betther. A little iv it lifts ye out iv th' mud where chance has thrown ye; a little more makes ye' think th' stains on ye'er coat are appylets."[87]

A late nineteenth-century graphic celebrated the Irish in America and their observance of St. Patrick's Day. A handsome group of men and women, elegantly dressed, one sporting a monocle and none with irregular facial features, stood before the parted drapes of an open window. Two landscape paintings depicting Ireland flanked the window. The genteel Irish party waved enthusiastically to the Irish militia companies

ST. PATRICK'S DAY PROCESSION

12. A nineteenth-century postcard depicts a group of elegantly dressed men and women cheering the St. Patrick's Day Procession. The saloon across the street with its sign framed by the window curtains emphasizes the linkages between Irish ethnicity and the public consumption of alcohol.

marching by. One of the paraders carried aloft a flag with a harp, while above the marching Hibernians, could be seen the word, "Saloon." The Irish landscape, the American-style parade, the harp as the ancient symbol, and the saloon, the Irish center of sociability, all came together.[88]

Irish Americans used music to celebrate the synergy between ethnicity and alcohol.[89] For decades Americans had characterized Irish men as drunkards.[90] By the last decades of the nineteenth century, Irish American songsters took up this theme themselves, knowing that audiences happily consumed images they "knew" to be true. The stereotype of that era was that of "Pat," the drunken Irishman addicted to his bottle.[91]

Ned Harrigan, for example, wrote an enormous corpus of musical pieces for the vaudeville stage of the latter part of the nineteenth century.

Harrigan, born in New York City's "Cork Row" neighborhood in 1844, sought in his many skits, sketches, and full-length plays to "be as realistic as possible . . . Each drama is a series of photographs of life today in the Empire City."[92] In his 1880 song "The Pitcher of Beer," featured in the play *The Mulligan Guard's Christmas*, the refrain went:

> Oh the child in the cradle, The dog at the door,
> The fires so cheerful and bright,
> Old folks at the table with plenty galore,
> For to welcome you in with delight,
> Their blessings they give, it's "long may you live,
> And so gaily glide o'er the year":
> Then they hand you a glass for to let the toast pass.
> And we drink from the pitcher of beer.

Did the "galore" on the table refer to food, which Harrigan did not list, or did it point to the contents of the beer pitcher?[93]

Harrigan's "My Dad's Dinner Pail" of 1883 spelled out an array of foods that the Mulligan family ate. But even when food got mentioned, alcohol still had greater emotive power. The song came from a play entitled *Cordelia's Aspirations*, a drama of an up-and-coming Irish family about to move out of its working-class neighborhood, Mulligan's Alley. The wife, Cordelia, insisted that they leave the old neighborhood for the tonier reaches of uptown. Dan Mulligan, her husband, lamented the move and experienced deeply conflicted feelings about abandoning the jumbled egalitarian world of the tenement district he had grown up in. While packing up to leave, Dan came across his father's growler. The growler served in this song, and in the play, as his mnemonic of the sweet days of childhood and of the innocent conviviality of poverty that would never happen "uptown."

> Preserve that old kettle, so blacken'd and worn,
> It belonged to my father before I was born,
> It hung in a corner, beyant on a nail,
> 'Twas an emblem of labor, was Dad's dinner pail.
> There's a place for the coffee, and also for the bread,
> The corned beef and praties, and oft it was said:

"Go fill it wid porter, wid beer, or wid ale,"
The drink would taste sweeter from Dad's dinner pail.[94]

"Sweet" did not describe the meat or potatoes, bread or coffee. Only the alcohol was embellished by the adjective.

The following year audiences heard "My Little Side Door," also by Ned Harrigan. Dan Mulligan, protagonist of the play *Dan's Tribulations*, again sacralized the growler as a symbol full of meaning.

> When the supper is spread with corn, meat and bread,
> It's "Take down the pail and go buy,
> A pint of buck-beer, oh the poor man to cheer
> A'toiling all day makes him dry."[95]

Neither corn, meat, nor bread could cheer a man worn out from hard work. Only the liquid in the pail could do that.

Alcohol linked the Irish in America to the emotionally satisfying world of past memory and ushered them into a comfortable world of friendship with others like themselves. Above all, it heightened their Irish identity. In saloons, under the influence of alcohol, they declared their unswerving loyalty to Ireland, the place they had left but claimed still to serve, while they articulated a deep American patriotism. Jeremiah O'Donovan on his American ramble found himself in a saloon in Galena, Illinois. A Mr. O'Reily sat down with him, and "we drank a little, of course, of the invigorating beverage . . . and swore to the hilt to stand immovably to sustain the stars and stripes which had been at the time beautifully unfurled by a gentle breeze over our heads, not forgetting our patriotism to the Emerald Isle."[96]

That drink trumped food in the performance of Irishness also can be seen by comparing Irish saloons with their urban analog, German saloons, which also came to be fixtures of nineteenth-century American cities. Irish saloon drinking happened in male homosocial groups. As in Ireland, saloons provided men a refuge from, or alternative to, home and heterosocial leisure. German "beer gardens" attracted whole families; men, women, and children sat, drank, and ate together.[97] Irish saloons, as opposed to German ones, or indeed most other working-class drinking establishments, put minimal emphasis on food. For others, eating lunch

13. Irish food establishments did not carry marks of ethnicity. Saloons did. The "Erin Go Bragh" saloon in Duluth, Minnesota, pictured here in 1875, with a harp on the sign, conveyed to the public that it was Irish-owned.

in a saloon was an important pre-Prohibition urban ritual practice. German saloons served "blut-wurst or blood sausage . . . Or, the hard and leathery cervelat or summer sausage," plus sardines, herring, ham, pig's feet, and rye bread. All sorts of items appeared in bars at lunchtime to encourage patrons to buy more liquor: hamburger, roast beef, corned beef, onions, pumpernickel bread, salads, cheeses, crackers, bologna, and pretzels, and so on.[98]

Irish bars had to provide food since they did not serve Irish customers only. But it was notable how little food they served, both in terms of quantity and variety. In the pre-Prohibition era, "most Irish barrooms were more distinguished for the facilities they lacked than those they contained," and chief among these were tables for sitting down and eating a full meal. The lunch in the Irish saloon was "more of a standard fare than something designed to attract crowds."[99] Jane Addams recalled the experience of an Italian immigrant, recently arrived in the United States, who ate dinner with her at Hull House. He expressed amazement at how many different foods were on the settlement house's table. It turned out he had done almost all of his "American" eating at an Irish bar, where he had seen nothing but potatoes to accompany the drinks.[100]

Alcohol had its liabilities. Drunkenness plagued the Irish in Ireland and America. It caused a range of problems detrimental to work, and related to poverty, accidents, illnesses, crime, and a host of other difficulties which Irish immigrants endured. Native born-American Protestants used Irish drinking to stigmatize the newcomers, bar them from jobs, and subject them to ridicule. Americans constructed the Irish as inherently predisposed to drunkenness and the moral crusades, which by the latter part of the nineteenth century fueled political movements, sought to separate Irishmen from their bottles. The entire history of the movements for alcohol regulation, temperance, and Prohibition grew out of the American invention of the drunken "Pat." The *New York Times* in the 1850s referred to Irish drinking as "drowning the shamrock." By taking away their drink, Americans hoped to remake the Irish, to strip them of this aspect of their cultural repertoire.[101]

Much of Irish male performance of identity played itself out through drinking and was contextualized in the companionship of the grog shops, groceries, and saloons. It also involved a defiant resistance to American culture. Irishmen (and women) drank not just because they had long used alcohol as food, or because they came from a culture which valorized social drinking, but because it helped them stake a claim to cultural authenticity. It was hard to miss the fact that Americans condemned them for just about everything in their cultural repertoire, their religion, accents, domestic arrangements, and drinking. The immigrants and their children were not going to give these up. The signs on Irish saloons, the slogans painted on barroom mirrors, the symbols of Irish nationalism–all were directed in part against those who sought to remake them.

Yet alcohol also deeply divided the Irish amongst themselves. In Irish communities in America a powerful temperance movement arose. Organized primarily as an alliance between the Irish clergy and Irish women, it sought to rid their families and communities of the scourge of drinking. The slogan "Ireland sober, Ireland free" achieved its greatest force in the 1830 campaign of the Capuchin monk Father Theobold Mathew.[102] Father Mathew took his movement to the worldwide Irish diaspora, and in America he was lionized by non-Irish and the Irish alike.[103] In almost every Irish American community a priest, often in league with a group of women, formed an Irish temperance society, pressuring men to give up drinking. Usually coalescing under the banner of the Catholic Total Abstinence Society, local Irish temperance groups tried to convince men that they were harming themselves and their families by drinking.[104] In Chicago in the 1880s, Father Maurice J. Dorney of St. Gabriel's Parish in the stockyards neighborhood, described by parishioners as "a haven and heaven for the Irish," labored to remove all drinking establishments from residential streets. When some saloon keepers, also parishioners, refused, Father Dorney retaliated by reading their names and addresses aloud at Mass.[105] In Cambridge, Massachusetts, Father Thomas Scully organized the women of his parish to vote in favor of a "no-license" ordinance, one which would have effectively made public purchase and consumption of alcohol illegal in the Boston suburb with its huge working-class Irish population.[106] Though many singers and listeners waxed eloquent and teary-eyed over "My Dad's Dinner Pail" and the alcohol flowing from it, the Irish temperance movement volleyed back with its own musical salvos. The Albany, New York, Catholic Total Abstinence Association sang:

> Her noble sons were once enslaved;
> Their gen'rous hearts were crushed with shame,
> Until the Temp'rance banner waved,
> And poured cold water on the flame.
> And then an army gladly rose
> To fight and conquer all its foes.

Did the British enslave them or did alcohol? Which foe did the C.T.A.A. hope to vanquish, the Protestant colonizers or the intoxicating beverage? Perhaps they were one and the same. Similarly, the Boston *Pilot* in 1849 printed the words to a temperance ballad, "Lament of an Irish Emigrant," which transposed the guilt of drinking to the personal:

I'm think on the night, Mary,
The night of grief and shame,
When with drunken ravings on my lips,
To Thee I homeward came,
And the curse of drink was in my heart,
 To make my love a bane.[107]

The Irish heaped much criticism on themselves for their attachment to drink. The economically better-off, more respectable among them looked with horror and shame at the poor who drank, and asserted that it was drinking that kept them down. John Francis Maguire, eager to prove how well his sisters and brothers in America had done, found one deep source of distress. "Were I asked," he addressed his readers in 1861,

> to say what I believed to be the most serious obstacle to the advancement of the Irish in America I would unhesitatingly answer— *Drink*; meaning thereby the excessive use, or abuse, of that which, when taken in excess, intoxicates, deprives man of his reason, interferes with his industry, injures his health . . . I believe this fatal tendency to excessive indulgence to be the main cause of all the evils and miseries . . . that have strewed the great cities of American with those wrecks of Irish honour, Irish virtue, and Irish promise.[108]

Alcohol may have provided the Irish with much that they cherished, but it brought with it a range of detrimental physiological and behavioral reactions. It caused much conflict within the Irish world and could not solidify community. It certainly could not serve the Irish as an entry into American respectability. In community after community it divided the Irish amongst themselves, with men taking the "pledge" in the millions, and then slipping back into the pleasurable culture of drinking. It emerged as a contentious issue dividing women and men, the respectable and the poor, the clergy and the laity. Alcohol symbolized Irish ethnicity, but it did not function as a constructive force for shaping community.

To the Irish, food was other people's cultural coin. In American cities they associated food with their neighbors of other immigrant communities—Italians, Germans, Jews, Greeks—who forged powerful links between food and identity.[109] Michael Donohue, who described his father's growler with loving detail and made an analogy between saloon and church, never once described *any* item of food as Irish. He recalled Italian fruit stands, which "were just like in Naples." He explored adjoining neighborhoods where "you could get kelbassa with your eggs or pollo con riso," but his Irish neighborhood had no foods it called its own.[110] In Fall River, Massachusetts, the Irish lived next to French Canadians and Poles. These two groups filled up their urban spaces with bakeries and other shops which sold the foods they needed in order to feel French or Polish.[111] Sara Walsh in Chicago never had Irish food, but remembered vividly German and Lithuanian bakeries.[112] Other people fused food and ethnic identity. The Irish did not.

They lacked a pre-migration elite whose foodways they wanted to adopt once they had access to more and better food. Moreover, they carried with them a bundle of memories about Ireland as a place where hunger and want defined national identity. When Irish women came to America, they were ushered immediately into the kitchens of hundreds of thousands of American homes and there made to feel incompetent. They saw the wide discrepancy between American bounty which they could partake of, and the scarcity in Ireland which they had left. Rather than push them towards creating a food culture because of that disjunction, remembered hungers prevented them from doing so.

On one occasion, in August 1908, the nationalist organization Clan na Gael held a picnic outside of Chicago in Ogden Grove. The sounds of hornpipes reverberated. The crowd watched the races and games and enjoyed the "jig and step dance" competitions. And they listened to speeches. While no one thought it worth reporting to the Irish American press what the picnickers ate that afternoon, they did report the words of Professor M. G. Rohan of Marquette University. Rohan, a Fenian admirer, "explained why the potato is the great Irish food staple and deplored the dependence of the Irish people upon the yearly success of this one crop." The potato, according to Rohan, represented Ireland's oppression:

When the people, harassed and reduced, were driven into poverty [forced] to support themselves by the cultivation of bits of land, they soon found the potato gave them the maximum nourishment, and since then they have cultivated it. It failed in 1822 and dire distress followed. When again in 1847 it failed, a great wave of emigration set in, and those who could not emigrate, were reduced literally to starvation.[113]

Rohan's remarks could have destroyed the appetites of those who listened, or at least might have made it difficult to revel in the stuff they took out of their baskets as representing their Irish identity.

Their silence about what they ate in America and their inability to use food as a medium for community solidarity revealed the rawness of the wounds which hunger inflicted upon them. This legacy made it impossible for them to create a distinctive Irish food in America. Part of their identity was forever fused with memories of hunger. By giving up those memories, they would have given up much of what they constructed as authentically and profoundly Irish.

6

A SET TABLE: JEWISH FOOD
AND CLASS IN EASTERN EUROPE

Desperate with worry, a poor woman ran to the town rabbi, two freshly slaughtered geese tucked under her arms. She had planned to feed them to her family during the upcoming Passover week, the annual celebration marking the exodus from Egypt. But something about them looked suspicious, and she feared that the fowl might not meet strict standards of *kashrut* (ritual purity). So she sought the advice of the community's religious authority, the rabbi, who would inspect them and decide if they could be eaten. His permission was needed for her to roast the geese. He would judge if she might stuff the skin of their necks, the *helzel*, with onions and crushed matzah, to be sewn up and then cooked in the drippings of the festive birds until hot and brown. Only he could determine if she could render their fat into *schmaltz* for frying and offer her husband and children a prized eastern European Jewish delicacy, *gribenes* (cracklings). His words would decide if her otherwise poor table would be transformed into a rich one for the holiday of freedom.[1]

The rabbi studied the geese and declared that, alas, a minor imperfection rendered them *treyf* (forbidden). The law was the law. The "set table" countenanced no deviation.[2] They could not be eaten. No roast bird, no *helzel*, no *schmaltz*, no *gribenes*, no table changed from bare bones to bounty to mark the sacred time. As the woman wept, the rabbi offered words of consolation: "You should not despair, poor woman! Jews are charitable! You can support yourself by begging!"[3]

The poet Yehuda Leib Gordon, a key figure of the Jewish enlightenment, the *Haskalah*, created this fictional encounter between Jewish law and the food needs of the poor to make a point about the inequities of Jewish food practices.[4] The fictional poor woman of "Barburim Abusim," or fattened geese, represented the complex conjoining of the Jewish class system, gender, religious law, and the *gravitas* of food in Jewish culture. The term "barburim" linked Gordon's work to the sacred knot, tying food—good food—to holy time. Gordon's readers knew the word "barburim," a rare term, from a Friday night table song, "Mah Yedidut," which celebrated Sabbath meals and Sabbath pleasures as the closest one could come on earth to the bliss of paradise.[5] "Barburim Abusim" mocked the ideal of luxurious ritual feasting in the lives of the poor.

As Gordon saw it, the Jewish poor were trapped by a system which cared more about the punctilious observance of *halachah* (Jewish law) than about their hunger. But the story had other dimensions as well. To the woman who had invested so much time in getting the geese ready, the idea of the holiday and of eating well on it were one and the same. Without certain iconic food on her table, she would have no holiday at all. Her community understood this, and what may have seemed like the rabbi's cruelty was indeed a statement of fact. East European Jewish communities considered providing the poor with food at sacred times a deep, non-negotiable obligation. The Passover food, the dietary laws which rendered some foods acceptable and others not, and the bond of food which linked Jews to each other, were fixed.

Eastern European Jews lived in a world where food was sacred for all, but in which scarcities loomed for most. It was a rare text—novel, poem, short story, personal memoir—that failed to connect the sanctity of Jewish food to the inequitable distribution of resources. Few missed the connection. The Yiddish writer Leon Kobrin, born in Vitebsk in White Russia, created a fictional Lithuanian village of B—where people ate, "bread and groats, sometimes with milk and sometimes without. That was for weekdays. For the Sabbath and the holidays the good Lord betimes sent a fish or two and a piece of meat."[6] The hoped for "fish or two" and "piece of meat" underlay their food culture. Food gave meaning to Jewish life, but that meaning became complicated by the inner class divisions of the Jewish world. Good food, particularly at holy times, enhanced sanctity. But when individual Jews could not afford food, then the reality of economic inequality diminished the intensity of sacred times.

Food, as depicted by Gordon and Kobrin, revealed the differences within the Jewish world. But food also made Jews different from their non-Jewish neighbors. By the laws of *kashrut*, they could not mix meat and dairy and could only eat meat of certain animals slaughtered according to specific standards.

This was not, however, just an east European story. A worldwide people, Jews adopted local foodstuffs and adapted them to their laws. They created cuisines blending Jewish law and practice with the produce and styles of the lands of their dispersion. The greater a Jewish family's wealth and the more extensive its networks, the greater its knowledge of exotic foods and novel tastes. A journey to a new place for business or religious reasons brought Jews into contact with new foods and modes of preparation. Those who had money incorporated these into their diets.

Even poor Jews knew that the world was a place of many tastes. The vast area of Europe east of the Elbe River supported a range of styles of Jewish food.[7] The Jews of Rumania, for example, cooked with spices exotic to the palates of Polish Jews. While Polish Jews preferred sweet *gefillte* fish, Ukrainian or Lithuanian Jews ate it savory. The sweet *gefillte* fish went along with a common Polish Jewish dish called *farfl* ("cut squares or pellets of dough") not consumed elsewhere in Jewish eastern Europe.[8] Sometimes Jews used the same food word for different items. Those who lived in the more northerly and easterly regions ate a soup called "rosl" made of beets, while those living towards the southwest made "rosl" without beets. They knew *rosl* as a meat soup, more akin to a pot roast than to the beet soup of their "fellow" eastern European Jews.[9]

Enough regional variations existed within eastern Europe for folklorist Israel Furman to publish a specialized article on baking terminology common only to the Jews of Bukovina and eastern Galicia.[10] Hinde Shmulevitz had enough material to write a piece examining "words from Lodz that are connected to food." Lodz Jews, according to Shmulevitz, had unique words for certain kinds of peaches, refined sugars, a local variety of plums, particular types of noodles, and specific parts of beef tongue distinctively prepared. The editors of the New York journal *Yiddishe Sprakh* sensed that this 1943 article had such resonance among its readers that they wanted to explore the subject further. "Perhaps there are among you other old housewives who come from different cities and from different regions who will honor us their recollections of the old home?"[11]

For all classes, eastern European Jewish social life fostered culinary cosmopolitanism, as the centrifugal nature of ordinary life exposed most people to variations in Jewish food. The Jewish economy taught them about different kinds of Jewish cooking. Peddlers traversed the region, oblivious to borders, and carried goods and information with them. They relied on Jews to feed them in their homes, inns, or if they were really poor, in a community lodging house for poor travelers, the *hachnassat orchim*. As a people with a strong commercial presence, albeit usually at the lowest levels, Jewish women and men traveled to fairs and markets beyond their localities. There they ate with other Jews and learned about other ways of cooking. Marriage arrangements often brought together husbands and wives from different regions, and families or individuals picked up and moved across borders, and traversed culinary zones in pursuit of better lives. Contemporary with the Jewish emigration out of eastern Europe, an internal Jewish migration within eastern Europe also took place. Jews from smaller communities gravitated to the larger cities, Warsaw, Lodz, Kiev, Lemberg, Lublin, Krakow, Vilna, Minsk, Kharkov, Bialystok, places where economic prospects beckoned for the impoverished masses. These cities became Jewish culinary melting pots, blending different styles and ingredients from near and distant places.[12]

Jewish movements in and out of towns and cities continually expanded eastern European Jewish ideas about taste. Lillian Gorenstein had been a child in the Russian province of Volyn in the years around World War I. Sometime during the war she got a box of chocolate. "We had never tasted chocolate before," she wrote in wonder. She and her family considered it "one more miracle from God."[13] The aunt of a poor Jewish boy in a small Polish town in the 1920s traveled to Berlin and brought back a pineapple. Seventy years later he still recalled that "no one in our house had ever eaten a pineapple, or probably ever seen one. . . . When we opened it the aroma was like nothing we had ever experienced."[14]

Other widespread Jewish practices exposed them to diverse foodways. Yeshiva students, rich and poor, traveled across eastern Europe in pursuit of higher learning. In Mir, Volozhin, Chernovitz, Kletzk, Lublin, and all the other yeshiva towns, boys studied and ate.[15] They enumerated the days of the week according to where they ate, calling them *essen teg*, or eating days. Each day they went to another home, eating as such at many tables. Charles Madison's father suggested to his son that he ought to delay a bit his entry into the yeshiva. "You might as well enjoy mother's meals while you can," he counseled his son, who only too soon found himself eating with other families and "did not fail to note which woman skimped on his portion and which added morsels to his plate."[16] In a narrative of his yeshiva days, a young man from a poor family from the Polish town of Rozhinoy went to pursue his learning in Slonim. The Jews of Slonim feasted, he reported, upon a unique Sabbath dish called *gutman*, "a sort of pudding of buckwheat meal, sauteed in fried onions and rose oil." So at the same time that students at the Slonim yeshiva learned all sorts of lofty and important subjects—Talmud, commentary, Torah—they also learned to eat and enjoy the town's culinary specialty.[17]

Followers of hassidic rabbis journeyed considerable distances to celebrate holidays in the courts of their spiritual leaders. There Jews from many places met, prayed together, made matches for their children, and ate from each other's pots.[18]

The flow of the Jewish calendar fostered adventures with exotic foods. Memoirs described the childhood pleasures of eating oranges, dates, or a bunch of figs imported from distant places, sometimes even the land of Israel, on Purim, a midwinter festival, and on Tu b'Shevat, the new year of the trees. Biting into them, even if only once or twice a year, strengthened the bond between the sacred and the knowledge of the larger world as a place of many tastes.

This consumption helped forge the idea that the rich ate these wonderful foods regularly, while the poor got them only at holy days.[19] Within the Jewish world of food, a world that extended beyond the boundaries of localized communities, class mattered. Wherever they went, Jews saw the connection between money and food. Wealth determined who ate what and how they ate it. Even at sacred times, it was more than likely that good food came to the poor by way of communal charity.

Food for Jews meant more than calories for survival. It transcended pleasure. For poor and rich, regardless of place and time, food in the Judaic system stood squarely at the center of the sacred zone. It "articulated in terms of who eats what with whom under which circumstances, the most important languages in which Jews conceived and conducted social relations among human beings and between human beings and God."[20] Food embodied a palpable manifestation of Jewish conceptions of divine will. It functioned as a blueprint for human relations instituted by texts considered the word of God, and buttressed by law. The Judaic system assumed that food contained within it manifestations of holiness and commanded that human beings should not only eat but should "be satisfied."[21]

In the Jerusalem Talmud, Tractate *Kiddushin*, human beings were warned that in the final judgment to take place in the world to come, they would be punished if they had failed to partake of the good foods which their eyes had seen.[22] *Gittin*, the section of the Talmud dealing with divorce, allowed a man to institute divorce proceedings against his wife if she burnt his soup, thereby hampering him in his enjoyment of food.[23] From biblical sources through modern writings, the intimate connection between food and holiness, between good food and good life, defined Jewish ideas of consumption.

The examples in Jewish texts are legion. Moses met his fiercest opposition from the children of Israel when they got hungry as they journeyed to their promised land, a place defined in part by limitless "milk and honey," fruit, grains, and oils. "We remember," they whined, "the fish we ate in Egypt freely, the cucumbers, and the melons, and the leeks, and the onions and the garlic."[24] Rather than chiding them for their obsession with food, God pacified them with manna, a neutral substance which tasted however each person imagined it. The prophet Isaiah depicted the "end of days" as a time, when "the Lord of hosts will make for all peoples a feast of fat things, a feast of wine . . . of fat things full of marrow."[25]

The Friday night table, ushering in the Sabbath, was defined in post-exilic Jewish texts as a *mizbeach*, an altar, similar to the one which stood at the heart of the holy temple in Jerusalem. The food served on it, Kabbalists wrote, represented the sacrifices made there.[26] By eating their Sabbath meal, every Jewish family performed on and at their table a reenactment of the days before exile.[27]

The preparation and consumption of food informed Judaism and Jewish ritual practice, shaping what foods could be eaten and how. *Halachah* prescribed what should be done before and after the consumption of food, calling for different blessings for different categories of food. Fruit grown on a vine required a different blessing from that of a tree. Food from under the earth needed its own special words.

The elaborate laws of *kashrut*, of biblical and later Talmudic origins, divided the universe of foods into the edible and the inedible. Complicated strictures determined what could be eaten when, how, and with what. Some foods always lay beyond the permissible. They were *treyf*. Others "traveled." A pat of butter might be just fine, if one could afford it, on a piece of bread at one time of the day, and utterly unacceptable at another, if consumed too close to the eating of meat. Bread underlay the Jewish diet of eastern Europe, and eating it required a special blessing. But eight days out of the year, during Passover, a minute crumb of it polluted Jewish space. Dietary laws obligated all Jews, regardless of age, sex, or class, to know what they ate, how they ate it, and to always understand that what they ate derived from the intentions of God, who, as expressed in the blessing after the meal, "feeds the world with his goodness, with grace, with righteousness and with mercy."

Each and every ordinary homey object connected to the preparation and eating of food throbbed with sanctity, and hence with potential danger. Pots and pans, spoons and forks, tables and sinks, bowls and boards were of utmost significance. As the guardians of their own bodies and souls and of those of their families and communities, Jews had a role to play in keeping sanctity in and pollution out. Vigilance, care, and an overriding eye toward food informed Jewish life, from the private world of the home to the public world of the community.

Knowledge of the anatomy of cows and chickens, care in the treatments of glass bowls versus wooden ones, constituted sacred information. Rabbis derived part of their authority from knowing all this kitchen detail. Religious functionaries, always men, interpreted sacred texts and examined crockery, cutlery, and pieces of food, determining what Jews could and could not put into their mouths. Men supervised the communal preparation of food. Rabbis, slaughterers, and butchers formed a communal chain of command, with rabbis the ultimate judges of *kashrut*.[28]

But ordinary women in their homes, alone or with the aid of servants, with husbands deeply invested in the process, also inspected and judged food. They usually spotted problems first. As their families' cooks they

14. Judaism deeply informed what and how Jews ate. Despite the crisis of World War I, Jews in Lodz, Poland, brought their dishes for ritual purification to make them usable during Passover.

stood as the sentinels of *kashrut*. They could choose to ignore a problem or expose it. In their hands lay the integrity of the system.

Home and community functioned as overlapping spaces. The housewife in her kitchen and the community leaders in their formal bodies created community through food. Because Jewish communities and Judaism invested so much importance in what got eaten, they venerated food. People brought up in this world constantly talked and wrote about food as a marker of identity.[29]

The vast bulk of east European Jewish narratives, regardless of the writer's sex, class, geography, and ideology, described food in exquisite detail, their words catching tastes, smells, and sights. Joseph Cohen, born in 1878 in Russia, boasted, for example, about his grandmother's *gribenes*. They were "dry crisp on the outer side with a soft full juicy center that made the delicacy melt in the mouth."[30]

An expressive culture celebrated Jewish foodways in song and satire. Yiddish folk sayings made ample use and fun of their foodways. "Jewish heads—complain and cry and eat *kreplach*," was one of many food aphorisms collected by Y. L. Cahan, an early twentieth-century Jewish folklorist.[31] A 1920 collection of Yiddish proverbs mixed sardonic humor with observations about food, class, and piety: "It is good to eat *kugel* with a Jew, but not from the same plate, because he will grab it." Another considered someone stupid who made "*hamotzie* [the blessing over bread] on a radish!"[32] Purim parodies typically allowed Jews to laugh at themselves and their eating habits. One such vignette from Hungary from the early decades of the twentieth century parodied a talmudic treatise on "The Seven Laws Governing Card Playing." In the fourth Law, Jews were reminded that "It is better to play in a restaurant where food and drink are available, but in an emergency, private homes may be substituted. And although one leaves such homes like a burned person, this does not matter, for one's food budget is fixed in Heaven on New Year, but money for card playing is unlimited."[33]

Eastern European Jews lived in a world shaped by love of food. As simple, common, and universal a practice as the tradition by which little boys, starting their first day of school, were given a slate of Hebrew letters written in honey to lick, brought to life the connection between good tastes and holy moments.[34] Memoirs, songs, and literary offerings pointed to a widely shared belief that eating well enhanced life.[35] Eastern European Jews derived tremendous pleasure from food, reveled in the sensuality of taste, and did not consider interest in food to be a low order of concern. The socialist theoretician Chaim Zhitlovsky noted that his father, "who was very learned in the Talmud and qualified as a rabbi . . . often spoke of culinary delights, like mushrooms marinated with little cucumbers."[36]

Asceticism played little part in fostering Jewish piety. Jews did not correlate spirituality with a lack of interest in food. Hassidic rabbis and their followers emphasized good eating in the context of communal celebration. Their hearty banquets fostered religious ecstasy. At the court of the Kozhentes rebbe, "tables were laden with appetizing dishes." Appropriately, "no one touched them until the Rebbe made a blessing and distributed them," but then the crowd of followers "went wild and grabbed much more food than they could possibly have consumed."[37] Young

David Toback went to break the Yom Kippur fast at the home of "a Zinkover Hassid." Gathered there was a crowd of his followers who had just spent a day confessing their sins (including that of gluttony): "Many Hassidim were gathered around a table set with platters of gefilte fish, roast chicken, potatoes, sweetened carrots, and other delicacies, the odor of which rose like incense. The congregants made a toast to end the long fast, and what we tasted was like a feast from heaven."[38]

The Jewish calendar moved from holiday to holiday, from Sabbath to the six days of the work week, from one life cycle event to another, along a food trajectory. Each holiday called for its own special dishes. Few had any textual sanction. While Jewish law mandated eating matzah for Passover to remember the haste with which the children of Israel left Egypt, and a morsel of bitter herbs to recall the anguish of their slavery, Hanukkah by custom would not have been Hanukkah without *latkes* (potato pancakes) fried in oil, nor would Purim have actually been celebrated to the fullness of its merriment and burlesque without *hamantashen* (three-cornered pastries) filled with poppy seeds or prunes. Rosh Hashanah, the Jewish New Year, was ushered in by the sounding of the ram's horn. But it also brought with it *lekakh* (honey cake), carrot *tzimmes*, and sweetened fish. Dairy dishes like cheesecake and cheese blintzes accompanied the spring holiday of Shavuot, the day Moses received the Torah. These foods made the holiday.

A young girl whose family got caught up in the displacement and hunger of World War I wrote in her diary of life in the Polish town of Siedlice on May 19, 1915: "On Shavuot we're *supposed* [emphasis added] to decorate the house with long, green leaves and eat dairy dishes: beet borsht enriched with beaten raw eggs, blintzes in sour cream, cheese cakes. But not everyone can afford these delicacies now. My mother cooks a barley soup with milk and some fish. Good enough. Others don't have this much."[39]

The Sabbath emerged as the most powerful sacred food experience for Jews. Every week they organized the seventh day, from Friday sundown until Saturday night, around what they could not do. They could not handle money, make fire, write, chop wood, sew, all defined as work. They also organized the day around what they did do. They lit candles to usher in the Sabbath. They listened to the reading of the Torah in the synagogue on Saturday morning. Some men studied sacred texts. Families visited with each other, and children played. They sang. Married couples enjoyed conjugal relations.

And they ate. The Sabbath meals, three of them, eaten Friday night, Saturday midday, and Saturday evening, stood out from the weekly food cycle for their richness and elaborateness, just as the Sabbath stood out from the rest of the week for its liberation from work and worldly worries. Memoirs of Jewish life in eastern Europe recalled chicken soup, roasted meat, *gefillte* fish, *tcholent* (a mixture of beans, meats, potatoes, other vegetables) cooked long and slow, usually in communal ovens, and cakes and fruits, as the embodiment of Jewish family and communal life. Childhood memories so deeply valorized Sabbath pleasures with food that one memoirist called the Saturday afternoon nap the "after-the-*tcholent*" sleep. Depicting a typical Sabbath in her home, Bela Terner, who left her town in eastern Galicia in the late 1920s for Havana, Cuba, wrote, "I remember: A wintry Shabbes afternoon. Mother and Father have fallen into a delightful sleep after the tcholent." Terner even used the adjective "geshmak"—tasty—to describe their sleep.[40]

Memoirists emphasized elaborate preparations and week-long scrimping so that even the poor could eat something special on the Sabbath. They intermingled memories of Sabbath, home, and food. Morris Raphael Cohen juxtaposed his everyday impoverished boyhood in Mir with the sensual relief of "the savory Sabbath *tcholent* (a baked dish of meat and potatoes), the white bread, and the *tzimis* (a compote of turnips and carrots) were the green oases in the desert of our early life."[41] To Maurice Hindus the food of Sabbath provided "the one glimmer of light in our lives . . . we waited for its arrival . . . we were sure of getting a slice of white bread at each meal and sugar for our tea and meat at least during one meal."[42] Louis Lozowick, also a poor child in the Ukraine, sometimes had Sabbath meals with better-off relatives,

And what a meal it was. . . . Everything was so tasty, it melted in one's mouth: chicken noodle soup, chopped liver with onions and chicken fat, roast chicken and a compote of carrots and prunes. I was given a special treat—a gizzard and a little yellow ball . . . a premature chicken egg. . . . And last, the crowning glory of the Sabbath meal, the *kugel* . . . made of noodles or potatoes filled with raisins and other goodies. My father would probably not have another meal like it for many months to come.[43]

Different individuals remembered the different tastes that made Sabbath an earthly approximation of Eden. To Lillian Gorenstein it was a "flat bun," a *pletsl*. Close to 80 years after coming to America, she wrote with eloquence about her mother's Sabbath baking. "The aroma of the *pletslekh* and our anticipation of getting them . . . [were] indescribable. . . . Slowly we started to nibble and in no time the *pletslekh* were gone. Nothing in the world tasted as good as those warm *pletslekh*."[44] Another woman, from a wealthier home, pictured herself as a young girl:

> I sit down on the steps leading to the courtyard and allow the Sabbath smells to envelop me. The pungent fragrance of the *gefullte* fish, the odor of dill dropped into the chicken broth, the smell of the newly baked *challe* (special white Sabbath loaves) and the *kichlach* (yeast cakes filled with chopped almonds, raisins and cinnamon). I know, too that soon they will be putting the *tzimmes*, *tscholent* and *kugel* into the oven.[45]

Louis Borgenicht, a poor Galician child, told a relatively similar story. He remembered his family Sabbath through a "fine midday meal as was—and is—the custom in most Jewish homes." Of all the tastes, he remembered most sharply the dessert, "a special delicacy, generally a kind of potato cake with a golden crust on it." He claimed decades later he could still see and taste "this "kugel," and how he would "plunge a luscious forkful" into his mouth.[46]

The Sabbath and its foods elevated ordinary time and ordinary lives to transcendence and bore witness to the intimate connection between sanctity and food. A young girl growing up in Minsk at the beginning of the twentieth century told the same story. "At the end of week," wrote Minnie Fisher, "of course, the struggle was always how did one provide for the Sabbath, for the holidays. No matter how poor a Jewish person was, the rest of them put together money and gave it to him so that his family would at least have what they *required* [emphasis added] for the Sabbath." Fisher considered "lots of baked goods," "fish and meat, and all kinds of wonderful dishes: chicken soup was a must every Friday night. And a dessert called *tsimmis*."[47] However poor, all families believed themselves entitled to good food at holy moments. They did not feel unworthy of eating well, and did not believe that perpetual scarcity ought to be their lot in life.

Those who knew hunger also knew that other Jews were satisfied. They condemned this disparity. As one folk saying put it: "The rich man eats meat, the poor man eats the bones." The number who gnawed at bones, as opposed to those who feasted on the meat, grew in the last quarter of the nineteenth century. By the latter decades of the nineteenth century a large proportion of eastern European Jewry was poor, indeed poorer than they had been earlier. (The Jewish birth rate had skyrocketed despite impoverishment.) From 20 to 25 percent of the Jews of eastern Europe lived "at miserably low economic levels."[48] Anti-Jewish, restrictive legislation, such as the May Laws in Russia of 1881, further limited economic options, while worldwide depressions in the 1870s and the 1890s reverberated across the Pale of Settlement.[49] During this period the number of poor Jewish artisans "under the impact of industrialization . . . was rapidly increasing." They were forced to compete against each other for a shrinking market among the poorest of them. Tailors and shoemakers "occupied a commanding position within the artisan group."[50] While rates of pauperization varied from region to region, the overall portrait was one of endemic poverty. In some places the destitute—"those devoid of skills, resources, and specific occupations and largely or even wholly dependent on charity"—constituted nearly half of all Jews. Others "were crowded overwhelmingly into occupations, crafts, and trades . . . that were very poorly remunerated."[51] A Russian statistician in the 1860s recorded that for the Grodno province, "the bulk of the Jews . . . are poor. . . . It is not uncommon for a three- or four-room dwelling to house as many as twelve families. . . . In most cases a pound of bread, a herring, and a few onions represent the daily fare of an entire family."[52] Increasing numbers of Jewish poor taxed Jewish communal resources. From the 1860s onward the situation worsened, and would be somewhat relieved only by emigration.

Pauperization made the quest for food a daily Jewish crisis. Famines broke out, and local crop failures brought about intensified deprivations. In the late 1860s a widespread famine in western Russia, including Suvalk

15. In Krakow, M. S. Mandl's Bakery supplied kosher bread to Jewish residents at the turn of the twentieth century. Jews throughout the world depended upon their own separate commercial infrastructure to sustain communal life.

and other parts of Lithuania, sent the first large contingent from that region to America.[53] Famines struck Russia in 1891–1892 and 1903–1905, while during World War I acute food shortages made daily life difficult for many.[54] By the last half of the nineteenth century the Jewish masses had been reduced to a poor diet, mostly of dark bread, potatoes, and herring. Many had to depend on the welfare rolls of the *kahal*, the Jewish community.

Ordinarily, eastern European Jews ate from a paltry repertoire characterized by few variations from meal to meal. Maurice Hindus's mother sometimes came upon an egg, and "she cut it into four parts and gave each of her children only one." They ate the morsel of egg with their staple, black bread.[55] Norman Salsitz, who grew up after World War I in the

MEHL MAKA
KLEIN VERKAUF   SPRZEDAŻ DETALICZNA
Stadt-Mehlverteilungs Komitee   Komitet Rozdziału Chleba Mąki

Łódź. Sprzedaż mąki.
Lodz. Mehlverkauf.

16. At times of crisis, east European Jews created formal and informal programs to feed the hungry. The larger the community, the more elaborate the feeding programs for those in distress. This bread line was photographed in Lodz during World War I.

town of Kolbuszowa in Poland, described his mother's "false soup," garlic or onion in boiling water. Most meals in his home "consisted of little more than a plate of potatoes or cereal, a piece of bread rubbed with onion or garlic and a cup of tea, chicory, or sometimes coffee." Up to half of his town's Jewish population was poor, and "in a large majority of households food was always scarce. People worried all the time about having money to buy food even in small amounts, and about having enough food particularly for the Sabbath."[56]

The massive study conducted by the Jewish Colonization Association in 1905, as well as various government and Jewish communal surveys, detailed the growing impoverishment of the Jews. According to an 1898 investigation of over 1,000 Jewish communities in Russia, 19 percent of the population needed to ask for assistance from the *kahal* in order to celebrate Passover, while in Vilna that figure stood at nearly 38 percent. Vilna Jews in the 1890s suffered acutely, "despite their industry and frugality . . . the majority of Jews failed to reach . . . a low standard of comfort . . . fully four-fifths of the Jewish population in the city did not know in the evening where they would obtain a meal the next morning."[57]

Personal stories revealed consciousness of class inequities.[58] Melech Epstein, born in 1889 in Ruzhany, a small town in Russia, described in detail the Jewish class hierarchy of his town, which he understood as a "de facto caste system." At the top he located a "well-to-do upper crust," followed by a "handful of learned men" and their families, and then the "storekeepers, artisans," and *melamdim*, the teachers. Towards the bottom clustered factory workers, and at the very bottom were the chimney sweeps and the *balegoles*, the draymen. His father was a *melamed*, a member of the middle class, so the family ate black bread, herring, which "cost a kopek," soup, and "sometimes even butter, milk and eggs, fish on Saturday, and occasionally even inexpensive meat." More often, though, they would simply wrap "a piece of herring in paper and put it on the burning stove. When the burnt paper was removed, the herring was sharp and delicious."[59] Solomon Berger, born in 1897 in the eastern Galician town of Zborow, claimed that 20 percent of the Jews in his town qualified as truly destitute, five percent enjoyed prosperity, and everyone else fell between, but closer to the bottom than the top.[60]

Louis Lozowick's autobiography resounded with themes of poverty, the class inequities of the Jewish society around him, and the resentment they fostered. Lozowick indeed opened his memoir with the recitation of a folk poem about the much hated impressment of poor Jewish boys into the czarist army:

> Little tots are kidnapped from the heder
> They are fitted out in soldiers' uniforms.
> Yankel, the rich man, has seven sons
> Not one of them goes into the army.
> But widow Leah's only child
> Is sacrificed for the community's sins.[61]

In 1890, the Yiddish writer Y. L. Peretz accepted a commission from Jan Bloch, a convert to Christianity, to research and write about the economic and social plight of the Jews. Peretz traveled through the towns surrounding his Polish city, Zamosc, meeting with Jews on the streets, in their homes, and at the marketplaces, compiling his observations in a series of sketches called *Impressions of a Journey Through the Tomaszow Region in the Year 1890*. The leitmotif of everyday Jewish life was poverty, with its partner, hunger. "On the stoves," wrote Peretz in a piece entitled "A Little Boy,"

> potatoes or else dumplings and beans should already be cooking in their pots of boiling water. The statistical data show the average per capita income of Tishevitz to be thirty-seven and a half rubles a year, or about ten kopecks a day. You can do the arithmetic: tuition fees; two sets of kitchenware and tableware: one for milk and one for meat; Sabbath and holy days; illness; something for those who pray efficaciously for you—add it all up and you will understand why the stoves are so seldom used for preparing a fine meal, why the dumplings are made without a single egg, and why the potatoes may be served dry. And those are not the worst houses.[62]

Life histories testified to the accuracy of Peretz's observations. Israel Pressman, born in Minsk in 1881, described his mother's long and arduous food preparations. In a family where they "struggled for a piece of black bread," his mother "cooked three times a day. In the morning, for breakfast, she made barley soup with oats; for dinner, potatoes in their skins with sour milk. Sometimes she also served a little pickled herring which made it a special meal. And for supper, she made barley with peas, sometimes with lima beans. This was a *fleyshik* [meat] meal in name only—there was no meat in it, but it was cooked with stale chicken fat."[63]

Most had only limited choices. Breakfast, lunch, and supper differed little from each other, and only bits of meat, a few vegetables, minute amounts of fat or sugar appeared on their tables. Dairy products were also scarce, though perhaps less so for those who lived in the smaller country towns.[64] Accounts list with monotonous regularity potatoes, bread, herring, *kasha* (buckwheat groats), and *krupnik* (vegetable soup). In the town of Swislocz, a Polish community, "*krupnik* was . . . on the menu of every Jewish home."[65] One writer estimated that before World War II no fewer than 90 percent of Lithuanian Jews subsisted on black bread and potatoes, spiced up with *zoiers*, "sours," notably beet borscht, cabbage, and schav, a sour sorrel soup.[66] Beatrice Baskerville, who spent eight years in Poland and published her impressions of Jewish life there in 1908, commented on the overwhelming smell and use of garlic and the ubiquity of herring on the Jews' tables.[67] Rumanian Jews, as poor as their Polish counterparts, ate as their staple *mamaliga*, a cornmeal product similar to polenta, and little else.[68]

In this period of volatile economic and political upheavals at the end of the nineteenth and beginning of the twentieth century, some people's fortunes went up, others managed to hang on, but many who used to be comfortable became impoverished. World War I, in particular, left its mark on the Jewish better-off classes. One young man, born in 1903 in Poland, recalled that he had begun life very well off. But wartime exigencies, increased taxes, military invasion, food shortages, all reduced the family's circumstances. Once rich, the family now confronted "a scarcity of food," and only the "miracle" of charitable food distributions helped in "preserving us from starvation." Years later he still felt the sting: "I cannot stop being moved emotionally, talking about it."[69] Aaron Sher came to Baraboo, Wisconsin, after World War I. Until the Great War, his comfortable family was supported by his father's large harness-making business in Kobrin. When the war broke out, his father was drafted into the Russian army, and the whole family faced starvation. The boy, just thirteen, "had to dig potatoes so the family would not starve."[70] Shlomo Noble did not know hunger until World War I. During the war years, when he turned thirteen, his "Bar Mitzvah was nothing, nothing. There was no food to give anybody. My mother wept. We were supposed to give something to eat to everybody, but what could we do when there wasn't a piece of bread around?"[71]

A small number of Jews benefited from the new economic realities and enjoyed prosperity. Wealthy Jews at the top rung of the class ladder lived well in nice houses, wearing fine clothes and driving sturdy vehicles. Servants, Jewish and non-Jewish, worked in their large homes. These Jews ate rich foods, including meats, fruits, imported wines, elaborate baked goods, noodles, dairy products, whatever they wanted. Miriam Shomer Zunser's 1939 autobiography gave considerable space to the comfortable home of her Pinsk grandfather, where the "larder was bursting with plenty, and the cellar of his house was stored with barrels of apples, potatoes, sauerkraut and pickles of grandmother's making." Her grandparents had a storehouse with flour, meal, dry beans and peas, and "great closets in the anterooms stocked with jars of rendered chicken fat, jams and preserves, and cupboards full of wheaten products—bread, rolls, *kuchen*, and cake."[72]

The contrast between their food and that of the mass, alongside the intimate social relations which bound all Jews together and bisected class lines, shaped the east European Jewish engagement with food in the modern era. Those who ate poorly knew in great detail what it meant to eat well. Those with empty larders also knew that rich and poor alike came under the same sacred laws governing the universe of food. Class distinctions had deep implications for Jewish foodways, particularly for *kashrut* and the communal system of regulating and providing kosher meat.

Starting in Poland in the seventeenth century, in Galicia and Posen in the eighteenth, then Russia in the early nineteenth, the sale of kosher meat came under a system of regressive taxation. Known in Poland and Russia as the *korobka* (meaning box, since whoever came to the kosher slaughterer to get meat had to put a coin in a box), the tax hit the poor harder than the rich. Like with any sales tax, the poorest paid the largest percentage of their income on the taxed item.

Meat symbolized the most desirable food possible. Holidays achieved their fullest expression of holiness through the eating of meat.[73] Meat symbolized plenty. The poor focused on eating meat as the mark of prestige, as the standard to which they aspired. In Morris Raphael Cohen's home "food was only occasionally seen in the house—such food consisting entirely of stale bread discarded or sold for next to nothing by certain warehouses." But he remembered how his grandfather put a toothpick in his mouth when he went outside. He wanted "to give the impression that he had eaten meat."[74]

The *korobka* at different times and places was levied on other items—silk, kosher wine, matches—as well as on the essential services, such as circumcision and the signing of betrothal papers. But it was taxation on kosher slaughtering, paid directly by consumers, that raised the greatest amount of money and was the one constant in the tax system.[75] The levy came from the state, but the *kahal* administered it and depended upon it to finance communal activities, including rabbis' salaries.

Abuses of the system were not infrequent, perpetrated by both *kahal* and state. Unscrupulous Jewish tax collectors could, and did, line their own pockets.[76] The *shochtim*, the slaughterers, held a monopoly and used their power to cut out competition from others who might charge a lower price. Even without abuses, the taxation system reflected and exacerbated the internal class biases of the Jewish world of eastern Europe. The leaders of the *kahal*, almost always the wealthy, controlled the public purse in concert with rabbis. They suffered little from the *korobka*, control of which added to their power and wealth. For the poor, the tax on ritually pure food deepened the burden of their poverty and heightened their resentment of their own elite.

Mendele Moykher-Sforim's play of 1869, *Di Takse, oder di Bande Shtot Baley-toyves* (The Tax [meaning the kosher meat tax] and the Gang of the Town Benefactors), took as its themes class inequities and the corruption of the *korobka*.[77] Mendele's use of the phrase "shtot baley-toyves" dripped with sarcasm. These men, who manipulated the tax for their own advantage, claimed that they did so in the name of the town's charitable enterprises. Mendele, the *nom de plume* of Sholem Abramovitch, knew better. His father, Chaim Moyshe Broyde, had been the *korobka* collector in Kapulye.[78] In *Di takse* Mendele portrayed the class divisions within the Jewish communities, writing what one literary critic has described as "one of the most radical, shrill, and effective exposes of social injustice within the Jewish community to be found in Yiddish literature."[79] A defender of *kashrut* admitted that Mendele's play "helped to awaken the hatred of the masses against their wealthy and respectable communal leaders, a feeling that accounts in great measure for that anomalous creature, the Jewish communist of a half century later."[80]

Kashrut had different financial consequences for the well-off and for the poor. It demanded that all Jews own multiple sets of dishes, cutlery, bowls, pots, and pans. The more meticulous the observance, the more it cost. One description of life in a fabulously wealthy *hassidic* home in eastern Europe at the end of the nineteenth century depicted a family, the grandparents of the author, rich enough to have a separate room for the consumption of meat dishes and another for dairy. They also maintained a "Passover apartment," separate rooms where breadstuffs had never been eaten. The memoirist, Ita Kalisch, remembered that her grandfather, the *rebbe* who presided over this palace, wore "separate kaftans for dairy meals and meat meals," lest accidental drippings of the two substances, which Jewish law mandated must not be consumed together, mix on his clothing.[81]

Poor married women bore the brunt of the food system. They carried the burdens of "keeping kosher" while feeding their husbands and children. They minded the foods which came into their homes and monitored the pots and pans and tableware, making sure that carelessness did not render a meat dish unusable because someone had sloppily used it to eat a dairy item. If they failed in their rigor, they had the community and their husbands to answer to, and they lost the use of the spoon or fork, dish or pot. *Kashrut* made cooking difficult, but particularly so for those of limited means. Just as the *korobka* made little impact on the rich who could afford to pay a tax on meat, so too the goose declared unkosher, or the dairy spoon polluted by contact with meat, would have been minor annoyances for someone with wealth. But for the poor these matters loomed large. The goose represented an investment of months of labor and money. The polluted spoon very well may have been the only one, shared by all family members.

To make matters worse, many poor women worked and could not cook for their families as they wanted to, or as society deemed they ought. They labored in the marketplace as sellers of goods, either working with husbands in a common concern or at their own marginal businesses. They could not spend their days cooking the tasty food they wanted for their families. Wealthier families, like that of Bella Chagall, employed servants who cooked while her mother managed the family store.[82] Poorer women, however, had no help. They merely had to make do.

Families in the middle, like that of Howard Weinshel, from eastern Galicia, "always had enough food." But his mother worked outside the home. Born in 1904, he remembered how "life for my mother was not easy because in addition to running the house, she had to help father in the store. As the children got older they helped with the chores, but she was still responsible for running the house and for the cooking and baking." He specifically made the point that although never hungry and part of the town's middle class, they could not afford a servant to help in cooking and other domestic chores. The onus for all the work fell upon his mother. "My mother would start preparing for the baking on Thursday evening, and she would get up early on Friday morning to get the fire in the oven started and to prepare the dough for the white egg bread *chalah* for the Sabbath. . . . we always looked forward to Friday. Mother's rolls, especially those with cottage cheese fillings, were delicious."[83]

Families situated on a lower economic level than the Weinshels suffered far more, and poorer women had less time to devote to cooking, an act they understood as binding them to their children and husbands and which made their homes sacred. Other than on the Sabbath and holidays, mealtimes were informal among poorer Jewish families. On ordinary days they did not sit down and eat on a fixed schedule. "One ate," wrote Hirsch Abramowitz in a volume memorializing the Jews of Lithuania, "when there was time, between things one grabbed a bite."[84]

Among the many stings of Morris Raphael Cohen's childhood poverty, he recalled with bitterness how his mother labored outside the home, so there were no regular meals for the family:

> I was walking along with my young sister and we passed a house where people in the front room were having their midday meal, at which I looked longingly. I was ashamed to ask for anything, but I turned to my sister and inquired, "Friedke (Florence), are you hungry?" The mother of the family gave us each a piece of bread dipped in soup and launched into a tirade against my mother for leaving us alone all day and not providing us with sufficient food. But the delightful taste of the food prevailed over my indignation and the disrespect to my mother.[85]

The gap between the rich and poor, between eating well and starving, intersected with the religious system. Hints of it ran through east European Jewish folk materials. A Yiddish children's "ABC" rhyme merged sacred motifs with food and class. Sung to the melody of the Shavuot chant of *Akdamut* (an Aramaic text describing the awesome power experienced when Moses received the Torah at Mt. Sinai), it told a food story of class difference. The melody would have been instantly recognizable to both Jewish children and adults in eastern Europe.

> Aleph—*Indikes est der nogid* (A: The rich man eats turkeys)
> Beys—*Beyndelach grizhet der oriman* (B: The poor man gnaws on little bones)

Gimel—*Gendzelch est der nogid* (C: The rich man eats little geese)

Daled—*Dem dalles hot der oriman* (D: The poor man has his poverty)

and so on, with the person of wealth savoring little chickens and rolls with butter, while the pauper consumed nothing. Sickness and pain consumed him.[86]

The masses of poor Jews represented to the wealthy elite a class of fellow Jews to whom they owed a series of communal obligations. The tradition decreed that "All of Israel are responsible, one for the other." Jewish communities organized around a number of charitable nodes to ensure, among other things, that the tables of the poor, empty or virtually empty most of the time, would be more amply covered at sacred times. Those who had means understood that they owed much to those who had little, and the latter knew that communal *mitzvot*, obligations, forced the rich to give, and entitled them—the poor—to a minimum standard of living below which the *kahal* would not let them fall.

Most food sharing grew out of sacred time. Jewish housewives set aside a portion of their Sabbath food for the poor. Men going to the synagogue on Friday night to usher in the Sabbath or on Saturday morning to hear the reading of the Torah *expected* and *were expected* to bring home visitors, strangers, or poor people with no Sabbath table of their own. In larger cities the *shamash*, the synagogue's factotum, arranged an orderly system by which those without a meal would be matched up with the householders who set the richest board.

Betrothal and wedding ceremonies did more than bring a bride and groom together. As joyous communal events, they celebrated the creation of a new Jewish family, and the feasts hosted by the families of the bride were open to the public. In the Lithuanian town of Eiyshishok before the 1920s and 1930s public feasting commonly accompanied the signing of the *tena'im*, the terms of the engagement contract.[87] Sh. Ansky (Shlomo Zanvl Rappoport), a folklorist and author of the play *The Dybbuk*, opened his play about forbidden love and the occult with the prospect of a public feast. Meyer, the *shamash* of the synagogue, engaged in some banter with the town loafers, who complained that so far that day they had eaten little more than a "crust of bread." As *shamash*, and privy to all sorts of information, Meyer counseled a bit of patience. "You just wait," he predicted with glee: "I have a feeling we'll be celebrating before long. Sender has gone off to inspect a bridegroom for his only daughter. Let's hope they come to some agreement, he'll provide us with a fine feast."[88] In smaller communities the third Sabbath meal, the *seudah shlishit,* took place in some public space, and the whole of "Israel" partook of the meal.[89]

Individual memoirs recalled generous relatives, mothers, fathers, grandparents from the "old home" who distributed food regularly to the poor. Jews who grew up in the eastern Galician town of Ustile described the ubiquity of food distribution as a form of Jewish communal charity. One Ustile man recalled how his mother "took out a portion of the meat that father brought home from the butcher before the Sabbath to give to the poor." She, with a group of other women, "went from house to house to collect money for a poor neighbor" for Sabbath foods. Another son of this town depicted a local woman, Shprintze, who walked around the town every Friday afternoon, with "a sack on her sunken back collecting *challah* for the *hekdesh* [poor house] and for other poor people generally."[90] Solomon Berger from Zborow, also in eastern Galicia, remembered that his brother Mannie distributed chicken and other foods to the town's poor. Some of them were relatives, a fact that muddled the line between helping strangers and sustaining family members.[91] Jacob Scarr described in detail how as a child he sat with the women of the community who were preparing for burial the corpse of his beloved grandmother, Bubba Feige:

> The women sat around Bubba and began to eulogize her and remember her good deeds. They recalled that she would tell Aunt Leah to bake six extra *challahs* on Friday for the poor families of the . . . city. They related that, when word got about that this or that widow did not have money for meat for the Sabbath meal, Bubba would fill a pot with a quarter of a chicken or a few slices of meat with potatoes, onion and garlic. She would wrap the pot in a linen towel and say, "Yankele, take this to Geetel, the widow, but you make sure you bring back the pot."[92]

Groups of neighbors, aware that a poor young woman was to get married or that a poor boy was to turn thirteen, which would mark his entry into adulthood, banded together to make the life cycle event truly sacred by providing food. David Toback's father, around the time of the boy's bar mitzvah in 1888, "had become so poor that he could no longer pay a tutor's wages." The boy taught himself, but it was the townspeople who made the feast. "How astonished and happy we were," he wrote in his memoirs, "that night when all those who had been at the services came to our home. People had decided in advance to all contribute a little and make a banquet in my honor. They carried pots of potatoes and cabbage, roasted lamb, and big loaves of bread."[93]

Communities set up soup kitchens for the town poor and for transients. The larger the community the more elaborate such institutions. Smaller towns had more informal arrangements. During World War I, towns which had previously relied on more casual ways of feeding the hungry instituted more structured methods to cope with demand. Tzirl Fleisher wrote in the Ustile *yizkor* (memorial) book that "the first communal project that I remember, and which I took a part in when I was of a young age, was the public kitchen that was founded . . . in 1915." After listing the other young people involved, she described how the kitchen "provided a hot meal every day to the poor population, and in particular to the families of the men who had been drafted into the war."[94] In the midst of the dislocation of the war, soup kitchens emerged as alternative sources of community power.[95] In Vilna and elsewhere the Bund, the Jewish workers' organization, opened its own soup kitchens, which dispensed education and cultural programs as well as soup. Other soup kitchens elected governing boards and sought to create consumer cooperatives to protect the poor from the vagaries of the marketplace.[96]

The various societies of the *kahal* staged annual dinners. Members contributed money and food and invited the town's poor to share in the festive fare. The *hevre kaddisha* (burial society) of the town of Horodets, for example, set a table for its annual feast in the winter, and, according to one participant, it resembled "the feasts of King Solomon in his day. Special challahs were baked. Large pieces of fish were served, along with meat, chicken, tsimmes, and compote." All this good stuff, along with wine and brandy, was shared by the members and the poor, whose presence transformed the banquet from pure hedonism to the fulfillment of a sacred communal obligation.[97] Likewise, in Kalvaria, the *hevra shas* (Talmud study group) held a mammoth feast to mark its *siyum*, held every seven years when the group completed its reading of the six books of the Mishnah. Every man was invited. Each "would bring his own knife and fork and spoon. There was no dearth of potables either; and there was such merry-making as to keep in the memory until the next *Siyum Hashas* seven years hence." The poor, even though they had not engaged in the scholarly enterprise, were invited as well.[98]

These public banquets, Sabbath food distributions, Friday night dinners, and the other practices which fed the poor were ubiquitous and universal. For the poor, they offered a momentary relief from hunger. They demonstrated Jewish cross-class relationships. They tightened the bond between food and holiness. They often gave the poor a chance to sit down at the same table with the rich, the learned, the elite, to eat what they ate, and to know how good it tasted.

But food obtained through charity came with an emotional price tag and created conflict between the desire for self-respect and the hunger for food. Charity exacerbated the resentment felt by the recipients. A young man who experienced the cycle of "eating days" as a yeshiva student in Minsk, recalled that "all of my benefactors acted as though they'd never heard of me. Tuesdays and Fridays were the worst. On Tuesdays I ate—or rather, I starved—at the home of one of my mother's relatives . . . They were rich people and owned several homes . . . they never asked me to come into the parlor. They fed me in the kitchen."[99]

The families that took turns sharing their meals fostered learning, a great value in and of itself. Memoirs of the men who had been on the receiving end as youngsters, the yeshiva students who went from house to house for their suppers, described the competition amongst themselves to eat in the richest homes that served the best food. Some fared well. "I could hardly believe," David Toback recalled, "the delicious feast that had been provided—onion rolls, pancakes, knishes, and pitcher of warm milk," a contrast to the foods he generally ate at home.[100]

Class chasms divided families, complicating further the obligations of those with means towards those without, and heightening the resentment of those on the receiving end. Memoirs frequently included references to a "rich uncle" or a "poor sister." A Hebrew memoir written by Israel Kasovich, born in 1859, described in detail how his "rich uncle" brought his poor uncle into his home to tutor his children. Kasovich's branch of the family also fell on the poorer side of the kinship spectrum, and the "rich uncle"—always referred to as such—offered to pay for his studies alongside his wealthy cousins. The rich cousins and the poor one studied and ate together. Kasovich recalled with bitterness the shame of dependence.[101] Chaim Grade described his mother as poor, overworked, and overwhelmed. Every Saturday afternoon she took him to "her sister's house for cholent. This meal was estimated as part of her wages, earned by wearing herself out working in that sister's store all week. Each week after the meal, the same conversation. . . . 'Some husband you've got!. . . . the husband who's supposed to take care of you, is letting you struggle alone.'"[102] "My uncle was the capitalist of the family," remembered Leah Rosenberg, who as a poor girl in 1912 went with her mother to live with rich relatives in Warsaw. The "affluent and childless" family members temporarily took in the poorer ones. In her retelling of her early life, the contrast between her poverty and their wealth, her privation and their "pastries . . . made with ground almonds," remained vivid.[103]

Similar contrasts manifested themselves in the many common spaces occupied by the Jewish poor and their economic betters. The sons of all classes studied and ate together in the *heder*, the Jewish elementary school. They sat together, studied the same texts and enjoyed, or suffered, the same strict discipline of the *melamed*. But when it came time for lunch, their paths parted. Alexander Bittelman recalled this sting in his memories of Berdichev of the 1890s. The children of "businessmen, merchants of various sorts, clerks or professionals" learned with him. But "only my father was a working man and what was really shameful, a shoemaker." The other boys "were dressed better and nicer than I and their lunch packages [were] richer and tastier." He remembered how his shame turned into anger at the boys, the system, and "the Almighty."[104] In Morris Raphael Cohen's memories of childhood, he remembered how "the wealthier children had some liquid food which their mothers put in . . . vessels strung together . . . and carried by the *rebbeh*'s assistant. Like the more plebeian boys I had only a piece of bread . . . which I carried in my pocket." Every day a woman came to the school with a pot of "freshly baked, steaming soft chick peas and sold it to the aristocrats who had a groschen." He never had the requisite coin and never got the midday treat.[105]

The resentment articulated and remembered by the poor grew out of the shared economy in which most functioned. Jews by and large employed other Jews.[106] The small class of rising Jewish industrialists in Russia "created jobs for over 93 percent of the Jewish industrial workers."[107] Most Jewish employers hired and supervised other Jews, if not exclusively, then predominantly.

Jewish servant women worked in Jewish, not gentile homes, although Jewish householders employed the domestic help of both groups.[108] In the 1880s Rose Schneiderman's aunt Luba "was employed as a domestic by a wealthy Jewish family, the only way a young woman could earn a living in our village."[109] Although Jewish women had broader options in larger towns in Russian Poland, the experience of Jewish women as domestic servants played a formative role in the shaping of class consciousness among the poor.[110] Young Jewish women from poor families went into service because their own families could not feed them. Working in a wealthy home gave them a chance to eat and to earn their own dowries, something their parents could not provide, but which the matrimonial system required.[111]

Rich and poor, and those from the many grades in between, Jews rubbed up against each other in the town marketplace. Beatrice Baskerville, an outsider, detected the class encounter in the food shops and stores where Jews sold to each other. There she saw rich soups, fat cuts of meat, pungent vanilla for flavoring baked goods, and other delicacies in great profusion. Baskerville also saw, eyeing the rich array, a poor woman, the wife of a workingman, buying "a few cucumbers or a loaf of bread and looking wistfully at dainties she cannot afford."[112]

Poor teachers ate nightly with town families, paying a bit of money for their meals, or eating in exchange for lessons. Chaim Aronson worked as a teacher in various towns of the Pale in the late nineteenth century. He moved from house to house, some serving better food, some worse. He had been in the town of Shadova for a few days, eating primarily at the home of a poor baker who provided paltry meals, when one of his students, a young woman, "lingered behind to talk with me. She asked about my circumstances and where I lodged and had my meals. She shook her head over my poverty. She said she would ask her parents to let me have my meals with them for the same charge which I paid the poor baker."[113] He switched and commenced to eat better with the wealthier family.

The constant contrast between rich and poor and the deeply held belief about food as an entitlement of all Jews emerged as a powerful theme in east European Jewish texts, a theme as significant in their world view as their fear of anti-Jewish violence at the hands of non-Jews around them. The constant specter of hunger set against the full stomachs of the Jewish elite emerged as a powerful theme in Yiddish literature. Writers such as Mendele, Sholem Aleykhem, and Y. L. Peretz identified the plight of the poor Jewish masses as their inspiration and took it up as their cause.

In his novel *Fishke der Krumer*, published in 1869, Mendele explored the world of Jewish beggars. Their miserable existence resulted from fundamental class injustices which divided Jewish communities. In *Fishke*, Mendele commented acidly:

> Once a Jew has broken himself of the vile passion of eating, food ceases to be a matter of importance to him and he can spend the rest of his life requiring nothing. To this very day . . . many a Jew can be found who has only the remnants of a stomach—truly, the size of an olive pit. And there are great hopes that with the passing of time—if only the kosher meat tax is kept . . . Jews will drift further and further away from eating, until among future generations there will be no trace left of the digestive system.[114]

The first piece of writing in which Sholem Rabinovitsh introduced himself by the pen name of Sholem Aleykhem also featured food as a way to show Jewish class inequities. In his 1883 story "Di Vibores" (The Elections), the Russian authorities had decreed that Jewish townspeople of Loubny had to vote for a new rabbi as their chief religious functionary. The election pitted the poor against the rich as backers of the two candidates for the coveted position. Everyone in the town showed up: "The hall was filled with people standing around, jammed together like a flock of sheep. They were of the lower class, the masses who must earn their piece of bread with their last bit of strength. At the sides, in arm-chairs and on benches, sat the genteel, well-fed men, with smooth round bellies and finely groomed beards."[115] Of course, the latter prevailed. The discrepancy in communal power followed the gap between the well-fed and hungry, and the poor could see quite clearly how political power went along with the ability to eat well.

One of the most widely known pieces of writing penned by the latest of the "three greats" of Yiddish literature, Y. L. Peretz, was his short story "Bontshe Shvayg" (Silent Bontshe). Bontshe represented the paradigmatically poor eastern European Jew, the classic loser. "No wine," wrote Peretz, "was drunk at Bontshe's circumcision, no glasses clinked in a toast." So inconsequential was Bontshe, that after he died, "the wind blew away the wooden sign marking his grave. The grave digger's wife found it some distance away and used it to boil potatoes." The story took place in heaven where the court of judgment sat in deliberation, weighing Bontshe's actions on earth to determine his fate in the world to come. One angel presented the case and described his life of privation. His mother died when he was young, and his cruel stepmother "fed him moldy bread and gristle, while she feasted herself on coffee with cream." No matter what happened to him, he never complained, and even "when half-dead from hunger, he never begged except with his eyes." The court decided that Bontshe had led a pure life and deserved whatever he might want for all of eternity. "Ask for anything you wish," the judge told him, and the bewildered Bontshe, who had never asked for anything, hesitatingly asked only for "a warm roll with fresh butter every morning."

Peretz's tale can be read in many ways. Bontshe might be the greatest of heroes. He had lived a life utterly unblemished by evil or selfishness. His final request, a roll with butter in the morning, could be interpreted as a celebration of simplicity. Unlike the greedy, wealthy Jews who stuffed themselves in Peretz's other stories, poor Bontshe's spartan desires ennobled him. Yet Peretz could also have intended to show that Bontshe's humility and lack of a sense of entitlement to good food had an effect in the "other world." This story indicted the Jewish class system, which had beaten down this poor man so badly that he could not even beg for food. He had been so tormented by his schoolmates, his neighbors, his family that he had never developed a conception of pleasure and plenty. After hearing the utter simplicity of Bontshe's wish, "The judges and angels hung their heads in shame. The prosecutor laughed."[116]

Unlike the protagonist of the Peretz story, the masses of east European Jews who knew hunger considered themselves worthy and entitled, as Jews, to eat well. Their concern for food and their understanding of food as the marker between ordinary and sacred, pure and impure, Jewish and "goyish," was shared with their social and economic betters who never worried about the source of their next meal. All believed that God intended them to eat well because their own sacred texts told them so. When Jews finished eating, whether good and rich fare or spartan foods acquired through communal assistance, they were required to "bentch," to thank God for the food just eaten. They praised God who "gives bread to all living things." They also intoned, "I was a boy, and I also grew up, and I never saw a righteous person [*tzaddik*] abandoned or his children begging for bread."

Eastern European Jewish foodways grew out of a particular context which connected food, sanctity, community, class, and the gendered nature of everyday responsibilities Jews bore to each other. These realities played a shaping role in the migration to America, an act best understood as a search not just for bread, but for meat and fish, noodles and soups, and all the sweet stuffs that the less well-off got only at sacred time.

Immigrants to America came from the ranks of the lower, although not the lowest income groups, who were unable to benefit from new economic conditions.[117] Skilled workers and artisans made up over 60 percent of the immigrants, although accounting for less than 40 percent of the Jewish population. Common laborers and servants also showed up among those who left in numbers greater than their proportion among east European Jews.[118] That the less observant of the east European Jews immigrated to America, and the most traditional stayed put, further demonstrated the selectivity of the exodus to America.

East European Jews emigrated primarily in response to economic conditions. While they also left Russia because of anti-Jewish violence, the search for work that would enable them to buy good food propelled the exodus. That quest was informed by the desire of ordinary Jews to control their own consumption. They knew America as a place of plentiful food, where pre-migration hierarchies tumbled. In Leon Kobrin's fictional small town in Lithuania the poor Jews could not believe the words that came to them in the "first letter from America," informing them that, "On the very sidewalk lay precious things such as I only wish you could have on your table for the holidays . . . they eat of the very best here. They don't lack even bird's milk! Roast hens in the middle of the week and so many other dainty dishes that I don't know how to name them."[119]

In perhaps the most well-known song of the migration era, the lullaby written by Sholem Aleykhem, a mother crooned to her child that, before long, the father, now in America, would send them passage money. They would join him there, where, as everyone knew, they could have chicken soup and *challah* in middle of the week.[120]

Those who left went to a place where food cost little, where choice abounded, and where men and women assumed different roles and relationships towards each other and to Jewish communities. Food still lay at the heart of their culture, but it, like the culture itself, went through a process of renegotiation.

7

FOOD FIGHTS: IMMIGRANT JEWS
AND THE LURE OF AMERICA

In the world they left behind, the 2.5 million east European Jews who came to America considered themselves entitled to eat well. Judaism itself put food in the foreground, with its strict rules and commands to honor the holy days by eating well. If people had no food, as happened with frightening regularity, then the better-off Jews bore the responsibility of sharing something fine from their Sabbath and holiday tables with the hungry. But in daily life sharp differences divided the classes.

In America, however, once hungry Jews felt sufficiently empowered to challenge the idea that only the rich could eat well all the time. They strove vigorously to have good food regularly, and to feast as they wanted upon luxuries once associated with the sacred times. They saw the meals on their tables as America's gift and the fruit of their own aggressive efforts to get what they wanted.

The tastes and smells of their new home attracted and engaged them, offering them chances to try out novelties, some of which challenged traditional boundaries. Yet east European Jews in America also retained a commitment to foods emblematic of their culture. Certain foods anchored them to the past and tradition. They celebrated those foods and waxed eloquent about their sensory satisfaction, even while pursuing novelty.

That pursuit shook up community stability. American realities shattered the orderliness of east European Jewish consumption, which was based on a relatively broad consensus over *kashrut*. Most Jews observed the laws, and Jewish foodways before migration separated Jews from non-Jews. America challenged that basic way of life.

Minnie Fisher, born in a "very remote town" in the province of Minsk, White Russia, arrived in New York on the eve of World War I as a teenager. Her new life in America allowed her to embrace American choices.

> We got together a few youngsters and made a club, called the Yiddishe Yugend [the Jewish youth] where we discussed the problems of the world . . . I started going to the Yiddish theatre and saw that the theatre reflected the life of our people, which inspired us to write and put on our own little plays . . . We started to go every Saturday to different theatres, first to the Yiddish theatre, and then we learned to go to the English-speaking theatre.

Her group affiliated with a satirical publication, *Kundes*, and congregated in its East Broadway offices. "The editor's sister ran a restaurant nearby where everybody came because it was homemade cooking and because of the atmosphere." By the 1920s Fisher attended the Yiddishe Arbeiten Universitett, the Jewish Workers University, sponsored by the left-wing International Workers Order. Working as a milliner, she lived in "what today you would call a students' commune." She married a classmate, and they decided to "start out across the country, hitchhiking." In their year on the road, they saw America, "so vast and beautiful, and the contact with the people . . . so stimulating." Amidst all this heady novelty, she also recalled traditional practice: "we still lived under the respect of the family: Friday night was the big dinner. Where it came to your home life, life went on as if it were a continuation of the European experience."[1]

Her recollections reflected much of the east European Jewish immigrant encounter with food in America. The East Broadway restaurant associated with *Kundes* constituted a small part of a highly elaborate, vast public world of Jewish food. Even if it served "homemade cooking," it was divorced from home and family, free from restraints. Indeed, Fisher did not think to mention if its food was kosher. It defied real home cooking as experienced once a week in the "big" dinner of the Sabbath.

Access to food outside the family broadened preferences, raised standards, and complicated the meaning of food to people who had once lived with hunger. It confirmed their sense of entitlement to good and plentiful food. By eating foods once the reserve of the Jewish upper classes, they engaged in an act of class reversal. The formerly poor started to eat *blintzes, kreplach, kasha-varnitchkes, strudel*, noodles, *knishes*, and, most importantly, meat every day. Their once meager cabbage or beet *borschts* now glistened with fat pieces of meat.

By eating food once reserved for Sabbath or holidays every day, they also reversed their relationship to time. Marcus Ravage came from Rumania to New York in 1900 to join relatives. He was stunned at his first American meal, which included "Cake for breakfast! If I had been offered swan's eggs or steak or broiled pigeons . . . I should have kept my self-possession. But the very idea of serving cake for breakfast struck me as an extravagant fancy." Even more discordant, "In New York, every night was Friday night and every day was Saturday, as far as food went. . . . Why, they even had twists instead of plain rye bread, to say nothing of rice-and-raisins (which is properly a Purim dish) and liver paste and black radishes," anytime and every time.[2]

Except for a small and mostly unheeded handful of traditionalists who lamented the embrace of America, a "treyf" land, most greeted American possibilities as positive.[3] Few questioned the beneficent outcome of the migration. They viewed America as eastern Europe's antithesis and saw their old world as limited, narrow, a modern-day Egypt, shaped by persecution and scarcity. America meant freedom and food. Whatever their politics in their new home, their unalloyed celebration of its opportunities transcended political ideology. In their embrace of this new promised land, few swerved in their self-identification as Jews. Many renegotiated details of Jewish religious practice, but few questioned their basic identity.

Food in America opened up new forms of consumption for immigrant Jews. The ability to purchase meat and other luxury items for everyday enjoyment escalated expectations. They had felt entitled to eat well before migration, but the realities of scarcity made that impossible. In America satisfaction lay within their means, and they challenged anyone who stood in their way.

No aspect of Jewish food in America proved as contentious as *kashrut*. What had functioned historically as a sacred system that held Jews together and separated them from non-Jews took a different turn in America. *Kashrut* became one of the most divisive issues in the American Jewish world, turning Jews against each other, sundering families, causing suspicion to fall on neighbors, and engendering an erosion of trust in institutions. *Kashrut* and its discontents in America complicated the class-based journey of the once hungry who came to a place where food happened to be abundant and inexpensive. While some immigrants emphatically rejected traditional food restrictions, adopting the anti-religious sentiment of left-wing politics, most Jews tried to live with the sacred system. A very small Orthodox group at the other extreme lamented the corrosiveness of *treyf* America. In sermons, editorials, pamphlets, and posters rabbis appealed to Jews to observe the dietary laws. To them, the decline in observance served as an ominous omen of the erosion of the boundaries between Jews and other Americans.

In part the problem of *kashrut* in America grew out of the basics of the political structure. The absence of state sanction for religious functionaries, along with a general commitment to *laissez-faire* economics, made communal supervision chaotic. The disinterest of the government, federal or state,[4] in the requirements of religious communities gave Jewish butchers, slaughterers, and other food purveyors a relatively free hand to sell whatever they wanted and call it "kosher."[5] This disorder caused a number of traditional New York congregations in 1887 to form the Association of American Orthodox Hebrew Congregations. The Association imported Rabbi Jacob Joseph from Vilna to be America's "Chief Rabbi." They expected him to supervise the morass of kosher slaughtering and the sale of kosher meat.[6] To pay his salary and that of the cadre of rabbis who came to form a *bet din* (religious court), Jacob Joseph added a half-cent tax on every kosher chicken. Chickens were tagged with a metal clip bearing witness to their ritual purity. Other rabbis protested. This system robbed them of their livelihood, as they too derived income from slaughtering and supervision.[7] Immigrant Jews reacted negatively to the new tax; it smacked to them of the hated *korobka* of eastern Europe.

Most, however, wanted to be Jewish and eat Jewish foods without too much fretting over the details. "If I had a kosher *shochet* [slaughterer]," lamented a woman who migrated from Russia to the small town of Elman, Wisconsin, in 1908, "I would keep kosher."[8] No *shochet* ever came to her town, yet she stayed on. Not prepared to opt for vegetarianism, she decided to eat ritually impure meat. But despite her consumption of "treyf" meat, she continued to define herself and her family as living a Jewish life. Kosher meat would have been nice, but it was not essential to her identity as a Jew.

On the whole, though, wherever the immigrant east European Jews settled, they tried to get kosher meat. They felt obligated to do so and went to considerable lengths to observe the law. Sol Bloom's family came in 1879 to New York from Szyrpcz, Poland and set out on a journey to California. Bloom remembered with pride that they would not eat in any gentile establishment, and on the transcontinental train his mother cooked their food on a pot-bellied stove. Until he was twelve or thirteen, he boasted, he had never eaten even "a mouthful of food that was not kosher."[9]

In small towns, the hinterlands to larger Jewish communities, kosher meat came by horse and wagon and later by train.[10] In Stamford, Connecticut, no *shochet* had yet arrived in the late 1880s, so the town's Jews brought kosher meat and bread back with them from New York or Port Chester. If no one was making the trip to these better stocked communities, Stamford Jews would hire a courier.[11] Rose Engel lived in Pewaukee, Wisconsin, having come from Hungary in the early twentieth century. Kosher meat came to Pewaukee on the train from Milwaukee, and as a young girl she had the job of waiting at the depot to unload the meat for the handful of Jews who lived in this satellite community.[12] Small-town congregations even advertised in Jewish newspapers to secure the services of a *shochet* so as to not have to depend on their big-city co-religionists.[13]

But for all the efforts of individual Jews and their communities to "keep kosher," *kashrut* divided rather than united them. Standards of observance splintered families, particularly when it came to deciding where to live. In 1908 Joseph Orenstein, a Galician immigrant, left New York City to try farming in Ohio. He hired on with local farm families, who fed him "beef and chicken, five different cooked vegetables, a tossed salad, four kinds of preserves, home-made butter, and cucumber relish." Orenstein liked this life. Over time he bought his own farm, went back to Galicia to marry his longtime sweetheart, and brought her to America to become a farmer's wife. Therein ensued years of conflict between Bertha and Joe. He loved farming and the rural life, and did not care if they ate kosher food. "'Yossel, I love you,'" their son remembered was his mother's constant refrain, "'but I can't live like this. I just can't do it. There isn't even a bit of Kosher food. I want to go live in the city.'" The family moved between the farm and the city, where Bertha could get her ritually approved foods and serve "chopped liver, stuffed neck, boiled sides of beef, strudel and sweet wine."[14]

In most places Jews could get kosher meat. But wherever they did, fights of one kind or another arose. Writing in 1938, Maurice Karpf, a Jewish communal worker, expressed the hope that the Jewish community councils sprouting up across America would bring some order to the kosher meat industry.[15] *Kashrut* spawned communal chaos. In Brownsville kosher meat wars raged in 1894. Street fights broke out, crowds thronged, and one local rabbi, Rabbi Wisinetzky, was even attacked. A mob turned over his buggy and beat him up because of his support for those butchers and *shochtim* whom the rioters opposed.[16] A 1915 study issued by New York's *Kehillah* claimed that only 40 percent of the butchers purporting to sell kosher meat actually did so.[17]

Small towns had their own *kashrut* battles. The Jewish community of Beaver Falls, Pennsylvania, split down the middle over the matter of a butcher, the calf he slaughtered, and his standards of *kashrut*. So intense was the fracas that a rabbinical court from Pittsburgh had to come in to adjudicate, although hard feelings lingered and the community remained split.[18] In Madison, Wisconsin, in the 1920s, two kosher butchers, Shapiro and Morgenstein, "fought constantly" over customers.[19] The community lined up behind one or the other. Even efforts at communal good will were complicated by suspicions over standards of observance. Jews in Rochester, New York, maintained two Jewish orphanages, the Hebrew Children's Home and the Hebrew Sheltering and Guardian Society. Rochester did not have an enormous number of dependent Jewish children, but "slight differences about the critical matter of *kashrut*" divided charitable efforts.[20]

Individuals working in Jewish institutions had to be vigilant about what they ate in public and who saw them. In 1895 a scandal erupted at the Jewish Theological Seminary when its Rabbinical Preceptor Joshua Joffee was temporarily removed from his job. Someone accused him of entering a non-kosher restaurant, and he had to defend himself against such "medieval" charges.[21]

Not only did maintaining dietary laws prove to be a problem for immigrant Jews in their homes and institutions, but many of their children felt constrained by these rules. As Jews increasingly encountered the American mainstream, they sensed keenly the difference between what they could eat and what was on the American table. Immigrants' children who aspired to move from the Jewish working class into the American middle class had to make decisions about what to eat relatively early on in their American lives. Schools obviously provided one place where food challenged integration.

Here they often experienced their first confrontations with the forbidden and the social discomfort of food. One young woman remembered her acute awkwardness of having to eat *matzah* in school during Passover, while her non-Jewish classmates ate bread. "Zoln zey zikh oyshtekhen di oygn (let them stare their eyes out)," her father cursed, when she complained about the taunts she endured in her Farmingdale, New Jersey, public school of the early 1930s. "I did not like eating matzos so publicly because I felt it reminded the other children, who might otherwise have forgotten, that I was Jewish. And it reminded me too."[22] Abraham Alderman's parents immigrated from Russia sometime in the early twentieth century and settled in New Haven, Connecticut. He attended Yale University while living at home. Once during his college years Abraham (class of 1923) accepted an invitation to dine at a professor's home. The formality of the dinner made him uncomfortable. He had no idea what foods would be served and whether he could, or should, eat them. What would happen if he refused pork or shellfish? After the horror of the meal, he breathed a sigh of relief, hoping never to get such an invitation again.[23]

Rabbi Mordecai Kaplan, the founder of the Reconstructionist movement, understood the conflict between "fitting in" and observance. In calling for a new articulation of Judaism in the 1920s and 1930s, he warned that "To demand a scrupulous observance of the Dietary Laws is to place a handicap upon pioneer efforts on the part of the Jew who wants to remain loyal to his faith."[24] To a congregant in 1922 he confessed that he had a hard time defending *kashrut*'s strict practice in light of American realities. He predicted that "sooner or later Judaism will have to get along without dietary laws."[25]

America weighed heavily with the newcomers, as they sought entry into its mainstream. They did not found parochial schools, and many daughters and sons of immigrants started going to college. As outwardly and upwardly mobile new Americans, the masses of Jews had in mind two potentially irreconcilable goals. They wanted to have broad access to all the good stuff America had to offer and still be good Jews.

Most looked for ways to do both. They divided the world in half: keeping a kosher home, but eating non-kosher food in restaurants. Rather than strictly adhering to law, they opted for Jewish tastes and flavors, creating a food system which they called "kosher style."[26] Chicago's Jews, who by the 1920s had left the area of first settlement, offered a case in point.

> The latest avenue of escape from the ghetto is represented by the rapid influx of Jews into the apartments and residential hotels of the city, particularly of Hyde Park and the North Shore. So popular have these hotels become with the Jewish population that a "Jewish Hotel Row," as it is called by the real estate men of the district, is rapidly springing up. Many of these hotels, while not advertising Kosher food, are nevertheless catering to the traditional tastes of the Jews.[27]

The Jewishness of style reminded these Chicagoans of who they were, and that counted more than *Halachah*.

They did not see their desire to become Americans, send their children to American public schools, enjoy American popular culture, celebrate its basic values, venerate its heroes, and sample its foods as antithetical to being Jewish. They wanted to have and be both. The dream of America, in contrast to the nightmare of east European hunger, resonated in personal experiences. A woman who immigrated to Pittsburgh remembered, "It was lovely here—so much food. Plenty to eat."[28] Harry Roskolenko's parents received a letter in the early part of the century from Russia. "It's from Gidalya," his father announced. "He wants to come to America. He has four sons and a wife and they are hungry."[29]

Almost everything about Jewish foodways changed in America. Domestic technology such as running water and gas improved the Jewish immigrants' standard of living and eased women's burdens. "One of the greatest conveniences," Morris Raphael Cohen wrote, "which made life simpler for my mother in this country was the availability of gas for lighting and especially for cooking. . . . Just by lighting a match the business of cooking could be quickly achieved."[30] Immigrant Jewish women in America expressed no longing for the conviviality of the town well, nor did they miss carrying their Sabbath *tcholent* to communal ovens.[31]

More Jews ate more good food than ever before. Even as relatively poor laborers, they ate well.[32] Although many immigrant families endured poverty, few among the industrial laborers and those who eked out a living as junk dealers, grocers, and peddlers suffered systemic hunger. In Roskolenko's working-class family—his father labored as a presser in a garment shop, his mother, who had lost an arm in an accident, operated a newspaper stand—lived a life in which "the thick meat borscht was always on tap."[33] In the immigrants' new surroundings food scarcities were temporary aberrations, not lifelong grinding realities.[34]

Samuel Golden, a child of the immigration, recalled how the family table, which almost always displayed hearty meals, responded to economic swings. At "periodic unemployment seasons, during which my father earned no money . . . slowly but surely the food we ate underwent a complete change. Tastier dishes disappeared and the menu eventually consisted almost entirely of bread, butter, herring and potatoes," somewhat better than the ubiquitous and omnipresent menu of poor Jews in eastern Europe. But "The happiness of my childhood was hardly affected by this change . . . because there were many religious holidays which mother celebrated by doing all kinds of extra baking and cooking of special holiday foods, like *taglach* [sweet pieces of dough]." The family rarely went without meat and other foods of the American standard.[35]

They struggled to get this good food. Relatively poor Jews strategized to eat well on limited budgets. Taking in boarders helped cut down the cost of housing so that they did not have to skimp on food. Women developed elaborate marketing rituals, hunting for ends, seconds, throwaways, foods of a slightly lesser quality. Emma Beckerman's mother came to New York in 1904 from Galicia. During hard times she "scoured the neighborhood for day-old bread; fish was bought at closing time, when it was almost give-away; liver and lungs, cheapest of meats, were chopped, sauteed, pot-roasted, broiled or fried." Jewish women's constant haggling with merchants got them more food at lower prices.[36]

Yet immigrant Jews also experienced situations in which they needed food relief. Some among them—orphans and other children in distress in particular—needed assistance.[37] Constant cycles of expansion and con-

17. The obligation of Jews to feed each other continued in the United States. Newly arrived immigrants Jews who landed in Boston in 1921 sat down to a Passover seder, followed by a lavish meal provided by Boston Jewish charities.

traction of the American economy also took a toll. Workers in the garment trade, which employed so many, repeatedly rolled from one slack season to the next. When factories closed, Jewish neighborhood merchants also suffered.

Jewish immigrants arriving after the 1870s entered into a well-structured and complex universe of Jewish philanthropy set up to cushion distress. Middle-class Jews with longer roots in America helped newcomers who could not feed themselves. In 1895, at the height of the migration, more affluent Jewish women from Congregation Keneseth Israel in Philadelphia created a kosher soup kitchen in "the southern section of the city, for the benefit principally of the poor Jewish residents."[38] The Hebrew Immigrant Aid Society, HIAS, worked out an arrangement with officials at Ellis Island to provide kosher food for Jewish detainees.[39] In Milwaukee, as in every sizable Jewish community, the Federated Jewish Charities reported yearly on how much food, particularly milk, eggs, and butter, organizations such as the Ladies Benevolent Society gave to Jews in need. The Society set up special milk stations for poor Jewish children and maintained a *Hachnosas Orchim*, or "Jewish Shelter House," which in 1919 provided "3 to 4 days food at an expense of about $1,000" to transient Jews. The Milwaukee branch of the National Council of Jewish Women, through the Federated Jewish Charities, employed a full-time Nutrition Worker to focus on children's food needs. The community sponsored a summer camp, and while the youngsters may have thought only of playing in the fresh air, the sponsoring organization considered it "essentially a nutritional camp." In 1923 the directors beamed with pride, claiming that they were "coming a little nearer to our goal" of universal weight gain.[40]

Aid did not just emanate from the top down. Immigrant Jewish workers and small shopkeepers helped those who had less. May Weisser Hartman, the daughter of Bessarabian immigrants, was born in New York in 1900. Although of quite humble means, her family along with their *landsleit* (townspeople) formed the Bessarabian Verband Association, a *landsmanshaft* (hometown society). In 1914 it sponsored the Hebrew National Orphan Home for boys. The Home began small, admitting at first "four pitiful little brothers, parentless and neglected, who were brought in by a very sick grandmother." In the early years of the home the women of the *landsmanshaft* "took turns looking after the children. Each day one would bring in the meals prepared in her own kitchen. Another stayed with the children during the day, until another relieved her in the evening."[41]

Those who had food shared with those who did not. A woman who grew up in the immigrant Jewish community of Rochester, New York, recalled her grandmother:

a true old time Jewish woman with a great heart . . . she made it a project during the depression years to make baskets in her home, *erev shabbes* [before the Sabbath]. She would call Alfred Hart [a local merchant] and ask him for all of his seconds on Thursday. . . . She made these packages for all the people. She made it a personal project to find out where all the people were who had no food . . . She would never tell us the names of the people.[42]

Despite formal and informal assistance, however, some immigrant Jews went hungry. The imaginative literature of the era told of struggles to put bread on the table. In the writings of Morris Rosenfeld, the laureate of the "sweatshop poets," fear of hunger and deprivation stalked the workers who slaved for a living:

> Tears that are seething,
> Soak into my thin little banquet of bread—
> I choke on the food—I cannot swallow a morsel.[43]

In one of his "Among the Pushcarts" sketches, he described a "pale young man, poorly dressed and poorly shod, his total appearance revealed a 'slack' worker or a striker, he goes around, perhaps, without having eaten." The hungry worker peered at pushcarts laden with food, "bagels . . . fruit,"[44] and in the name of his fellow sweatshop workers, the poet declared:

> And if it's a grand celebration, a ball,
> Where all are invited as brothers,
> Then I too, should sit in the banqueting-hall—
> My portion as large as the others'.
> I, too, am well able to eat what is good;
> A choice bit of meat gives me pleasure;
> The blood in my veins is as red as the blood
> Of those who are swollen with treasure.[45]

Another poem, published in the 1930s in the children's magazine *Kinder Zhurnal*, pointed out to young readers the inequities in food distribution. The poet, F. B. Ravitzky, constructed an imaginary dialogue between "Der Marantz un die Kartoffel," the orange and the potato:

> An orange,
> With a red smoothness,
> Said to the potato:
> —"You are dirty, you are low,
> Poor people eat you.
> I am beautiful,
> Sparkling, clean.

I am brought from far away.
There is no chance,
That just anyone can have pleasure from me."
The potato answered:
"Actually the truth is,
I feed the hungry, and the satisfied."[46]

Most immigrant Jews in America expected to eat both exotic oranges and prosaic potatoes. Most rejected the idea that back home foods tasted better and were more authentic. They expressed little emotional longing either for the old tastes and smells or for back home altogether. Occasional exceptions cropped up. One of the most popular Yiddish songs written in America, Aaron Lebedeff's "Rumania, Rumania" from the mid-1920s, was a musical panegyric to a land "so sweet and so nice . . . a land so sweet and so fine." The song went on:

To live there was a pleasure,
Whatever the heart wanted, it could get.
A *mamelige* [polenta],
A *karnatsele* [a spicy sausage] and a glass of wine.
In Rumania it is good,
One knows of no worries, sorrows.
They drink wine there everywhere,
Eating a *kashtaval* [a Rumanian cheese] with it.[47]

Other bits of food nostalgia surfaced occasionally. The grandmother of Yiddish actress Molly Picon came from the Russian town of Rezshishtchov to Philadelphia in 1880. As her granddaughter remembered it, every time someone complimented the old woman on the bounty of her Sabbath table, she retorted, "'You think this is nice?' And off my grandmother would sail on a sea of recollections. 'If you think this is nice, you should have seen the meals we used to prepare in Rezshishtchov. . . .' Every time my grandmother remembered how it used to be, the meals seemed to get better."[48] A 1939 Yiddish film, *A Brivele der Mamen*, depicted a HIAS aid worker eating a meal in eastern Europe and commenting on how long it had been since he had tasted such "emesdike" (real) food. The *borscht* in the film tasted better in its authentic setting.[49]

Yet these were minor exceptions. The lyrics of "Rumania, Rumania" ought not be taken as a genuine ode to that country's cuisine. Few Jews who emigrated from Rumania went back. Lebedeff himself, born in Homel, White Russia, never lived in Rumania. He also churned out other catchy songs like "Mottke from Slobodke," "Gibe Mir Bessarabia," "Slutzk, My Shtetele," "A Wedding in Odessa," "Galitzye," about places to which his listeners had no desire to return. *Mamelige, karnatsele*, and *kashtaval* played no role in the formation of an American Jewish food system. Jewish audiences may have loved the song for its humor, its tongue-twisting lyrics, its fusion of food and sex, and its jangly rhythm, but Rumanian foods did not tempt them (except for pastrami).

The lack of nostalgia for old country foods among east European Jews grew out of the fundamental character of migration. The immigrants intended to stay.[50] Women and men migrated in equal number. In some families husbands arrived first, paving the way for wives to join them once they had saved enough money. Fathers brought their older children with them, daughters as well as sons. The presence of women in large numbers, relatively early on, meant that the families' cooks could be counted upon to prepare customary foods and keep familiar foodways in place. The age structure of Jewish migration also fostered this continuity. Although typically east European Jewish immigrants, like most others, were young adults able to work, children and older people constituted a sizable minority, about one quarter. Both groups influenced the immigrant Jewish negotiation with food in America.

The older immigrants served as repositories of Jewish knowledge, skills, and standards. Older women cooked and baked familiar foods. As their age took them out of the work force, it doubtless also rendered them less flexible and less willing to experiment in the kitchen. They harbored set ideas about consumption. A 1905 commentator on Jewish life in Philadelphia made this point: "The old mother immediately [upon arriving in America] assumes the duties of the household. Glad as they are of the fine appearance of their children . . . they cannot suppress a sigh at beholding their shaved chins or at seeing them eat their breakfast without having put on their phylacteries, prayed, washed their hands and pronounced the blessing before and after the meal."[51]

The immigrants and their children told the same story. Rita Seitzer arrived in America in 1921 at age nineteen. She admitted that "It took a little time to get used to it [America] . . . I started night school to learn English . . . I was determined to learn English." Not so her mother. "My mother did not learn English. She never adjusted. She was an old-fashioned woman . . . She just remained the same as she was. She practiced her religion. She just stayed with us and did the cooking . . . It used to be she'd use two kinds of dishes. We were supposed to use kosher meat . . . It hurt her to see her children not to observe the old ways, but she never said anything. I know she was hurt."[52]

Daughters of "old mothers" rarely recalled either learning to cook or being forced to help in the kitchen. They complained mightily about endless hours of cleaning, tending smaller children, doing laundry, working in a family store. But cooking they rarely mentioned. They cooked during crises, but not routinely. Their failure to cite cooking or learning to cook under their mothers' tutelage reflected the realities of the young women's working lives, their pursuit of education and leisure, and their mothers' intentions of holding on to power through the kitchen. Mothers also had aspirations for their daughters which did not center on futures in front of the stove.[53]

Immigrant children, those below age fourteen, also affected American Jewish foodways. The presence of youngsters may have nudged mothers and grandmothers toward conservatism. The older women, guardians of Jewish culture, used food to connect Americanizing children to the world of tradition. The women knew that food was fundamental to their way of life and that children would absorb its tastes and smells at an early age. Older women cooked to sustain that life and to pass it on.

Immigrant parents invested in their children the aspirations and anxieties surrounding the move to America. Born in 1907 in New York, Harry Roskolenko stated this boldly, pointing out that his mother had given birth to eight children in the Ukraine, all of whom died in infancy. She gave birth to six children in America, all of whom lived. "We, Americans all, were tougher, burlier, hardier, and better fed." As Americans, "we had," he recalled, "more possibilities if less God; though my father tried to give us both with the bread my mother baked, the wine he made."[54]

Children described with warm details how parents, mothers and fathers, made sure that children got the best and the most food. Rose

Cohen worked with her father in a shop. He went out of his way to feed her. "Father," she lovingly recalled, "made the life as easy as he could. . . . Father used to buy me an apple and a sweetened roll" from the peddler who went from sweatshop to sweatshop selling food. "At noon we had our big meal. Then father would send me out for a half pound of steak or a slice of beef liver and a pint of beer which he sometimes bought in part-nership with two or three other men. He used to broil the steak in the open coal fireplaces where the presser heated his irons and cut it into tiny squares. He always picked out the juiciest bits and pushed them to my side of the plate."[55]

Alfred Kazin offered a vivid picture of the parent-child encounter and "the veneration of food in Brownsville families" in the 1920s:

> I can still see the kids pinned down to the tenement stoops, their feet helplessly kicking at the pots and pans lined up before them, their mouths pressed open with a spoon while the great meals are rammed down their throats. *Eat! Eat! May you be destroyed if you don't eat! What sin have I committed that God should punish me with you! Eat! What will become of you if you don't eat! Imp of darkness, may you sink ten fathoms into the earth if you don't eat! Eat!* We never had a chance to know what hunger meant. At home we nibbled all day long as a matter of course.[56]

The obsession with children's consumption, the belief that food in-dicated love and ensured health, grew out of the immigrants' pre-migration encounter with hunger and America's possibilities. Harry Golden, a child of immigrants from eastern Europe, grew up in lower Manhattan in the early twentieth century. His childhood food experi-ences emerged as a constant theme in his later humorous journalism.[57] He mocked in retrospect his parents' food anxieties and their desire that he eat a lot.

> The first words a Jewish child heard were, "*Ess, ess mein Kindst* [Eat, eat, my child]." A fifteen-year-old boy already weighing one hun-dred and forty-five pounds was an object of concern to his mother if he dawdled over his supper. "Look at him, nothing but skin and bones," said Mama, near tears. . . . And, when you went off on a

week's vacation, the first question everybody asked you when you returned was, "How much weight did you gain?" I was a fat kid myself and I remember my mother saying, "In America the fat man is the boss and the skinny man is the bookkeeper."[58]

Sara Sandberg's mother, a successful furrier from eastern Europe, believed, as did "most Jewish mothers of that time [that] no tragedy was so great as having a 'child who wouldn't eat.'" The Sandbergs' servants did the cooking, while their employers attended charity dinners to support Jewish philanthropies. When Sara would not eat, her mother wept bitterly, "'What did I ever do,' Mother would appeal to heaven, 'to be tortured like this!' She would stagger away. 'I can't bear to watch.'"[59]

Immigrant parents and their children blended the familiar with the new, the eastern European Jewish and the American. They continued to eat certain familiar foods of pre-migration Europe and still talked about herring, dark bread, *borscht, gefillte* fish, *tzimmes,* and *kugel.* The first three, along with potatoes and cabbage, they ate pretty much all the time in America. But increasingly dark bread was pushed aside in favor of white and rye. Furthermore, evening meals began to consist of meat stews, meatloaf, and meat soups, along with the old familiar dishes. Jewish consumers did not so much reject older foods as make them secondary to newer, decidedly richer ones.

Although they no longer ate meat only on Sabbath, they did differentiate between the "seventh day and the six days of labor." Friday night meals still stood out for their exuberant bounty. Valorizing the Sabbath and its foods reflected not only the importance of marking Jewish sacred time, but also represented an accommodation to economic realities. The majority of Jews made a living in small businesses, and commonly, Jewish families lived above, behind, or near their stores. They maintained little separation between work and family, and weekday cooking and meals happened haphazardly, according to the rhythms of the store. In Mary Antin's childhood years in Boston, her mother tended the store and cooked the family's food at one and the same time. "In the intervals of slack trade, she did her cooking. . . . Arlington Street customers were used to waiting while the storekeeper salted the soup or rescued a loaf from the oven."[60] The business of business and the business of family food had to accommodate each other.

But on Friday night families and guests sat down to large and sumptuous meals on the best dishes. Those American Sabbath meals differed from east European ones in the amounts of food available and the relative lack of struggle by which the bounty came to them. Golda Meir's family, for example, came from Kiev to Milwaukee in the early twentieth century. The young girl who would become Prime Minister of Israel recalled that her shopkeeper mother

> was forever cooking and baking. . . . She was a very good cook. . . . On Friday evenings, when we sat down for the Sabbath meal— chicken soup, gefilte fish, and meat braised with potatoes and onion, with a carrot-and-prune tzimmes on the side—in addition to father, Clara, and me, there would almost always be guests from out of town. . . . When I try to remember her at this period, I hear the sound of her laughter in the kitchen as she fried onions, peeled carrots and chopped fish for Friday night.[61]

Alfred Kazin's *Walker in the City* stands out as the most eloquent autobiography of an American child of east European Jewish immigrants. His Sabbath recollections took place in "the kitchen," the title of an entire chapter in a book of four. Sensual recollections of holy time came from food. When he returned home from school on Friday afternoons, his nose took in with delight "the warm odor of a coffee cake baking in the oven." Everything scrubbed and shining in his working-class home served as a backdrop for

> the long white tablecloth . . . the "company" dishes, filled for some with *gefillte* fish on lettuce leaves, ringed by red horseradish, sour and half-sour pickles, tomato salad with a light vinegar dressing; for others, with chopped liver in a bed of lettuce leaves and white radishes; the long white *khalleh*, the Sabbath loaf; chicken soup with noodles *and* dumplings; chicken, meat loaf, prune and sweet potatoes that had been baked all day into an open pie; compote of prunes and quince, apricots and orange rind; applesauce; a great brown nut cake filled with almonds, the traditional *lekakh;* all surrounded by glasses of port wine, seltzer bottles with their nozzles staring down at us . . . a samovar of Russian tea, *svetouchnee* from the little red box.[62]

Sophie Turpin's family made a migration decision decidedly different from that of the Kazin family, who like the majority of Jews chose New York, or the Mabeson family [Meir's maiden name], who settled in another large Jewish community. They headed in 1904 for North Dakota, to join the minuscule world of Jewish farmers on the western prairies. There Friday night meant potato *kugel,* "made from fresh potatoes, onion, eggs, a little flour, and baked with plenty of goose fat." Having no access to fresh fish other than herring, they could not eat *gefillte* fish. One Jewish neighbor "had attempted to make something like it with the white breast of chicken but it tasted nothing like it should have," and as "*gefillte* fish cannot be compared to any other dish, and it can only be made with fresh fish," they gave up. The Turpins put the herring on the table, since they believed that Sabbath dinner required fish; they set the table with "a white linen tablecloth," and more often than not a Jewish peddler shared their Sabbath meal.[63]

Communal biographies, the histories of Jewish enclaves across America resounded with details of immigrant women and men preparing Sabbath foods. "Thursday" in the Chicago ghetto, wrote Louis Wirth, "is 'chicken day,' when the Jewish customers lay in their supplies for the Friday evening meal. . . . Thursday is also 'fish day' on Maxwell Street," the ghetto's marketing hub. "The turnover of some these street-stands and stores is enormous." Chicago's immigrant Jewish housewives patronized the many "basement fish stores to gratify the tastes of the connoisseur with a variety of herrings, pike, and carp, which Jewish housewives purchase . . . in order to serve the famous national dish of *gefillte* fish at the sumptuous Friday evening meal." They scoured the neighborhood's "Kosher bake-shops with rye bread, poppy seed bread, and pumpernickel daily, and a kind of doughnut known as *beigel* for Shabboth."[64]

Sabbath was the high point of the Jewish food week in Europe and America. But in America the Jewish marketplace throbbed with abundance all week long. Those markets functioned as the spines of the Jewish communities. Jews lived primarily where they could buy Jewish food.[65] Residential choices and culinary choices coincided. Anything else, clothing, furniture, paper, pens, needles, thread, crockery, they could buy elsewhere. Food for home they bought in their own neighborhoods. Grocery stores, fish markets, bakeries, butcher shops, restaurants, cafes,

18. The buying and selling of food at open air markets characterized the street culture of immigrant Jewish enclaves. The buyers here evaluated the fish available at the stands underneath the Williamsburg Bridge in New York City. What they bought would likely make its way onto their Sabbath tables in the form of *gefillte* fish.

and cafeterias in the larger cities, delicatessens in even smaller ones, defined Jewish urban space.[66] So for immigrant Jewish merchants the food business offered an obvious occupational choice. One memoirist described how when her grandfather "came to America, he couldn't speak a word of English, naturally. So the brothers-in-law, his wife's brothers, opened a grocery for them in a Jewish neighborhood."[67]

So complex and large had Jewish food marketing become by the late nineteenth century that it supported Yiddish-language food trade publications, such as *Der Groceryman, Die Shpize Tzytung, Der Yiddisher Retail Shpize Hendler, Die Grocer's Shtimme*, and so on. By 1936 dozens of such publications had seen the light of day.[68] Selling Jewish food provided the foundation for Jewish communal life no matter the size of the community. In the small Jewish world of Johnstown, Pennsylvania, most east European immigrant Jews made a living selling merchandise to Slavic steelworkers and coal miners. Even here, Jewish food selling and Jewish community formation went together. Johnstown's first rabbi functioned as its first *shochet*, and its one Jewish food emporium, the kosher butcher shop, opened in 1903 next to the railroad station. It "served as a referral service for passengers just off the train. If they were transient, travel assistance was provided by women of the *Hakhnoses Orkhim*," the traditional Jewish traveler's aid society.[69]

New York obviously stood in a category of its own in terms of size. It supported a dazzling array of Jewish food stores. An 1899 survey of the city's Eighth Assembly District, which encompassed much of the Jewish immigrant enclave, enumerated 631 foodmongers that

> catered to the needs of the inhabitants of this area. Most numerous were the 140 groceries which often sold fruits, vegetables, bread and rolls as well as the usual provisions. Second in number were the 131 butcher shops which proclaimed their wares in Hebrew characters. The other food vendors included: 36 bakeries, 9 bread stands, 14 butter and egg stores, 3 cigarette shops, 7 combination two-cent coffee shops, 10 delicatessens, 9 fish stores, 7 fruit stores, 21 fruit stands, 3 grocery stands, 7 herring stands, 2 meat markets, 16 milk stores, 2 matzo . . . stores, 10 sausage stores, 20 soda water stands, 5 tea shops . . . 11 vegetable stores, 13 wine shops, 15 grape wine shops, and 10 confectioners.[70]

Those who lived there and wrote about the neighborhood described its food culture as ubiquitous. The New York Jewish "ghetto" of the early twentieth century was the site of "flamboyant displays" of food, where "the bakeries, with their pushcart adjuncts, sold the various breads of the world. Russian, Polish, Hungarian, Austrian, German—all heavy, all good, all the breads with or without every variation of *kiml*, or caraway seed, were there. None of the breads had paper wrappings because nothing came that way then; and one had to touch and smell the bread before it was shoved into the great shopping bags that all mothers carried." Orchard Street was "devoted to the enormous barrels of brine containing herring from every part of the world . . . You came by holding your mother's hand or her big shopping bag. . . . The bag was cavernous, capable of containing fifty pounds of herring, potatoes, huge amounts of black bread, smoked fish, red cabbage for the borscht."

The New York world of Jewish food allowed individuals to eat away from family as well. Cafes and restaurants, "coffee and cake parlors," dotted the neighborhood. "Cafes and saloons opened early and closed late. Many sold food—bean soup, borscht, cold fish, Russian dishes, Jewish dishes, and something pronounced *samitch* [obviously, sandwich]." The cafes "were named after their European cities, villages, streets and towns. There was, I recall, the Odessa Café on East Broadway, a few thousand miles from its original geography. Others were called Krakow, Moscow, Kiev, Lublin, and Warsaw." One of the neighborhood's children recalled that on Second Avenue there "bloomed on every corner . . . a Yiddish theater, a café, a cuisine that was intellectual as *tsimes*."[71]

In *every* Jewish enclave in every American city food drew Jewish men and women to the streets. In the immigrant and first American-born generations, Jews lived in relatively compact Jewish neighborhoods. The provision of food to Jews by Jews enhanced the sense of community.

Immigrant Jewish food culture also played itself out in organizational life. Benevolent societies, lodges, and family clubs served a range of social purposes. Eating together was one. Commensality functioned alongside camaraderie. Bernard Horwich belonged to the Golden Eagle Lodge of the Somech Noflim (assisting those who have fallen) Society in Chicago in the 1890s. An organization of east European immigrants of various national backgrounds, the lodge gave members a chance to "become acquainted with one another . . . always speak their minds, no matter how poor their English." It provided medical care in times of illness, death benefits, and burial. Food events punctuated its annual calendar. Dinners and picnics helped create fellowship, and lodge brothers took very seriously the details of organizing food events. They debated intensely who should provide which items for upcoming feasts and boasted about the gustatory success of previous food functions. One member claimed that the excellent "smoked beef for sandwiches" he brought had made the event successful. A second one took credit for getting a bargain price on "the pop"; yet another "peddled around among the bakers . . . procured almost all of the bread . . . without any cost."[72]

The richness of Sabbath meals, the dense connection between Jewish residence and food marketing, and the numerous communal events built around food anchored immigrants into a repertoire defined as Jewish. But continuity existed in new forms. Jews had many places within their reach, economically, geographically, and culturally, where they could eat. Ruth Katz, who came to Chicago in 1913 from Poland, worked as a sewing machine operator and boarded with a Jewish family. "I didn't cook," she remembered. "You could get for twenty cents a good dinner in a restaurant. So about three times a week I used to go out. The rest I used to buy smoked fish, cheese, cream, lox."[73]

The public and commercial nature of American Jewish eating represented a deep shift in the immigrants' lives. Inns had existed in eastern Europe, providing kosher food and lodging for travelers, but few memoirs mention eating at commercial establishments. In America's Jewish enclaves countless places mushroomed where Jews could eat away from family, or eat away from home with family members.[74] This magnified individuals' choices, exposed them to new styles of cooking, and challenged conventions about food consumption and preparation.

Restaurants, cafes, delicatessens, and summer resorts all attracted Jewish newcomers. May Weisser Hartman, a Lower East Side child, described in detail the neighborhood's restaurant landscape, waxing eloquent about Manny Wolf's, Jack Silverman's Old Roumanian, Burger's, Ratner's, Cafe Boulevard, Lorber's, Monopole, Cafe Royale, Moskowitz, Lupowitz, and Milgrim's as just a few of the popular spots of her childhood.[75] The first Jewish summer resort opened in 1899.[76] By the 1930s candy stores with soda fountains flourished in elaborate profusion in Jewish neighborhoods. All of them offered, for a relatively modest price, a chance to eat food unavailable at home.[77] Lillian Gorenstein remembered her first American dinner. "We all sat around the table on which were cakes that the guest brought and that Ma baked. Ma served tea, and the guests talked about America and how people lived in America. They described the restaurants, the chicken dinners, the theater, the artists."[78]

As of 1903, the word *oyesessen* (eating out) appeared in the *Jewish Daily Forward*, a newspaper famous for its English-Yiddish fusions and neologisms. *Oyesessen* "is spreading every day, especially in New York."[79] The newspaper considered the growing interest in eating outside the home a positive step in immigrants' education and part of a larger process of social evolution. Among the immigrants, "the restaurants [are] the latest response to the steadily growing social instinct and material development of the East Side." Contemporary observers chronicled the steady Jewish trajectory from home to "coffee and cake parlor" and finally to the restaurant.[80]

Just as surely as free public education and democracy, these eating places symbolized America's novelty. From the most prosaic to the gaudiest, the restaurants, clustering in New York between Houston Street and Delancey, blended the familiar with the new. These places for *oyesessen* served as nodes of recreation for local residents, as alternatives to eating at home, and as centers for Jewish employment. They also illustrated the intra-Jewish food exchange which took place in America. East European newcomers began to enjoy the cold cuts sold in the German Jewish delicatessens which dotted their neighborhoods. Corned beef, frankfurters, and salami quickly entered their food repertoire. Eddie Cantor, an orphan, was raised by his Russian-born grandmother in New York. He supplemented her meager earnings as a matchmaker by delivering packages for Isaac Gellis's kosher sausage factory on Essex Street. Gellis had immigrated from Berlin, where he got his start in manufacturing sausage and other cured meats typical of German Jewish cuisine.[81] By 1872 Gellis produced mountains of kosher sausages, frankfurters, and other cold cuts in New York, and sold them to Jewish consumers all over America. Cantor, whose family had come from Russia where such foods did not exist, became, as a result of working for Gellis, the self-proclaimed "world's supreme delicatessen eater, absorbing more salami, pastrami, bologna, and frankfurters in that short span than most families do in a lifetime."[82]

These items became standard fare for Jewish immigrants, and the delicatessens which sold them emerged as social centers in their neighborhoods. Although east European Jews had not eaten these foods before migration, as American Jews they learned to think of them as traditional.[83] In Alfred Kazin's Brownsville, neighborhood delicatessen food was "our greatest delight in all seasons . . . hot spiced corned beef, pastrami, rolled beef, hard salami, soft salami, chicken salami, bologna, frankfurter 'specials' and the thinner, wrinkled hot dogs always taken with mustard." The streetscape of his exclusively Jewish neighborhood was dominated by "the electric sign . . . lighting up the words Jewish

National Delicatessen, it was as if we had entered into our rightful heritage."[84]

This culinary exchange was fueled by residential patterns. East European immigrants moved into neighborhoods already inhabited by their co-religionists from Central Europe beginning in the 1870s and 1880s.[85] For decades their living space overlapped, and the delicatessens and other food markets of the earlier Jewish denizens attracted the newcomers. Cantor ate Gellis's prepared meats, and Sophie Ruskay, the child of Galician immigrants, recalled sitting on the stoop of her East Broadway apartment building with a friend, "munching with relish a sour vinegar pickle, purchased from the German delicatessen store around the corner."[86] The exchange also went the other way. In 1935 a German Jewish Reform congregation in Newark, New Jersey, Oheb Shalom, marked its 75th anniversary with an elegant meal. At the banquet the most celebratory of eastern European Jewish foods, *gefillte* fish, showed up on the menu, along with "Tongue, Sauce Polonaise."[87]

The larger the Jewish enclave, the more specialized the variations. In New York, the behemoth of communities, Galician, Hungarian, Polish, Russian, "Levantine," Lithuanian, German, and Rumanian Jews lived near each other. Each consumed its own foods. Marcus Ravage, proud of his Rumanian origins, recounted the triumph of "Little Rumania" over the other Jewish neighborhoods. It, he boasted, had produced "more restaurants than the Russian quarter . . . with . . . platters of liver paste, chopped eggplant, and other distinctive edibles in the windows. On Rivington Street and on Allen Street the Rumanian delicatessen-store was making its appearance, with its goose-pastrami and kegs of ripe olives and tubs of salted vine-leaves." Food and politics separated Rumanian Jews from all others. "Unlike the other groups of the Ghetto, the Rumanian is a *bon-vivant* and a pleasure-lover; therefore he did not long delay to establish the pastry-shop (while his Russian neighbor was establishing the lecture platform)."[88] By 1902 collectors of American Jewish statistics confirmed Ravage's boast, estimating that in New York Rumanians owned 150 restaurants, 200 wine cellars which all had lunch rooms, as well as 30 coffee shops.[89]

Other intra-Jewish ethnic rivalries manifested themselves in food. Alfred Kazin learned as a child that in every way Lithuanians trumped

Galicians, who "were coarse-grained, had no taste, took cream with herring, and pronounced certain words in so uncouth a manner that it made you ache with laughter just to hear them."[90] Such differences, however, made little impact on the creation of an east European American Jewish food culture. Jewish marriage patterns eroded the importance of European birth places. Although within their homes Friday night *gefillte* fish retained nationally specific styles, in public Jews sampled from a vast and rich cuisine.

Public sites for Jewish food consumption also shortened the distance between areas of first settlement and newer neighborhoods to which Jews moved in search of better housing. However far from the original places they settled, the Jewish marketplace of food drew them back. A writer in Los Angeles in the 1930s wrote about Boyle Heights, the old immigrant enclave: "[T]here are 'ritzy' cars from Beverly Hills . . . unloading Jews who wouldn't think of 'living in Boyle Heights,' but who are tied to the Ghetto by a bond that is stronger than race or religion—the mouth-watering desire for a good piece of Russian rye bread, a herring . . . and a lox sandwich. Gustatorial Jews coming back to give lip and tooth service to their own people."[91]

On the other coast the same food pilgrimages took place. A feature piece on the Jewish cabarets of New York's East Side in the *Jewish Daily Forward* of 1926 charted the way these tony restaurants served as magnets for newly minted "uptown" Jews:

Within a radius of a few blocks are Moskowitz's and Lupowitz's Roumanian Rathskeller, Kumonin's, Pearlman's Oriental, Phillip's Russian Bavaria. . . . Of course, Schwartz's "Little Hungary" on Houston Street . . . The food most frequently Roumanian cooking with steaks running high in favor. On Saturday and Sunday nights the automobiles of uptown guests line the curbs and their owners . . . beam in the warmth of familiar speech and countenance and gorge themselves on the delicacies with which no night club lobster *a la Newburg* can compare. . . . One can get jazz in any cabaret—but not with such food. A platter of bread anticipates the appetite, and abundant pickles, sour tomatoes and kraut. The waiters are . . . disdainful of finicky appetites. Eat and drink, and be merry, for tomorrow you're uptown again. Here a man may talk in Yiddish . . . and draw neither stares or sneers.[92]

Like restaurants, the constant dinners and banquets of Jewish societies, synagogues, and charitable and benevolent organizations blended new and old. As banquets played a key role in philanthropy, the quality of the food helped determine the success or failure of events. A good dinner, well-cooked, set amidst convivial company, enhanced fundraising. Menus generally steered a middle course between novelty and comfort. The banquet of the Nikolaever *landsmanshaft* in Chicago included at its 1937 event a variety of new foods, including "Fruit Cocktail, with Celery and Olives," as well as pineapple and lettuce, mashed potatoes, dill pickles, and orange ices for dessert, and to drink, "pop" and ginger ale. But chicken soup with "mandel and farfel," *gefillte* fish, and strudel anchored the meal to tradition. Roast chicken, the main course, bridged the two zones.[93]

Recollections of immigrant Jewish children rang with the allure of food for sale on the streets. In Chicago in the Maxwell Street market, "hot dog stands were on almost every corner."[94] A young girl growing up on East Broadway at the end of the nineteenth century described walks with her immigrant grandfather, which "meant stopping whenever I wished and being treated to all the good things displayed by vendors on their carts: a sliver of luscious watermelon, ice cream dabbled on a bit of paper, an ear of corn taken out of a steaming kettle and liberally sprinkled with salt and butter, chestnuts roasting in their blackened tin ovens over the charcoal burner, and best of all the taffy-apple with its hard sugar coating of dazzling red. Every season had its appointed goodies as I had discovered when out walking with my *Zadie* [grandfather]."[95]

America also functioned for east European Jewish immigrants as a literal melting pot. Here they met not only other Jews, but other "others," non-Jews. Immigrant Jews not only ate new Jewish foods, but began to appreciate "goyishe" tastes. They often learned about foods consumed by Italian immigrants, since they lived and worked together in many cities. In the garment shop where Elizabeth Hasanovitz worked, Jewish women brought sandwiches of bologna and corned beef while their Italian co-workers carried from home "eggplant fried in olive oil." Hasanovitz prided herself on being one of the few Jewish girls who eschewed tasting the Italians' foods. The others were tempted and ate.[96] Sara Sandberg found her walks through Italian Harlem, the neighborhood just beyond her own, enlightening. It seemed "a place of fascinating foods displayed in grimy windows."[97] Simon Moss grew up in Madison's predominantly Italian "Bush" neighborhood in the 1920s. His family kept a kosher home and owned a kosher bakery, but his friendship with Italian boys brought him into their homes. "I ate so much spaghetti and meatballs at Frank's house," he remembered, "I should be Italian by now."[98] Italian cheeses gave the air a "damp sweetness" in Alfred Kazin's olfactory memories, although he wondered as a child if anyone really ate the "clumps of red and brown meat dripping off the sausage rings."[99] A Yiddish short story of the late 1910s, "The Goat in the Backyard," by Boruch Glasman, told of Jewish and Italian next-door neighbors in the Bronx. Amity flourished between them, and the Italian man shared with the Jewish family his homemade goat cheese.[100] In their descriptions of Italian food, Jews expressed interest, engagement, and fascination.

Some of the first Yiddish cookbooks published in America included Italian food words and styles. In Hinde Amchanitzky's 1901 Yiddish cookbook, she addressed "Jewish daughters" who wanted to learn how to "excite her husband and family with the best, tastiest foods, which will excite the soul and strengthen the body." She "Italianized" the east European Friday night classic "lokshen yokh" by calling it "chicken zup mit macaroni."[101] A 1914 Yiddish cookbook by H. Braun offered immigrant readers a chance to learn how to cook Italian food as part of the project to teach them to cook American.[102]

Chinese food, one of the other ethnic magnets which drew Jewish culinary attention, had a somewhat different trajectory.[103] Memoirs and autobiographies of the immigrant era made few reference to eating Chinese food. Sophie Ruskay recalled that a childhood friend told her, "Chinamen eat mice, you know."[104] Yet the Jewish social pattern of going out to Chinese restaurants emerged quite early. In the 1890s the *American Hebrew*, a magazine oriented to the English-reading middle-class traditional Jews, reported on the trend and criticized it.[105] In 1928 *Der Tog*, a New York daily Yiddish newspaper, ran an article entitled, "Di Milkhome tsvishn Tshap-sui un Gefilte Fish" (The War between Chop Suey and

Gefillte Fish).[106] Although slightly tongue-in-cheek, the article's juxtaposition of the Chinese dish with the symbol of Jewish cultural continuity as embodied in food hinted at challenges to Jewish practice.

Earlier arrivals taught more recent immigrants about American culinary diversity. Rose Pesotta arrived as a young girl in America three days before Thanksgiving, journeying from the Ukraine to her uncle in Harlem. They celebrated the American holiday with a dinner at his home. And there, "besides succulent roast turkey with stuffing and cranberry sauce, we had pineapple pie and bananas, my first time for both, and I liked them greatly."[107]

The encounter with food in America in the context of novelty and abundance also subverted a culture built around food taboos. Food, so central to the Judaic sacred system and the promise of America, got caught up in a complicated set of internal Jewish fights about class, immigrant status, religion, generation, and gender. Because they venerated food, and because so much about their food world changed in America, it became a locus of contestations and conflict.

The contest over Jewish food took place in public. Jews relied upon their own system of food preparation and distribution. They relied upon Jewish butchers and bakers, for example, to provision the community with ritually acceptable and familiar foods. This made Jewish consumers dependent upon the food merchants. But the merchants were equally dependent upon Jewish laborers to actually do the work and the Jewish shoppers who needed to trust the food being sold.

Friction between consumers and producers quickly escalated into a war between Jewish housewives and Jewish merchants allied with the religious establishment. Boycotts by Jewish women against Jewish butchers and grocers who charged "too much" for meat, bread, milk, and other essential items demonstrated the volatility of the Jewish marketplace. This war also pointed to women's sense of entitlement.[108] As they developed an American standard, they demanded good food and expected the Jewish community to make it affordable. They successfully organized in New York, Boston, Chicago, Cleveland, Providence, and elsewhere to ensure that their families could eat like Americans and Jews.[109] They formed associations, met, planned, and strategized how best to bring meat, bread, milk, onions, and potato prices down. They picketed butcher shops and attacked those willing to cross their lines.

Women demanded that the entire Jewish communal infrastructure—butchers, wholesalers, kosher slaughterers and the rabbis who supervised them—subscribe to their vision of a proper and acceptably priced family meal.

These guardians of their families' tables did not mind being criticized in the Jewish and citywide press. It did not bother them if butchers castigated them or even if they got arrested for their unlawful behavior. The first of the Jewish women's food protests in New York in 1902, described in the *New York Times* as a riot, led to the arrest of 70 women and 15 men.[110] In Boston in 1892 angry Jewish women responded militantly to an announcement that the kosher butchers of the immigrant North End had formed a trust to stabilize meat prices. The women met in a neighborhood synagogue. They decried the actions of the butchers for manipulating meat prices and upbraided all the players in the Jewish food chain for selling meat that was probably less than kosher.[111] They twinned an American consciousness of themselves as entitled to eat meat with their concerns about Jewish standards.

Jewish workers in the Jewish food industries also fought with employers. They asserted their right to earn a decent wage in order to live well, even if their actions threatened the supply of Jewish food. Although food for them was sacred, it was not beyond the sphere of labor strife. Jewish food workers, like workers in the garment industry, organized, thereby expressing class resentment toward their Jewish employers. Over the course of the late nineteenth and into the early twentieth century, Jewish laborers in New York's Jewish-owned bakeries, seltzer water plants, abattoirs, butcher shops and delicatessens, as well as clerks in Jewish grocery stores and waiters working in Jewish restaurants, organized and, when necessary, struck.[112]

These were all active unions. They launched massive membership drives, demanded recognition from employers, and when they had to, withheld their labor. In the process they threatened the Jewish community's foodstuffs. In 1915 the Jewish waiters called for a general strike and for three weeks closed down all the East Side restaurants. Later that year the strikes spread to the Jewish restaurants of Harlem and the Bronx. By 1929 the various Jewish waiters' unions enrolled over 1,900 members, controlling about 800 restaurants.[113]

The earliest unions in the baking industry were formed in 1887. The seltzer-workers organized in 1889 and the butchers in 1892, all predating the organization of Jewish needle-trade workers.[114] Even more than in the garment industry, Jewish food wars engendered bitter intra-communal conflict, involving the manipulation of Jewish symbols and appeals to communal loyalty. Jewish employers played upon the fellow-ship that existed between them and the workers. In the early years of the east European Jewish migration, employers hired relatives and towns-people. They considered giving a "greenhorn" a job in a rat-infested cel-lar bakery a favor.[115] The bonds of familiarity between workers and em-ployers made workers dependent on precisely those whose economic interests kept them poor. Bakery workers boarded with employers in the early years of the industry.[116] Employers fed workers, although the work-ers' "stray bites" contrasted sharply with the "hot dinner" owners ate, heightening laborers' awareness of the need to organize.[117]

Employers understood that Jewish consumers wanted to eat Jewish bread and kosher meat. The buying public considered those foods funda-mental to the practice of Judaism. This gave the owners a monopoly and decided advantage. Someone wanting kosher meat could only shop in stores they knew and trusted. *Hallah* (braided bread for holidays) made according to Jewish standards, with a pinch of dough thrown into the fire, did not exist outside Jewish neighborhoods.[118] Pumpernickel, rye bread, distinctive rolls formed the core of the immigrants' food reper-toire. Shoppers depended on the Jewish food network dominated by a handful of large concerns. Merchants appealed to ideals of intra-communal trust to keep customers loyal and weaken the hands of the unions.

Employers linked the bread they sold to Jewish customers to sacred symbols in highly visible ways. Aaron Messing, owner of the largest of New York's commercial Jewish bakeries, let the public know that he in-toned special blessings on his *hallahs* and rolls. Those blessings made his baked goods taste better than the competition's. Messing did not just rely on prayers to convey the connection between his breads and Judaism. "As long as Messing's bakery was an open shop, the non-union members, af-ter a 12–14 hour night of hard work, were compelled to go, together with the bosses to the synagogue to pray and recite Psalms, perhaps as a sign that the *bulkes* [buns] would come out tasty from the oven, and the public would buy them up."[119] East Side residents could see the Messing employees marching from the bakery to the synagogue, connect the two, and assume that Messing's bread was more "Jewish."

Messing and the other owners believed that workers would be pacified and consumers would support them over the unions. They erred. Jewish bakers went on strike in New York, Pittsburgh[120], Boston, Philadelphia, Chicago, Newark, Jersey City, and dozens of other cities, dramatizing the contentiousness of the Jewish food world.[121] By withholding their labor in order to improve working conditions, bakery workers made it impossible for Jewish families to crown their Sabbath tables with *shabbesdike hallah*. So, too, strikes among poultry handlers and butchers jeopardized the availability of kosher meat for Friday night.

Like their employers, union activists understood food to be sacred. To the Jewish public they argued that workers, fellow Jews, also should be able to have bread and meat, and a degree of economic security. Consumers overwhelmingly sided with the workers. They themselves often engaged in labor disputes with their employers. So they understood that they were choosing between kosher food and familiar bread on the one side, and guaranteeing the rights of Jewish workers on the other. They decided that the latter was more important, and in the short run they could do without the former. More important, they believed, was to force employers, those who never worried about what they would feed their own children, to recognize the fundamental rights of the food workers. "The big strike," remembered a Jewish baker from Pittsburgh, "was against Caplan's bakery in 1907 . . . in 1906 I stood on a wagon and persuaded the people not to buy bread without a union label."[122]

The support the consumers gave to the striking workers proved powerful. A 1910 report on unionizing among all bakery workers in New York marveled at the strength of the Jewish effort:

> It was in the face of these conditions that the 3,000 Jewish union bakers gave up work on May 1, 1909. So universal was the spirit of unrest among the bakers of this race that in seven weeks almost all their shops had struck, over 3,000 men were enrolled in the unions and the bosses could not find a man to work for them . . . with the help of the people of the East Side, who demanded bread bearing

the union label . . . the Jewish bakers took the first steps toward some measure of leisure and opportunity for normal living, with standards of personal and shop cleanliness.[123]

"Bread strikes" and other highly public labor disputes over Jewish food ripped through the larger communities. Jewish consumers boycotted non-union shops, forcing employers to guarantee an American standard of living to Jewish laborers. The unions' message that Jewish workers deserved an American standard of living outweighed Aaron Messing's blessing over his breads and the parade of his workers going to recite morning prayers.

Conflicts over food took place in the domestic sphere as well. Families negotiated between American food and Jewish definitions of the familiar. Charles Angoff, born in 1902, grew up in Boston alongside a childhood friend, Kivvie Greenberg. Their families reacted differently to American food. The Greenbergs, wrote Angoff, "were the opposite of us. They became Americanized in record time. Less than six months after they arrived in this country, they served ice cream at dinner or supper every Sunday . . . [were] the first to spice their food with ketchup, the first to go to the movies . . . and the first to eat such strange vegetables as celery and lettuce." Agnoff's father scoffed at these foods. Ketchup, "he was sure wasn't kosher, no matter how many rabbis' signatures were on the bottle, and he considered it as fit only for pigs." He "looked upon ice cream as on the whole a shameful thing, and as children's food at best. Whenever he'd see any of his children eat it—and we did manage to get a cone of strawberry or vanilla or chocolate ice cream every now and then, largely through the connivance of our mother—he'd look at one condescendingly and say, 'A strange place, America, a very strange place!'" He condemned American food and "wouldn't wish it upon the worst Russian hooligan."[124]

The father looked down on ice cream, but his children ate it with pleasure. He proved powerless against the American food dynamo. Suspicion of food novelty and family repeated itself throughout the immigrant Jewish world. Witness a family memoir typical of its genre, *The Katsiv Chronicles*, which traced through interviews the many branches of a Ukrainian Jewish family transplanted to Chicago. Shmulik Katsiv came to America in 1913 with his son Eli Leib from the town of Ladouka, in the province of Kiev. He and his son, the more traditional of the two, sparred with each other, as well as with one of his daughters, over a lowly bowl of cereal. As his granddaughter, Eva Leiter, who witnessed the argument, remembered:

> Everything had to be strictly kosher, kosher, ultra-kosher for Eli Leib. My grandfather [Shmulik], on the other hand, was devout— he went to shul every single day—but whatever my mother put in front of him, he knew that she kept a kosher home, he knew that it was okay for him to eat. Eli Leib comes in one day and he sees my grandfather eating cereal and he says in Yiddish, of course, *"Vas este? Es trayf?"* [What are you eating? Is it *trayf?*] So my grandfather says, "Elka wouldn't give me anything *trayf*."[125]

Such anecdotes revealed a complex world of choices, which in turn brought to the surface cultural conflicts. Even when new foods were not necessarily unkosher, their unknown origins challenged a conventional food system.

One way to make such foods acceptable was to render them both familiar and demonstrate their *kashrut*. Commercial manufacturers recognized a potential for selling to immigrant Jews, perceiving them rightly as poised to try new foods. The critics among them needed to be silenced. But once some immigrant Jews ate particular foods, others would surely follow. By the 1910s such companies as Gold Medal Flour, Uneeda Biscuits, Quaker Oats, H. J. Heinz, Coca-Cola, and other giant producers of foods, routinely advertised in the Yiddish press.[126] In 1913 *Di Froyen Velt* (translated by its publishers as "The Jewish Ladies Home Journal," but literally the Women's World) carried a two-page advertisement for Borden's Eagle Brand canned milk. One page sang the product's praises, contrasting the sickly condition of Indian children on the Pine Ridge Reservation in South Dakota who did not drink it with the robust health of the one white child who lived among them and drank the Borden product. The next page directly connected Borden's canned milk to Americanization. "Every President of the United States Can Claim Immigrant Origins," declared the advertising copy, explaining that good health came from good nutrition, which in turn spelled success in America. Borden's milk would ensure that trajectory for the mothers who read *Die Froyen Velt*. Unspoken was the promise that with just enough Borden's milk, their American born sons, too, could become president.[127]

With the exception of the flour company, these firms marketed products unknown before migration. Canned soups, crackers, canned milk, soda pop, ketchup, mustard, were all new. These companies spent their advertising dollars wooing Yiddish readers, understood to be culinary adventurers, although potentially pulled back by communal conservatives.[128] A cozy bond developed between food purveyors and in particular Jewish women willing to try new products, cook familiar foods better, and experiment with new ones. In the early 1930s the Sarasota Flour company placed a notice in Chicago's Jewish newspapers announcing a contest for recipes using its product. "They got fifty entries at least," all in Yiddish. Company officials asked a Minneapolis rabbi for help, and he recommended Laura Rapaport to translate them. "The Jewish contestants," it turned out, "used the opportunity to tell how they came to America, and how they had suffered, as well as demonstrating their kitchen skills." In May 1925 in Fargo, North Dakota, a group of largely immigrant Jewish women, under the aegis of the Hebrew Ladies' Aid Society, staged a picnic at which company agents demonstrated the benefits of Mazola corn oil. "It was decided," remembered one of them, "to serve doughnuts and some are supposed to be made in the mazo [sic] oil, to demonstrate to the ladies how good the oil is." The picnic taught the Jewish women about a new product, the oil, an American food, doughnuts, and for every gallon sold the society, a *hevrat nashim* [a women's burial society], received a contribution.[129]

The year 1912 was a key moment in forging the bond between food manufacturers and the Jewish public. That year Proctor and Gamble of Cincinnati launched a nationwide campaign for its newly created vegetable-based shortening, Crisco. The Jewish market seemed a promising field for this product. Neither meat nor dairy (hence *pareve)*, it was versatile, did not need refrigeration, and handled more easily than oil. To attract Jewish cooks, Proctor and Gamble enlisted the support of one of American Jewry's most notable orthodox rabbis, Rabbi Moshe Zevulun Margolies (the "Ramaz") of New York, to endorse Crisco as ritually pure. "The Hebrew Race," the advertisement boldly announced, "had been waiting for 4,000 years" for a solution to its shortening problems, and now, with the rabbi's blessings, it had Crisco.[130]

Just as Proctor and Gamble provided Jews with a product that their history lacked, on all sides massive campaigns were directed at Jewish newcomers about what to eat and how to eat it. Within immigrant communities, large ones in particular, radical Jewish health reformers preached in the immigrants' own language about the evils of the Jewish diet and the pitfalls of the foods they enjoyed.[131] Ben-Zion Lieber, a Rumanian who came to New York in 1904, published for seven years a Yiddish monthly journal, *Unzer Gezund* (Our Health), in which he advocated a vegetarian diet. He extolled this same diet in a column for the Yiddish women's magazine, *Di Froyen Velt*.[132] He also allied himself with Jewish vegetarians who published Yiddish pamphlets, broadsides, and cookbooks decrying Jewish eating. Aaron Frankel's *Lo Tirtzach*, (You Shall Not Kill) excoriated Jews and Judaism for carnivorous brutality and for the evil of thinking that "it is a *mitzvah* to feast on meat and fish on the Sabbath and that it is one of the greatest *mitzvot* to eat a sheep's head on Rosh Hashanah." The pamphlet claimed that Moses and the Torah had intended Jews to be vegetarians.[133] Supporters of the cause opened vegetarian restaurants as alternatives to the popular pastime of eating corned beef, steaks, and pastrami. In 1913 *Di Froyen Velt* displayed an advertisement blaring "Meat Is Unhealthy," and encouraged readers to try a vegetarian eatery, Pythagoras, at 42 Norfolk Street.[134]

Although Frankel and the other vegetarians used biblical words and metaphors, they participated in a contemporary, broad-based intra-Jewish criticism of Jewish foodways. Newspapers, social welfare workers, and dieticians censured Jews, and women in particular, for their preparation of food. Jewish women, they claimed, were poor cooks. Different critics offered different criticisms, but they agreed that all was not right in American immigrant Jewish kitchens. Chicago's Yiddish *Daily Jewish Courier* commented that "It is a great error to think that women are capable of only raising children and taking care of a house." It documented the "hundreds of Jewish women [who] carry on a business alone, work in shops, and canvass from door to door." But, the *Courier* moralized, "The tragedy of such families cannot be overestimated . . . food is never dished out in proper time or proper manner."[135]

Women themselves joined the chorus of critics. Various educated Jewish women, daughters of immigrant families and those with somewhat longer roots in America, entered the newly professionalized field of nutrition.[136] Jewish charities hired trained nutritionists to oversee the many food operations under their aegis. Boston's Federated Jewish Charities brought onto its staff S. Etta Sadow as Head Worker for its Bureau of Home Economics, while Milwaukee's Jewish charitable federation employed a Nutrition Worker. Whatever they called these professionals, Jewish institutions all over the country hired trained women to bring science to bear upon the food served at old age homes, orphanages, day nurseries, hospitals, camps, and other institutions where Jews fed Jews. As a result, directors and boards of institutions felt compelled to provide scientifically appropriate food.[137]

These Jewish women stood between immigrant households and American nutrition culture. S. Etta Sadow of Boston explained the intricacies of the Jewish diet to her nutritionist colleagues, members of the Massachusetts Dietetic Association, in 1928:

> Polish and Russian Jews emphasize lokshen (noodles), gefillte fish, and kashe, a cereal made of barley or grits and generally eaten with meat instead of a vegetable. Borsht, a soup of beets or cabbage is a favorite. Galicians and Lithuanians share in a great many of these characteristic foods and add carrots, potatoes and prunes—a sort of compote, cooked with meat, to the list. The taste for herring, pickles and cucumbers comes from Holland, while a fondness for oil as a frying medium comes from Spain and Portugal and the Orient. The sweet and sour stewing of vegetables and meat comes from Germany.

Like many Jewish commentators, she defined Jewish foodways as a problem to be solved.[138] She ended her lecture on a negative note. "The diet in general is over rich and poorly balanced; the chief fault lies in the use of too few vegetables."[139]

Nutritionists were respected members of the Jewish communal infrastructure. Florence Greenbaum had earned a bachelor's degree in home economics at Hunter College and got her first job as a cooking and domestic science instructor at New York's Young Women's Hebrew Association. When the city's Jewish leaders created the communal governing board, the Kehillah, in 1908, they formed within it an Association of Jewish Homemakers, with Greenbaum as its director. Just as Kehillah leaders believed that Jewish education and charity needed scientific rationalization, so too they considered the home and its food a problem to be solved by planning, rationalization, and order.[140]

Jewish social and philanthropic workers believed that the culinary inadequacies of Jewish women explained the relatively high rates of men's desertion of their families. Solomon Lowenstein of the Hebrew Orphan Asylum noted in 1905 that most deserted women gave their husbands, "unpalatable, ill-cooked food." Five years later Morris Waldman remarked that men drifted away from home because they could get better food in restaurants than they could get at home. After eating away from home, some just decided not to come back.[141]

Yiddish journalistic vignettes intended to be humorous ridiculed Jewish women's cooking. A comic sketch in the *Yiddishe Tageblatt* of 1915 spoofed the Passover *haggadah* and the food Jewish women prepared. The article, "The Suffragists Haggadah," asked: "How is this Passover night different from all other nights? *She'b'khol halaylos* [on all other nights], the men eat sometimes in restaurants and sometimes at home. This night, of Passover, they are all at home. . . . All other nights they have complaints that the food does not appeal to them."[142] Somehow, the article chuckled, on this sacred night wives managed to make an edible meal.

By the 1910s leaders of American Jewry—writers, rabbis, teachers, and communal activists from within and without the immigrant community—asked repeatedly why Jewish homes seemed to be, as they saw them, such hotbeds of tension and discord. Bad food was high on their list of answers. Poet Morris Rosenfeld, in his *Epigrams* (1912), entitled one piece "Shalom Bayiss," or peace in the household. He advised husbands to take the lead in promoting domestic tranquility:

> Praise the soup and praise the *kitkes* [twisted rolls]
> And it will be good for your Yenta
> Soon forgotten and forgiven
> A thousand burdens of your life.[143]

Health workers noted high levels of Jewish parental distress about food and children's eating habits. As they saw it, mothers particularly fretted about their children's food.[144] Louis Wirth's 1925 master's thesis on "Culture Conflicts in the Immigrant Family" was based on his experience as a case worker for Chicago Jewish Charities. Wirth, who worked with troubled families, linked the parental obsession with feeding children to a "symbolization of food." Parents worked hard for what they put on the table, and believed food was essential to being Jewish. Children, knowing what food meant to their parents, often refrained from eating what was offered in order to stake out their independence.[145]

Social workers recognized the power of food, and tried to use it to bridge the generational divide. In 1913 Boris Bogen organized a "Jews of Many Lands" exposition in Cincinnati. He intended the pageant to demonstrate to American-born Jewish children the richness of their parents' immigrant culture. Bogen organized an exhibition of "Jewish housewives" who "prepared delicacies famed in their birthlands."[146] Such a public display of Jewish foodways, he thought, might patch up the Jewish generational rift.

Jewish women, as the objects of a multipronged food campaign, were offered much advice. The many American Yiddish-language cookbooks provided guidance on negotiating between novelty and familiarity. Some came from American food companies, like that issued by Gold Medal Flour in 1921. Typical of the genre, this particular one included dishes made with Parmesan cheese and anchovies, Hungarian goulash and hollandaise sauce, as well as *kneydlach* and *gefillte* fish.[147]

Not surprisingly, Jewish women also wrote Yiddish cookbooks. Hinde Amchanitzky instructed Jewish women in the making of *gefillte* fish along with "French Soup," "French Cutlets," "French Balls," "Lemon Pie," "Lemon Short Pie," and so on.[148] That cookbook authors wrote in Yiddish indicated their intended readership: older women, neither American-born nor American-educated. Had these older women been comfortable with English they would not have needed to learn to cook in Yiddish. Plenty of English-language kosher cookbooks existed.[149]

So too immigrant Jewish women flocked to cooking classes, demonstrating both their anxieties and aspirations about food and its Jewish and American meanings. In many American Jewish communities—including New York, Chicago, Milwaukee, San Francisco, and Philadelphia—Jewish settlement houses and community centers offered classes on preparing American food and traditional east European fare.[150] Jewish women responded positively to opportunities to learn to cook "receipts [recipes] typical of our people and the novel dainty dishes to tempt most palates," as well as American-type foods.[151]

א פרעהליכער שבת

סוך בל סוך זועט איהר
נעברויבען קיין אנדערע ווי

גאלד מעדאל מעהל
גענוג קאהב-ווים נאבדאפם

19. In 1921 Gold Medal Flour published a Yiddish cookbook with both classic
east European recipes and American novelties. The cookbook's cover promised
that its flour, with its "clear whiteness," ensured "health" and "nutrition" along
with the warmth and piety of the Sabbath meal.

Milwaukee's Lizzie Black Kander, under the aegis of the Abraham
Lincoln House of the National Council of Jewish Women, decided in
1901 to publish a cookbook as a fundraiser. Collecting recipes from Jewish women in her classes as well as from non-Jewish neighborhood
women, she published them as *The Settlement Cookbook*.[152] Its very title
bore witness to the complexity of the project. Subtitled *The Way to a*

Man's Heart, the book, as well as the cooking classes and the decision by Jewish women that they needed to improve their cooking, all revealed a dense social drama. Immigrant Jewish women understood that they had something to gain by enhancing the food they served, making it more American yet anchored in Jewish tradition.

The cooking classes offered in Milwaukee could never accommodate the number of women who wanted to enroll. Generally older women, not in the workforce, attended. In 1906 none of the classes scheduled during the daytime had any vacancies, and there were even long waiting lists.[153] This high demand continued into the 1920s, attracting Jewish housewives concerned about the path to their husbands' hearts.[154] Women who did not work outside the home had less exposure to American norms, behaviors, and styles, as opposed to husbands who went off to jobs and children who worked and studied in the larger world. Cooking classes offered married Jewish women a chance to enter America through their kitchens. One woman, the daughter of a student in the Milwaukee Jewish cooking class, remembered how "the women in the class were from many countries; and the teacher asked each to tell about her favorite food. As they recited she corrected their grammar and pronunciation."[155] That they spent time and money on learning to cook traditional Jewish food showed both their continued commitment to a particular repertoire and their sense that they had not learned it well enough from their mothers.

Each episode in the immigrant Jewish food encounter with America highlighted the basic theme of fulfillment and its attendant conflict. These women and men had been formed by a culture which entwined food with Jewish identity. They came to a land that they embraced for its political and religious freedom, as well as for the opportunities it opened up to them to earn a living and spend some of their money on good and tasty food. That food helped transform them into Americans. In the process, they redefined what had once been venerated as God's reward and the embodiment of Jewishness and made it into one of their new nation's gifts to them.

The very success of the migration, however, created tensions. In communities and families, newcomers focused on the limitations which Judaism placed on their entry into American life. America's food, like its culture as a whole, represented something they wanted to embrace. But in doing so, they upset the boundaries between sacred and ordinary, Jewish and non-Jewish.[156] Jews and their children came to America with visions of meat and other good foods which they got, albeit with effort. The ability to eat well in America helped erase the harsh class divisions between them and their own well-fed elite. But in the process, the fulfillment of their desire to eat well every day divided the Jewish people in America amongst themselves.

8

WHERE THERE IS BREAD,
THERE IS MY COUNTRY

The stories of Nanni, Mary Butler, and the woman with no name who wept over her *treyf* geese, linked to those of Rosolino Mormino, Elizabeth Gurley Flynn, and Minnie Fisher, reveal America as an immigrant destination. They, and so many other fragments of the past, contain worlds of food, culture, and identity.

On the biggest canvas, these stories stand for the long chain of human migration across the earth. More specifically, they reveal the allure of the United States for hungry people around the world and show how its abundance shaped the identities and practices of its many communities. Their stories, as memory and as imaginative literature, testify to the lucidity of Isaac Bashevis Singer's insight about the simultaneous universality and variability of hunger. Personal food preferences might well be opaque. But on the level of the group, food choices and the meaning of food might in fact be discerned and understood through the common themes that join particular histories.

Each story revealed the power of hunger to shape human behavior, and beyond this the connection between food knowledge and social relations. Aspirations for better and more reliable food spurred migration, while powerful memories of food and hunger influenced the way people confronted new realities. Even when the change brought material improvement, recollections of past deprivation did not fade. Rather, as hungry people found food within their reach, they partook of it in ways which resonated with their earlier deprivations. How they remembered those hungers allows us to see how they had once lived them, and how they then understood themselves in their new home without them.

This nexus between hunger and food, class and migration, was informed by the specific histories of Ireland, Italy, and Jewish eastern Europe. The fictional peasant Nanni of "Pane Nero," the poor woman in Y. L. Gordon's "Barburim Abusim" who would have no kosher meat to serve her family during Passover, and pamphleteer Mary Butler, who sought to infuse Irish homes with the aura of cultural authenticity but without food, were paradigmatic of the worlds they lived in and which millions left. Their American counterparts—Rosolino Mormino laboring on a sugar cane plantation in southern Louisiana, Elizabeth Gurley Flynn, reteller of her grandfather's Famine memories, and Minnie Fisher, the exuberant embracer of American food who spent Friday nights eating the traditional Sabbath meal with her family—performed the legacies of pre-migration social life. The long histories of food and hunger endured by their forbears strongly shaped how they made sense of themselves and their opportunities.

Verga's Sicily, where the imaginary Nanni lived and died, was a world of vast differences in food built around the intricate divides of class structure. There food represented a key element in identity. The poor defined themselves as the consumers of "pane nero," black bread. The Italians who chose to migrate had watched the rich eat a cuisine praised by some as one of the world's best, in the piazzas of their towns' cafes and restaurants. Their daughters, like one of Nanni's, went into the homes of the elite to work and in the process saw, prepared, and ate good food. Poor families ate bits of that food—macaroni, cheese, wine, and olive oil—meted out to them by landowners as payment in kind for their labors. They and their sons and daughters tasted such rich food at holy times, when the ordinary boundaries between rich and poor, landowner and laborer, employer and employee were temporarily erased. Food for Italy's people served as an occasional bridge across the lines of class. But the foodways of the elite also became a model to which they and their children aspired. Such bounty represented to them the good life.

Like Verga's characters, Gordon's poor woman was paradigmatic of the world she inhabited. She lived in a complex web of class, religion, and food which dominated Jewish life in eastern Europe. In this world the sanctity of food derived from holy texts, codified by law. Food brought all

Jews together, figuratively, around their set table, but class divided them. A few among them did not have to worry about the ritual purity of any particular goose. If one was defective, well-off Jews had a whole flock of geese to choose from. Because of their wealth, they bore the obligation to nourish their hungry sisters and brothers. Rich and poor stood within the same sacred realm of *halachah*, which fostered communal order and provided a floor below which no one, no matter how poor, would fall.

The poor had ample information about the tables and pantries of the rich. Through domestic service, communal banquets, "essen teg," and Sabbath and holiday food distributions, those who habitually hungered took peeks into paradise. Their glimpses and tastings of rich and satisfying meals fostered a deep sense of resentment against those who had more. Food, in the ideal, bridged the class divide that ran through the Jewish communities of eastern Europe. Yet it also pulled the unequal parts further asunder. The poor ate with bitterness and a deep sense of social outrage. They considered themselves entitled to eat well and resented deprivation.

Mary Butler could not have listed food as a way to make homes more Irish. The idea of food as pleasure and food as a symbol of group identity ran counter to the course of modern Irish history. The particular ways in which England exercised its domination over Ireland and the seemingly unbridgeable gap between the small number of Protestant landowners and vast majority of landless Catholics created a colonial situation in which the elite and the masses shared no common ground.

Here was a historic drama in which food embodied a deep political struggle. The vast majority of Irish Catholics experienced life and the deadly ravages of famines through the one food they all ate—the potato—which was also the food that had been imposed upon them. British administrators brought in the potato not to "civilize" the Irish, but to take over Irish lands and ensure a work force that was just adequately fed.

As a colonial power, the British made no effort to enculturate the Irish to a "better" food system, to teach them to eat as their "betters" did, and to encourage them to become British. As a colonized people, the Irish rejected the styles of the hated occupiers of their land. They had few venues for learning what rich folks ate, and few reasons to want to eat like the alien elite in their midst.

The nature of the potato, the ease of cooking it, the rudimentary equipment needed to prepare and serve it, and the lack of skill and food lore which defined female networks further marginalized food. The variant of Catholicism which flourished in Ireland made little room for sensuality of any kind, sexual or culinary, and religious worship disconnected the life of the spirit and the life of the body. No one had a stake in making food meaningful except inasmuch as Irish bodies needed calories to survive and work.

Had Mary Butler come up with food suggestions for the mothers of Ireland, she would have acted in a manner counter to the entire weight of Irish culture. She would in essence have been diminishing Irishness. Likewise, had the daughters and sons of Ireland who came to America used food to celebrate their new identities as Irish Americans, they would have violated a deeply held cultural norm. That Elizabeth Gurley Flynn recalled her grandfather's memories of destroying salmon rather than eating and enjoying them bore witness to the political power of hunger. In constructing an American identity that fused Irish imagery with the realities of their new home, Irish Americans could not fit food into their communal repertoire. Not that they did not eat and enjoy food. But the foods consumed could not embody the idea of Irish identity. Inasmuch as the Irish understood Ireland as a repository of hunger, they could not enact identity by means of food. This made them unique among immigrants to America. Only in their communities did food shops lack the symbols of ethnic pride. Only in their families did home and institutional rituals downgrade food, either as unimportant or disconnected to ideas about group identity.

The inability of the Irish to use food for the construction of ethnicity was compounded by their widespread employment in domestic service. The Irish women who took their first American steps through the back doors and into the kitchens of Yankee homes were hounded and ridiculed for their lack of skill at the stove and table. Although many of them went on to create their own homes, what they had learned on the job was not Irish. Having to cook someone else's food, under someone else's supervision, and according to someone else's rules drove another wedge between Irish culture and food culture.

The memories Irish immigrants brought to America and the ethnic practices they created differed radically from those of eastern European Jews. Jews, before and after migration, put food at the center of their sacred system and imbued the preparation and consumption of food with deep meaning. But as it was with Irish immigrants, the memories of past deprivation structured the nature of Jewish encounters with America.

Minnie Fisher might very well have served as a model for the daughter of the fictional woman who mourned her geese. Had Gordon written a sequel to "Barburim Abusim," he could have allowed his tragic character, left at the end of the narrative begging for alms to feed her family, to decide that eastern Europe held very little for her. But we need not speculate. Minnie Fisher recalled childhood privation in Russia and consistently contrasted its scarcity and restrictions with the seemingly boundless opportunities of America. Just as she reveled in the youth culture, theater life, and educational opportunities of New York in the early twentieth century, so too did she enjoy the good food which she could buy for herself.

She and others like her did not give up on Jewish food or reject the tastes of the past. Some food had a specifically Jewish place, in the home, in communal institutions, at banquets and other food functions that made up organized Jewish life in America. But the foods associated with past practice made room for novelty, innovation, and experimentation.

In setting aside certain times and places for new food and others for traditional food, Jews were not so different from most immigrants. The bifurcation of immigrants' lives into spaces for being "American" and others for being Poles, Japanese, French-Canadians, or Dominicans has typified the construction of ethnic identity in America.

The complications of *kashrut* distinguished the Jewish variant on this nearly universal process. Jewish dietary laws functioned powerfully in the sacred universe to maintain group distinctiveness, keeping Jews separate and apart from the people around them. In most of the places Jews lived before their migration to America, they accepted the rationale of *kashrut*. In eastern Europe they indeed used the phrase "goyishe tam" (gentile taste) to mean something repulsive and unattractive. But just as America as a society and a culture attracted them, so too did its foods. Instead of repulsed, Jews were lured by American food novelties.

They cherished American ideas about individual choice, personal preference, and limitless opportunities, however much those clashed with the underlying rationale of *kashrut*. The "kosher wars" that ripped through the immigrant enclaves in America were not just about the legal problems of supervision. Parents and children, husbands and wives, clubs and charitable institutions, rabbis, butchers, and slaughterers all struggled over the implications of the inherent conflict between freedom of choice and the "set table."

The distinctiveness of the east European Jewish involvement with food in America also grew out of their passion for food. For a group of people who venerated food and described their hopes, dreams, and deepest memories in terms of food, conflict was unavoidable. Jewish women, those most intimately associated with cooking, bore the brunt of that conflict, which in turn exacerbated gender tensions. A cadre of critics publicly chided Jewish women for their allegedly poor cooking skills, blaming them and their tasteless meals for the disorganization of the Jewish home. Advertisers, nutritionists, social workers, rabbis, and journalists cajoled and appealed to Jewish women to save their families and their communities by serving better food. No wonder that their daughters, with eyes already trained on entering the middle class and the professions, viewed their mothers' lives in the kitchen as narrow and not worth replicating. This too made the Jewish story different from all others.

The food drama played out between Nanni, his children, and Rosolino Mormino may have been the least complicated of these three immigrant histories. People already used to a sparse diet but fearing even greater hunger, emigrated to a place where food abounded. They understood that their new home was not without its difficulties, yet freedom from hunger outweighed all the negatives. That freedom allowed these immigrants to behave in new ways.

Much of the food world, which immigrants from up and down the Italian peninsula constructed in America, was new. That they called the foods they ate "Italian" was new. That their communities were dominated by clubs, stores, markets, festivals, and restaurants to eat those food was new as well. Thus the fundamental details of their American consumption represented a break with the past. But no matter how great the chasm between what had been and what they achieved in terms of food in America, they believed that they were behaving in traditional ways. They invested the foods which they ate in America with the aura of authenticity.

Food seemed to cause them no problems. Families did not fight over it. Community institutions were not ripped apart by it, and all agreed upon the Italian American food consensus that emerged. Across gender and generation lines, Italians in America believed that what they ate was vastly superior to what anyone else ate, and they made little effort to try items associated with other immigrant groups. Food marked off who they were and set them apart from everyone else. Preparing and eating Italian food offered them a place of distinction in American society. That others, initially only the adventurous and the off-beat, wanted to try those foods, made it possible for these immigrants to demonstrate an expertise that no one else had. As a group often stigmatized by the dominant culture for its low aspirations and violent character, Italian Americans pointed to an area of public culture where they claimed superiority and a contribution to their new home. They had a stake in performing their food identity for others, so that they could present their cultural distinctiveness as rich and worth preserving to themselves and their children.

The Italian story may best represent the experiences of most immigrants. The Irish and the Jewish stories were too laden with inner conflict, too fraught with problems to be paradigmatic. The Italian story, as framed by Verga's "Pane Nero" and Mormino's letter, could be retold as a Mexican story, a Jamaican story, a Greek story, or a Swedish one. Hungry people embraced plenty in a new setting and played out the injuries of class remembered from back home through a new and exuberant production of "traditional" foods, reheated in American ovens with richer ingredients, and enjoyed by all as the embodiment of both the group itself and its American variant.

It is risky to assert that these real, remembered, and fictive narratives can represent the experiences and sensibilities of all the women and men who ate and hungered in Italy, Ireland, and Jewish eastern Europe, only some of whom made their way to America. Those societies were complex and defy generalizations. Regional variations, changes over time, idiosyncrasies and variations among families and individuals render blanket statements problematic. But woven into these stories, however limited their geographic and chronological scope, are some basic, universal truths about food and hunger.

For all people at all times food matters. What and how people eat reveals a dense world of behavior and belief that extends far beyond mundane details of ingredients, equipment, responsibilities, and meal formats. Food as actual practice and as a set of ideas about the appropriate order of things characterizes all human societies. Regardless of time and place, differences in wealth usually mean differences in food. Those who have the most and best resources—cattle, land, pelts, money, whatever the historically specific measure of wealth—eat the most, the best, and worry the least about being hungry. Those who have the least wealth by definition eat the least and the worst food and spend much of their time worrying about feeding themselves and their families.

No people's history is devoid of episodes of want. No people can be said to have escaped completely the reality of food deprivation, the growling of empty bellies, the panic of staring at empty sacks, empty bowls, and empty baskets, or the anguish of parents who must explain to children that they do not know when they will eat again. For the vast majority of human beings who ever lived, food has been the most vexing of all human needs, and it, rather than sex, shelter, or clothing, gave them the urgency to organize societies and construct social institutions.

Saints and ascetics excepted, human beings have strategized how to fill their plates and mouths. Human migrations have been inspired in large measure by the search for steady sources of food. But while many of the migrations which scattered human beings to every habitable continent were simply flights from starvation, most modern geographic movements had more complicated origins. Most migrants did not come from the ranks of the most comfortable. Neither were they the most impoverished—those who lacked the means and possibly the emotional resources to relocate to a new place. Rather, they represented in food terms not so much the starving as the hungry. They had lived out their hungry years in specific places. They knew that they lived next to people who hungered more deeply and more frequently, reminding them of how they might end up if they did not seize the opportunity to leave.

This is obviously a historic drama which did not come to an end with the cessation of open immigration to America in the 1920s, the point at which this study concludes. Ethnic food still stands out, eight decades later, as the most visible and palpable manifestation of America's immigrant legacy. What is different at the beginning of the twenty-first century is not that immigrants since the late 1960s are making their way to America from places that had in the early part of the twentieth century not sent any (or many). The difference is that technology makes it infinitely easier to send information and ingredients from place to place than had been the case earlier. Immigrants cross oceans by jet in a matter of hours, not weeks. They pick up the telephone and call friends and family around the globe and swap recipes and food stories. They can carry back from villages in the Dominican Republic, Pakistan, or Thailand foods prepared by mothers and grandmothers who are not joining them in the United States. Likewise, in the cities and towns of those countries, American food establishments have sprung up which introduce potential immigrants to the tastes they will encounter if they do decide to emigrate.

America at the beginning of the twenty-first century, in the age of multiculturalism, is also a different place from the America encountered by Rosolino Mormino, Minnie Fisher, or Tom Flynn. Americans have come to be much more interested in eating what they define as "authentic" ethnic food. Having broken out of their previous culinary conservatism, Americans, particularly in larger cities, sample foods from Thailand, Lebanon, Ethiopia, Cuba, Japan, Mexico, China. When they think and talk about ethnic food, as readers of the food section of local newspapers, as restaurant goers, as visitors to festivals and street fairs, as urban explorers venturing out to neighborhoods other than their own, Americans look for such authenticity, assuming a yardstick of tradition.

They measure food accordingly. Does the restaurant cater to tourists or group members? Are the people milling about the booths voyeurs like themselves or genuine consumers of the ethnic food, who know quality when they taste it? Do the shelves of the stores, marked on the outside by words and symbols referring to far away places, display mass-produced packaged goods, or handmade food from "back home"?

If the latter, then the food must be an exact recreation of the stuff consumed before migration, the real thing from a far away place. In this new century, Americans assume the existence of something genuine in the ethnic food cultures developing around them, and celebrate them as exemplars of continuity.

It may be that the fusions taking place in contemporary America and the high level of interest which Americans now express in the new foodways of arriving immigrants will make a difference, and the histories of these immigrant cuisines will take a very different course than those presented in these pages. However that plays itself out, certain forces will no doubt be present and will replicate the histories of the east European Jews, the Irish, and the Italian immigrants who made their way to America from the middle of the nineteenth century through the 1920s.

This encounter with America and its food took its shape from three powerful forces. First, the class structures in the countries they left marked people with particular memories of hunger and ideas about food, which, more than the food itself, traveled to America. The sharper the divisions and the more complicated the class structure, the greater the gap between those who ate well and those who got their meager bread by the sweat of their brows.

The creation of ethnic foodways in America also grew out of the very details of the migrations, namely, the balance between men and women, children and adults. The food cultures which developed in America were shaped by the intentions of the migrants—whether they saw themselves as permanent immigrants or temporary sojourners. The basic nature of American plenty left a deep imprint on the various ethnic food cultures which developed among the immigrants. Food was available at a price and in quantities which staggered the imagination of women and men who had been hungry. Meat, sugar, fat, fruit, vegetables, soft and fine white bread, ice cream, beer, coffee were within their grasp at last.

The individual histories of ethnic immigrant groups stand by themselves. No one story encapsulates the experiences of all others. Each one was shaped by the confluence of past hungers, the nature of the migrations, and the ways in which each immigrant group saw its prospects in America. No story is good or bad, rich or deficient. Each represents a particular experience which can be seen, described, and explained.

In placing the Italian, Irish, and East European Jewish experiences side by side, we can see much that was similar, particularly the role of American abundance in stimulating migration and changing the conditions of life for people who once feared hunger. That bounty, set against pre-migration scarcity, functions as a shaping element in a common American culture. Food for all, at low prices and in great variety, became an every day reality, consumed at every meal.

These three histories also tell us much about the pressures of the past and the choices people made. The women and men of the immigrant groups had choices in America about what to eat, when to eat it, and how. But their preferences were deeply affected by the experiences they

NOTES

INDEX

NOTES

1 WAYS OF EATING, WAYS OF STARVING

1. Isaac Bashevis Singer, "Afterword: Knut Hamsun, Artist of Skepticism," in Knut Hamsun, *Mysteries* (New York: Noonday Press, 1998), pp. 341–342.

2. See E. Parmalee Prentice, *Hunger and History: The Influence of Hunger on Human History* (Caldwell, Idaho: Caxton, 1951).

3. Mary Douglas, *Purity and Danger: An Analysis of the Concepts of Pollution and Taboo* (London: Routledge, 1992); Marvin Harris, *Good to Eat: Riddles of Food and Culture* (New York: Simon and Schuster, 1985), Frederick J. Simoons, *Eat Not This Flesh: Food Avoidances from Prehistory to the Present* (Madison: University of Wisconsin Press, 1994).

4. Audrey I. Richards, *Hunger and Work in a Savage Tribe: A Functional Study of Nutrition Among the Southern Bantu* (Glencoe, Ill.: Free Press, 1948), p. xii.

5. Jean Anthelme Brillat-Savarin, *The Physiology of Taste, Or, Meditations on Transcendental Gastronomy*, M. F. K. Fisher, tr. (New York: Heritage Press, 1949), p. 1.

6. Margaret Cussler and Mary L. DeGive, *'Twixt the Cup and the Lip: Psychological and Socio-Cultural Factors Affecting Food Habits* (New York: Twayne, 1952), pp. 36–37.

7. Joan W. Scott, *Gender and the Politics of History* (New York: Columbia University Press, 1998), p. 2.

8. William A. McIntosh and Mary Zey, "Women as Gatekeepers of Food Consumption: A Sociological Critique," *Food and Foodways* 3, 4 (1989), pp. 317–332.

9. Horace M. Miner, *St. Denis: A French-Canadian Parish* (Chicago: University of Chicago Press, 1939), p. 141; Pat Caplan, "Engendering Knowledge:

The Politics of Ethnography," in Shirley Ardenor, ed., *Persons and Powers of Women in Diverse Cultures: Essays in Commemoration of Audrey I. Richards, Phyllis Kaberry and Barbara E. Ward* (New York: Berg, 1992), pp. 75–77; Cora Du Bois, "Attitudes Towards Food and Hunger in Alor," in Leslie Spier, A. Irving Hollowell and Stanley S. Newman, eds., *Language, Culture, and Personality: Essays in Memory of Edward Sapir* (Menasha, Wis.: Sapier Memorial Publication Fund, 1941), p. 277; Cora Du Bois, *The People of Alor: A Social-Psychological Study of an East Indian Island* (Minneapolis: University of Minnesota Press, 1944); Michael S. Laguerre, *American Odyssey: Haitians in New York City* (Ithaca: Cornell University Press, 1984), p. 110.

10. Bridget O'Laughion, "Mediation of Contradiction: Why Mbum Women Do Not Eat Chicken," in *Women, Culture and Society*, Michelle Zimbalist Rosaldo and Louise Lamphere, eds. (Stanford: Stanford University Press, 1974), pp. 301–318.

11. Miriam Kahn and Lorrain Sexton, "The Fresh and the Canned," *Food and Foodways* 3, 1–2 (1988), pp. 1–18.

12. Jack Goody, *Cooking, Cuisine, and Class: A Study in Comparative Sociology* (Cambridge: Cambridge University Press, 1982).

13. Fernand Braudel, *The Structures of Everyday Life: The Limits of the Possible* (London: Collins/Fontana, 1985), p. 163.

14. Sidney W. Mintz, *Sweetness and Power: The Place of Sugar in Modern History* (New York: Penguin, 1985).

15. Eric Hobsbawm and Terence Ranger, *The Invention of Tradition* (Cambridge: Cambridge University Press, 1983).

16. Pierre Bourdieu, *Distinction: A Social Critique of the Judgement of Taste*. Richard Nice, tr. (Cambridge, Mass.: Harvard University Press, 1984), p. 79; Peter Farb and George Armelagos, *Consuming Passions: The Anthropology of Eating* (Boston: Houghton Mifflin, 1980), p. 4.

17. Marcel Proust, *Remembrance of Things Past*, vol. I (*Swann's Way*), C. K. Scott Moncrieff, tr. (New York: Random House, 1934), p. 34.

18. Thomas J. Jablonsky, *Pride in the Jungle: Community and Everyday Life in Back of the Yards Chicago* (Baltimore: Johns Hopkins University Press, 1993), pp. 78–79.

19. Roger Cohen, "A Nigerian Discovers America," *New York Times Magazine* (June 6, 1999), p. 136.

20. Jackson Lears, *Fables of Abundance: A Cultural History of American Advertising* (New York: Basic Books, 1994), pp. 26–33.

21. Quoted in David M. Potter, *People of Plenty: Economic Abundance and the American Character* (Chicago: University of Chicago Press, 1954), p. 78; T. Kenneth Jackson, *Crabgrass Frontier: The Suburbanization of the United States* (New York: Oxford University Press, 1985); Andrew Heinze, *Adapting to Abundance: Jewish Immigrants, Mass Consumption, and the Search for American Identity* (New York: Columbia University Press, 1990).

22. J. Hector St. John Crevecoeur, *Letters from an American Farmer* (1781) (New York: Fox, Duffield, and Company, 1904), pp. 52, 54, 90.

23. James T. Lemon, *The Best Poor Man's Country: A Geographical Study of Early Southeastern Pennsylvania* (Baltimore: Johns Hopkins University Press, 1972), pp. 154, 159.

24. Werner Sombart, *Why Is There No Socialism in the United States* (1906) (White Plains, N.Y.: International Arts and Science Press, 1976), pp. 86, 106.

25. Peter Roberts, *Anthracite Coal Communities: A Study in the Demography, the Social Educational and Moral Life of the Anthracite Region* (1904) (New York: Arno, 1970), p. 34.

26. Stuart M. Blumin, *The Emergence of the Middle Class: Social Experience in the American City, 1760–1900* (Cambridge: Cambridge University Press, 1989), pp. 110–111.

27. Rita Moonsammy, "A Comparison of British and American Foodways As Observed by Travellers of the Early Nineteenth Century," *Digest* 2, 3 (Spring, 1979), pp. 7–14.

28. Horace P. Batcheler, *Jonathan at Home* (London: W. H. Collingridge, 1864), p. 45.

29. Jackson Turner Main, *The Social Structure of Revolutionary America* (Princeton: Princeton University Press, 1965) p. 131.

30. Harvey Levenstein, *Revolution at the Table: The Transformation of the American Diet* (New York: Oxford University Press, 1988), p. 32.

31. Peter R. Shergold, *Working-Class Life: The "American Standard" in Comparative Perspective, 1899–1913* (Pittsburgh: University of Pittsburgh Press, 1982), pp. 90–115, 179–198; Peter Shergold, "'Reefs of Roast Beef': The American Worker's Standard of Living in Comparative Perspective," in Dirk Hoerder, ed., *American Labor and Immigration History, 1877–1920s: Recent European Research* (Urbana: University of Illinois Press, 1983) pp. 78–105; Dorothee Schneider, "'For Whom Are All the Good Things in Life?' German-American Housewives Discuss Their Budgets," in Hartmut Keil and John B. Jentz, eds., *German Workers in Industrial Chicago, 1850–1910: A Comparative Perspective* (DeKalb: Northern Illinois University Press, 1983), pp. 145–160.

32. Robert Fogel, Stanley L. Engerman, James Trussell, Roderick Floud, Clayne L. Pope, and Larry T. Wimmer, "The Economic Morality in North America, 1650–1910: A Description of a Research Project," *Historical Methods* 11 (1978), pp. 75–108; Stanley Engerman, "The Height of U.S. Slaves," *Local Population Studies* 16 (1976), pp. 45–50; Richard H. Steckel, "A Peculiar Population: The Nutrition, Health, and Morality of American Slaves from Childhood to Maturity," *Journal of Economic History* 46 (1986), pp. 721–742.

33. John Komlos, *Nutrition and Economic Development in the Eighteenth-Century Habsburg Monarchy: An Anthropometric History* (Princeton: Princeton University Press, 1989), p. 26.

34. Franz Boas, *Changes in Bodily Form of Descendants of Immigrants* (New York: Columbia University Press, 1912).

35. W. O. Atwater, *Errors in Our Food Economy* (Washington, D.C.: Farmers Bulletin, 23, 1894).

36. Richard Horowitz, *Hog Ties; Pigs, Manure, and Mortality in American Culture* (New York: St. Martin's Press, 1998); Eric B. Ross, "Patterns of Diet and Forces of Production: An Economic and Ecological History of the Ascendancy of Beef in the United States Diet," in Eric B. Ross, ed., *Beyond the Myths of Culture: Essays in Cultural Materialism* (New York: Academic Press, 1980), pp. 181–225.

37. George Rogers Taylor, *The Transportation Revolution, 1815–1860* (New York: Harper and Brothers, 1951).

38. Richard Wade, *The Urban Frontier: Pioneer Life in Early Pittsburgh, Cincinnati, Lexington, Louisville, and St. Louis* (Chicago: University of Chicago Press, 1959).

39. Edgar W. Martin, *The Standard of Living in 1860: American Consumption Levels on the Eve of the Civil War* (Chicago: University of Chicago Press, 1942).

40. Lawrence Glickman, *A Living Wage: American Workers and the Making of Consumer Society* (Ithaca: Cornell University Press, 1997).

41. Margaret Byington, *Homestead: The Households of a Mill Town* (New York: Russell Sage, 1910), p. 70.

42. Lizabeth Cohen, *Making a New Deal: Industrial Workers in Chicago, 1919–1939* (New York: Cambridge University Press, 1990), p. 112.

43. Carl Sandburg, "Chicago," in *Chicago Poems* (New York: Henry Holt, 1916), p. 3.

44. Victor Greene, *The Slavic Community on Strike: Immigrant Labor in Pennsylvania Anthracite* (Notre Dame: University of Notre Dame Press, 1968), p. 45.

45. Harvey Levenstein, *Revolution at the Table*, p. 26.

46. Sophonisba P. Breckenridge, *New Homes for Old* (New York: Harper and Brothers, 1921), pp. 55–56.

2   BLACK BREAD, HARD BREAD

1. Giovanni Verga, *Pane Nero and Other Stories* (Manchester: Manchester University Press, 1962), pp. 48–75.

2. Henry Hearder and D. P. Waley, *A Short History of Italy: From Classical Times to the Present Day* (Cambridge: Cambridge University Press, 1966); Stuart Joseph Woolf, *A History of Italy, 1700–1860: The Social Constraints of Political Change* (London: Methuen, 1979).

3. Joseph Lopreato, *Peasants No More: Social Class and Social Change in an Undeveloped Society* (San Francisco: Chandler, 1967), p. 151.

4. Dennis Mack Smith, "The Prehistory of Fascism," in A. William Salomone ed., *Italy from the Risorgimento to Fascism: An Inquiry into the Origins of the Totalitarian State* (Garden City, N.Y.: Doubleday, 1970), p. 106.

5. Frederick Wright, *The Italians in America* (New York: Missionary Educational Movement of the United States and Canada, 1913), p. 9.

6. Filippo Sabetti, *Political Authority in a Sicilian Village* (New Brunswick, N.J.: Rutgers University Press, 1984), pp. 57–58.

7. Francis E. Clark, *Our Italian Fellow Citizens: In Their Old Homes and Their New* (Boston: Small, Maynard, 1919), p. 79.

8. Norman Douglas, *Old Calabria* (1915) (Evanston, Ill.: Marlboro Press/ Northwestern University, 1993), p. 33.

9. Robert E. Dickinson, *The Population Problem in Southern Italy: An Essay in Social Geography* (Syracuse, N.Y.: Syracuse University Press, 1955).

10. Salvatore Saladino, *Italy from Unification to 1919: Growth and Death of a Liberal Regime* (New York: Thomas Crowell, 1970) p. 58.

11. Giuseppe Giarizzio, "La Sicilia e la Crisi Agraria," in Giuseppe Giarizzio, G. Manacorda, Francesco Renda, and P. Mangranaro, *I Fasci Siciliani*, vol. 1, *Nuovi Contributi a una Riconstruzione Storica* (Bari: De Donato, 1975).

12. Leonard W. Moss, "The Passing of Traditional Peasant Society in the South," in Edward R. Tannenbaum and Emiliana P. Noether, eds., *Modern Italy: A Topical History Since 1861* (New York: New York University Press, 1974), p. 151; Credito Milano, *The Economic Resources of Italy: Their Development during the Last Twenty-Five Years and Their Present Condition, 1895–1920* (Milan: Credito Milan, 1920), vol. 1, p. 8.

13. Graeme Barker, *A Mediterranean Valley: Landscape Archaeology and Annales History in the Biferno Valley* (London: Leicester University Press, 1995), p. 33.

14. Pino Arlacchi, *Mafia, Peasants, and Great Estates: Society in Traditional Calabria*, Jonathan Steinberg, tr. (Cambridge: Cambridge University Press, 1983).

15. Sydel F. Silverman, "An Ethnographic Approach to Social Stratification: Prestige in a Central Italian Community," *American Anthropologist* 68, 4 (August 1966), pp. 899–921; John S. McDonald and Leatrice McDonald, "Italian Migration to Australia: Manifest Functions of Bureaucracy Versus Functions of Informal Networks," *Journal of Social History* 3, 3 (Spring 1970), pp. 249–273.

16. Salvatore Salomone-Marino, *Costumi e Usanze dei Contadini di Sicilia*, Rosalie N. Norris, tr. (Rutherford, N.J.: Farleigh Dickinson University Press, 1981), p. 11.

17. Martin Clark, *Modern Italy, 1871–1925* (London: Longman, 1984), p. 13.

18. Harry Hearder, *Italy in the Age of the Risorgimento: 1790–1870* (London: Longman, 1983).

19. Robert Lumley and Jonathan Morris, *The New History of the Italian South: The Mezzogiorno Revisited* (Exeter: University of Exeter Press, 1997); Jane Schneider, ed., *Italy's "Southern Question": Orientalism in One Country* (Oxford: Berg, 1998).

20. Roland Sarti, *Long Live the Strong: A History of Rural Society in the Apennines Mountains* (Amherst: University of Massachusetts Press, 1985), p. 82.

21. Jane Schneider and Peter Schneider, *Culture and Political Economy in Western Sicily* (New York: Academic Press, 1976), p. 29.

22. Pietro Orsi, *Modern Italy, 1748–1898* (New York: G. P. Putnam, 1900), p. 344.

23. Tommaso Tittoni, *Modern Italy: Its Intellectual, Cultural and Financial Aspects* (New York: Macmillan, 1922), p. 133.

24. Sydel Silverman, "An Ethnographic Approach," p. 902; see also Sydel Silverman, *Three Bells of Civilization: The Life of an Italian Hill Town* (New York: Columbia University Press, 1975), p. 902.

25. Donna Gabbaccia, "Migration and Peasant Militance," *Social Science History* 8, 1 (Winter 1984), pp. 67–80.

26. Pino Arlacchi, *Mafia, Peasants, and Great Estates*, p. 2.

27. William A. Douglass, *Emigration in a South Italian Town: An Anthropological History* (New Brunswick, N.J.: Rutgers University Press, 1984), p. 1.

28. Antonio Gramsci, *Antologia degli Scritti*, Mario Spinella and Carlo Salinari, eds. (Rome: Editori Riuniti, 1963), vol. 1, p. 74; see also Sidney G. Tarrow, *Peasant Communism in Southern Italy* (New Haven: Yale University Press, 1967).

29. Luigi Villari, *Italian Life in Town and Country* (New York: G. P. Putnam, 1902) p. 2.

30. Leonard Moss and Stephen C. Cappannari, "Estate and Class in a Southern Italian Hill Village," *American Anthropologist* 64, 2 (Spring 1964), pp. 287–300.

31. Jane Hilowitz, *Economic Development and Social Change in Sicily* (Cambridge, Mass: Schenkman, 1976), p. 53.

32. Marta Petrusewicz, *Latifundium: Moral Economy and Material Life in a European Periphery* (Ann Arbor: University of Michigan Press, 1996).

33. Russell King, *Land Reform: The Italian Experience* (London: Butterworths, 1973), p. 36.

34. Sidney Sonino, *I Contadini in Sicilia* (1876) (Florence: Vallecchi Editore, 1925).

35. See Frank Snowden, *Violence and Great Estates in the South of Italy: Apulia, 1900–1922* (Cambridge: Cambridge University Press, 1986).

36. Napoleone Colajanni, *Gli Avvenimenti di Sicilia a le Loro Cause* (Palermo: R. Sandron, 1894), pp. 65–66.

37. Roderick Aya, "The Missed Revolution: The Fate of Rural Rebels in Sicily and Southern Spain, 1840–1950," *Papers on European and Mediterranean Societies: Anthropoligisch-Sociologisch Centrum Universitet Van Amsterdam* 3 (1975), p. 17.

38. Anton Blok, *The Mafia of a Sicilian Village, 1860–1960: A Study of Violent Peasant Entrepreneurs* (Prospect Heights, Ill.: Waveland Press, 1974).

39. Giuseppe Medici, *Land Property and Land Tenure in Italy* (Bologna: Edizioni Agricole, 1952), p. 125.

40. Dino Cinel, *The National Integration of Italian Return Migration, 1870–1929* (New York: Cambridge University Press, 1991), p. 57.

41. Grazia Dore, "Some Social and Historical Aspects of Italian Emigration to America," *Journal of Social History* 1, 2 (Winter 1968), p. 97.

42. Francesco Saverio Nitti, *Inchiesta sulle Condizioni dei Contadini in Basilicate e Calabria*, quoted in Francesco Cordasco and Michael Vaughn Cordasco, *The Italian Emigration to the United States, 1880–1930: A Bibliographical Register of Italian Views, Including Selected Numbers from the Italian Commissariate of Emigration, Bollettino Dell'Emigrazione* (Fairview, N.J.: Junius-Vaughn Press, 1990), p. 9.

43. Frank Snowden, *Violence*, p. 4.

44. Quoted in Gary Mormino, *Immigrants on the Hill: Italian-Americans in St.Louis, 1882–1892* (Urbana: University of Illinois Press, 1986), p. 33.

45. Caroline White, *Patrons and Partisans: A Study of Politics in Two Southern Italian Communi* (Cambridge: Cambridge University Press, 1980), pp. 12, quote, p. 21.

46. Mimmetta Lo Monte, *Classic Sicilian Cookbook* (New York: Simon and Schuster, 1990).

47. Artui Pellegrino, *La Scienza in Cucina e l'Arte di Mangiar Bene* (1891) (Turin: Einaudi, 1970).

48. Piero Camporesi, *Exotic Brew: The Art of Living in the Age of Enlightenment*, Christopher Woodall, tr. (Cambridge: Polity Press, 1990).

49. Luigi Villari, *Italian Life*, pp. 113–115.

50. Constantine Panunzio, *The Soul of an Immigrant* (New York: Macmillan, 1922), pp. 21, 24.

51. Stella J. Sonier, *Small Potatoes* (Block Island, R.I.: J. Stella Sonier, 1993), p. 8.

52. Elizabeth Mathias and Richard Raspa, *Italian Folktales in America: The Verbal Art of an Immigrant Woman* (Detroit: Wayne State University Press, 1985), pp. 5, 25, 34–36.

53. Guido Orlando, *Confessions of a Scoundrel* (Philadelphia: John C. Wiley, 1954), pp. 2–5.

54. Carlo Levi, *Christ Stopped at Eboli: A Story of a Year* (New York: Farrar, Straus, 1947), pp. 54, 21, 174.

55. Ottavio Cavalcanti, *Il Materiale, il Corporeo, il Simbolico: Cultura Alimentare ed Eros nel Sud* (Rome: Gangemi, 1984), pp. 32, 38, 41.

56. *Inchiesta Parlamentare sulle Condizioni dei Contadini nelle Provincie Meriodionali e Nella Sicilia: Basilicata e Calabria* vol. 5 (Rome: Tipografia Nazionale Di Giovanni Bertero, 1909), p. 476.

57. Robert F. Foerster, *The Italian Emigration of Our Times* (Cambridge, Mass.: Harvard University Press, 1924), p. 95.

58. Leonard Covello, *The Heart Is the Teacher* (New York: McGraw-Hill, 1958), p. 11.

59. Quoted in Michael La Sorte, *LaMerica: Images of Italian Greenhorn Experience* (Philadelphia: Temple University Press, 1985) p. 3.

60. Paolo Sorcinelli, *Gli Italiani e il Cibo: Appetiti, Diguini e Riunance dalla Realta' Contadina all Societa' del Benessere* (Bologna: Cooperativa Libraria Universitaria Editrice Bologna, 1992) p. 47.

61. Cited in Dino Cinel, *From Italy to San Francisco: The Immigrant Experience* (Stanford: Stanford University Press, 1982), p. 39.

62. Quoted in Anton Blok, *The Mafia*, p. 51.

63. Francis E. Clark, *Our Italian Fellow Citizens*, p. 131.

64. Conte Stefano Jacini, *Frammenti dell'Inchiesta Agricole Agraria* (Rome: Forzani T. P. del Senato, 1883).

65. Gian-Paolo Biasin, *The Flavors of Modernity: Food and the Novel* (Princeton: Princeton University Press, 1993).

66. Giovanni Verga, *The House by the Medlar Tree* (New York: Grove Press, 1953), p. 35.

67. *Little Novels of Sicily* (in Italian, *Novelle Rusticane*, 1883) D. H. Lawrence, tr. (Oxford: B. Blackwell, 1925); on using Verga, a fiction writer, as a historical source, see Maureen Giovanni, "A Structural Analysis of Proverbs in a Sicilian Village," *American Ethnologist* 5, 2 (May 1978), p. 331; Leonard W. Moss and Walter H. Thompson, "The Southern Italian Family: Literature and Observation," *Human Organization* 18, 1 (Spring 1959), pp. 35–41; Dennis Mack Smith, *Modern Italy: A Political History* (Ann Arbor: University of Michigan Press, 1997), p. 209.

68. Olga Ragusa, *Verga's Milanese Tales* (New York: S. F. Vanni, 1964), p. 99.

69. Ibid., pp. 12, 159.

70. Giovanni Verga, *House*, p. 23.

71. Quoted in Frank Snowden, *Violence*, p. 24.

72. Roland Sarti, *Long Live the Strong*, p. 133.

73. Jane and Peter Schneider, *Culture and Political Economy in Western Sicily* (New York: Academic Press, 1976), pp. 33, 60.

74. Valerie Mars, "Spaghetti—But Not on Toast: Italian Food in London," in *Food in Motion: The Migration of Food Stuffs and Cookery Techniques: Proceedings of the Oxford Symposium, 1983* (Leeds: Prospect Books, 1983), p. 143.

75. Dennis Mack Smith, *Modern Italy*, p. 209; William A. Douglass, *Emigration in a South Italian Town*, p. 86.

76. Bolton King and Thomas Okey, *Italy To-Day* (London: James Nisbet, 1909), p. 131.

77. Rudolph M. Bell, *Fate and Honor, Family and Village: Demographic and Cultural Change in Rural Italy since 1800* (Chicago: University of Chicago Pres, 1979), p. 77.

78. Jan Brogger, *Montevarese: A Study of Peasant Society and Culture in Southern Italy* (Bergen: Universitets-Forlaget, 1971), p. 65.

79. Donna Gabbaccia, *Militants and Migrants: Rural Sicilians Become American Workers* (New Brunswick, N.J.: Rutgers University Press, 1988), p. 23.

80. *Inchiesta Parlamentare sulle Condizioni dei Contadini nelle Provincie Meridionali e nella Sicilia: Basilicata*, vol. 5 (Rome: Tipografia Nazionale Di Giovanni Bertero, 1909), p. 54.

81. Robert Foerster, *The Italian Emigration*, p. 95.

82. Massimo Livi-Bacci, *Population and Nutrition: An Essay On European Geographic History* (Cambridge: Cambridge University Press, 1991), pp. 31–33, 87, 93–97, 106.

83. "Peter Mossini," in *In Their Own Words: Ellis Island Interviews* (New York: Checkmark Books, 1997), p. 44.

84. *Inchiesta Parlamentare, Basilicata e Calabria*, p. 476.

85. Quoted in Dennis Mack Smith, *Modern Italy*, p. 208.

86. Douglas B. W. Sladen, *In Sicily, 1896–1898–1900* (London: Sands, 1901), p. 101.

87. Marta Petrusewicz, "The Demise of Latifondismo," in Robert Lumley and Jonathan Morris, *The New History*, p. 26.

88. Giovanni Verga, "Rosso Malpelo," in *Italian Stories/ Novelle Italiane: A Dual-Language Book*, Robert A. Hall, Jr., ed. (New York: Dover, 1989) p. 87.

89. John E. Zucchi, *Italians in Toronto: Development of a National Identity, 1875–1935* (Kingston: McGill-Queens University Press, 1988), p. 27.

90. Jan Brogger, *Montevarese: A Study of Peasant Society and Culture in Southern Italy* (Bergen: Universitets-Forlaget, 1971), p. 43.

91. Robert Foerster, *The Italian Emigration*, p. 95.

92. Quoted in Gary Ross Mormino, *Immigrants on the Hill*, p. 26.

93. Salvatore Salomone-Marino, *Costumi e Usanze*, pp. 69–102.

94. Jerre Magione, *An Ethnic at Large: A Memoir of America in the Thirties and Forties* (New York: G. P. Putnam's 1978), p. 182.

95. Leonard Covello, *The Social Background of the Italo-American School Child: A Study of Southern Italian Family Mores and Their Effect on the School Situation in Italy and America* (1944) (Leiden, Netherlands: E. J. Brill, 1967), p. 88.

96. Charlotte Chapman, *Milocca: A Sicilian Village* (Cambridge, Mass.: Schenkman, 1971), p. 126.

97. Louise Caico, *Sicilian Ways and Days* (New York: D. Appleton, 1910), pp. xii–xiii, 153–154.

98. Charlotte Chapman, *Milocca*, p. 130.

99. Donna Gabaccia, "In the Shadows of the Periphery: Italian Women in the Nineteenth Century," in Marilyn J. Boxer and Jean H. Quatert, *Connecting Spheres: Women in the Western World, 1500 to the Present* (New York: Oxford University Press, 1987), pp. 166–176; Donna Gabaccia, "Italian Immigrant Women in Comparative Perspective," in *The Columbus People: Perspectives in Italian Immigration to the Americas and Australia*, Lydio F. Tomasi, Piero Gastaldo, and Thomas Row, eds. (New York: Center for Migration Studies, 1994), pp. 391–401.

100. Salvatore Salomone-Marino, *Costumi e Usanze*, p. 41.

101. Ibid., p. 41.

102. John H. K. Davis, *Land and Family in Pisticci* (London: Athlone, 1973), p. 49.

103. Quoted in Bolton King and Thomas Obey, *Italy To-Day*, p. 136.

104. Carlo Levi, *Christ Stopped at Eboli*, p. 185.

105. King and Obey, *Italy To-Day*, p. 136.

106. Helen S. Mitchell and Natalie F. Joffee, "Food Patterns of Some European Countries: Background for Study Programs and Guidance of Relief Workers," *Journal of the American Dietetic Association* 20, 10 (November, 1944), p. 681; Charlotte Chapman, *Milocca*, p. 13.

107. Charlotte Chapman, *Milocca*, p. 131.

108. Donna Gabaccia, "Sicilians in Space: Environmental Change and Family Geography," *Journal of Social History* 16, 2 (Winter 1982), p. 55; *From Sicily to Elizabeth Street* (Albany: State University of New York Press, 1984).

109. Salvatore Salomone-Marino, *Costumi e Usanze*, p. 57.

110. Frank Snowden, *Violence*, p. 45.

111. A. L. Maraspini, *The Study of an Italian Village* (Paris: Mouton, 1968), p. 143.

112. "Peter Mossini," in *Ellis Island Interviews: In Their Own Words*, Peter Morton Coan, ed. (New York: Checkmark Books, 1997), p. 43.

113. Jane C. Schneider and Peter T. Schneider, *Festival of the Poor: Fertility Decline and the Ideology of Class in Sicily, 1860–1980* (Tucson: University of Arizona Press, 1996), pp. 107–108, 137, 229–231.

114. "Bruna Pieracci," in Sal La Gumina, *The Immigrants Speak: Italian Americans Tell Their Story* (New York: Center for Migration Studies, 1979), p. 33.

115. Charlotte Chapman, *Milocca*, p. 38.

116. See, for example, Elizabeth Mathias and Richard Raspa, *Italian Folktales in America*, p. 35.

117. Maura O'Connor, *The Romance of Italy and the English Political Imagination* (London: St. Martin's, 1998); *Viaggio nel Sud: Centro interuniversitario di recherche sul "Viaggio in Italia"* (Geneva: Slatkin, 1992).

118. Louise Caico, *Sicilian Ways.*

119. Angelo M. Pellegrini, *The Unprejudiced Palate* (New York: Macmillan, 1948), p. 15.

120. Katherine Hooker, *Through the Heel of Italy* (New York: Rae D. Henkle, 1927), p. 156; see also Norman Douglas, *Old Calabria.*

121. Russell King, *Land Reform: The Italian Experience* (London: Butterworths, 1973), p. 25.

122. Constantine Panunzio, *The Soul of an Immigrant* (New York: Macmillan, 1921) p. 24.

123. Anton Blok, *The Mafia*, p. 22.

124. Norman Douglas, *Old Calabria*, p. 232.

125. Frank Snowden, *Violence*, p. 41.

126. Sydel Silverman, *Three Bells.*

127. Giuliano Procacci, *The Italian Working Class from the Risorgimento to Fascism: Three Lectures* (Cambridge: Harvard University Press, 1979), p. 8.

128. Stuart J. Woolf, *A History of Italy, 1700–1860* (London: Methuen, 1979), p. 284; Samuel J. Surace, *Ideology, Economic Change, and the Working Classes: The Case of Italy* (Berkeley: University of California Press, 1966), p. 36; Pasquale Villari, *Le Lettere Meridionali ed Altri Scritti sulla Questione Sociale in Italia*, Francesco Barbagallo, ed. (Napoli: Guida Editri, 1979), pp. 47–48.

129. Guido Orland, *Confessions*, p. 11.

130. Douglas Brooke Wheelton Sladen, *In Sicily, 1896–1900, with Maps and over 300 Illustrations* (London: Sands, 1901), p. 63.

131. Francis E. Clark, *Our Italian Fellow Citizens*, p. 135; Luigi Ciani, *Il Viaggio per l'Italia de Giannettino*, quoted in Phyllis Williams, *South Italian Folkways*, p. 51.

132. Egano Lambertini, Enrico Volpe, and Antonio Guizzaro, *La Cucina nella Storia di Napoli: Venticinque Secoli di Gastronomia nella Storia e nel Costume di una Città* (Naples: Edizioni Scientfiche Cuzzolin, 1996), pp. 112, 116.

133. George Gissing, *By the Ionian Sea: Notes of a Ramble in Southern Italy* (London: Jonathan Cape, 1901), p. 216.

134. Giuseppe Prezzalini, *Spaghetti Dinner: A History of Spaghetti Eating and Cooking* (New York: Abelard-Schuman, 1955), pp. 25–26.

135. Marie Hall Ets, *Rosa: The Life of An Italian Immigrant* (Minneapolis: University of Minnesota Press, 1970), pp. 18, 29.

136. A. L. Maraspini, *The Study of an Italian Village* (Paris: Mouton, 1968), p. 167; Sydel Silverman, *Three Bells*, pp. 59–60.

137. For a description of regionally specific Christmas foods, see "Christmas in Italy," in Instituto Italiano di Cultura, *Occasional Papers in Italian Folkore 37*, Center for Migration Studies, Series Division, Box 111.

138. Salvatore Salamone-Marino, *Costumi e Usanze*, p. 150.

139. Leonardo Sciascia, *Feste Religiose in Sicilia* (Bari: Leonardo Da Vinci Editrice, 1965).

140. *Inchiesta Parlamentare sulle Condizioni dei Contadini nelle Provincie Meridionali e nella Sicilia: Campania*, vol. 4 (Rome: Tipografia Nazionale Di Giovanni Bertero, 1909), p. 401.

141. Clement L. Valletta, "A Study of Americanization in Carneta: Italian-American Identity through Three Generations," Ph.D. diss., University of Pennsylvania, 1968, p. 23.

142. Anthony L. La Ruffa, *Monte Carmelo: An Italian-American Community in the Bronx* (New York: Gordon and Breach, 1988), p. 46.

143. Domenico Pisani, *L'Etica della Famiglia Siciliana Tra Passato e Presente: Lineamenti di Cultura, Feste e Spiritualità* (Ragusa: Liberoitaliano, 1994), p. 72.

144. Emilano Giancristofaro, *Tradizioni Popolari d'Abruzzo: Feste e Riti Religiosi, Credenze Magiche, Superstizioni, Usanze, Pellegrinaggi* (Rome: Newton Compton, 1995).

145. Maria Adele Di Leo, *Feste Popolari di Sicilia* (Rome: Newton and Compton, 1997), pp. 14, 25, 37–40, 44, 245.

146. Sydel Silverman, *Three Bells*, p. 160.

147. Bruce B. Giuliano, *Sacro o Profano? A Consideration of Four Italian-Canadian Religious Festivals* (Ottawa: National Museum of Canada, 1976), p. 15.

148. Peter Burke, *The Historical Anthropology of Early Modern Italy: Essays on Perception and Communication* (Cambridge: Cambridge University Press, 1987), pp. 132–149.

149. Carol Field, *Celebrating Italy* (New York: William Morrow, 1990), pp. 340, 18.

150. Piercarlo Grimaldi, *Il Calendario Rituale Contadino: Il Tempo della Festa e del Lavoro fra Tradizione e Complessità Sociale* (Milan: FrancoAngeli, 1993).

151. Carol Field, *Celebrating Italy*, p. 374.

152. Mark Wyman, *Round-Trip to America: The Immigrants Return to Europe, 1880–1930* (Ithaca, New York: Cornell University Press, 1993); Betty Boyd Caroli, *Italian Repatriation from the United States, 1900–1914* (New York: Center for Migration Studies, 1973).

153. Katherine Hooker, in *Through the Heel*, p. 13.

154. Francesco P. Cerase, "From Italy to the United States and Back: Re-

turned Migrants, Conservative or Innovative?" Ph.D. diss., Columbia University, 1971; George R. Gilkey, "The United States and Italy: Migration and Repatriation," *Journal of Developing Areas* 2, 1 (October 1967), pp. 23–63; George R. Gilkey, "The Effects of Emigration on Italy, 1900–1923," Ph.D. diss., Northwestern University, 1950.

155. Angelo Pellegrini, *Unprejudiced Palate*, p. 22.

156. Quoted in Gary R. Mormino and George E. Pozzetta, *The Immigrant World of Ybor City: Italians and Their Latin Neighbors in Tampa, 1885–1985* (Urbana: University of Illinois Press, 1987), p. 15.

157. John E. Zucchi, *Italians in Toronto*, p. 29.

158. Roland Sarti, *Long Live the Strong*, p. 132.

159. Giorgio Lolli, Emidio Serianni, Grace M. Golder, and Pierpaolo Luzzatto-Fegiz, *Alcohol in Italian Culture: Food and Wine in Relation to Sobriety among Italians and Italian Americans* (Glencoe, Ill.: Free Press, 1958), pp. 50, 53. William A. Douglass, *Emigration in a South Italian Town*, p. 107.

160. Dino Cinel, *The National Integration*, pp. 206, 227–228.

161. Francesco Ventresca, *Personal Reminiscences of a Naturalized American* (New York: Daniel Ryerson, 1937), pp. 16–17.

162. Pietro Militello, *Italians in America* (Philadelphia: Franklin, 1973), p. 1.

3 "THE BREAD IS SOFT"

1. Communication from Gary Mormino, grandson of Rosolino Mormino, to author, Oct. 25, 1999.

2. Paul Radin, *The Italians of San Francisco: Their Adjustment and Acculturation* (1935) (San Francisco: R & E Associates, 1970), pp. 71–72, 96–97.

3. Peter Campon, *The Evolution of an Immigrant* (Brooklyn: Theo Gaus' Sons, n.d.), p. 63.

4. Thomas Kessner, *The Golden Door: Italian and Jewish Immigrant Mobility in New York City, 1880–1915* (New York: Oxford University Press, 1977).

5. Antonio Stella, *The Effects of Urban Congestion on Italian Women and Children* (New York: William Wood, 1908), p. 21.

6. Humbert S. Nelli, *The Italians in Chicago, 1880–1930: A Study in Ethnic Mobility* (New York: Oxford University Press, 1970), pp. 51–53, 55–66, 140–142.

7. See Colleen L. Johnson, *Growing Up and Growing Old in Italian-American Families* (New Brunswick, N.J.: Rutgers University Press, 1985), p. 34.

8. "Italian Interviews, Informant no.7," W.P.A. Archives, University of Connecticut, Storrs, Connecticut, Box 22.

9. June Namias, *First Generation: In the Words of Twentieth-Century American Immigrants* (Boston: Beacon Press, 1978), p. 23.

10. Antonio Mangano, "The Italian Colonies of New York City," M.A. thesis, Columbia University, 1903, p. 51.

11. Donald Tricario, *The Italians of Greenwich Village: The Social Structure and Transformation of an Ethnic Community* (New York: Center for Migration Studies, 1984) p. 23

12. Joseph Kirkland, "Among the Poor of Chicago," in *The Poor in Great Cities* (New York: Charles Scribner's Sons, 1895), p. 201.

13. Carroll D. Wright, *The Italians in Chicago: A Social and Economic Study* (Washington: Government Printing Office, 1897), p. 47.

14. Antonio Stella, *The Effects of Urban Congestion on Italian Women and Children*, p. 21.

15. Eliot Lord, John J. D. Tremor and Samuel J. Barrows, *The Italian in America* (New York: B. F. Buck, 1905), p. 201.

16. Frank J. Sheridan, "Salari, Ore di Lavoro, Consumi e Risparmi degli Italiani negli Stati Uniti," in *Gli Italiani negli Stati Uniti* (Rome: Presso la Rivista Popolare, 1909), pp. 16–21.

17. Louis C. Odenkrantz, *Italian Women in Industry: A Study of Conditions in New York City* (New York: Russell Sage, 1919), p. 198.

18. Quoted in Luciano John Iorizzo, "Italian Immigration and the Impact of the Padrone System," Ph.D. diss., 1966, Syracuse University, p. 58.

19. Richard N. Juliani, "The Social Organization of Immigration: The Italians in Philadelphia," Ph.D. diss., University of Pennsylvania, 1971, p. 206.

20. Carlo Bianco, *The Two Rosetos* (Bloomington: Indiana University Press, 1974), pp. 134–136.

21. Clement L. Valletta, "A Study of Americanization in Carneta: Italian-American Identity through Three Generations," Ph.D. diss., University of Pennsylvania, 1968.

22. Angelo Pellegrini, "An Italian Odyssey: From Famine to Feast," in James P. Shenton, et al., *American Cooking: The Melting Pot* (New York: Time-Life Books, 1971), pp. 31–31.

23. Carlo Bianco, "Migration and Urbanization of a Traditional Culture: American Italian Experience," in Richard Dorson, *Folklore in the Modern World* (The Hague: Mouton, 1978), pp. 55–63.

24. Niccolà de Quattrociocchi, *Love and Dishes* (Indianapolis: Bobbs-Merrill, 1950), pp. 30, 49.

25. Judith G. Goode, Karen Curtis, and Janet Theophano, "Meal Formats, Meal Cycles, and Menu Negotiation in the Maintenance of one Italian-American Community," in *Food in the Social Order: Studies of Food and Festivities in Three American Communities*, Mary Douglas, ed. (New York: Russell Sage Foundation, 1984), pp. 143–218.

26. Charlotte Adams, "Italian Life in New York," *Harper's Magazine 62*

(April 1881), p. 676; Harvey Zorbaugh, *Gold Coast and Slum: A Sociological Study of Chicago's Near North Side* (Chicago: University of Chicago Press, 1926), p. 165.

27. Mary Sherman, "Manufacturing of Foods in the Tenements," *Charities* 15 (Feb. 10, 1906), pp. 669–670.

28. John W. Briggs, *An Italian Passage: Immigrants to Three American Cities, 1890–1930* (New Haven: Yale University Press, 1978), pp. 167–168.

29. Erasmo S. Ciccolella, *Vibrant Life, 1886–1942: Trenton's Italian Americans* (New York: Center for Migration Studies, 1986), pp. 26, 112.

30. James J. Divita, *The Italians of Indianapolis: The Story of Holy Rosary Catholic Parish, 1909–1984* (Indianapolis: Holy Rosary Parish, 1984), p. 44.

31. United States Department of Agriculture, Office of Experiment Stations, *Dietary Studies in Chicago in 1895 and 1896: Conducted with the Cooperation of Jane Addams and Caroline L. Hunt, of Hull House* (Washington: Government Printing Office, 1898) p. 15.

32. Sadie Penzato, *Growing Up Sicilian and Female in America, in a Small Town in the Thirties* (New York: Bedford Graphics, 1991), p. 91

33. Seamus Cooney, *John Fante: Selected Letters, 1932–1981* (Santa Rosa: Black Sparrow Press, 1991), p. 39.

34. John Fante, *Wait Until Spring Bandini* (1938) (Santa Barbara: Black Sparrow Press, 1983), p. 13.

35. Lucy H. Gillett, "Factors Influencing Nutrition Work among Italians," *Journal of Home Economics* 14, 1 (Jan. 1922), p. 16.

36. Dorothy Gladys Spicer, "Health Superstitions of the Italian Immigrants," *Hygeia* 4 (May 1926), p. 266.

37. Saul D. Alinsky, *Reveille for Radicals* (New York: Random House, 1946), p. 81.

38. Gertrude Gates Mudge, "Italian Dietary Adjustments," *Journal of Home Economics* 15, 4 (April 1923), pp. 181–185; Lucy H. Gillett, "Factors Influencing Nutrition Work among Italians," pp. 14–19.

39. Lucy H. Gillett, "The Great Need for Information on Racial Dietary Customs," *Journal of Home Economics* 14 (June 1922), p. 260.

40. Louise More Boland, *Wage-Earners' Budgets: A Study of Standards and Cost of Living in New York City* (New York: Henry Holt, 1907), pp. 218–219.

41. *Report on Condition of Woman and Child Wage-Earners in the United States*, 61st Congress, Second Session, Government Document #645 (Washington: Government Printing Office, 1911), p. 283.

42. Mary Catherine Tripalin, *A Taste of Memories from the Old "Bush": Italian Recipes and Food Memories from People Who Lived in Madison's Greenbush District, 1900–1960* (Madison: Italian-American Women's Mutual Society, 1988), pp. 27, 33.

43. Quoted in Gary Mormino, *Immigrants on the Hill: Italian Americans in St. Louis, 1882–1982* (Urbana: University of Illinois Press, 1986), pp. 42–43.

44. Caroline Ware, *Greenwich Village: 1920–1930* (New York: Harper and Row, 1935), p. 109.

45. See Lucy H. Gillett and Penelope Burts Rice, *Influence of Education on the Food Habits of Some New York City Families* (New York: New York Association for the Improvement of the Conditions of the Poor, 1931); "Report of the New York School Lunch Committee," *Journal of Home Economics* 4 (Dec. 1912), pp. 482–492; Mable Hyde Kittredge, "The Need of the Immigrant," *Journal of Home Economics* 5, 4 (Oct. 1913), pp. 307–316; "Teaching Domestic Science to Different Nationalities," *Journal of Home Economics* 2, 3 (June 1910), pp. 271–273; Mabel H. Kittredge, "Experiments with School Lunches in New York City," *Journal of Home Economics* 2, 2 (April 1910), pp. 174–177.

46. Gertrude Gates Mudge, "Italian Dietary Adjustments," *Journal of Home Economics* 15, 4 (April 1923), pp. 181–185. Lucy H. Gillett, "Factors Influencing Nutrition Work among Italians," pp. 14–19.

47. Pietro di Donato, *Christ in Concrete* (1937) (New York: Penguin, 1993), pp. 12, 86, 189–190.

48. Leonard Covello, *The Social Background of the Italo-American School Child: A Study of the Southern Italian Family Mores and Their Effect on the School Situation in Italy and America* (Leiden: E. J. Brill, 1967), p. 295.

49. Angelo Pellegrini, *The Unprejudiced Palate* (New York: Macmillan, 1948), pp. 27–28.

50. Marie Hall Ets, *Rosa: The Life of an Italian Immigrant* (Minneapolis: University of Minnesota Press, 1970), p. 29.

51. Ibid., pp. 172, 175.

52. Ibid., pp. 189, 191.

53. Sophonisba P. Breckenridge, *New Homes for Old* (New York: Harper, 1921).

54. Sophonisba Breckenridge Papers, Regenstein Library, University of Chicago, Box I, folder 16.

55. Mangione finished out his memoir cycle with *An Ethnic At Large: A Memoir of America in the Thirties and Forties* (New York: G. P. Putnam's, 1978) and *Reunion in Sicily* (Boston: Houghton Mifflin, 1950).

56. Jerre Mangione, *Mount Allegro* (New York: Hill and Wang, 1942), p. 17.

57. Jerre Mangione, *An Ethnic*, p. 15.

58. Francesco Ventresca, *Personal Reminiscences of a Naturalized American* (New York: Daniel Ryerson, 1937), p. 24; Frederick Wright, *The Italians in America* (New York: Missionary Education Movement in the United States and Canada, 1913), p. 11.

59. Frederick A. Bushee, "Italian Immigrants in Boston," *The Arena* 17 (April 1897), pp. 722–734.

60. George La Piana, *The Italians in Milwaukee* (Milwaukee: The Associated Charities, 1915), pp. 12–13.

61. Antonio Mangano, "The Italian Colonies of New York City," p. 21.

62. Charles W. Churchill, "The Italians of Newark: A Community Study," Ph.D. diss. New York University, 1942, p. 140.

63. Giovanni E. Schiavo, *The Italians in Chicago: A Study in Americanization* (Chicago: Italian American Publishing, 1928), p. 41.

64. Frederick A. Bushee, *Ethnic Factors in the Population of Boston* (New York: Macmillan/S. Sonnenschein, 1903), p. 29.

65. Donald Tricarico, *The Italians of Greenwich Village*, pp. 9–10.

66. Jane Voiles, "Genoese Folkways in a Mining Camp," *California Folklore Quarterly* 3, 3 (July 1944), p. 214.

67. Lizabeth Cohen, "Embellishing a Life of Labor: An Interpretation of the Material Culture of American Working-Class Homes, 1885–1915," in Dirk Hoerder, ed., *Labor Migration in the Atlantic Economies: The European and North American Working Classes During the Period of Industrialization* (Westport, Conn: Greenwood Press, 1985) p. 333.

68. Gary R. Mormino and George E. Pozzetta, *The Immigrant World of Ybor City: Italians and Their Latin Neighbors in Tampa, 1885–1985* (Urbana: University of Illinois Press, 1987), p. 242.

69. Donna R. Gabaccia, *From Sicily to Elizabeth Street: Housing and Social Change among Italian Immigrants, 1880–1930* (Albany: State University of New York Press, 1984), p. 93.

70. Eliot Lord, John J. D. Trenor, and Samuel J. Barrows, *The Italian*, p. 108.

71. Mari Tomasi, *Like Lesser Gods* (1949) (Shelburn, Vt.: New England Press, 1988), p. 29.

72. Robert A. Woods and Albert J. Kennedy, *The Zone of Emergence* (Cambridge, Mass.: Harvard University Press, 1962), p. 123.

73. North Bennet Street Industrial School Papers, Schlesinger Library, Series II, 47, 1135.

74. John Foster Carr, *Guide for the Italian in the United States of America* (New York: Doubleday, Page, 1911), p. 23.

75. The clipping about broccoli, courtesy of Gary Mormino, is from *San Jose Mercury*, Sept. 6, 1942. On truck farming see Luigi Villari, *Gli State Uniti d'America e l'Emigrazione Italiana* (Milan: Fratelli Treves, 1912), pp. 169–171, 255–259; Kansas City & Memphis Railway Company, *History of Tontitown: The Gem of the Ozarks* (1901); Frissco Lines, *Colonia Italiana: Tontitown, Arkansas, Stati Uniti D'America* (St. Louis: 1899).

76. Konrad Bercovici, *Around the World in New York* (New York: Century, 1924), p. 127.

77. James J. Divita, *Italians of Indianapolis*, pp. 10–12.

78. George Schiro, *Americans by Choice: History of the Italians in Utica* (Utica: George Schiavo, 1940), p. 151.

79. For the various cities see: George Pozzetta, "The Italians of New York

City, 1890–1914," Ph.D. diss., University of North Carolina at Chapel Hill, 1971, pp. 307–308, 317; Richard N. Juliani, *Building Little Italy: Philadelphia's Italians before Mass Migration* (University Park: Pennsylvania State University Press, 1998), pp. 240–241; Nelli, *The Italians in Chicago*, pp. 73, 209; Deanna Paoli La Gumina, *The Italians of San Francisco, 1850–1930* (New York: Center for Migration Studies, 1978), pp. 79–108.

80. See Lizabeth Cohen, *Making a New Deal: Industrial Workers in Chicago, 1919–1939* (New York: Cambridge University Press, 1990).

81. Dennis J. Starr, *The Italians of New Jersey: A Historical Introduction and Bibliography* (Newark: New Jersey Historical Society, 1985), p. 15.

82. Joseph W. Carlevale, *Who's Who Among Americans of Italian Descent in Connecticut* (New Haven: Carlevale Publishing, 1942) and *Leading Americans of Italian Descent in Massachusetts* (Plymouth, Mass: Memorial Press, 1946); Giovanni Schiavo, *Four Centuries of Italian-American History* (New York: Vigo Press, 1958).

83. David Nicandri, *Italians in Washington State: Emigration, 1853–1924* (Tacoma: Washington State American Revolution Bicentennial Commission, 1978), p. 45.

84. Guido Orlando, *Confessions of a Scoundrel* (Philadelphia: John C. Winston, 1954), pp. 14–15.

85. Jean Ann Scarpaci, "Italian Immigrants in Louisiana's Sugar Parishes: Recruitment, Labor Conditions, and Community Relations, 1880–1910," Ph.D. diss., Rutgers University, 1972, pp. 120–121.

86. Dino Cinel, *From Italy to San Francisco: The Immigrant Experience* (Stanford: Stanford University Press, 1982), pp. 217–218.

87. WPA in the State of Nebraska, *The Italians of Omaha* (Omaha: Independent Printing, 1941), p. 39.

88. Frank J. Palescandolo, *Remembrance of a Restaurant: The Decameron of Dining Tales of the Table of a Little Bit of Naples in Coney Island* (no publication data, Center for Migration Studies), pp. 24, 431.

89. Konrad Bercovici, *Around the World in New York*, p. 128.

90. Donald Tricarico, *The Italians of Greenwich Village.*

91. Emelise Aleandri, "Women in the Italian American Theater of the Nineteenth Century," in *The Italian Immigrant Woman in North America: Proceedings of the Tenth Annual Conference of the American Italian Historical Association*, Betty Boyd Caroli, Robert F. Harney, and Lydio Tomasi, eds. (Toronto: Multicultural History Society of Ontario, 1978), pp. 358–368.

92. "The Roma," Warshaw Collection, Box 2, "P,Q,R," Smithsonian Institution Archives Center.

93. Michael Immerso, *Newark's Little Italy: The Vanished First Ward* (New Brunswick: Rutgers University Press, 1997).

94. Albert Pecorini, "The Italians in the United States," *Forum* 45 (Jan. 1911), pp. 15–29.

95. George Pozzetta, "The Italians of New York City, 1890–1914," pp. 337–339.

96. Judith E. Smith, *Family Connections: A History of Italian and Jewish Immigrant Lives in Providence, Rhode Island, 1900–1940* (Albany: State University of New York Press, 1985), pp. 157–158.

97. For Ronzoni's promotional material, which stressed both its connection to Italian tradition and the modern factory system, see Warshaw Collection, "Ronzoni Macaroni, Long Island City, New York," Smithsonian Institution/National Museum of American History, Archives Center.

98. BTW, Local 3, Box 2, 86, Tamiment Library, New York University.

99. See *La Società Italiani negli Stati Uniti del'America del Nord nel 1910* (1910), in Francesco Cordasco and Michael V. Cordasco, *The Italian Emigration to the United States, 1880–1930: A Bibliographical Register of Italian Views, Including Selected Numbers from the Italian Commisariate of Emigration, Bollettino Dell' Emigrazione* (Fairview, N.J.: Junius-Vaughn, 1990), p. 139; Ellen Calomiris, "Conflict, Cooperation, Acceptance: The Italian Experience in Delaware," *Delaware History* 20, 4 (Fall–Winter, 1983), pp. 270–290.

100. Mary Brown Sumner, "A Strike for Clean Bread," *Charities* 24 (June 18, 1910), pp. 483–487.

101. Samuel L. Baily, "The Italians and the Development of Organized Labor in Argentina, Brazil, and the United States, 1880—1914," *Journal of Social History* 3, 2 (Winter 1969–70), pp. 123–134.

102. Edwin Fenton, "Immigrants and Unions: A Case Study: Italians and American Labor, 1870–1920," Ph.D. diss., Harvard University, 1957; Charles W. Churchill, "The Italians of Newark: A Community Study," p. 11.

103. Robert D. Parmet, *Labor and Immigration in Industrial America* (Boston: Twyane, 1981), pp. 129, 137, 140.

104. Charles P. Ferroni, "The Italians in Cleveland: A Study in Assimilation," Ph.D. diss., Kent State University, 1969, p. 122.

105. "An Open Letter from a Member of the Circolo Italo-Americano di Boston," 1908, in *Italians in the United States: A Repository of Rare Tracts and Miscellania* (New York: Arno Press, 1975), p. 2.

106. Gloria Nardini, *Che Bella Figura! The Power of Performance in an Italian Ladies' Club in Chicago* (Albany: State University of New York Press, 1999), p. 64.

107. John Daniels, *American Via the Neighborhood: The Acculturation of Immigrant Groups into American Society* (New York: Harper and Brothers, 1920), p. 198.

108. Italian Welfare League, *Annual Report: 1927* (New York: Italian Welfare League, 1927), p. 13; Report, August 21–23, 1918, Italian Welfare League Papers, Box 15, Center for Migration Studies.

109. Salvatore Primeggia and Joseph A. Varacalli, "The Sacred and Profane among Italian American Catholics: The Giglio Feast," *International Jour-*

nal of Politics, Culture and Society 9, 3 (Spring 1996), pp. 423–450; Margaret Hobbie, *Italian American Material Culture: A Directory of Collections, Sites, and Festivals in the United States and Canada* (New York: Greenwood Press, 1992), pp. 85–138.

110. Denise Mangieri DiCarlo, "The Interplay of Ritual for Italians in Multicultural Society," in Jerome Krase and Judith N. DeSena, *Italian Americans in a Multicultural Society: Proceedings of the Symposium of the American Italian Historical Association, 1993*, pp. 110–111.

111. Helen Barolini, *Festa: Recipes and Recollections of Italian Holidays* (New York: Harcourt Brace Jovanovich, 1986).

112. Denise Mangieri DiCarlo, "The History of the Italian Festa in New York City: 1880's to the Present," Ph.D. diss., New York University, 1990.

113. Rudolph J. Vecoli, "Prelates and Peasants: Italian Immigrants and the Catholic Church," *Journal of Social History* 2, 3 (Spring 1969), pp. 217–238.

114. WPA, *The Italians of Omaha*, p. 99.

115. Edward Orsi, *The Madonna of 115th Street: Faith and Community in Italian Harlem, 1880–1950* (New Haven: Yale University Press, 1985).

116. Charles Speroni, "The Observance of Saint Joseph's Day among the Sicilians of Southern California," *Southern Folklore Quarterly* 4, 3 (Sept. 1940), pp. 135–139.

117. Antonio Stella, *Some Aspects of Italian Immigration to the United States: Statistical Data and General Considerations Based Chiefly Upon the United States Census and Other Official Publications* (New York: G. P. Putnam's, 1924) p. 11.

118. Caroline Ware, *Greenwich Village*, p. 42.

119. Robert F. Harney, "Men without Women: Italian Migrants in Canada, 1885–1930," *Canadian Ethnic Studies* 11, 1 (1979), pp. 29–47.

120. See as one of many examples, Salvatore LaGumina, *From Steerage to Suburb: Long Island Italians* (New York: Center for Migration Studies, 1988), p. 27.

121. Quoted in Jean Ann Scarpaci, "Italian Immigrants in Louisiana," p. 131.

122. Edith Abbott, *The Tenements of Chicago: 1908–1935* (Chicago: University of Chicago Press, 1936), pp. 353–354.

123. John Potesto, "Itinerant Grimaldesi: Paesani on the Railways of North America," in *Italian Immigrants in Rural and Small Town America*, Rudoph Vecoli, ed. (New York: American Italian Historical Association, 1987) pp. 50–61.

124. Edith Abbott, *The Tenements*, p. 354.

125. Geneoffa Nizzardini and Natalie F. Joffe, "Italian Food Patterns and Their Relationship to Wartime Problems of Food and Nutrition," Committee on Food Habits, National Research Council, Social Welfare Archives, University of Minnesota, La Guardia House papers, Box 1, folder 8, p. 5.

126. Antonio Mangano, "The Italian Colonies of New York City," pp. 11–

13; J. H. Senner, "Immigration from Italy," *North American Review* 162, 475 (June 1896), pp. 649–656; William P. Shriver, *At Work with the Italians* (New York: Missionary Education Movement of the United States and Canada, 1917), p. 11; Folger Barker, "What of the Italian Immigrant," *Arena* 34 (August 1905), pp. 174–176; Julius G. Rothenberg, "A Glance at a 1911 Self-Help Book for Italian Immigrants," *Italian Americana* 3, 1 (Autumn 1976), p. 48; John E. Zucchi, *Italians in Toronto: Development of a National Identity* (Kingston, Ont.: McGill-Queen's University Press, 1988), p. 47; and most importantly, Luciano J. Iorizzo, "Italian Immigration and the Impact of the Padrone System."

127. Constantine Panunzio, *The Soul of an Immigrant* (New York: Macmillan, 1912), p. 285.

128. Luciano Iorizzo, "Italian Immigration," p. 178.

129. Richard Raspa, "Exotic Foods among Italian-Americans in Mormon Utah: Food as Nostalgic Enactment of Identity," in *Ethnic and Regional Foodways in the United States: The Performance of Group Identity*, Linda K. Brown and Kay Mussell, eds. (Knoxville: University of Tennessee Press, 1984), p. 186.

130. Joseph Conlin, *Bacon, Beans, and Galantines: Food and Foodways on the Western Mining Frontier* (Reno: University of Nevada Press, 1986), p. 181.

131. Maria Sermolino, *Papa's Table d'Hote* (Philadelphia: J. B. Lippincott, 1952), pp. 13–15.

132. "An Italian Dinner," *American Kitchen Magazine* 8, 6 (March 1898), pp. 4, 6.

133. Richard N. Juliani, "The Social Organization of Immigration: The Italians in Philadelphia," pp. 171–172.

134. Edith Abbott, *The Tenements*, p. 354.

135. Quoted in Salvatore LaGumina, *From Steerage*, p. 27.

136. Judith E. Smith, *Family Connections*, p. 48; Gary Mormino, *Immigrants on the Hill*, p. 113; Virginia Yans-McLaughlin, *Family and Community: Italian Immigrants in Buffalo, 1880–1930* (Ithaca: Cornell University Press, 1977), p. 165.

137. Garibaldi M. LaPolla, *The Grand Gennaro* (New York: Vanguard, 1935), pp. 18–19, 23, 25, 31.

138. Anthony M. Gisolfi, *Caudine Country: The Old World and an American Childhood* (New York: Senda Nueva de Ediciones, 1985), p. 118.

139. Harvey W. Zorbaugh, *The Gold Coast and the Slum*, p. 168.

140. Garibaldi LaPolla, *Grand Gennaro*, p. 319.

141. Nizzardini and Joffe, *Italian Food Practices*, p. 5.

142. Antonio Mangano, *Sons of Italy: A Social and Religious Study of the Italians in America* (New York: Russell and Russell, 1917), pp. 147–149.

143. North Bennett Street Papers, Series I, 4; "The Work of the North Bennett Street Industrial School from 1891 to 1892," Ser. I, 1, 1.

144. Marie Josephine Concistre, "Adult Education in a Local Area: A Study of a Decade in the Life and Education of the Adult Italian Immigrant in East Harlem, New York City," Ph.D. diss., New York University, 1943, pp. 135, 164, 174, 195–196.

145. Cecile L.Greil, "L'Economia per Cibi," in *I Problemi della Madre in un Paese Nuovo* (New York: National Board, YWCA, 1919), pp. 67–71.

146. Charles D. Ferroni, "The Italians in Cleveland: A Study in Assimilation," pp. 251–263.

147. Maxine Seller, "Protestant Evangelism and the Italian Immigrant Woman," in *Italian Immigrant Woman in North America*, p. 131; Enrico Sartorio, *Social and Religious Life of Italians in America* (Boston: Christopher House, 1918), pp. 57–58.

148. Marie J. Concistre, "Adult Education," p. 346.

149. Robert A. Orsi, *The Madonna of 115th Street*, pp. 50–106.

150. Quoted in Richard N. Juliani, "The Settlement House and the Italian Family," in *Italian Immigrant Woman in North America*, pp. 118–119.

151. Genoeffa Nizzardini and Natalie F. Joffee, "Italian Food Patterns," p. 9.

152. Mary Jane Capozzoli, *Three Generations of Italian American Women in Nassau County, 1925–1981* (New York: Garland, 1990), p. 27.

153. Caroline Ware, *Greenwich Village*, p. 145; William F. Whyte, *Street Corner Society: The Social Structure of an Italian Slum* (Chicago: University of Chicago Press, 1943), p. 255; Herbert J. Gans, *The Urban Villagers: Group and Class in the Life of Italian-Americans* (Glencoe, Ill.: Free Press, 1955).

154. Marie J. Concistre, "Adult Education," p. 341.

155. Donald Tricarico, *The Italians of Greenwich Village*, p. 21.

156. Carlo Bianco, *The Two Rosetos*, p. 29; James J. Divita, *The Italians of Indianapolis*, p. 44.

157. Catherine Tripalin Murray, *A Taste of Memories*, p. 42.

158. Donald Tricarico, *The Italians of Greenwich Village*, p. 23.

159. Anthony Gisolfi, *Caudine Country*, pp. 118–120.

160. Jerre Mangione, *An Ethnic*, p. 15; "On Being Sicilian," in Frances Cordasco, *Studies in Italian American Social History*, pp. 40–49.

161. Leonard Covello, *Social Background*, p. 343.

162. Virginia Yans-McLaughlin, *Family and Community*.

163. Rocco Brindisi, "The Italian and Public Health," *Charities* 12 (May 7, 1904), pp. 483–486.

164. Leonard Covello, *The Heart Is the Teacher* (New York: McGraw-Hill, 1958).

165. Leonard Covello, "The Social Background of the Italo-American School Child: A Study of the Southern Italian Family Mores and Their Effect

on the School Situation in Italy and America," Ph.D. diss., New York University, 1944, p. 337.

166. Joseph Wilfred Tait, *Some Aspects of the Effects of the Dominant American Culture upon Children of Italian Parentage* (New York: Teachers College, Columbia University, 1942), p. 49.

167. Leonard Covello, "The Social Background of the Italo-American School Child," p. 341.

168. Ivan Childs, *Italian or American? The Second Generation in Conflict* (New Haven: Yale University Press, 1943).

169. Ibid., pp. 110–111, 138.

170. Philip M. Rose, *The Italians in America* (New York: George H. Dorrance, 1922), p. 65.

4 "OUTCAST FROM LIFE'S FEAST"

1. Alan O'Day and John Stevenson, *Irish Historical Documents Since 1800* (Savage, Maryland: Barnes and Noble Books, 1992), p. 133.

2. Joyce, James, "A Painful Case," in *Dubliners* (New York: Penguin Books, 1968), p. 117.

3. The Irish were hardly alone in their use of alcohol as a source of food and social satisfaction. Throughout northern Europe the same pattern could be found. See James S. Roberts, *Drink, Temperance, and the Working Class in Nineteenth Century Germany* (Boston: George Allen and Unwin, 1984). Roberts commented that for German workers "the alcohol problem had more to do with diet than with drunkenness." *Kartoffelschnaps*, a cheap liquor made from potatoes, provided a more available source of calories than food in its solid form.

4. Kenneth Connell, "Illicit Distillation," in Kenneth H. Connell, *Irish Peasant Society: Four Historical Essays* (Dublin: Irish Academic Press, 1996), p. 1.

5. On the vast amounts of Irish-grown grain which went into distilled beverages see S. R. Dennison and Oliver MacDonagh, *Guinness, 1886–1939: From Incorporation to the Second World War* (Cork: Cork University Press, 1998); St. James's Gate Brewery, *History and Guide* (Dublin: A. Guinness, 1931). On other aspects of drink in Ireland see Elizabeth Malcom, "The Rise of the Pub: A Study in the Discipline of Popular Culture," in James S. Donnelly, Jr. and Kerby A. Miller, eds., *Irish Popular Culture, 1650–1850* (Dublin: Irish Academic Press, 1998), pp. 50–77; E. B. Maguire, *Irish Whiskey: A History of Distilling, the Spirit Trade and Excise Controls in Ireland* (New York: Barnes and Noble, 1973); Hewitt S. Thayer, "Distilling Spirits and Regulating Subjects: Whiskey and Beer in Romantic Britain," *Eire-Ireland* 30, 3 (Fall 1995), pp. 7–13.

6. Helen Sheil, *Falling into Wretchedness: Ferbane in the Late 1830's* (Dublin: Irish Academic Press, 1998), pp. 17, 53–54.

7. S. J. Connolly, *Priests and People in Pre-Famine Ireland, 1780–1845* (Dublin: Gill and Macmillan, 1982), p. 185.

8. Desmond J. Keenan, *The Catholic Church in Nineteenth-Century Ireland: A Sociological Study* (Dublin: Gill and Macmillan, 1983), pp. 23, 101; Emmet Larkin, "The Devotional Revolution in Ireland, 1850–1875," *American Historical Review* 78, 3 (June 1972), pp. 625–652.

9. Ray Sokolov, *Why We Eat What We Eat: How the Encounter Between the New World and the Old Changed the Way Everyone on the Planet Eats* (New York: Summit Books, 1991); Sidney Mintz, *Sweetness and Power: The Place of Sugar in Modern History* (New York: Viking, 1985).

10. E. P. Thompson, *The Making of the English Working Class* (New York: Penguin Books, 1963), pp. 347–348.

11. C. F. Longworthy, *Potatoes and Other Root Crops as Food: United States Department of Agriculture, Farmers Bulletin no. 295* (Washington, D.C.: Government Printing Office, 1910), p. 295.

12. Redcliffe Salaman, *The History and Social Influence of the Potato* (Cambridge: Cambridge University Press, 1949), p. 188.

13. *Ibid.*, p. 274.

14. Quoted in E. Margaret Crawford, "The Irish Workhouse Diet, 1840–1890," in *Food, Diet and Economic Change Past and Present*, Catherine Geissler and Derek J. Oddy, eds. (Leicester: Leicester University Press, 1993), p. 83.

15. Cormac O'Grada, *The Great Irish Famine: Prepared for the Economic History Society* (Cambridge: Cambridge University Press, 1989), p. 8.

16. General Report of the Census Commissioners, *The Census of Ireland for 1851* (1856), p. 2087, table xxxiii.

17. John Mitchel, *The Last Conquest of Ireland (Perhaps)* (Glasgow: Cameron, Fergeson, 1980), p. 219.

18. Quoted in James S. Donnelly, Jr., "The Construction of the Memory of the Famine in Ireland and the Irish Diaspora, 1850–1900," *Eire-Ireland* 31, 1–2 (Spring-Summer 1996), pp. 28–29.

19. Austin Bourke in *"The Visitation of God"? The Potato and the Great Irish Famine* (Dublin: Lilliput Press, 1993) concluded that the imagery of memory departed dramatically from statistical reality. Total exports of grain in the Famine years fell below the annual averages.

20. Christopher Morash, ed., *The Hungry Voice: The Poetry of the Irish Famine* (Dublin: Irish Academic Press, 1989), pp. 190–192, 287.

21. Joel Mokyr, *Why Ireland Starved: A Quantitative and Analytical History of the Irish Economy, 1800–1845* (London: Allen and Unwin, 1983).

22. Helen E. Hatton, *The Largest Amount of Food: Quaker Relief in Ireland, 1654–1921* (Montreal: McGill-Queen's University Press, 1993), p. 5.

23. Alexis Soyer, *Charitable Cookery; or, the Poor Man's Regenerator* (London: Simpkin, Marsha and John Oliver, 1847).

24. Ibid., pp. 10, 15.

25. E. R. R. Greene, "Agriculture," in *The Great Famine: Studies in Irish History, 1845–1852*, R. Dudley Edwards and T. Desmond Williams, eds. (Dublin: Browne and Nolan, 1956), p. 121.

26. Louis M. Cullen, "Irish History Without the Potato," *Past and Present* 40 (1968), pp. 72–83; Kenneth H. Connell, "The Potato in Ireland," *Past and Present* 23 (Nov. 1962), pp. 57–71; L. M. Cullen, "Population Growth and Diet, 1600–1850," in J. M. Goldstrom and L. A. Clarkson, eds., *Irish Population, Economy, and Society: Essays in Honour of the Late K. H. Connell* (Oxford: Clarendon Press, 1981), pp. 89–111.

27. E. P. Thompson, *Making of the English Working Class*, p. 348.

28. Kenneth Connell, "The Potato in Ireland," pp. 59–60.

29. Cecil Woodham-Smith, *Great Hunger* (London: Penguin, 1962), p. 50; James S. Donnelly, Jr., *The Land and the People of Nineteenth-Century Cork: The Rural Economy and the Land Question* (London: Routledge and Kegan Paul, 1975), pp. 245; E. Margaret Crawford, "Indian Meal and Pellagra in Nineteenth-Century Ireland," in J. M. Goldstrom and L. A. Clarkson, eds., *Irish Population*, pp. 113–133.

30. David N. Doyle, "Unestablished Irishmen: New Immigrants and Industrial America, 1870–1910," in *American Labor and Immigration History, 1877–1920s: European Research*, Dirk Hoerder, ed. (Urbana: University of Illinois Press, 1983), p. 212.

31. According to the European Union, the Irish in the 1990s still eat more potatoes than the people of any other member nations. In 1993 average Irish potato consumption was 143 kg a year, as opposed to Portugal which registered 107 kg., Spain, 106kg. and the United Kingdom, 99kg. See *Eurostat: Basic Statistics of the Community* (Luxembourg: Statistical Office of the European Community, 1993), Table 5.9.

32. Kenneth Connell, "The Potato in Ireland," p. 67.

33. Richard White, *Remembering Ahanagran: Storytelling in a Family's Past* (New York: Hill and Wang, 1998), p. 15.

34. Tim P. O'Neill, "The Persistence of Famine in Ireland," in *The Great Irish Famine*, Cathal Poirteir, ed. (Dublin: Mercier Press, 1995), p. 210.

35. Annie Greely to John Dillon, March 31, 1896; Letter to John Dillon, June 2, 1896, "Milltown, County Kerry" Dillon Papers, 6810, Trinity College, Dublin.

36. Redcliff Salaman, *History and Social Influence*, pp. 299, 321.

37. Victor A. Walsh, "The Great Famine and Its Consequences," *Eire-Ireland* 23, 4 (Winter 1988), p. 14; James S. Donnelly, Jr., *The Land and the People of Nineteenth-Century Cork*, p. 244.

38. Cormac O'Grada, "The Rise in Living Standards," in *From Feast to Famine: Economic and Social Change in Ireland, 1847–1997*, Kieran A. Kennedy, ed. (Dublin: Institute of Public Administration, 1998), p. 14.

39. Louis M. Cullen, *The Emergence of Modern Ireland, 1600–1900* (New York: Random House, 1981).

40. Maurice O'Sullivan, *Twenty Years A-Growing* (Oxford: Oxford University Press, 1933), p. 242.

41. Conrad Arensberg, *The Irish Countryman* (Garden City, N.Y.: Natural History Press, 1937), p. 52.

42. Patrick Kavanagh, *Tarry Flynn* (Dublin: Pilot Press, 1948), p. 18.

43. Patricia Lysaght, "Continuity and Change in Irish Diet," in *Food and Change*, Alexander Fenton and Eszter Kisban, eds. (Edinburgh: John Donald, 1986), pp. 80–96.

44. E. Margaret Crawford, "Subsistence Crises and Famines in Ireland: A Nutritionist's View," in E. Margaret Crawford, ed., *Famine: The Irish Experience: 900–1900* (Edinburgh: John Donald, 1989), pp. 207–209.

45. James S. Donnelly, *The Land and the People of Nineteenth-Century Cork*, pp. 25–26.

46. Rita M. Rhodes, *Women and the Family in Post-Famine Ireland: Status and Opportunity in a Patriarchal Society* (New York: Garland Press, 1992), pp. 15–16.

47. E. Estyn Evans, *Irish Heritage: The Landscape, The People and Their Work* (Dundalk: W. Tempest, Dundalgan Press, 1942), p. 73.

48. Ibid.

49. Thomas Reid, *Travels in Ireland, in the year 1822, exhibiting brief sketches of the moral, physical, and political state of the country, with reflection on the best means of improving its conditions* (London: Longman, 1823), p. 203. See also William Wilde, "The Food of the Irish," *Dublin University Magazine* 43 (1876), p. 131.

50. Mary E. Daly, *Women and Work in Ireland* (Dublin: Dundalgan Press, 1997), p. 24.

51. Conrad Arensberg and Solon Kimball, *Family and Community in Ireland* (Cambridge, Mass.: Harvard University Press, 1940).

52. John Millington Synge, *The Aran Islands* (1907) (London: Penguin, 1992), pp. 22–23.

53. Quoted in Sarah McNamara, *Those Intrepid United Irishwomen: Pioneers of the Irish Countrywomen's Association* (Limerick: published by the author, 1995), p. 23; see also Diarmaid Ferriter, *Mothers, Maidens and Myths: A History of the Irish Countrywomen's Association* (Dublin: FAS, 1950); and the major scholarly analysis of this phenomenon, Joanna Bourke, *Husbandry to Housewifery: Women, Economic Change, and Housework in Ireland, 1890–1914* (Oxford: Clarendon, 1993).

54. Horace Plunkett, Ellice Ilkington, and George Russell, *The United Irishwomen, Their Place, Work and Ideals* (Dublin: Maunsel, 1911), p. 1.

55. Frank O'Connor, *An Only Child* (Syracuse: Syracuse University Press, 1997), pp. 12, 19.

56. Emiko Ohnuki-Tierney, *Rice As Self: Japanese Identities Through Time* (Princeton: Princeton University Press, 1993).

57. Thomas Vennum, Jr., *Wild Rice and the Ojibway People* (St. Paul: Minnesota Historical Society, 1988), pp. 3, 58, 188, 194, 297.

58. Jeffrey M. Pilcher, *Que Vivan Los Tamales: Food and the Making of Mexican Identity* (Albuquerque: University of New Mexico Press, 1998).

59. Julia Floyd Smith, *Slavery and Rice Culture in Low Country Georgia, 1750–1860* (Knoxville: University of Tennessee Press, 1985); Judith A. Carney, *Black Rice: The African Origins of Rice Cultivation in the Americas* (Cambridge, Mass.: Harvard University Press, 2001).

60. John Blassingame, *The Slave Community: Plantation Life in the Antebellum South*, rev. and enl. ed. (New York: Oxford University Press, 1979); Deborah Gray White, *Ar'n't I a Woman? Female Slaves in the Plantation South* (New York: Norton, 1985).

61. Jacqueline Jones, *Labor of Love, Labor of Sorrow: Black Women, Work, and the Family from Slavery to the Present* (New York: Basic Books, 1985), p. 230; quoted in James R. Grossman, *Land of Hope: Chicago, Black Southerners, and the Great Migration* (Chicago: University of Chicago Press, 1989), p. 155.

62. Ralph Ellison, *Invisible Man* (New York: Random House, 1952), p. 229. Ellison's use of yams and food in general is discussed in Doris Witt, *Black Hunger: Food and the Politics of U.S. Identity* (New York: Oxford University Press, 1999), p. 84.

63. Ruth Schwertfeger, *Women of Theresienstadt, Voices From a Concentration Camp* (New York: Berg, 1989), p. 38.

64. Cara De Silva, ed., *In Memory's Kitchen: A Legacy from the Women of Terezin* (Northvale, N.J.: Jason Aronson, 1996). See also Marion Kaplan, "Jewish Women in Nazi Germany: Daily Life, Daily Struggles, 1933–1939," *Feminist Studies* 16, 3 (Fall 1990), p. 600.

65. James Joyce, *Ulysses* (New York: Random House, 1961), p. 55.

66. Sean O'Casey, *Juno and the Paycock and The Plough and the Stars* (New York: St. Martin's Press, 1966), pp. 4, 13, 17.

67. Liam O'Flaherty, "The Pedlar's Revenge," in *The Pedlar's Revenge & Other Stories, Selected and Edited by A. A. Kelly* (Dublin: Wofhound Press, 1976), pp. 17–33.

68. William Carelton, "The Death of a Devotee," in *The Oxford Book of Irish Short Stories*, William Trevor, ed. (New York: Oxford University Press, 1991), pp. 52–72.

69. Kevin Danaher, *In Ireland Long Ago* (Dublin: Mercier Press, 1964) in-

cluded a chapter on "traditional" Irish breads and bread lore. Unfortunately his descriptions lacked any kind of historicization. It is impossible to know if the breads he described and the methods of baking them referred to 1650 or 1890, that is, well before the widespread adoption of the potato, or after the liberation of the Irish from it.

70. Patricia Lysaght, "Continuity and Change in Irish Diet," pp. 81–84.

71. C. Anne Wilson, *Food and Drink in Britain from the Stone Age to the 19th Century* (Chicago: Academy Chicago Publishers, 1991), pp. 65–67, 210.

72. Kenneth Milne, *The Irish Charter Schools, 1730–1830* (Dublin: Fourcourts, 1997), pp. 76–79.

73. Regina Sexton, *A Little History of Irish Food* (Dublin: Gill and Macmartin, 1998), pp. 34, 55.

74. Caoimhin O'Danachair, "Irish Folk Customs," *Eire-Ireland* 2, 1 (Spring 1967), p. 9.

75. Anthony Bluett, *Things Irish* (Cork: Mercier Press, 1994), pp. 49, 54; Darina Allen, *The Festive Food of Ireland* (West Cork: Roberts Rinehart, 1992) and Regina Sexton, *A Little History of Irish Food.*

76. Regina Sexton, *A Little History of Irish Food,* p. 82.

77. Kevin Danaher, *Folktales from the Irish Countryside* (Dublin: Mercier Press, 1967); William Butler Yeats, *Irish Fairy and Folk Tales* (New York: Modern Library, 1994).

78. E. Estyn Evans, *Irish Heritage,* p. 77.

79. Kenneth Connell, "The Influence of the Potato," in *The Population of Ireland, 1750–1845* (Oxford: Clarendon, 1950), pp. 121–162.

80. Patrick J. Duffy, "Carrickmacross," in *More Irish Country Towns,* Anngret Simms and J. H. Andrews, eds. (Dublin: Mercier Press, 1995), p. 77.

81. See Peter Somerville-Large, *The Irish Country House: A Social History* (London: Sinclair-Stevenson, 1995).

82. Selina Crampton, Journal Book for 1817, Crampton Papers, Trinity College, Dublin, 4197.

83. Crampton Papers, 4199, Trinity College, Dublin.

84. Eliza Jane Alcock, Wilton Castle, County Wexford, 1810–1834, "Cookery," TCD, 10166–7.

85. Quoted in Kevin Whelan, "An Underground Gentry? Catholic Middlemen in Eighteenth-Century Ireland," pp. 130–131.

86. Kerby Miller, *Emigrants and Exiles: Ireland and the Irish Exodus to North America* (New York: Oxford University Press, 1985), p. 5.

87. Robert L. Wright, *Irish Emigrant Ballads and Songs* (Bowling Green, Ohio: Bowling Green State University Press, 1975), pp. 90–93.

88. Gale E. Christianson, "Landlords and Land Tenure in Ireland, 1790–1830," *Eire-Ireland* 9, 1 (Spring 1974), pp. 25–58.

89. Oliver MacDonagh, "The Irish Famine Emigration to the United States," *Perspectives in American History* 10 (1976), p. 363.

90. Helen Sheil, *Falling Into Wretchedness*, p. 17.

91. Robert J. Scally, *The End of Hidden Ireland: Rebellion, Famine, and Emigration* (New York: Oxford University Press, 1995), p. 30.

92. Gearoid O'Tuathaigh, *Ireland Before the Famine, 1798–1848* (Dublin: Gill and Macmillan, 1972), p. 133.

93. Robert Scally, *The End of Hidden Ireland*, p. 33.

94. William Gacquin, *Roscommon Before the Famine: The Parishes of Kiltoon and Cam, 1749–1845* (Dublin: Irish Academic Press, 1996), p. 54.

95. Alexis de Tocqueville, *Journeys in England and Ireland*, G. Lawrence and K. P. Mayer, eds. (New Haven: Yale University Press, 1965), p. 164.

96. James Ebenezer Bischeno, *Ireland and Its Economy: Being the Result of Observations Made in a Tour Through the Country in the Autumn of 1829* (London: J. Murray, 1830), pp. 251–252.

97. Robert Scally, *The End of Hidden Ireland*, p. 35.

98. Ronald E. Seavoy, *Famine in Peasant Societies* (New York: Greenwood Press, 1986), p. 300.

99. Redcliffe Salman, *History and Social Influence*, p. 335.

100. See Robert Scally, *The End of Hidden Ireland*, pp. 82–104; Marilyn Silverman and P. H. Gulliver, *In the Valley of the Nore: A Social History of Thomastown, County Kilkenny, 1840–1983* (Dublin: Geography Publications, 1986), p. 145.

101. William Gacquin, *Roscommon Before the Famine*, pp. 18, 30.

102. Ignatius Murphy, *Before the Famine Struck: Life in West Clare, 1834–1845* (Dublin: Irish Academic Press, 1996) p. 39, 45.

103. Cormac O'Grada, *Ireland Before and After the Famine: Explorations in Economic History, 1800–1925* (Manchester: Manchester University Press, 1988), p. 65.

104. Jim Gilligan, *Graziers and Grasslands: Portrait of a Rural Meath Community: 1854–1914* (Dublin: Irish Academic Press, 1998) p. 15.

105. J. G. Kohl, *Travels in Ireland* (London: Bruce and Wyld, 1844), p. 316; Ned McHugh, *Drogheda Before the Famine: Urban Poverty in the Shadow of Privilege, 1826–1845* (Dublin: Irish Academic Press, 1998).

106. Patrick O'Flanagan, "Bandon," in *Irish Country Towns*, Anngret Simms and J. H. Andrews, eds. (Dublin: Mercier Press, 1994) p. 91.

107. Helen Sheil, *Falling into Wretchedness*, p. 31.

108. Mona Hearn, *Below Stairs: Domestic Service Remembered in Dublin and Beyond, 1880–1922* (Dublin: Lilliput Press, 1993).

109. Peter Somerville-Large, *The Irish Country House*, p. 168.

110. David Fitzpatrick, "The Modernisation of the Irish Female," in *Rural Ireland, 1600–1900: Modernisation and Change*, Patrick O'Flanagan, Paul Ferguson, and Kevin Whelan, eds. (Cork: Cork University Press, 1987), p. 166.

111. Richard White, *Remembering Ahanagran*.

112. Marilyn Silverman and P. H. Gulliver, *In the Valley of the Nore*, p. 9.

113. Mark Bence-Jones, *Life in an Irish Country House* (London: Constable, 1996).

114. For a few of the rare examples, see Peter Somerville-Large, *The Irish Country House.*

115. James S. Donnelly, *The Land and the People of Nineteenth-Century Cork,* pp. 25–26.

116. Louis M. Cullen, "Comparative Aspects of Irish Diet, 1550–1850," in *European Food History: A Research Review,* Hans J. Teuteberg, ed. (Leicester: Leicester University Press, 1992), p. 47.

117. Quoted in Kerby A. Miller, *Emigrants and Exiles,* p. 51.

118. Ibid., p. 204.

119. On the differences between pre- and post-Famine Ireland see Thomas W. Guinnane, *The Vanishing Irish: Households, Migration, and the Rural Economy in Ireland, 1850–1914* (Princeton: Princeton University Press, 1997).

5   THE SOUNDS OF SILENCE

1. Elizabeth Gurley Flynn, *The Rebel Girl: An Autobiography, My First Life (1906–1926)* (New York: International Publishers, 1955), pp. 24–25.

2. William Forbes Adams, *Ireland and the Irish Emigration to the New World from 1815 to the Famine* (New York: Russell and Russell, 1932); Roger Daniels, *Coming to America: A History of Immigration and Ethnicity in American Life* (New York: HarperCollins, 1990), p. 129

3. Patrick J. Blessing, "Irish," in *Harvard Encyclopedia of American Ethnic Groups,* Stephan Thernstrom, ed. (Cambridge, Mass.: Harvard University Press, 1980), p. 528; *Commission on Emigration and Other Population Problems* (Dublin: Ministry of Social Welfare, 1954), pp. 309–311.

4. James P. Myers, Jr., "'Till Their Bog Trotting Feet Get *Talaria*': Henry D. Thoreau and the Immigrant Irish," in Patrick O'Sullivan, *The Creative Migrant* (Leicster: Leicester University Press, 1994).

5. Quoted in Arnold Schrier, *Ireland and the Immigration* (Minneapolis: University of Minnesota Press, 1958), p. 24.

6. Kerby Miller, *Emigrants and Exiles: Ireland and the Irish Exodus to North America* (New York: Oxford University Press, 1985).

7. Hasia R. Diner, *Erin's Daughters in America: Irish Immigrant Women in the Nineteenth Century* (Baltimore: Johns Hopkins University Press, 1983).

8. David Katzman, *Seven Days a Week: Women and Domestic Service in Industrializing America* (New York: Oxford University Press, 1978); Daniel Sutherland, *Americans and Their Servants: Domestic Service in the United States from 1800 to 1920* (Baton Rouge: Louisiana State University Press, 1981); Faye E. Dudden, *Serving Women: Household Service in Nineteenth-Century America*

(Middletown, Conn.: Wesleyan University Press, 1983); Elizabeth O'Leary, *At Beck and Call: The Representation of Domestic Servants in Nineteenth-Century American Painting* (Washington, D.C.: Smithsonian Institution Press, 1996); Hasia Diner, *Erin's Daughters in America.*

9. Robert A. Woods and Albert E. Kennedy, *Young Working Girls: A Summary of Evidence from Two Thousand Social Workers* (Boston: Houghton Mifflin, 1913), p. 58.

10. Emmett Corry, "A Gathering of the Clans," *New York Irish History* 11 (1997), pp. 28, 30–31.

11. See also Margaret Gralton, "The Big Apple Seventy Years Ago," *Leitrim Guardian* 30 (1998), pp. 33–35.

12. Mary Ellen West, "Domestic Service," *Our Day* 4, 3 (1889), pp. 401–405.

13. Dale T. Knobel, *Paddy and the Republic: Ethnicity and Nationality in Antebellum America* (Middletown, Conn.: Wesleyan University Press, 1986).

14. "Restaurant," Box 1, Warshaw Collection, Smithsonian Institution, National Museum of American History/Archives Center.

15. *Women's Journal*, Dec. 7, 1895, p. 389.

16. Quoted in Faith Dudden, *Serving Women*, p. 66.

17. Ibid., p. 121.

18. Harriet Spofford, *The Servant Girl Question* (Boston: Houghton Mifflin, 1881), pp. 15–16.

19. *Puck*, 13, 322 (May 9, 1883).

20. *Harper's New Monthly Magazine*, 13 (Oct. 1856), p. 717.

21. James Michael Curley, *I'd Do It Again: A Record of All My Uproarious Years* (Englewood Cliff, N.J.: Prentice-Hall, 1957), pp. 9–10.

22. Quoted in Marie Fitzgerald, "The St. Patrick's Day Parade: The Conflict of Irish-American Identity in New York City, 1840–1900," Ph.d. diss., State University of New York at Stony Brook, 1993, p. 71.

23. Mary C. McLaughlin, "Mary Mallon: Alias Typhoid Mary," *Recorder of the American Irish Historical Society* 40 (1979), pp. 44–57; Alan Kraut, *Silent Travellers: Germs, Genes, and the "Immigrant Menace"* (New York: Basic Books, 1994), pp. 97–103.

24. Alan Kraut, *Silent Travellers*, p. 165.

25. David Doyle, "Unestablished Irishmen: New Immigrants and Industrial America, 1870–1910," in *American Labor and Immigration History, 1877–1920s*, Dirk Hoerder, ed. (Urbana: University of Illinois Press, 1983), pp. 193–220.

26. Dennis Clark, *The Irish in Philadelphia: Ten Generations of Urban Experience* (Philadelphia: Temple University Press, 1973); Robert Ernst, *Immigrant Life in New York City, 1825–1863* (New York: King's Crown Press, 1948).

27. Hasia Diner, *Erin's Daughters in America*, p. 75.

28. Suellen Hoy "The Journey Out: The Recruitment and Emigration of

Irish Religious Women to the United States, 1812–1914," *Journal of Women's History* 6, 4/7, 1 (Winter/Spring 1995), pp. 65–98.

29. A. A. McGinley, "The Catholic Life of Boston," *Catholic World* 68, 397 (1898), pp. 20–34.

30. Roy Rosenzweig and Elizabeth Blackmar, *The Park and the People: A History of Central Park* (Ithaca: Cornell University Press, 1992), pp. 63–64.

31. Philip L. White, "An Irish Family on the New York Frontier," *New York History* 48, 2 (April, 1967), p. 188.

32. Quoted in James P. Myers, Jr., "Thoreau and the Irish."

33. Quoted in Kerby Miller, *Emigrants and Exiles*, p. 274.

34. Jack Walsh to his mother, June 3, 1930, in a hand-copied letter book, "A Legacy of Jack and Kate Walsh," compiled by Michael Birch, in the possession of the author.

35. Richard White, *Remembering Ahanagran: Storytelling in a Family's Past* (New York: Hill and Wang, 1998), pp. 174–176.

36. Frank McCourt, *Angela's Ashes: A Memoir* (New York: Scribner, 1996), pp. 11–46.

37. Robert Coit Chapin, *The Standard of Living among Workingmen's Families in New York City* (New York: Charities Publication Committee, 1909), p. 141.

38. Ruth S. True, "Boyhood and Lawlessness," in Pauline Goldmark, *West Side Studies* (New York: Russell Sage, 1914), pp. 58–63.

39. Katherine Conway, Lalor's Maples (Boston: The Pilot, 1901), in *The Exiles of Erin: Nineteenth Century Irish-American Fiction*, Charles Fanning, ed. (Notre Dame, Ind.: University of Notre Dame Press, 1987), pp. 241–250.

40. Ellen Skerritt, "Irish Americans in Chicago, 1880–1920," in Timothy J. Meagher, *From Paddy to Studs: Irish-American Communities in the Turn of the Century Era, 1880 to 1920* (Westport, Conn.: Greenwood Press, 1986), p. 134.

41. James T. Farrell, *Studs Lonigan*, (1932) (Urbana: University of Illinois Press, 1993) pp. 12, 123–124. Thomas H. O'Connor, *South Boston: My Home Town: The History of an Ethnic Neighborhood* (Boston: Quinlan Press, 1988), p. 79, also talks of the obligatory Sunday dinner after church as a hallmark of South Boston Irish culture.

42. Laurie K. Mercier, "We Are Women Irish: Gender, Class, Religious, and Ethnic Identity in Anaconda, Montana," *Montana: The Magazine of Western History* 44, 1 (Winter 1994), p. 33.

43. John Francis Maguire, *The Irish in America* (London: Longmans, Green, 1868), p. 256.

44. Daniel J. Walkowitz, *Worker City, Company Town: Iron and Cotton-Worker Protest in Troy and Cohoes, New York, 1855–1884* (Urbana: University of Illinois Press, 1978), pp. 116–117.

45. Thomas M. Truxes, *Irish-American Trade, 1660–1783* (Cambridge: Cambridge University Press, 1988), pp. 147–169.

46. Marion Casey, "Ireland, New York and the Irish Image in American Popular Culture," Ph.D. diss., New York University, 1998, p. 182.

47. Martin G. Towney, "Kerry Patch Revisited: Irish Americans in St. Louis in the Turn of the Century Era," in *From Paddy to Studs*, Timothy Meagher, ed., pp. 139–159.

48. Dennis P. Ryan, *Beyond the Ballot Box: A Social History of the Boston Irish, 1845–1917* (Rutherford, N.J.: Fairleigh Dickinson University Press, 1983), p. 83.

49. Robert Ernst, *Immigrant Life*, pp. 84–85, 87; Paul A. Gilje, "The Development of an Irish American Community in New York," in Ronald Bayor and Timothy Meagher, eds., *The New York Irish* (Baltimore: Johns Hopkins University Press, 1996), p. 76.

50. Marion Casey, "'From the East Side to the Seaside:' Irish Americans on the Move in New York City," in Ronald Bayor and Timothy Meagher, eds., *The New York Irish*, pp. 403–404.

51. See John T. Ridge, *Erin's Sons in America: The Ancient Order of Hibernians* (New York: Ancient Order of Hibernians 150th Anniversary Committee, 1986).

52. David M. Emmons, *The Butte Irish: Class and Ethnicity in an American Mining Town, 1875–1925* (Urbana: University of Illinois Press, 1989), pp. 67–68.

53. Jeremiah O'Donovan, *A Brief Account of the Author's Interview with His Countrymen, . . . During His Travels Through Various States of the Union In 1854 and 1855* (Pittsburgh: privately published, 1864).

54. Jeremiah O'Donovan, *A Brief Account*, pp. 72, 92, 98.

55. Mary Higgins Clark, "My Wild Irish Mother," *The Recorder of the American Irish Historical Society* 38 (1977), p. 31.

56. Michael and Ariane Batterberry, *On the Town in New York: The Landmark History of Eating, Drinking, and Entertainments from the American Revolution to the Food Revolution* (New York: Routledge, 1999) pp. 98–99.

57. *Picture of New York* (New York: Homans and Ellis, 1846).

58. Trade cards for Gallagher's and Cavanagh's can be found in the Warshaw Collection.

59. Hasia Diner, *Erin's Daughters in America*, p. 96.

60. Unidentified clipping, Dillon Papers, 6844/111, Trinity College, Dublin.

61. *Irish World*, May 22, 1897, quoted in John T. Ridge, "Irish County Societies in New York, 1880–1914," in Ronald H. Bayor and Timothy Meagher, *The New York Irish*, p. 285.

62. Clipping, Nov. 8, 1897, Dillon Papers, 6869, TCD.

63. Program, *Annual Irish Picnic and Games, Saturday Aug. 10, 1912*, State Historical Society of Wisconsin, Madison, Wisconsin.

64. Colleen McDannell, "Going to the Ladies' Fair: Irish Catholics in

New York City, 1870–1900," in Ronald Bayor and Timothy Meagher, eds., *The New York Irish*, p. 237.

65. Paul A. Gilje, "The Development of an Irish American Community in New York City before the Great Migration," in Ronald Bayor and Timothy Meagher, *The New York Irish*, p. 72; Earl F. Niehaus, *The Irish in New Orleans, 1800–1860* (Baton Rouge: Louisiana State University Press, 1965), p. 117.

66. On non-Irish guests at Irish communal banquets, see Brian Mitchell, *The Paddy Camps: The Irish of Lowell, 1821–1861* (Urbana: University of Illinois Press, 1988), p. 47.

67. Kenneth Moss, "St. Patrick's Day Celebrations and the Formation of Irish-American Identity, 1845–1875," *Journal of Social History* 29, 1 (Fall 1995), pp. 125–148.

68. Crimmins Collection, Smithsonian Institution, National Museum of American History/Archives Center.

69. See Dennis Clark, *Erin's Heirs: Irish Bonds of Community* (Lexington: University of Kentucky Press, 1991), p. 28. He described a Philadelphia banquet of the Friendly Sons of Saint Patrick at which guests ate oysters, turtle soup, pate, salmon, beef, chicken, terrapin, had four deserts, and drank seven wines.

70. Stephen Mennell, *All Manner of Food: Eating and Taste in England and France from the Middle Ages to the Present*, 2nd ed. (Urbana: University of Illinois Press, 1996).

71. Crimmins Collection, Smithsonian Institution, Museum of American History/Archives Center. This 1919 menu was the most "Irish" in its presentation.

72. Marion Casey, "Ireland, New York and the Irish," p. 215.

73. J. C. Beckett, *A Short History of Ireland: From the Time of St. Patrick to the Present* (New York: Harper and Row, 1968), pp. 161–162.

74. Marion Casey, "Ireland, New York and the Irish," pp. 190–191.

75. Dennis Clark, *Irish in Philadelphia*, pp. 65–73.

76. Robert Ernst, *Immigrant Life*, p. 86.

77. Carole Groneman Pernicone, "The "Bloody Ould Sixth": A Social Analysis of a New York City Working-Class Community in the Mid-Nineteenth Century," Ph.D. diss., University of Rochester, 1973, pp. 111–112.

78. James H. Mundy, *Hard Times, Hard Men: Maine and the Irish, 1830–1860* (Scarborough, Maine: Harp Publications, 1990), p. 109; Roy Rosenzweig, *Eight Hours for What We Will: Workers and Leisure in an Industrial City, 1870–1920* (New York: Cambridge University Press, 1983) p. 41.

79. Brian Mitchell, *Paddy Camps*, p. 110.

80. Perry Duis, *Public Drinking in Chicago and Boston, 1880–1920* (Urbana: University of Illinois Press), p. 152.

81. *Michael Donohue: An Oral History: Starting off from Dead End* (New York: Community Documentation Workshop, 1980), p. 6.

82. See Louis R. Biscegalia, "The McManus Welcome: San Francisco, 1851," *Eire-Ireland* 16, 1 (Spring 1981), p. 11.

83. Dennis Clark, *The Irish Relations: Trials of an Immigrant Generation* (Rutherford, N.J.: Fairleigh Dickinson University Press, 1982), p. 69.

84. George Ade, *The Old-Time Saloon: Not Wet-Not Dry, Just History* (New York: Long and Smith, 1931), pp. 119–120.

85. Kenneth E. Nilsen, "The Irish Language in New York, 1850–1900," in Ronald Bayor and Timothy Meagher, *The New York Irish*, p. 260.

86. Edward J. Bander, *Mr. Dooley and Mr. Dunne: The Literary Life of a Chicago Catholic* (Charlottesville, Va.: Michie, 1981), p. 31.

87. Ibid., p. 246.

88. "St. Patrick's Day Procession," "Irish," Box 1, "Postcards/letters/decals," Warshaw Collection, SI/NMAH/AC.

89. William H. A. Williams, *'Twas Only an Irishman's Dream: The Image of Ireland and the Irish in American Popular Song Lyrics, 1800–1920* (Urbana: University of Illinois Press, 1996), pp. 149–157.

90. Dale Knobel, *Paddy and the Republic.*

91. Richard Stivers, *A Hair of the Dog: Irish Drinking and American Stereotype* (University Park: Pennsylvania State University Press, 1976).

92. Quoted in William H. A. Williams, *'Twas Only an Irishman's Dream,"* p. 160.

93. Ibid., pp. 150–151.

94. Ibid., p. 166.

95. Ibid., p. 166.

96. Jeremiah O'Donovan, *A Brief Account*, pp. 31–33.

97. Ray Oldenburg, *The Great Good Place: Cafes, Coffee Shops, Community Centers, Beauty Parlors, General Stores, Bars, Hangouts and How They Get You Through the Day* (New York: Marlowe, 1989), p. 99.

98. Madelon Powers, *Faces Along the Bar: Lore and Order in the Workingman's Saloon, 1870–1920* (Chicago: University of Chicago Press, 1998), pp. 214–215.

99. Perry Duis, *The Saloon: Public Drinking in Chicago and Boston, 1880–1920* (Urbana: University of Illinois Press, 1983), p. 153; Madelon Powers, *Faces*, p. 214.

100. Jane Addams, *Twenty Years at Hull House* (1910) (New York: New American Library, 1960), p. 102.

101. Quoted in Marie Fitzgerald, "The St. Patrick's Day Parade," p. 70.

102. Elizabeth Mathew, *"Ireland Sober, Ireland Free": Drink and Temperance in Nineteenth Century Ireland* (Syracuse, N.Y.: Syracuse University Press, 1986); George Bretherton, "Against the Flowing Tide: Whiskey and Temperance in the Making of Modern Ireland," in *Drinking: Behavior and Belief in Modern History*, Susannah Barrow and Robin Room, eds. (Berkeley: University of California Press, 1991), pp. 147–164.

103. Lawrence J. McCaffrey, *Textures of Irish America* (Syracuse, N.Y.: Syracuse University Press, 1992), p. 58; John F. Quinn, "Father Mathew's American Tour," *Eire-Ireland* 30, 1 (Summer, 1995), pp. 91–104; Sister Joan Bland, *Hibernian Crusade: The Story of the Catholic Total Abstinence Union of America* (Washington, D.C: Catholic University of America Press, 1951).

104. Humphrey J. Desmond, "Early Irish Settlers in Milwaukee," *Journal of the American Irish Historical Society* 29 (1931), p. 109; Thomas H. O'Connor, *South Boston: My Home Town*, p. 46; Dennis Ryan, *Beyond the Ballot Box*, pp. 43, 115, 119; Timothy Meagher, "'Why Should We Care for a Little Trouble, or a Walk Through the Mud': St. Patrick's and Columbus Day Parades in Worcester, Massachusetts, 1845–1915," *The New England Quarterly* 58, 1 (March 1985), pp. 10–11; James H. Mundy, *Hard Times*, p. 99, and Dennis Clark, *The Irish in Philadelphia*, p. 103, represent just a handful of the references in the Irish community history literature that documented the rise of an Irish movement for temperance in America.

105. Eileen M. McMahon, *What Parish Are You From? A Chicago Irish Community and Race Relations* (Lexington: University of Kentucky Press, 1995) pp. 20–21.

106. Hasia Diner, *Erin's Daughters in America*, p. 150.

107. Robert R. Grimes, *How Shall We Sing in a Foreign Land? Music of Irish Catholic Immigrants in the Antebellum United States* (Notre Dame, Ind.: University of Notre Dame Press, 1996), pp. 42, 141.

108. John F. Maguire, *The Irish in America*, p. 281.

109. Frank McCourt, *Angela's Ashes*, pp. 26, 32–34; James T. Farrell, *Studs Lonigan*, pp. 228, 288, 409, 422.

110. *Michael Donohue: An Oral History*, pp. 6, 36.

111. Louise Lamphere, *From Working Daughters to Working Mothers: Immigrant Women in a New England Industrial Community* (Ithaca: Cornell University Press, 1987), pp. 99–110.

112. Richard White, *Remembering Ahanagran*, p. 123.

113. Clipping, August 16, 1908, Dillon Papers, 6870/191, Trinity College, Dublin.

6 A SET TABLE

1. Beatrice Weinreich, "The Americanization of Passover," in Raphael Patai, Francis Lee Utley and Dov Noy, *Studies in Biblical and Jewish Folklore* (Bloomington: Indiana University Press, 1960), p. 329–365.

2. "Set table" is the literal translation of the highly authoritative sixteenth-century code of Jewish law, the *Shulchan Aruch*, edited by Joseph Caro.

3. Yehuda Leib Gordon, "Barburim Abusim," in *Kol Shire Yehuda Leib Gordon* (Vilna: Dfus ha'Almanah ve-ha'Ahim Rom, 1899), pp. 152–159.

4. See Michael Stanislawski, *For Whom Shall I Toil: Judah Leib Gordon and the Crisis of Russian Jewry* (New York: Oxford University Press, 1988).

5. Shmuel Elizer Shtern, *Seder Kiddush le-Rabotenu ha-Rishonim* (Bene Berak: Mekhon "Pardes," 1991).

6. Leon Kobrin, *A Lithuanian Village* (New York: Bernard G. Richards, 1927), p. 2.

7. Steven Lowenstein, "The Shifting Boundary Between Eastern and Western Jewry," *Jewish Social Studies* 4, 1 (Fall 1997), p. 63; Hayyim Schauss, *The Jewish Festivals: A Guide to Their History and Observance* (New York: Union of American Hebrew Congregations, 1938), p. 32.

8. Marvin I. Herzog, *The Yiddish Language in Northern Poland: Its Geography and History* (Bloomington: Indiana University Press, 1965), p. 18.

9. Rosaline B. Schwartz, "The Geography of Two Food Terms: A Study in Yiddish Lexical Variation," in *The Field of Yiddish: Studies in Language, Folklore, and Literature: Third Collection*, Marvin I. Herzog, Wita Ravid, and Uriel Weinreich, eds. (The Hague: Mouton, 1969), pp. 240–266.

10. Y. Fuhrman, "Terminolgia fun Bakerfakh in Bukovina un Mizrakh Galitzia," *Yidishe Shprakh* 33, 1–3 (1974), pp. 32–37.

11. Hinde Shmulevitz, "A Pekl Verter fun Lodz Voss Hobn a Shykhis Tzum Essen," *Yidishe Shprakh* 3, 3 (May-June 1943), pp. 88–89.

12. Edouard De Pomiane, *The Jews of Poland: Recollections and Recipes*, Josephine Bacon, trans. (orig. 1929; Garden Grove, Calif.: Pholiota Press, 1949).

13. Lillian Gorenstein, "A Memoir of the Great War, 1914–1924," *YIVO Annual* 20 (1991), p. 143.

14. Norman Salsitz, *A Jewish Boyhood in Poland: Remembering Kolbuszowa* (Syracuse: Syracuse University Press, 1992), p. 83.

15. Louis Greenberg, *The Jews in Russia: The Struggle for Emancipation: 1772–1880* (New Haven: Yale University Press, 1944), p. 58.

16. Charles Madison, "Autobiography," pp. 22, 27. Unpublished, Addendum, Box 1, Charles Madison Papers, Tamiment Library, New York University.

17. Jonathan Boyarin and Jack Kugelmass, trans. and eds., *From a Ruined Garden: The Memorial Books of Polish Jewry* (New York: Schocken Books, 1983), pp. 107–109.

18. Herman Dicker, *Piety and Perseverance: Jews from the Carpathian Mountains* (New York: Sepher-Hermon, 1981), p. 163.

19. Bittelman, Alexander Papers, Box 1, p. 31, Tamiment Library, New York University.

20. Gillian Feeley-Harnick, *The Lord's Table: The Meaning of Food in Early Judaism and Christianity* (Washington, D.C.: Smithsonian Institution Press, 1981), p. 72.

21. Isaiah 55:1–3.

22. Talmud Yerushalmi, *Kiddushin* 4:12; 66b.

23. Mishnah *Gittin* 9:10; Judith Hauptman, *Rereading the Rabbis: A Woman's Voice* (Boulder, Col.: Westview Press, 1998), p. 65.

24. Numbers 11:17.

25. Isaiah 25:6

26. *Shulhan Aruch, Orech Chaim,* 167:8.

27. Elliott K. Ginsburg, *Sod ha-Shabbat: The Mystery of the Sabbath from the Tola'at Ya'aqov of R. Meir ibn Gabbai* (Albany: State University of New York Press, 1989), p. 118.

28. Yaffa Eliach, in *There Was Once a World: A 900-Year Chronicle of the Shtetl of Eishyshok* (Boston: Little, Brown, 1998), p. 103.

29. Abram der Tate (Leib Blekhman), *Bletter fun Mine Yugent: Zikhrones fun a Bundist* (New York: Unzere Zeit, 1959), p. 13.

30. Joseph Jacob Cohen, *The House Stood Forlorn: The Legacy of Remembrance of a Boyhood in the Russia of the Late Nineteenth Century* (Paris: Editions Polyglottes, 1954), pp. 22–23.

31. Y. L. Cahan, *Der Yid: Vegen Zikh un Venegen Andere In Zine Shprekhverter un Redensorten* (New York: YIVO, 1933).

32. Leah Rachel Yoffie, "Yiddish Proverbs, Sayings, etc., in St. Louis, Mo.," *Journal of American Folk-Lore* 33, 128 (April–June 1920), pp. 134–165.

33. Herman Dicker, *Piety and Perseverance*, p. 172.

34. Ivan Marcus, *Rituals of Childhood: Jewish Acculturation in Medieval Europe* (New Haven: Yale University Press, 1996).

35. Zachary M. Baker, "Bibliography of Eastern European Memorial (Yizkor) Books," in *From a Ruined Garden: The Memorial Books of Polish Jewry*, Jack Kugelmass and Jonathan Boyarin, trans. and eds., 2nd ed., expanded (Bloomington: Indiana University Press, 1998), pp. 273–298.

36. Chaim Zhitlowsky, "The Jewish Factor in My Socialism," in Lucy Dawidowicz, *Golden Tradition* (New York: Schocken, 1984), p. 416.

37. Jonathan Boyarin and Jack Kugelmass, *From a Ruined Garden*, 1st ed., p. 83.

38. Carole Malkin, *The Journeys of David Toback: As Retold by His Granddaughter* (New York: Schocken Books, 1981), p. 52.

39. Anne Kahan, "The Diary of Anne Kahan: Siedlice, Poland, 1914–1916," *YIVO Annual* 18 (1983), p. 183.

40. Aryeh Avinadav, ed., *Kehillah Ustele: B'vinyanah Ub'Khurbana* (Tel Aviv: Irgun Yotzei Ustile B'Yisrael Ubatifutzot, 1962) p. 233.

41. Morris Raphael Cohen, *A Dreamer's Journey: The Autobiography of Morris Raphael Cohen* (Boston: Beacon Press, 1949), p. 18.

42. Maurice Hindus, *Green Worlds: An Informal Chronicle* (New York: Doubleday, Doran, 1938), p. 7.

43. Louis Lozwick, *Survivor from a Dead Age: The Memoirs of Louis Lozwick* (Washington, D.C.: Smithsonian Institution Press, 1997), pp. 19–20.

44. Lillian Gorenstein, "A Memoir," p. 135.

45. Miriam Shomer Zunser, *Yesterday: A Memoir of a Russian Jewish Family* (1939) (New York: Harper and Row, 1978), p. 35.

46. Louis Borgenicht, *The Happiest Man: The Life of Louis Borgenicht as Told to Harold Friedman* (New York: G. P. Putnam's Sons, 1942), p. 8.

47. Minnie Fisher, *Born the Year Before the 20th Century: An Oral History* (New York: Community Documentation Workshop, 1976), p. 8.

48. Simon Kuznets, "Immigration of Russian Jews to the United States: Background and Structure," *Perspectives in American History* 9 (1975), p. 79.

49. Salo W. Baron, Arcadius Kahan, and Others, *Economic History of the Jews*, Nachum Gross, ed. (New York: Schocken Books, 1975), pp. 97–98.

50. Arcadius Kahan, "Impact of Industrialization on the Jews in Tsarist Russia," in *Essays in Jewish Social and Economic History* (Chicago: University of Chicago Press, 1986), p. 25.

51. David Vital, *A People Apart: The Jews in Europe, 1789–1939* (London: Oxford University Press, 1999), pp. 302–305.

52. Quoted in Louis Greenberg, *The Jews in Russia*, p. 160.

53. Hasia R. Diner, *A Time for Gathering: The Second Migration, 1820–1880* (Baltimore: Johns Hopkins University Press, 1992), pp. 244–245.

54. Arcadius Kahan, "Impact of Industrialization," p. 31.

55. Maurice Hindus, *Green Worlds*, pp. 6–7.

56. Norman Salsitz, *A Jewish Boyhood in Poland*, p. 19.

57. Israel Cohen, *Vilna* (Philadelphia: Jewish Publication Society of America, 1943), p. 337.

58. Morris Schulzinger, *The Tale of a Litvak* (New York: Philosophical Library, 1985), p. 80.

59. Melech Epstein, *Pages from a Colorful Life: An Autobiographical Sketch* (Miami Beach: Block, 1971), p. 5.

60. Solomon Berger, *The Jewish Commonwealth of Zborow* (New York: Regsol, 1967), pp. 1, 36, 40, 43–44.

61. Louis Lozwick, *Survivor from a Dead Age*, pp. 19–20, 26–27, 30–31.

62. Y. L. Peretz, "A Ingele," in *Di Verk fun Y. L. Peretz* (New York: Farlag "Idish," 1920), II, pp. 36–38; see also the piece in its original format in *Bilder fun a Provints Rayze in Tomashover Paviat in York 1890* (Warsaw: Druck Halter ve-Auzonshtadt, 1894).

63. Israel Pressman, "Roads That Passed: Russia, My Old Home," *YIVO Annual* 22 (1995), p. 22.

64. Beatrice C. Baskerville, *The Polish Jew: His Social and Economic Value* (New York: Macmillan, 1906) p. 37.

65. Abraham Ain, "Swislocz: Portrait of a Jewish Community in Eastern Europe," *YIVO Annual* 4 (1949), p. 101.

66. Hirsch Abramowitz, "Akhilos bei die Yidden in Lite," in *Lite* (New York: Jewish-Lithuanian Cultural Society, 1951), vol. 1, p. 417.

67. Beatrice Baskerville, *Polish Jew*, pp. 18, 30.

68. Mordecai Kossover, "Yiddishe Makholim: A Shtudyie in Kultur-Geschichte in Shprachforshung," in *Yudah A. Yaffe-Bukh*, Yudl Mark, ed. (New York: YIVO, 1958), pp. 1–145.

69. "Abraham Livshein," in *Ellis Island Interviews: In Their Own Words*, Peter Morton Coan, ed. (New York: Checkmark, 1997), pp. 156–162.

70. Interview with Aaron Scher, May 27, 1977, 6:25, 653A, Wisconsin Jewish Archives, State Historical Society of Wisconsin, Madison, Wis.

71. Jonathan Boyarin, *A Storyteller's Worlds: The Education of Shlomo Noble in Europe and America* (New York: Holmes and Meier, 1994), p. 55.

72. Miriam Shomer Zunser, *Yesterday: A Memoir of a Russian Jewish Family* (1939; New York: Harper and Row, 1978), pp. 23–24.

73. There is no blessing on meat, but meat was discussed as highly prized in traditional sources. "There is no joy without meat and wine," Talmud, Pes. 109a.

74. Morris Raphael Cohen, *A Dreamer's Journey*, p. 10.

75. Jeremiah J. Berman, *Shehitah: A Study in the Cultural and Social Life of the Jewish People* (New York: Bloch, 1941), p. 183; Israel Cohen, *Vilna*, p. 166.

76. Jeremiah Berman, *Shehitah*, pp. 196–197.

77. Mendele Moykher-Sforim (Sholem Abramovitsh), "Di Takse, Oder Di Bande Shotot Baley-Toyve," 2nd ed. (Vilna: Fin and Rosenkratz, 1872).

78. Marvin Zuckerman, Gerald Stillman, and Marion Herbst, eds., *Selected Works of Mendele Moykher-Sforim* (Malibu, Calif.: Pangloss Press, 1991), p. 8.

79. Dan Miron, *A Traveler Disguised: The Rise of Modern Yiddish Fiction in the Nineteenth Century* (Syracuse: Syracuse University Press, 1996) p. 141; on Mendele as a "historian" and critic of social hierarchies, see Ken Frieden, *Classic Yiddish Fiction: Abramovitsh, Sholem Aleichem, and Peretz* (Albany: State University of New York Press, 1995).

80. Jeremiah Berman, *Shehitah*, p. 198.

81. Ita Kalish, "Life in a Hasidic Court in Russian Poland Towards the End of the 19th and the Early 20th Centuries," *YIVO Annual* 8 (1965), pp. 267–268.

82. Bella and Marc Chagall, *Burning Lights* (New York: Schocken Books, 1946).

83. Howard Weinshel, *A Twentieth Century Jewish Journey: The Memoirs of Howard Weinshel* (Milwaukee: Wisconsin Society for Jewish Learning, 1993) p. 22.

84. Hirsch Abramowitz, "Akhilos bei die Yiden in Lite," p. 417.

85. Morris R. Cohen, *A Dreamer's Journey*, p. 18.

86. Ruth Rubin, "Nineteenth-Century History in Yiddish Folksong," *New York Folklore Quarterly* 15, 3 (Fall 1959), p. 221.

87. Yaffa Eliach, *There Once Was a World*, pp. 354–375.

88. S. Ansky, *The Dybbuk*, S. Morris Engel, trans. (Washington, D.C.: Regnery Gateway, 1974), p. 50.

89. Aryeh Avinadav's recollections, "L'khof Neharot (Perke Khaim V'Hevai Shel Ayara)," in *Kehillat Ustile*, p. 16.

90. *Kehillah Ustile*, pp. 94, 172.

91. Solomon Berger, *The Jewish Commonwealth of Zborow* (New York: Regsol, 1967), p. 94.

92. Jacob Scarr, *Listen My Children: A Grandfather's Legacy* (Philadelphia: Dorrance, 1972), p. 33.

93. Carole Malkin, *The Journeys of David Toback*, p. 5.

94. *Kehillah Ustile*, p. 71.

95. Anne Kahan, "The Diary of Anne Kahan, pp. 141–371.

96. Samuel Kassow, "Jewish Communal Politics in Transition: The Vilna *Kehila*, 1919–1920," *YIVO Annual* 20 (1991), p. 69.

97. Jonathan Boyarin and Jack Kugelmass, *From a Ruined Garden*, 1st ed., p. 41.

98. Israel Matz, "Memories of Kalvaria," *Menorah Journal* 48, 1–2 (Autumn–Winter 1960), p. 83.

99. Israel Pressman, "Roads That Passed," p. 16.

100. Carole Malkin, *The Journeys of David Toback*, p. 19.

101. Israel Isser Kasovich, *Shishim Shenot Hayim: Zikhronot Hayay ve-Haye Dori b'Yisrael* (Jerusalem: Dvir, 1923), pp. 25–26.

102. Chaim Grade, *Der Mames Shabosim* (Chicago: L. M. Stein, 1955), p. 48.

103. Leah Rosenberg, *The Errand Runner: Reflections of a Rabbi's Daughter* (Toronto: John Wiley, 1981) pp. 18–20.

104. Alexander Bittelman, unpublished autobiography, pp. 35–36.

105. Morris R. Cohen, *A Dreamer's Journey*, p. 23.

106. Yoav Peled, *Class and Ethnicity in the Pale: The Political Economy of Jewish Workers' Nationalism in Late Imperial Russia* (New York: St. Martin's Press, 1989).

107. Arcadius Kahan, "Impact of Industrialization," p. 22.

108. According to the Isaac M. Rubinow, "*Economic Condition of the Jews in Russia: Bulletin of the U.S. Bureau of Labor* 15 (1907), in the 1890s from one-fifth to one-quarter of all Jews in Russia fell into the work category of "Domestic and Personal Service," p. 502.

109. Rose Schneiderman, *All for One* (New York: Paul S. Eriksson, 1967), pp. 14–15.

110. Alexander Bittelman, unpublished autobiography, p. 32.

111. Sidney Stahl Weinberg, *The World of Our Mothers: The Lives of Jewish Immigrant Women* (Chapel Hill: University of North Carolina Press, 1988),

pp. 192–193; Rose Cohen, *Out of the Shadow* (Boston: George H. Doran, 1918), pp. 172–173.

112. Beatrice Baskerville, *Polish Jew*, pp. 28–29.

113. Chaim Aronson, *A Jewish Life Under the Tsars: The Autobiography of Chaim Aronson, 1825–1888* (Totowa, N.J.: Allanheld Osmun, 1983), p. 126.

114. *Ale Verk fun Mendele Moykher-Sforim* (New York: Hebrew Publishing Company, 1920), vol. 1, p. 171.

115. Sholem Aleykhem, "Di Vibores," in *Ale Verk, Band 1: Verk fun di Yohr 1883–1886* (Moscow: Melukhe-Farlag "Der Emes," 1948), pp. 50–53; for an English version see *The Three Great Classic Writers of Modern Yiddish Literature. Vol. II. Selected Works of Sholem Aleichem*, Marvin Zuckerman and Marion Herbst, eds. (Malibu, Calif.: Pangloss Press, 1994).

116. Y. L. Peretz, "Bontshe Shveyg," in *I. L. Peretz Reader*, Ruth Wisse, ed. (New York: Schocken Books, 1990), pp. 146–151.

117. Raphael Mahler, "The Economic Background of Jewish Emigration From Galicia to the United States" (orig. 1943) *YIVO Annual* 7 (1952), pp. 255–267.

118. Simon Kuznets, "Immigration of Russian Jews to the United States," pp. 35–124.

119. Leon Kobrin, *Lithuanian Village*, p. 168.

120. Saul M. Ginzburg and P. S. Marek, eds., *Yidishe folkslider in Rusland* (St. Petersburg, 1901; Ramat Gan, Israel: Farlag fun Bar Ilan Universitet, 1991).

7 FOOD FIGHTS

1. Minnie Fisher, *Born One Year before the 20th Century: An Oral History* (New York: Community Documentation Workshop, 1976).

2. Marcus Ravage, *An American in the Making*, (New York: Harper and Brothers, 1917), pp. 63, 75–76.

3. Moses Weinberg, *People Walk on Their Heads: Moses Weinberger's Jews and Judaism in New York*, trans. and ed. Jonathan D. Sarna (New York: Holmes and Meier, 1981).

4. Mark A. Berman, "Kosher Fraud Statutes and the Establishment Clause: Are They Kosher?" *Columbia Journal of Law and Social Problems* 1, 15 (1992), pp. 1–75; Samuel Buchler, *"Cohen Comes First" and Other Cases: Stories of Controversies before the New York Jewish Court of Arbitration* (New York: Vanguard, 1933), pp. 142–149.

5. Jeremiah J. Berman, *Shehitah: A Study in the Cultural and Social Life of the Jewish People* (New York: Bloch, 1941), pp. 273–395.

6. Abraham J. Karp, "New York Chooses a Chief Rabbi," *Publications of the American Jewish Historical Society* 44 (March 1954), pp. 129–188.

7. Moses Weinberger, *People Walk on Their Heads*, pp. 46–50; Harold P. Gastwirt, *Fraud, Corruption, and Holiness: The Controversy Over the Supervision of Jewish Dietary Practice in New York City 1881–1940* (Port Washington, N.Y.: Kennikat Press, 1974), pp. 55–73.

8. "Katz, Bessie, November 1, 1974," Tape 686H, State Historical Society of Wisconsin, Madison, Wis.

9. Sol Bloom, *The Autobiography of Sol Bloom* (New York: G. P. Putnam's, 1948), p. 12.

10. Jeremiah Berman, *Shehitah*, pp. 364–395.

11. Samuel Koenig, *An American Jewish Community: 50 Years, 1889–1939* (orig. 1940; Stamford: Stamford Jewish Historical Society, 1991), p. 27.

12. *Memories of Longtime Milwaukeeans* (Milwaukee: Milwaukee Jewish Home, 1984), pp. 3–4.

13. As one of many examples, see Irit Erez-Boukai, "On the Banks of the Wabash: Jewish Life in Greater Lafayette, Indiana, 1840–1960," *Indiana Jewish Historical Society*, 31 (August 1996), p. 31.

14. Jacob L. Ornstein-Galicia, *Jewish Farmer in America: The Unknown Chronicle* (Lewiston: Edwin Mellen Press, 1992), pp. 56, 73, 88.

15. Maurice Karpf, *Jewish Community Organization in the United States: An Outline of Types of Organizations, Activities, and Problems* (New York: Bloch, 1938), pp. 115–116.

16. Alter Landesman, *Brownsville: The Birth, Development and Passing of a Jewish Community in New York* (New York: Bloch, 1971), pp. 74–75.

17. Arthur A. Goren, *New York Jews and the Quest for Community: The Kehillah Experiment, 1908–1922* (New York: Columbia University Press, 1970), pp. 78–79.

18. Jonathan Boyarin, *A Storyteller's Worlds: The Education of Shlomo Noble in Europe and America* (New York: Holmes and Meier, 1994), pp. 120–127.

19. "Sweet, Nathan, July 27, 1979," Wisconsin Jewish Archives, 775A, State Historical Society of Wisconsin, Madison, Wis.

20. Howard Goldstein, *The Home on Gorham Street and the Voices of Its Children* (Tuscaloosa: University of Alabama Press, 1996), p. 46.

21. Sabato Morais to the President and Board of Trustees, March 12, 1895, Morais Papers, 7, 7, Center for Judaic Studies, Philadelphia; "Joshua Joffee, 6/29/02" RG 1, General Files Series, 1902–1942, Box 13, Jewish Theological Seminary, New York; Moses Weinberger, *People Walk on Their Heads*, pp. 46–50, 74–75.

22. Gertrude Wishnick Dubrovsky, *The Land Was Theirs: Jewish Farmers in the Garden State* (Tuscaloosa: University of Alabama Press, 1992), p. 208.

23. Dan A. Oren, *Joining the Club: A History of Jews and Yale* (New Haven: Yale University Press, 1985), p. 77.

24. Mordecai Kaplan, "The Society for a Jewish Renascence," *Macabbean* 34, 4 (Nov. 1920), p. 111.

25. Quoted in Mel Scult, *Judaism Faces the Twentieth Century: A Biography of Mordecai M. Kaplan* (Detroit: Wayne State University Press, 1993) p. 297.

26. Jenna Weissman Joselit, *The Wonders of America: Reinventing Jewish Culture, 1880–1950* (New York: Hill and Wang, 1994).

27. Louis Wirth, *The Ghetto* (Chicago: University of Chicago Press, 1928), pp. 257–258.

28. Ailon Shiloh, ed., *By Myself I'm a Book! An Oral History of the Immigrant Jewish Experience in Pittsburgh* (Waltham, Mass.: American Jewish Historical Society, 1972), p. 35.

29. Harry Roskolenko, *The Time That Was Then: The Lower East Side, 1900–1914: An Intimate Chronicle* (New York: Dial Press, 1971), p. 26.

30. Morris Raphael Cohen, *A Dreamer's Journey: The Autobiography of Morris Raphael Cohen* (Boston: Beacon Press, 1949), p. 67.

31. Ruth Cowan Schwartz, *More Work for Mother: The Ironies of Household Technology from the Open Hearth to the Microwave* (New York: Basic Books, 1983), pp. 40–68.

32. Thomas Kessner, *The Golden Door: Italian and Jewish Immigrant Mobility in New York City, 1880–1915* (New York: Oxford University Press, 1977); Ruth Jacknow Markowitz, *My Daughter, the Teacher: Jewish Teachers in the New York City Schools* (New Brunswick, N.J.: Rutgers University Press, 1993); Joel Perlmann, *Ethnic Differences: Schooling and Social Structure Among the Irish, Italian, Jews, and Blacks in an American City, 1880–1935* (New York: Cambridge University Press, 1988).

33. Harry Roskolenko, *The Time That Was Then*, p. 32.

34. Rose Schneiderman, *All for One* (New York: Paul S. Ericksson, 1967); Bella Spewack, *Streets: A Memoir of the Lower East Side* (New York: Feminist Press, 1995).

35. Samuel Golden, "Some Days Are More Important: A Memoir of Immigrant New York, 1903–1913," in *Jewish Settlement and Community in the Western Modern World*, Ronald Dotterer, Deborah Dash Moore, and Steven M. Cohen, eds. (Selinsgrove: Susquehanna University Press, 1991), pp. 167–199.

36. Emma Beckerman, *Not So Long Ago: A Recollection* (New York: Bloch, 1980) pp. 14, 23, 44–45, 53, 63, 69–70.

37. Howard Goldstein, *The Home on Gorham*; Hyman Bogen, *The Luckiest Orphans: A History of the Hebrew Orphan Asylum of New York* (Urbana: University of Illinois Press, 1992); Reena Sigman, *These Are Our Children: Jewish Orphanages in the United States, 1880–1925* (Hanover, N.H.: University Press of New England, 1994).

38. *American Hebrew* 56, 11 (Jan. 18, 1895), p. 330.

39. "Hebrew Sheltering and Immigrant Aid Society," Reel 13, 1913–1914, Case File 53620/84. Record Group 85, Records of the Immigration and Natu-

ralization Service, Entry, "General Correspondence, 1906–1932, National Archives and Records Administration.

40. Federated Jewish Charities of Milwaukee, Wisconsin, *Annual Reports.* Quotes from report of 1923, pp. 74–75.

41. May Weisser (Mary) Hartman, *I Gave My Heart* (New York: Citadel, 1960), pp. 28–29.

42. Howard Goldstein, *The Home On Gorham Street*, p. 90.

43. Itche Goldberg and Max Rosenfeld, eds., *Morris Rosenfeld: Selections from His Poetry and Prose* (New York: Yiddisher Kultur Farband, 1964), pp. 26–28.

44. "Tzvishn Pushcarts: Zikh Onge'essen," in Maurice Rosenfeld, *Gevellte Shriften* (New York: Forverts, 1912), II, pp. 178–179.

45. Itche Goldberg and Max Rosenfeld, *Morris Rosenfeld*, pp. 69–70.

46. F. B. Ravitzky, "Der Marantz un di Kartoffel," *Kinder Zhurnal* (Oct. 1938), p. 9.

47. Victor Greene, *A Passion for Polka: Old-Time Ethnic Music in America* (Berkeley: University of California Press, 1992), pp. 102–108; Irene Heskes, *Yiddish American Popular Songs, 1895–1950* (Washington, D.C.: Library of Congress, 1992).

48. Molly Picon, *So Laugh A Little* (New York: Paperback Library, 1962), p. 65.

49. J. Hoberman, *Bridge of Light: Yiddish Film Between Two Worlds* (Philadelphia: Temple University Press, 1991), pp. 288–292.

50. Jonathan D. Sarna, "The Myth of No Return: Jewish Return Migration to Eastern Europe, 1881–1914," *American Jewish History* 71, 2 (Dec. 1981) pp. 256–268; Jacob Shatzky, "Polish Jews Emigrate from America" (Yiddish) *YIVO Bletter* 20 (Sept. 1942), pp. 125–127.

51. Julius H. Greenstone, "Philadelphia: Religious Activities," in Charles S. Bernheimer, *The Russian Jew in the United States* (Philadelphia: John C. Winston, 1905), pp. 159–160.

52. "Rita Seitzer," in *Ellis Island Interviews*, Peter Morton Coan, ed. (New York: Checkmark Books, 1997) pp. 258–259.

53. Ruth J. Markowitz, *My Daughter the Teacher*; Sidney Stahl Weinberg, *The World of Our Mothers: Lives of Immigrant Jewish Women* (Chapel Hill: University of North Carolina Press, 1988).

54. Harry Roskolenko, *The Time That Was Then*, p. 14.

55. Rose Cohen, *Out of the Shadow* (New York: George H. Doran, 1918), p. 83.

56. Alfred Kazin, *A Walker in the City* (New York: Harcourt Brace, 1952), p. 32.

57. Golden's collected vignettes appeared in *Ess, Ess Mein Kindt* (Eat, Eat My Child) (New York: Putnam, 1966). Another Golden book, *For 2 Cents*

Plain (Cleveland: World Publishing, 1958), referred to the high levels of consumption of seltzer water by east European Jews in America.

58. Harry Golden, "Preface and Notes," in Hutchins Hapgood, *The Spirit of the Ghetto: Studies of the Jewish Quarter of New York* (New York: Schocken Books, 1965) p. 94.

59. Sara Sandberg, *Mama Made Minks* (Garden City, N.Y.: Doubleday, 1964), p. 26.

60. Mary Antin, *The Promised Land* (orig. 1912; New York: Penguin, 1997), pp. 155–156.

61. Golda Meir, *My Life* (London: Weidenfeld and Nicolson, 1975), p. 37.

62. Alfred Kazin, *A Walker in the City*, pp. 31–34.

63. Sophie Turpin, *Dakota Diaspora: Memoirs of a Jewish Homesteader* (Lincoln: University of Nebraska Press, 1984), pp. 110–111.

64. Louis Wirth, *The Ghetto*, pp. 224, 237–238.

65. Kate Levy, "Health and Sanitation: Chicago," in Charles Bernheimer, ed., *The Russian Jew in the United States*, p. 324.

66. See the many entries in the Jewish Oral History Project, Rare Books and Special Collections at the University of Rochester, Rochester, N.Y.

67. Ted Gostin, *The Katsiv Chronicles: A Genealogy of the Kite, Kaciff, Weprin, Wander, and Dorfman Families* (Los Angeles: Privately published, 1990), p. 31.

68. A. Goldberg, "Der Yiddisher Fakh-Zhurnalism in Amerika," in *Zamlbukh Lekoved dem Tzvey Hundert un Fuftzikt Yoren fun der Yidishe Prese, 1686–1936*, Jacob Shatzky, ed. (New York: YIVO, 1937), pp. 233–249.

69. Ewa Morawska, *Insecure Prosperity: Small-Town Jews in Industrial America, 1890–1940* (Princeton: Princeton University Press, 1996) p. 51.

70. Moses Rischin, *The Promised City: New York Jews, 1870–1914* (Cambridge, Mass.: Harvard University Press, 1962), p. 56.

71. Harry Roskolenko, *The Time That Was Then*, pp. 93, 99–100, 187, 191, 40.

72. Bernard Horwich, *My First Eighty Years* (Chicago: Argus Books, 1939), pp. 148–151.

73. Sydelle Kramer and Jenny Masur, *Jewish Grandmothers: A Vibrant Generation of Women* (Boston: Beacon, 1976) p. 146.

74. Joanne Finkelstein, *Dining Out: A Sociology of Modern Manners* (New York: New York University Press, 1989), pp. 5, 14.

75. Mary Hartman, *I Gave My Heart*, p. 26.

76. Stephan Kanfer, *A Summer World: The Attempt to Build a Jewish Eden in the Catskills, from the Days of the Ghetto to the Rise and Decline of the Borscht Belt* (New York: Farrar, Strauss, Giroux, 1989), pp. 47–48; *Catskills Ethnic Resorts: A Guide to Records* (Delhi, N.Y.: Delaware County Historical Association, 1994).

77. Jacob Scarr, *Listen My Children: A Grandfather's Legacy* (Philadelphia: Dorrance, 1972), p. 168.

78. Lillian Gorenstein, "A Memoir of the Great War, 1914–1924," *YIVO Annual* 20 (1991), p. 174.

79. Quoted in Irving Howe, *The World of Our Fathers: The Journey of the East European Jews to America and the Life They Found and Made* (New York: Harcourt, Brace, Jovanovich, 1976), p. 127.

80. A. H. Fromenson, "Amusements and Social Life, New York," in Charles H. Bernheimer, *The Russian Jew in the United States*, p. 223; Melech Epstein, in *"Pages From a Colorful Life": An Autobiographical Sketch* (Miami Beach, Fla.: I. Block, 1971), p. 51.

81. Hasia Diner, *A Time for Gathering: The Second Migration, 1820–1880* (Baltimore: Johns Hopkins University Press, 1992), p. 76.

82. Eddie Cantor, *My Life Is in Your Hands* (New York: Harper and Brothers, 1928), pp. 20–21, 288.

83. *The American Hebrew* 56, 11 (Jan. 18, 1895).

84. Alfred Kazin, *A Walker in the City*, pp. 33–34.

85. On the extent of the delicatessen culture in the immigrant Jewish enclaves and its Central European roots, see Barry Kessler, "Bedlam with Corned Beef on the Side," *Generations: The Magazine of the Jewish Historical Society of Maryland* (Fall 1993), pp. 1–7.

86. Sophie Ruskay, *Horsecars and Cobblestones* (New York: A. S. Barnes, 1948), p. 58.

87. Congregation Oheb Shalom, *Seventy Fifth Anniversary. Congregation Oheb Shalom. 1860–1935/5620–5695* (Newark, N.J.: n.p., 1935), New York Public Library, Jewish Division.

88. Marcus Ravage, *An American*, pp. 88–89.

89. *American Jewish Yearbook: 5662* (Philadelphia: Jewish Publication Society of America, 1901), p. 102.

90. Alfred Kazin, *A Walker in the City*, pp. 43–44.

91. David Weissman, "Boyle Heights—A Study in Ghettos," *Reflex* 6 (July 1935), p. 32.

92. Zelda F. Popkin, "Jewish Cabarets on the East Side," *Jewish Daily Forward*, May 9, 1926. Thanks to Riv-Ellen Prell for this article.

93. Sidney Sorkin, *Bridges to an American City: A Guide to Chicago's Landsmanshaften, 1870–1990* (New York: P. Lang, 1993), p. 271; see also Home of the Daughters of Jacob, *Fortieth Annual Dinner and Dance, 1896–1936* (New York: n.p., 1936), New York Public Library, Jewish Division.

94. Irving Cutler, *The Jews of Chicago: From Shtetl to Suburb* (Urbana: University of Illinois Press, 1996) p. 70.

95. Sophie Ruskay, *Horsecars and Cobblestones*, p. 90.

96. Elizabeth Hasanovitz, *One of Them: Chapters from a Passionate Autobiography* (New York: Houghton, Mifflin, 1918), p. 45.

97. Sara Sandberg, *Mama Made Minks*; see also Meyer Levin, *In Search: An Autobiography* (New York: Horizon, 1950), p. 14.

98. Catherine Tripalin Murray, *A Taste of Memories from the Old "Bush": Italian Recipes and Fond Memories from People Who Lived in Madison's Greenbush District, 1900–1960* (Madison, Wis.: Italian-American Women's Mutual Society, 1988) p. 81.

99. Alfred Kazin, *A Walker in the City*, pp. 166–167.

100. Boruch Glasman, "Goat in the Backyard," in *Pushcarts and Dreamers: Stories of Jewish Life in America* (Philadelphia: Sholem Aleichem Club Press, 1967), pp. 161–172.

101. Hinde Amchanitzky, *Lehr Bukh vie azoy tzu Kokhen un Baken* (New York: Abraham Fernberg, 1901), p. 12.

102. H. Braun, *Dos Familien Kokh-Bukh* (New York: Hebrew Publishing Company, 1914).

103. Gaye Tuchman and Harry Gene Levine, "New York Jews and Chinese Food: The Social Construction of an Ethnic Pattern," *Journal of Contemporary Ethnography* 22, 3 (Oct. 1993), pp. 382–407.

104. Sophie Ruskay, *Horsecars and Cobblestones*, p. 58.

105. *American Hebrew* 65, 5 (June 2, 1899).

106. *Der Tog*, August 20, 1928.

107. Rose Pesotta, *Days of Our Lives* (Boston: Excelsior Publishers, 1958), pp. 245–246.

108. Paula Hyman, "Immigrant Women and Consumer Protest: The New York City Kosher Meat Boycott of 1902," *American Jewish History* 70, 1 (Sept. 1980), pp. 91–105; Elizabeth Ewen, *Immigrant Women in the Land of Dollars: Life and Culture on the Lower East Side, 1890–1925* (New York: Monthly Review Press, 1985); Beth Wenger, *New York Jews and the Great Depression: Uncertain Promise* (New Haven: Yale University Press, 1996); Annelise Orleck, *Common Sense and A Little Fire: Women and Working Class Politics in the United States, 1900–1965* (Chapel Hill: University of North Carolina Press, 1995); Dana Frank, "Housewives, Socialists and the Politics of Food: The 1917 New York Cost-of-Living Protests," *Feminist Studies* 11, 2 (Summer 1985), pp. 255–285; William Frieburger, "War, Prosperity, and Hunger: The New York Food Riots of 1917," *Labor History* 25, 2 (Spring 1984), pp. 217–239.

109. Judith E. Smith, *Family Connections: A History of Italian and Jewish Immigrant Lives in Providence, Rhode Island, 1900–1914* (Albany: State University of New York Press, 1985), pp. 156–157.

110. Annelise Orleck, *Common Sense*, p. 28.

111. William Braverman, "The Emergence of a Unified Community, 1880–1917," in *The Jews of Boston*, Jonathan D. Sarna and Ellen Smith, eds. (Boston: Combined Jewish Philanthropies of Greater Boston, 1995), p. 79.

112. Bernard Weinstein, *Di Idishe Unions in America: Bletter Geshikhte un Erinerungen* (New York: United Hebrew Trades, 1929).

113. Ibid., pp. 507–508.

114. Paul Brenner, "The Formative Year of the Jewish Bakers' Union, 1881–1914," *YIVO Annual* 18 (1983), pp. 39–120.

115. Moses Rischin, *The Promised City*, p. 57.

116. Morris Hillquit, *Loose Leaves from a Busy Life* (New York: Macmillan, 1934), p. 24.

117. Joseph Belsky, *I, The Union: Being the Personalized Trade Union Story of the Hebrew Butcher Workers of America* (New York: Raddock and Brothers, 1952), p. 8.

118. "Hallah," *Encyclopedia Judaica* (New York and Jerusalem: Macmillan Company and Keter Publishing House, 1971), VII, pp. 1193–1196.

119. Bernard Weinstein, *Di Iddishe Unions*, pp. 436–437.

120. See Ailon Shiloh, *By Myself*, pp. 59–60.

121. Bernard Weinstein, *Di Iddishe Unions*, pp. 438–440.

122. Ailon Shiloh, *By Myself*, p. 58.

123. Mary Brown Sumner, "A Strike for Clean Bread," *Survey* 24, XX (June 18, 1910), p. 485.

124. Charles Angoff, *When I Was a Boy in Boston* (New York: Beechhurst Press, 1947), pp. 95–96.

125. Ted Gostin, *The Katsiv Chronicles*, p. 18.

126. See Andrew R. Heinze, *Adapting to Abundance: Jewish Immigrants, Mass Consumption, and the Search for American Identity* (New York: Columbia University Press, 1990), p. 159.

127. *Die Froyen Velt* 1, 6 (Sept. 1913).

128. For ketchup, see the Yiddish language advertisement for Silver Boy Brand of 1906. Silver Boy claimed that its ketchup was kosher. Warshaw Collection, Box 22, "Catsup, 2," Smithsonian Institution/National Museum of American History/Archives Center.

129. Linda Mack Schloff, *"And Prairie Dogs Weren't Kosher": Jewish Women in the Upper Midwest Since 1855* (St. Paul: Minnesota Historical Society, 1996), pp. 111–113.

130. Susan Strasser, *Satisfaction Guaranteed: The Making of the American Mass Market* (New York: Pantheon, 1989), pp. 12–14; Andrew Heinze, *Adapting to Abundance*, pp. 176–177.

131. Eli Lederhendler, "Guides for the Perplexed: Sex, Manners, and Mores for the Yiddish Reader in America," in *Jewish Responses to Modernity: New Voices in American and Eastern Europe*, Eli Lederhendler, ed. (New York: New York University Press, 1994), pp. 140–158.

132. Shelby Shapiro, "No Dust, No Microbes: Health, Hygiene and Sanitation in Two Yiddish Women's Magazines, 1913–1923," unpublished paper, American University, Dec. 1998, p. 13; Jacob Cohen, "Liber, Ben-Tsion," in *Leksikon fun der Nayer Yidisher Literatur*, Efraim Auerbach, Isaac Charlash and Moshe Starkman, eds. (New York: Congress for Jewish Culture, 1963), V, pp. 53–54.

133. Aaron H. Frankel, *Lo Tirtzakh: Ein Ubhandlung Iber "Vegetarianism"* (New York: B. Rabinowitz, 1899), pp. 27–31, 45–54; see also A. B. Misulow and Mrs. A. B. Mishulow, *Vegetarian Kokhbukh* (New York: Better Health and Correct Eating Institute, 1926); A. B. Mishulow, *Gezund un Shpeiz* (New York: Better Health and Correct Eating Institute, 1926).

134. *Di Froyen Velt* 1, 6 (Sept. 1913), p. 18.

135. *Daily Jewish Courier*, July 8, 1912.

136. Jacob Rader Marcus, ed., *The American Jewish Woman: A Documentary History* (New York: KTAV, 1981), pp. 721–727.

137. Harvey Levenstein, *The Paradox of Plenty: A Social History of Eating in Modern America* (New York: Oxford University Press, 1993); Elaine N. McIntosh, *American Food Habits in Historical Perspective* (Westport, Conn.: Prager, 1995); Laura Shapiro, *Perfection Salad: Women and Cooking at the Turn of the Century* (New York: Farrar, Straus, and Giroux, 1986).

138. See also Mary L. Schapiro, "Jewish Dietary Problems," *Journal of Home Economics* 11, 2 (Feb. 1919), pp. 47–59. Schapiro also criticized "the Jewish diet" and its managers, Jewish women, for not knowing much about a balanced diet.

139. S. Etta Sadow, "Jewish Ceremonials and Food Customs," *Journal of the American Dietetic Association* 4, 2 (Sept. 1928), pp. 97–98.

140. Florence Kreisler Greenbaum, *The International Jewish Cook Book* (New York: Bloch, 1918), n.p.

141. Quoted in Anna Igra, "Male Providerhood and the Public Purse: Anti-Desertion Reform in the Progressive Era," in *The Sex of Things: Gender and Consumption in Historic Perspective*, Victoria de Grazia, ed. (Berkeley: University of California Press, 1996), pp. 194, 197.

142. "Di Haggadah fun di Suffergetkes," *Yiddish Tageblatt*, March 29, 1915.

143. Maurice Rosenfeld, *Gevellte Shriften*, vol. 2, p. 260.

144. Robert Freed Bales, "The 'Fixation Factor,' in Alcohol Addiction: An Hypothesis Derived From a Comparative Study of Irish and Jewish Social Norms," Ph.D. diss., Harvard University, 1944, pp. 117–120.

145. Louis Wirth, "Culture Conflicts in the Immigrant Family," M.A. Thesis, University of Chicago, 1925.

146. Boris D. Bogen, *Born a Jew* (New York: Macmillan, 1930), p. 79.

147. *Gold Medal Meal Cook Book* (Minneapolis: Washburn-Crosby, 1921).

148. Hinde Amchanitzky, *Lehr Bukh*, pp. 10, 13, 18–19, 33; see also H. Braun, *Dos Familian Kokh-Bukh: Bearbytet nokh Amerikanishe, Frantzoyzishe, Italienishe, un Dietche Kokh-Bikher, Spetziel far der Idisher Kikh* (New York: Hebrew Publishing, 1914), Adela Kean Zametkin, *Der Froy's Handbukh* (Jamaica, N.Y.: 1930).

149. Sisterhood Temple Mishkan Tefila, *The Center Table* (Boston: Temple Mishkan Tefila, 1922); Mildred Bellin, *Modern Kosher Meals: Recipes and*

Menus Arranged for Each Month of the Year Based on Current Food Supplies (New York: Bloch, 1934); United Home for Aged Hebrews, New Rochelle, N.Y., Westchester Ladies' Auxiliary, *Home on the Range* (New Rochelle, N.Y.: 1937). Manischewitz Company issued a half-English, half-Yiddish cookbook., B. Manischewitz Company, *Ba'taaam'te Idishe Ma'a'kholim, Tsugegreyt fun Veltbarimte Manishevitinin's Matso-Produktn. Oysdervehlte Resipis vos Zaynen Osgeproyvt un Gutgeheysen Gevaren in di Manishevits Esperimentale Kitschens fun Mis F. O. Gahr* (Cincinnati: B. Manischewitz Company, 1930).

150. Morris Isaiah Berger, "The Settlement, The Immigrant and the Public School: A Study of the Influence of the Settlement Movement and the New Migration Upon Public Education: 1890–1924," Ph.D. diss., Columbia University, 1956, p. 59; Elizabeth Rose, "From Sponge Cake to Hamentashen: Jewish Identity in a Jewish Settlement House, 1885–1952," *Journal of American Ethnic History* 13, 3 (Spring 1994), pp. 3–23, discussed the contentiousness of the Jewish "content" of such settlements and their programs. See Ruth Rafael, *Continuum: A Selective History of San Francisco Eastern European Jewish Life, 1880–1940* (San Francisco: Judah L. Magnes Memorial Museum, 1976), pp. 29–32.

151. Harry Roskolenko, *The Time That Was Then*, p. 216.

152. Mrs. Simon [Lizzie Black] Kander, *The Settlement Cook Book* (Milwaukee: J. H. Yewdale and Sons, 1910).

153. Federated Jewish Charities of Milwaukee, Wis., *Fifth Annual Report*, p. 37.

154. Federated Jewish Charities of Milwaukee, Wis., *Annual Report: 1923*, pp. 45–46.

155. *Memories of Longtime Milwaukeeans*, pp. 11–12.

156. Michael Stanislawski, *For Whom Do I Toil? Judah Leib Gordon and the Crisis of Russian Jewry* (New York: Oxford University Press, 1988); Yehudah Leib Gordon, "Hakizu Ami," in *Kitvei Yehudah Leib Gordon: Shirah* (Tel Aviv: Devir, 1956), pp. 17–18.

INDEX

Immigrants in *(continued)*
Louisiana, 48, 65; Lowell, 126, 134; Madison, 57, 80, 183, 205; Maine, 75, 113; Maryland, 11; Milwaukee, 130, 182, 187–188, 195, 214, 216–218; Minneapolis, 212; Missouri, 63; Nebraska, 63; Newark, 63, 67, 70, 202, 209; New Haven, 63, 70, 82, 184; New Jersey, 62, 63, 127; New York, 11, 56, 60, 63, 121; New York City, 51, 52, 61–68, 70, 71, 74, 77, 78, 80–82, 116, 121, 123, 126–136, 138, 148, 179, 180–183, 186, 188, 193, 198–199, 200–202, 204–207, 209, 214, 216; North Dakota, 196; Ohio, 182; Oklahoma, 62; Omaha, 63, 66, 72; Oneonta, 49; Paterson, 127; Pennsylvania, 11, 12, 63; Pewaukee, 182; Philadelphia, 47, 63, 64, 70, 75, 79, 126, 127, 134, 135, 187, 190, 191, 209, 216; Pittsburgh, 63, 183, 209; Port Chester, 182; Portland, 134; Providence, 63, 68, 206; Rochester, 60, 63, 183, 188; Rhode Island, 11; Roseto, 53; San Francisco, 48, 63–66, 70, 75, 216; Seattle, 65; South Dakota, 211; Stamford, 182; Staten Island, 62; St. Louis, 57, 63; Tampa, 46, 62, 63; Trenton, 55; Troy, 126; Utah, 75; Utica, 55, 64; Vermont, 62; Virginia, 10; Wilmington, 70; Worcester, 122, 126, 134

Irish in America; alcohol, 121, 122, 123, 128, 133–143; attitudes toward food, 114–116, 119–121, 123, 124, 143–145, 222–223; bread, 119, 122, 123, 125, 133, 138; dietary habits, 120–124, 130–132, 139–141; domestic life, 119–125, 134; domestic service, 115–120, 223; economic mobility, 115–116, 120, 124–125, 132, 138, 143; food purveyors, 126, 132, 133–134; hospitality, 125–126; Irish foods, 121–122, 126, 132, 133; Irish stereotypes, 116–119, 136, 137, 141; meat, 116, 119, 124–126, 130, 132, 138; neighborhoods, neighbors 114, 122, 125–128, 134, 138, 142, 144; philanthropy, 115, 130; politics, 113, 114, 131–135, 141–144; potato, 115, 121–123, 125, 131–132, 138, 144–145; public occasions, 129–131, 144; pubs and saloons, 134–137, 139–141; religion, 114, 115, 121, 124, 125, 141–142, 144; sources of food knowledge, 115–116; St. Patrick's Day, 130–131, 133, 136–137; symbols of Irishness, 128–129, 131, 132, 135–137, 141; temperance movement, 141–142; tea, 122, 123, 125, 133

Irish in Ireland, 2, 85, 129–130; Aran Islands, 97; Ballykilcline, 107; Bandon, 109; Blasket Islands, 93; Carrick, 104; Cork, 98, 110, 116; County Clare, 126; County Galaway, 93, 116; County Kerry, 93; County Kilkenney, 110, 126; County Mayo, 113; County Monaghan, 104; County Sligo, 127; County Tyrone, 97, 119; County Wexford, 104; Donegal, 95; Drogeheda, 109; Dublin, 133; Ferbane, 107; Kildare, 92; Limerick, 122, 126; Meath, 109; Munster province, 109; Roscommon, 108; Thomastown, 110; Wilton Castle, 104; alcohol, 85–86, 103; agriculture, 86, 87, 89–90, 94, 106, 132; alienation between Irish and English, 89–91, 104–105, 107–110, 133, 135, 222; attitudes toward food, 84–85, 97, 99, 101–102, 105–106, 111–113; bread, 92, 103, 104; Catholics, Catholicism, 84, 86, 91, 105, 106–107, 108, 110, 111, 114, 223; charity, 109, 110; class and class consciousness, 89–91 104–107, 108–110; colonization of, 85, 90–91, 102, 106, 222; dairy, 86, 93, 94, 103, 104, 106, 110; demographics, 87–88, 106–107, 111–114; dietary habits of elite and middle class, 104–105; dietary habits of poor, 87, 92–99, 106, 110–111; domestic life, 84, 86, 92, 93, 95–99; domestic service, 110; famines, 2, 87–92, 93, 95, 100; folklore, 95, 102–104; Great Hunger, 2, 87–92, 94, 99, 113–114; housing, 93, 94–95, 107, 109; hospitality, 104–105; Irish foods, 103–104; Irish cultural revival, 84; meat, 86, 93, 94, 103, 104, 106; modernization, 85, 93; politics, 85–86, 89, 113; potato, 85–87, 89, 91–98, 101, 103–106, 110–111, 222–223; Protestants, Protestantism, 91,104, 106, 108, 110; public relief, 91–92; solidarity of poor, 107–108; stereotypes, 92; tea, 93, 97; taxes, 86, 91; trade, 89–91, 93, 106

Italians in America: alcohol, 51, 56, 61, 72, 77, 79; attitudes toward food, 49–51, 74, 75, 78, 80–82, 225–226; bread, 52, 64, 72, 75, 77, 80; charity, 55, 71; cheese, 56–58, 60, 61, 65, 66, 69, 75–77, 81, 205; coffee, 46, 59, 61, 75, 77; dietary habits, 51–53, 55–57, 58, 61–63, 73–78; domestic life, 53, 57, 60, 63, 72–74, 76–78, 79–82; economic mobility, 50, 56–57, 60, 61, 63–64, 69, 72–73; food purveyors, 54, 55, 63–69, 70–72, 74–77, 80; hospitality, 61, 72, 80; innovations, 53–54 , 60–61, 63–66, 70–72; "Italian" cuisine and foods, 49, 50, 53–55, 61, 63–69, 70–72, 74–77, 79, 80–81; meat, 50–61, 66, 68, 70–72, 75–77, 79, 81; neighborhoods, 50, 51, 53–56, 62–64, 66–68, 71–76, 78, 79, 80, 205; nutrition, 50, 57; politics, 68, 69–70; public occasions, 55, 71–73, 80; oil, 56–58, 60, 65, 66, 69, 75, 76, 81; pasta, 50–52, 55–59, 65–68, 70–72, 75–77, 79–81, 105; religion, 55, 71–73; sauce, 61, 69–71, 76, 77, 79–81

Italians in Italy, 21–22, 86; Abruzzo, 46; Agrigento, 51; Alba, 36; Alia, 48; Amalfi, 66; Apennines, 24, 25, 46; Apulia, 28, 31, 40, 68, 75; Aquila, 29; Avellino, 68; Avigliano; 29; Barisciano, 29; Calabria, 25, 27, 29, 30, 33, 40, 66, 68; Campania, 68, 77; Cosenza, 49; Catania, 53; Cuggiono, 53, 57, 59; Florence, 65; Foggia, 53; Genoa, 40, 65, 66; Lombardy, 27, 28, 43; Lucca, 65, 71; Luciana, 36, 53; Milan, 40, 48; Montegegatesi, 31; Naples, 31, 40, 61, 66; Palermo, 26, 35, 40, 48, 54;

Piedmont, 36, 62; Rome, 2, 22, 24; San Donato, 49; Sicily, 23, 24, 31, 32, 34, 35, 39, 43, 44, 46, 48, 53, 54, 58, 60, 64–68, 72–74, 81, 221; Turin, 40, 62; Tuscany, 27, 38, 45, 58; Veneto, 28; Vesuvius Mt., 66; agricultural life, 23–27; alcohol, 27, 28, 30, 33, 34, 39, 44; attitudes toward food, 27–28, 31, 39, 34–35, 44–47; bread, 21, 27–30, 33, 35, 39, 40, 42–44, 48; charity, 43–45; cheese, 27, 28, 33, 34, 39, 40, 44; class and class consciousness, 22–23, 25–27, 29, 31, 33, 34, 39, 40, 43–45; corn and rice, 24, 27, 29–35; demographics, 23; dietary habits of elite and middle class, 27–29, 31, 38–43; dietary habits of poor, 23, 27, 29–34, 36–37, 43–45; domestic life, 35–38; food purveyors, 33, 38–39, 40–44, 46; hospitality and gift-giving, 34–35, 43–45, 61; housing, 39–40; influence of America, 45–47, 59; meat and fish, 27–33, 39, 40, 43, 44; oil, 27, 28, 30, 43, 44; pasta, 27, 28, 30, 31, 40, 42–44; *polenta*, 27, 31, 35, 42–44, 58; politics, 21–23, 26, 29; religion, 31, 42–45; soup, 27–30, 43

Japan, Japanese, 99, 228

Jews in America: attitudes toward food, 178–180, 184–186, 192–194, 215–216, 225; attitudes toward Jewish religious practice, 179–185, 191–192, 194–196, 204–205, 208–209, 224; bread, 180, 194–196, 198–199, 203, 206, 208–210; charity, 183, 186–188, 194, 198, 204, 215, 217; dairy, 187–188, 211–212; deli, delicatessen, 191, 197, 201–202, 207, 213; dietary habits, 179, 180, 182, 186, 191–192, 200–202, 204–206, 211–216; dietary laws, 178–179, 180–185, 192, 210–211, 218–219, 224–225; domestic life, 179, 185–186; economic mobility, 184, 185, 192, 203, 205; food purveyors, 173, 181–183, 187, 196–199, 205–212; innovations, 180, 194, 198–199, 200–206, 211–212, 216–218; meat and fish, 180–183, 186, 192–196,

CPSIA information can be obtained
at www.ICGtesting.com
Printed in the USA
BVHW042006140821
614063BV00003B/12

9 780674 011113